More Praise for *Winning with Customers*

From Business Leaders . . .

"The CVC Management System is a game-changing approach to developing a business growth strategy. Our work with Alderman and Pigues resulted in a deeper understanding of our customers. Winning with Customers is an impressive 'how to' guide for business leaders to move the concept into action. This is a must-read."

Sue Sears, Vice President, Global Market Development,
Kimberly-Clark Professional

"Keith is one of the people I turn to when I need to learn something about smart marketing! Keith and Jerry's book, *Winning with Customers,* is picture perfect!!!"

Jeffrey Hayzlett, CMO, Kodak

"Winning with Customers and the CVC Value Management system directly address the CEO's #1 priority, which is to drive profitable growth. CEOs are looking for pragmatic solutions based on real-world best practice experience—this is exactly what Pigues and Alderman deliver in this research work. This book is a must-read."

David Frigstad, Chairman, Frost & Sullivan

"Utilizing the approach outlined in *Winning with Customers* will move your business from one that is based on the 'best deal' or 'lowest price' to one that is fully aligned, metrics based, with mutual creation of value for both you and your customer."

Randy Marcuson, CEO (Retired), Embrex

"*Winning with Customers* cuts through all the fog and shows you how to deliver and then measure your value to the customer. *Winning with Customers* is a road map for creating indestructible customer loyalty and increasing sales."

David Pitts, President and Founder, Classic Graphics

"Pigues and Alderman have really struck dead center. In business today, B2B strategies often end up being developed like consumer market strategies, taking the focus off the true need of the business customer—their profits. This 'play book' will help develop customer relationships, where you are as knowledgeable about what drives your customer's growth and profit as you are about your own—a sure recipe for growth."

Steve Brozovich, PHD,
Business Strategy Advisor, Snap On Incorporated

"In too many business texts, the idea of customer focus simply doesn't extend beyond platitudes. *Winning with Customers* teaches a rigorous methodology around which the entire organization can align, making its approach real, practical, and quantifiable."

Donald M. DeLauder, Executive Director,
Corporate Innovation, MEDRAD, Inc.

"CVC is a comprehensive approach that lays out a measurable plan to maximize customer value and build a sustainable advantage in any B2B market you serve. The approach Pigues and Alderman have laid out is fresh, practical, relevant, and actionable . . . and will be a part of every strategy I implement in the future!"

Blair Schrum, Co-founder,
ZC Sterling Corporation

"*Winning with Customers* is a powerful, refreshing reminder to all that it's not about what you have to sell but rather who you are selling it to and the metrics to validate the value they're getting from it."

Cos Malozzi, CEO, Gibbs & Soell

"The authors' breakthrough contribution to the field of Management is an exciting new method ('CVC') that enables companies to impact customer value with rigorous, scientific precision."

Steven Fabry, CEO and Founder,
Compendia Exchange

From Business Education and Media . . .

"In this powerful and practical work, built on the work of two recognized and proven thought leaders, marketers will find a trove of new ideas, powerful tools, and new answers they need to grow profitably in the markets of the coming decade."

Ralph A. Oliva, Executive Director,
Institute for the Study of Business Markets

"A refreshing, new way for evaluating business success: How are our 'customers' doing? Unfortunately, few organizations take this vital measurement. Pigues and Alderman provide a thorough and clear game plan for creating a truly customer-centric company."

Ellis Booker, Editor, *BtoB Magazine*

"Strategic Sales Managers should spend more time understanding their customer metrics: procurement managers are receptive to productivity solutions vs. just price provided they are given clearly quantified economic gains. This book shows you how."

Bernard Quancard, CEO, Strategic
Account Management Association

"With this ground-breaking book and the CVC Management System, Pigues and Alderman provide a playbook to articulate, quantify, and certify the impact of differentiated value on sales—relevant for CEOs and their customers. A must-have!"

Navdeep Sodhi, Managing Director,
Six Sigma Pricing, Author of *Six Sigma Pricing*

"*Winning with Customers* and the CVC Management System represent the most significant breakthrough in managing profitable customer relationships in decades. It is a must for every B2B business to consider."

Patrick Farrey, Executive Director,
Business Marketing Association

"*Winning with Customers* provides a clear pathway for sustainable profitable growth for B2B businesses. The CVC Management System will help management teams align and focus their energy and resources toward creating greater customer value and thereby increasing the value of the B2B business"

Mark L. Frigo, Director, DePaul University Center for Strategy, Execution and Valuation, Author of *DRIVEN: Business Strategy, Human Actions and the Creation of Wealth*

"*Winning with Customers* stands out above the clutter. Pigues and Alderman's insights on understanding your customers' perspectives and showing what's possible through specific examples and quantitative results helps you move from lip service about winning with your customers to measurable success. A must-read."

Pete Krainik, Founder and CEO, The CMO CLUB

"Pigues and Alderman have developed a transformational pathway to sustained profit growth. Their Playbook is a must-have tool for all businesses small and large."

Tony Rome, President and CEO, Maven Strategies

"Pigues and Alderman have delivered a ground-breaking piece of work that Chief Marketing Officers and the other members of the C-suite will find of value as they chart the course for profitable top-line growth. Best of all, their guidance on implementation results in a valuable 'how to' manual for companies to win."

William L. Koleszar, Editor, *The Chief Marketing Officer Journal*

"The book's cover says it all—do your customers make more money doing business with you? If you cannot answer in the affirmative, or simply don't know, what are you waiting for? The authors lay out a practical and very accessible game plan to help you and your customers 'win' and achieve profitable and sustainable growth in the B2B marketplace."

Richard Ettenson, Ph.D., Associate Professor & Thelma H. Kieckhefer Fellow Thunderbird School of Global Management

"As an academic/business consultant who has toiled in the B2B marketing field for 30+ years, it is unusual to find a no-nonsense, practical guide to winning with customers. Their guide to create value for customers will benefit both the novice and experienced manager develop and execute marketing programs that meet customer needs, make money for both them and their customers, and will result in a stickier relationship with their customer base. This book should be on every marketing executive's must-read list."

Robert Spekman, Ph.D., Tayloe Murphy Professor of Business Administration University of Virginia - Darden School

"Pigues and Alderman offer an extremely insightful and practical book that shares valuable real company experiences, while providing proven integrated frameworks for creating and capturing value. This is a must for executives who want to create competitive advantage by building stronger more profitable customer relationships."

David Hopkins, Managing Director, Carlson School of Management University of Minnesota

From the Investment Community . . .

"Pigues and Alderman have developed a jewel. Winning with Customers and the CVC concept is a powerful approach to differentiate yourself in a highly competitive marketplace. This is a valuable tool that will help us as investors in the middle market."

Jeffrey A. Dombcik, Managing Director, Triangle Capital Corporation

"As a B2B bank, we are always looking for ways to differentiate ourselves from the competition. The CVC approach to winning with customers shows us how to do just that. The authors brilliantly lay out a unique management system that is rigorous, quantitative, and easily implementable, while affordable—allowing businesses like ours to build this critical capability in-house, without a team of consultants."

Eddie Blount, Executive Vice President, KeySource Commercial Bank

"Our life is built upon and made richer by the depth and sincerity of our relationships. So are our businesses. Yet, our customer relationships are often transactional and tactical versus strategic and collaborative. Pigues and Alderman make the case, in *Winning with Customers*, that if we are deliberate, thoughtful, and quantitative in our customer dialogue then our customers can make more money and we can too—and have deeper, more sustainable relationships to show for it. This book won't make it to my bookshelf; it will stay within arm's reach where other worn reference materials reside."

H. Beecher Hicks III, Partner, Red Clay Capital Holdings, LLC

"*Winning with Customers* puts the focus on the single most important value to any business . . . the customer. This concept reminds us that the reason any company is in business is to successfully serve the customer. The ability to leverage outside-in-thinking consistently keeps the focus on the customer, which translates into sales, profits, and increased customer value. The opportunity to systematically leverage the analysis of customer input is a transforming idea that today's leaders need to take advantage of."

Richard E. Stewart, President of Investment Banking,
Galen Capital Corporation

"As a private equity investor, I am always looking for ways to grow and enhance profitable customer relationships with our respective portfolio companies. *Winning with Customers* will be a great tool to use as a value creator for each company we acquire. Understanding 'why we win' provides a guide to learn how to create meaningful and profitable relationships with vendors and customers alike. Pigues and Alderman's real-world experience provides the context that distinguishes this book from the typical 'academic' marketing/customer relationship book."

Kelvin Walker, Partner, 21st Century Group, LLC

Winning with Customers

Winning with Customers

A Playbook for B2B

D. Keith Pigues
Jerry Alderman

WILEY

John Wiley & Sons, Inc.

Published by John Wiley & Sons, Inc., Hoboken, New Jersey.
Published simultaneously in Canada.

For general information on our other products and services or for technical support, please contact our Customer Care Department within the United States at (800) 762-2974, outside the United States at (317) 572-3993 or fax (317) 572-4002.

Wiley also publishes its books in a variety of electronic formats. Some content that appears in print may not be available in electronic books. For more information about Wiley products, visit our Web site at www.wiley.com.

Library of Congress Cataloging-in-Publication Data

Pigues, D. Keith.
   Winning with customers : a playbook for B2B / D. Keith Pigues, Jerry Alderman.
      p.   cm.
   Includes index.
   ISBN 978-0-470-54799-1 (cloth); ISBN 978-0-470-76849-5 (ebk);
   ISBN 978-0-470-76850-1 (ebk); ISBN 978-0-470-76851-8 (ebk)
      1. Customer relations—Management.   2. Consumer satisfaction.   3. Customer services—Management.   I. Alderman, Jerry D.   II. Title.
   HF5415.5.P544   2010
   658.8'04—dc22

                                                                         2010005942

Printed in the United States of America

10 9 8 7 6 5 4

To Monica: You are the love of my life and my biggest inspiration. Thanks for your never-ending encouragement and unconditional love.

To Christian, Caleb, Levi, and Chloe: I love you. You are incredible gifts from God. Pursue your dreams and serve God with excellence along your exciting life journey with Him.

To my brothers: Cottrell, Joseph, Kevin, Wyndon, and Terrance. Continue the legacy we were left by the greatest business person of all time, our dad, Alonzo Pigues. He left us a great gift.

To my Mom and Dad: Thank you and I love you.

—*D. Keith Pigues*

To Tracy, Kirbey, Carlie, Kelli, and McKenzie: You are special people in this world, especially to me. Never let anyone make you think your goals are out of reach. Be happy!

And to my Mom and Dad: I love you.

—*Jerry Alderman*

Contents

Foreword

Karel Czanderna, Group President, Building Materials, Owens Corning

Jerry, Keith, and the team have created one of the first systems I have found that truly allows us to learn what our customer values and use that information in the daily operation of the business, from investments to sales planning, and execution. The logic of what they have done is flawless and brilliant. What is even more powerful is that it is all based on an approach that creates tools and capability that will generate benefits for our customers and our company for years to come.

We have come a long way in our almost three years with Valkre, and we still have a long way to go. Maybe the single biggest compliment one could make about the power and potential of this approach is that we are still excited after three years, and the momentum continues to build. That is quite a testimony, considering the challenging building markets over the past couple years. We are focused on initiatives that are adding value to our customer and our shareholders . . . and this is guiding both.

I started my career in research, product development, and manufacturing, and I did not meet a customer for 10 years until I led a team servicing office copiers in the field. When I finally did, it changed my career. It was then that I recognized the challenge of people and just how hard it is to move an organization of thousands of employees to pursue and deliver what matters to the customer. It is no easy task because it permeates every function in the organization, from marketing to innovative product development to logistics to capital and operational planning to selling and so much more. And you know what? My experiences at three great brand companies showed that not all of the customers value everything you do in the same way or even at the same level. In the end, the journey of understanding what is valuable to each customer through to creating a sustainable competitive advantage for your company does not happen by accident. It takes diligent management and requires the organization to build a competency for doing so. The book you are about to read will go a long way to helping you develop or expand your competency. I wish Jerry, Keith, and team had developed this holistic system sooner, as I sure could have used it throughout my tenure in business.

Right now is absolutely the time to be working harder than ever to understand what will persuade customers to buy from you. The competency of understanding and executing against what creates value for customers relative to your competition is not a "nice to have"; it is a "must have." Waiting to develop this competency is akin to waiting to be successful, and success most often occurs from acting, not waiting. So read on, and proactively build your own Playbook.

Preface

This book has many pages. We are not sure yet why it has so many and who the heck wrote them all! We recognize that some of you will read every page, others will read selective portions of the book, and many (hopefully) will use the book as a reference or guide on your journey to "win with customers." We thought a quick road map up front might help you to navigate the material and use it best to meet your needs.

How Is the Book Organized?

There are 10 chapters and an afterword in the book. The first three chapters are:

1. "Why We Lose"
2. "Define Winning"
3. "The Playbook"

These chapters provide an executive overview of our formula for winning with customers. In these chapters you find the Six Big Ideas that help your organization accelerate profitable growth. We also discuss the four breakthroughs contained within our winning formula, which we believe sets our approach apart from others. And we share the real experiences from real companies that have delivered significant results using our approach. We talk about those companies and share their business cases in depth.

The next five chapters are:

4. "Winning Metrics"
5. "What Does Your Customer Think?"
6. "Informing Decisions"
7. "Executing Value Creation and Value Capture"
8. "The Scoreboard"

These are the "winning plays," as we like to call them. These chapters are filled with lots of practical information to help you put the winning formula into practice in your organization. This is where practitioners can learn with reasonable detail how to do the work of winning with customers and understand if your customers make more money by doing business with you relative to competitors. The next chapters are:

9. "Getting Started"
10. "Sustaining and Scaling: The Maturity Model"
"Afterword"

These chapters help you get on the path to action within your organization. They also cover some of the pitfalls we have experienced along the way—providing helpful advice whether you are undertaking a small project or one that involves an organization with 10,000 employees. We must admit that we have not discovered the unifying theory on the subject of change management. It is still a lot of hard work. We do share some insights from years of work with many companies that will help you successfully implement this approach in your business. And then we conclude with a summary of the book, which our English teachers suggested we always include. Here we capture the key highlights and takeaways from the book.

More detail on each chapter follows.

Chapter 1: "Why We Lose." This chapter was designed to describe the problem we are focused on, give you some insights as to why we are writing the book, let you know who we are writing it for, and discuss what we hope you will learn.

Chapter 2: "Define Winning." This book is focused on winning with customers. Here we define what winning with customers means and we introduce measures we have found to work. We also set up the playbook of winning plays to help you win.

Chapter 3: "The Playbook." This chapter provides the overall construct of the system we have collectively used to lead companies in developing their own outside-in customer capability. For each of the plays, we provide some background on why they are in the playbook and how they help you succeed.

Chapter 4: "Winning Metrics." This chapter describes in detail the metrics we use. We get to the bottom of understanding if your value proposition creates value for your customers—helping you move from anecdotes and gut feelings alone to sound metrics of success.

Chapter 5: "What Does Your Customer Think?" Here we discuss resources that you need to collect your customer's perspective on the value you create for them. We point out why your customer loves the conversation and we review the pros and cons of getting the various members of your team involved in this portion of work.

Chapter 6: "Informing Decisions." We show how you can generate a quantified (dollars of value to your customer) list of opportunities informed by your customers. We then discuss how this list is combined with your own internal ideas for improvement to generate a prioritized list of the most valuable ideas informed by you and your customers to improve the differential value you deliver to customers.

Chapter 7: "Executing Value Creation and Value Capture." We also like to call this bridging the say-do gap. Meaning, we always say we listen and respond to customers but we seldom do so in a way that our customers see and understand. This chapter is all about translating the knowledge generated about what our customers value (from the list of opportunities) and developing customer plans that can be executed by the organization, understood by the sales force, and communicated effectively to customers.

Chapter 8: "The Scoreboard." The scoreboard chapter discusses how we link value creation for the customer and value capture for ourselves. It also goes into how we can start to better predict our own profit improvements as a result of creating value for customers.

Chapter 9: "Getting Started." This chapter particularly focuses on organizational dynamics. Who needs to be involved, and how you go through the steps of transitioning this kind of work from a project to a way of doing business. How long does it take? How much does it cost? What are the benefits?

Chapter 10: "Sustaining and Scaling." This chapter is all about how to move from the initial implementation and learning within your organization to get the full value by ramping up the effort. This chapter addresses how to make it a way of doing business throughout the organization.

"Afterword": This chapter provides a brief overview of what we discuss throughout the book. It highlights the key frameworks and summarizes why companies lose, and why they win. It provides a high-level review of how to get your company into action.

For each chapter we set out the objectives and provide a summary of those objectives at the end. Each chapter also has practical examples and cases embedded to provide you with as many real-life examples as possible.

Case Study

The book is driven by case studies—we provide examples of how others used this approach. We introduce the cases in Chapter 1 and carry them through the entire book, developing their stories and providing practical insights and outcomes directly from the people who have done this work in their organizations. Where possible, we carry examples from one chapter to the next so you can follow the logic as we develop the concepts. There are instances where this is not possible due to the confidential nature of the outcomes and insights. We're sure you understand. When your successes are featured in the next version of the book or as cases on the companion web site (and we hope you will share), we will likewise ensure that your competitive insights are not disclosed.

Web Site and Community

We spent quite a bit of money building this web site so you better use it. Ha! . . . Just kidding! But seriously, we know that everything you need to win with customers cannot be contained within a book. The companion web site (www.winningwithcustomers.com) was designed to be used with the book. It provides online exercises, forums, and spreadsheets to help you begin implementation within your company. It also provides the outcome of your work to share with others in your organization by using formats that we have found to be effective.

Also on the web site we included two Appendixes. Appendix A: "Our Approach to Certification and Building Capability" provides more detail on the tools you can use to train your people and certify your organization to become proficient in using this approach to win with customers. Appendix B: "A Little More Background on Outside-In" is a carryover from our last book to help you better understand the opportunities and challenges of truly becoming an organization whose decisions are shaped by valuable outside-in customer data.

The web site also serves as a community for continued learning from peers and thought leaders, as well as additional reading and cases. You also find access to the CVC Institute, which is a destination for continued education on the topic of Customer Value Creation. There are blogs, discussion forums, and access to continuing education courses and conferences to help you learn and connect with other kindred spirits along your journey. You can also buy a book here as a gift for colleagues, family, and friends. Warning: We gave our kids a book as a gift and it did not turn out that well!

Acknowledgments

D. Keith Pigues

My contribution to this book would not be possible without the support and guidance of some very special people. My wife and children (the loves of my life) have been my fan club throughout the process of writing this book—when the words were flowing and during the countless hours of staring out of the window or at the keyboard waiting for the words to come. I thank them for their willingness to allow me to go off to my "writing place" to bring the ideas to life, put the words on the page, and exercise my gifts. I only hope I am as a big of a fan and supporter as they exercise their gifts and talents and pursue their dreams.

My mother, Verna Pigues, and my brother Kevin Pigues have always been in my corner through every endeavor. And once again, they encouraged me to tackle another new challenge—providing encouragement and support every step of the way.

My business experience foundation and many of the important lessons I've learned were shaped by my father (the late Alonzo Pigues) during my formative years working with him and my brothers at Pigues Tire Company—those were special times. While he had no formal education, he knew more about business, understanding customers, meeting their needs, and running a profitable business than most.

The completion of this book would not be possible without the contributors (Brian Kiep, Alex Monacelli, Matt Cobb, and Gabriel Lerner). Their sharp minds and tireless efforts were a big part of this effort—thank you. And I am grateful for the incredible partnership with Jerry Alderman. Without his knowledge and passion for helping customers win, this book would not be possible.

The review and feedback from Dave Hofmann and Margaret Woodard were invaluable—providing very valuable perspectives from a professor and practitioner, respectively, to ensure the soundness and practicality of this "how to" book.

Judy Howarth and the editorial team at Wiley & Sons provided invaluable counsel and guidance as we navigated through the process from ideas and experience to the creation of the book.

Jerry Alderman

Anyone who has ever taken on the challenge of writing a book knows it takes a team. This is especially true in this case of our book, *Winning with Customers*, as the book is not so much about the ideas and philosophies of the authors as it is about the actual work this team has accomplished over the course of several years. I thank the team for their passion in our collective journey, the willingness to dig in and drive results, and the intellectual genius each has added. Most of all, I thank their families for supporting them and us in completing this gratifying piece of work. Thanks Brian and Alyson, Alex and Susanna, Matt and Jennifer, and Gabe.

If not for the success of Valkre, there would be no book. There have been so many people and companies who have helped us. Our advisors Glenn Dalhart and Jim McClung work to keep us grounded and generally guided in the right direction. My uncle, John Edwards, is always generous with his banking and financial assistance. And most important, our customers are everything to us. Owens Corning in particular has been the most amazing collaboration partner any company or any person could have. They have challenged our Valkre team and made us better. Thanks to all of you.

And finally we thank Keith for doing this project with us. Keith has been one of our biggest fans for years. Anyone who knows him knows that he is an inspiration to have in your corner. Thanks for being in our corner, Keith, and we look forward to hanging with you in Hawaii!

Introduction

Glenn Dalhart, Retired Partner, Ernst & Young management consulting

This book captures the invaluable lessons learned from a nearly decade-long journey focused on perfecting the business science of creating value for customers in the so-called business-to-business (B2B) segment of commerce. Keith and Jerry have clearly arrived at an important destination. Not only has the customer value creation (CVC) science been significantly advanced, it has been proven by real-world applications in numerous B2B settings. This book provides a deep insight into the discoveries that can help you win with your customers and ultimately increase the value of your business.

I have had the distinct pleasure to participate in and witness this journey from its beginnings in the early 2000s. Keith and Jerry have come a great distance since working together in a client-consultant relationship at RR Donnelley. Keith has been a consistent CVC advocate, practitioner, and spokesperson. Jerry has maintained an unwavering focus on developing the CVC solution through a series of consulting organizations leading to his new company Valkre Solutions, Inc.

I have had a wide-ranging 35-plus year career in management consulting as a partner with Ernst & Young and several other prominent consultancies. In all my years of experience, I cannot point to a more powerful solution in the B2B setting than CVC. I truly believe that when a B2B business enterprise is aligned around CVC, it will not only create value for its customers but as a by-product it will create shareholder value for itself—most often many times greater than the returns enjoyed by its customers. This is the somewhat counterintuitive but perhaps the most exciting result of the CVC process. This is the ultimate "win-win" proposition.

I believe that CVC draws its power from the ingenious combination of three powerful business principles: outside-in thinking, competitive advantage, and continuous improvement (e.g., Kaizen/Six Sigma). First, CVC is absolutely focused on understanding and measuring value from the customer's point of view. This point of view is critical and is differentiated from the approach taken by most businesses that ask the question: "How profitable (to me) is this customer?" CVC turns that table and asks a much different and more powerful question: "Do you (the customer) make more money doing business with us than with our competitors?" Second, CVC embraces the well-established principle of relative performance when it comes to understanding competitive advantage. CVC applies this principle at the customer level by measuring its value proposition relative to its competitors—as you will learn, this measurement is central to the CVC solution and is called the differential value proposition (DVP). Last, CVC embraces the continuous improvement principles of Kaizen/Six Sigma by embedding DVP measurement within a closed-loop process: Discover – Analyze – Execute – Measure.

The CVC solution is truly unique. Although it resides primarily in the "Customer Intelligence" space, the CVC solution is truly different from the typical "Customer Loyalty," "Customer Satisfaction," "Voice of Customer," or "Customer Relationship Management" solutions. CVC is differentiated through the analytical rigor of its DVP measurement process and through the "relative to competition" measurement framework. Perhaps most important, CVC is an active, forward-looking solution that answers the question: "What can we do to create additional value for our customers?" Most "Customer Intelligence" solutions are passive, backward-looking, and ask: "How loyal/satisfied are our customers?" The collection of answers to the CVC question from many customers across the value chain and from various channels provides valuable enterprise-level perspectives that inform critical investment decisions. In this way, CVC morphs into a powerful closed-loop management decision-making system that aligns and impacts all functional areas of a business.

In forming Valkre, Jerry has taken the bold step to transform his company from a consulting focus to a software product focus. This development makes it possible for businesses to readily institutionalize CVC. Along with consulting support, Valkre offers two powerful software platforms, Render® and Academy, which allow businesses to effectively institutionalize and maintain CVC without ongoing consulting help. Additionally, both products are offered in a "Software as a Service" format that reduces implementation and maintenance complexities.

To most effectively benefit from this book, you may need to put aside the current paradigms you apply to B2B relationships. An open mind will allow you to more fully grasp the powerful new ideas that are offered by Keith and Jerry. After reading this book, I think you will agree that Keith and Jerry have made several important breakthroughs in the B2B business setting.

Winning with Customers

Chapter 1

Why We Lose

We show up every day and do the things we believe are necessary to run the business, grow profits, and increase the value of the company. We create demand for products, manufacture these products, sell the products to customers, deliver service to provide a good customer experience, develop additional products and services, and measure and report the results of our efforts to interested parties. We take actions and make investments that we believe will generate acceptable profit today and grow profit in the future.

Sometimes we achieve the sales and profit goals and sometimes we do not. There are many variables and moving parts in every business that contribute to the results—some we control and others are completely out of our control. All too often, we do not have a good handle on whether the actions and investments we pursue actually work and can be repeated.

The efforts to reduce production or manufacturing costs, by their very nature, are easier to manage, measure, and repeat. We typically have control of most of these costs and they are more easily identified and quantified. The systems used to reduce these costs and predict future cost reductions are proven and readily available thanks to Six Sigma, Lean Manufacturing, and other cost management systems.

Conversely, the actions and investments undertaken to provide customers what they value most—value propositions that contribute to their profits—are not as easy to manage, measure, or repeat. Identifying the specific components of the value proposition that contribute most to customer value and profits is difficult because it requires an in-depth knowledge of the customer's business. The relative impact of the value proposition versus that of competitors is more difficult to quantify and measure. Your value proposition has a direct impact on customer profits and represents the best opportunity to gain and maintain a true competitive advantage. Systems to manage these actions are not proven or readily available, making success difficult to repeat. This is where we focus the attention of this book.

Why? It is because of the absence of a rigorous business management system to tackle the challenges described above. Without such a business management system, organizations lack the ability to consistently and predictably create more value for customers. This results in being outmaneuvered by competitors and losing in the marketplace. Yes, we lose more than we would like.

After reading this chapter you will be able to:

- Understand why this books matters to you and your organization
- Understand what it means to Lose with Customers
- Define the six reasons Why We Lose
- Understand how this book, its authors and its partners can help you Win

Six Reasons Why We Lose

There are six reasons why companies lose.

Why We Lose

1. We don't understand the customer's perspective.
2. There is not enough quantitative rigor.

3. Data collected never finds its way into planning or execution.
4. We rely on individual surveys versus a continuous process.
5. The organization is not aligned or involved.
6. There is no systematic playbook.

We Lose Because We Don't Understand the Customer's Perspective

Before you react, let us elaborate on what we mean by losing. When our customers do not make more money doing business with us versus our competitors, we lose. If we do not know where we stand relative to our competitors in generating profits for our customers, we lose. If our organization lacks the ability to stay on top of customers' ever-changing needs and adjust our investments and actions customer-by-customer to beat competitors, we lose.

We lose potential profits from these customers and in some cases we lose the customers. If we do not maximize profit and profit growth from customers period after period, we lose out on opportunities to create more value for our stakeholders—we may lose our jobs. These are real losses with real impact on us and our business.

Why does this happen? Why do we lose? Well, we believe there are several contributing factors. However, the single greatest reason we lose is because we do not truly understand the customer's perspective of how to grow their profits. While this is a bold statement, it is not one that we make without significant proof from our experience and the experience of others with deep knowledge in this area.

First a personal story: I recall a strategic planning meeting with fellow members of the management team in a former company. We were going through the traditional process of strategic planning—identifying the key strategic growth issues and developing supporting strategies to pursue. A heated debate ensued about what customers really need, how much value they would receive if we met their needs, and how much money we could make in the process. The debate was great—we were wrestling with the key issues that would determine our success.

Each member of the team had an opinion supported by great anecdotes from customer visits and input from the sales organization. It was striking that each member of the team had a different opinion about the relative value of the various customer needs. There appeared to be no way to reach consensus and select the most important areas of customer needs to address. So I asked the question: "Do we really know what customers value from their perspective and do we have data to help us understand quantitatively how valuable these needs are to the customer?"

After a prolonged period of deafening silence, one of the team members mumbled: "Of course we don't." We had come to the recognition that we clearly did not understand how we could help customers grow their businesses. What followed is, unfortunately, something that we and many others have experienced. The leader of the business, in an effort to meet the timeline to complete the strategic plan to present to corporate, stated in a decisive voice, "Let's stop debating what customers need and get back to running the business."

Need we say more? This is an all-too-common occurrence in many B2B companies. There is a lack of understanding of the customer perspective and the value it brings. Yet we just move on and "get back to running the business" without having the fuel to run the business better—the customers' perspective. This behavior results in decision after decision about priorities, actions, and investments built on anecdotes, opinions, and gut feelings. This begs the question: "How do we maximize profits without incorporating the customer perspective in all we do?" We believe it is impossible.

To amplify the challenge we have personally experienced, here are the views of a few additional thought leaders and professionals.

> *"The profitable growth challenges of B2B companies will not be fully addressed until a true, unfiltered and quantitative understanding of customer's needs replaces the anecdotal and qualitative information that drives decision making in many organizations today."*
> —Ralph Oliva, Executive Director of the Institute for the Study of Business Markets (ISBM)

> *"When organizations move from over-reliance on discrete market research as the primary means to introduce customer input into the planning process, in favor of a more systematic approach to capture and*

include the customer perspective at the center of the planning process, management decisions will become truly customer centric and yield better results."

—Patrick Farrey, Executive Director,
Business Marketing Association

"Even companies with the most effective strategic account management and sales organizations are challenged to systematically capture customer input and use it to align the entire organization to deliver winning value propositions. This continues to be an area of great opportunity to create and sustain competitive advantage in the marketplace."

—Bernard Quancard,
CEO Strategic Account Management Association

"There were multiple definitions of 'winning' with our customers prior to Customer Discovery. Those definitions typically evolved on a customer-by-customer basis with an underlying theme of 'We grow and prosper only when our customers grow and prosper.' It all sounds great until you get into the metrics and attempt to understand if in fact growing and prospering is really taking place with a customer. The metrics typically had a disproportionate amount of Owens Corning's business metrics and not much, if any at all, customer-focused metrics. Said another way, I am not sure we had a good grasp on translating what we were doing into how it impacted the customer. We didn't have a good understanding or visibility to what it meant to their business . . . but we typically had a great understanding of what it meant to our business, our goals and our sales plans."

—Chad Fenbert, Director of Sales, Owens Corning

"We were spending so much energy trying to get the most out of the marketing investments we were making, that we really hadn't invested the time and energy to decide if we were making the right decisions."

—Christian Nolte, Director of Strategic
Marketing, Owens Corning

So we are not alone! Ensuring you include the customer perspective in the management of your business is not a "nice to have"; it is a "must have." And you know what? There is no easy button for incorporating the customer view into the fabric of your business. It is a journey and an ongoing commitment to build capability within your organization at a pace that out flanks your competitors. Throughout the book, we will share the latest tools, practices, and techniques we have used to improve business performance by incorporating the customer's point of view into the management of business.

We Lose Because There Is Not Enough Quantitative Rigor

Existing methods of measuring what customers' value and the impact these things have on their profits are not quantitative or rigorous enough. It is difficult to use outside-in customer perspectives unless you have some idea of the potential for improving business performance in dollars and cents. Being able to communicate within your organization what customers want in terms of profit dollar potential tends to get more attention than a litany of qualitative concepts.

It is quite amazing how important and even risky decisions are made to invest in new markets, new products, new services, more sales people, and so on without a quantitative understanding of how these investments impact customers' profits.

Let's be honest, what would happen if a business case was presented to the executive team for a plant expansion with only qualitative support, such as "Our largest customer thinks this is a good idea" or "We feel comfortable it will reduce costs and improve our competitive position." Oh, and I love this one: "The customer will walk and we'll lose all of their business if we don't do it." In most cases, the proposal would be dismissed without a quantitative and more substantive estimate of the operational and financial impact on the company.

However, business cases are presented and approved to invest significant sums in revenue-generating programs or other improvements to the company's value proposition with the equivalent qualitative support. Even if there is a quantitative assessment of the financial impact on the company, it is not accompanied by a quantitative assessment of the impact on the customers' operations and profits.

How is it possible to develop a sound assessment of the value that will be captured by the company without first assessing the value that will be created for the customer? A quantitative measure of the value that will be created from the investment is a prerequisite to assessing the value that can be captured in the form of sales and profits. A quantitative measure of the value created for customers is not often completed. As a result, we make estimates and develop business cases that are more risky and do not deliver the expected results in the marketplace. We lose because we do not use enough quantitative rigor.

A Brief Discussion of Outside-In and Improved Decision Making

We use the phrase outside-in consistently throughout the book. Before going further it makes sense to provide more background to what goes through our heads when we use the phrase.

We explored this in the previous book, titled *Beyond Six Sigma, Profitable Growth through Customer Value Creation* (John Wiley & Sons, 2006). Although we explored this concept in our last book, we did not come up with the idea of outside-in. We are not really sure who did. But we give much credit to Dr. Daniel Kahneman, a professor at Princeton University, who won the the 2002 Nobel Prize in Economics for his proofs that we tend to be overconfident in our beliefs. This overconfidence bias yields decision making that can be faulty. The point of outside-in is that we need to use more outside-in information to combat our own overconfidence and eliminate a powerful yet natural bias in our decision making. If you boil this whole book down to its core, it is about finding rigorous and systemic approaches to breaking these overconfidence biases that we all have.

There are plenty of books and cases on the legitimacy of injecting outside-in customer perspectives that go well beyond our simple treatment here or in our last book. Books written by far smarter and famous people than us. We are huge fans of Richard Thaler, Chicago Booth Professor, and his work on

(Continued)

decision making whether it be corporate or personal. One of his recent books, *Nudge*, is a brilliant and practical piece on getting inside the brains of people and understanding how they think and make decisions.

Barbara Bund, MIT Professor, wrote a book titled the *Outside-In Corporation* that chronicles several well-documented cases of companies prospering from the use of outside-in customer information. Her book also documents how difficult it is to establish and maintain an outside-in culture.

Rick Kash's book *The New Law of Demand and Supply* does a nice job of establishing how more and more markets are being driven from the customer back (outside-in) and not from the supplier out (inside-out).

Bill Hass and Shep Pryor, friends of ours, recently completed a book, *The Private Equity Edge*, that discusses how private equity markets can take advantage of their nimbleness and use outside-in customer knowledge to outperform the markets.

These previous works and many more serve as foundational thinking to shape the approach to collect and use outside-in customer information. In this book, we focus on our experiences on using this proven concept to provide you with more of a "so what do I do in the operation and management of my B2B company?"

We Lose Because the Organization Is Not Aligned or Involved

These companies do not have the functions of their organizations really vested in using an outside-in customer perspective to improve their decision making. The responsibility for collecting and making use of the outside-in customer information is far too silo'd within a functional area, either sales or marketing.

As a result, other critical parts of the organization do not provide input into the process and do not buy in. When the new offerings are developed and ready for launch, these groups become onlookers rather than participants. Execution is doomed from the start when this happens.

When the uninvolved groups are coerced or forced into participation, there is not a clear understanding on how they specifically contribute to delivering the value to customers.

Creating and delivering value to customers is a team sport! Getting the team on the same page seems a simple enough concept but the reality of day-to-day business is that it is not so easy to accomplish. We will talk about how to get this done.

We Lose Because the Data Collected Never Finds Its Way into Planning or Execution

This is almost a universal problem. In this case, companies may have some form of outside-in customer information but fail to use the information in their planning processes. In our years of doing this work, we have found a miniscule number of examples where customers who provided feedback would say their feedback was heard and resulted in change.

It is commonplace to have the marketing or market research organization conduct research to assess customer growth opportunities. Yet, the results of the research are not often used to shape the development of customer offerings or the growth strategy of the company. Thus, the information and valuable customer knowledge gained through the research is wasted.

Many organizations seem to be on autopilot, using the same anecdotal or historical view of customer needs to drive planning and execution. The research is reviewed and then is stored on a favorite hard drive or flash drive, yet operations, sales, marketing, customer service, R&D, and other functions do not change priorities consistent with the findings from customers. Customers continue to be dissatisfied with the relative value we bring to bear on their business versus competitors. The new learning or insight is not acted on and we lose opportunities for innovation in the way we serve customers and help them succeed, while also losing the opportunity to generate more profit for the business.

All of the successes and failures we have been a part of during our journey have hinged on execution. No surprise. It is such a complex road between successfully understanding what your customer really values through to executing on the insights and knowledge gained. To the comments we made earlier, it seems like we get all excited, figure out what really matters to the customer, and then come back to the farm where you get a big dose of "Okay, that's great but let's get back to running the business." Using outside-in customer information must become part of how you do work and not something extra. We'll talk more about this in the chapters ahead.

We Lose Because of Reliance on Individual Surveys versus a Continuous Process

Surveys work better to determine how a company is doing in deploying its inside-out approach to business rather than serving as a source of outside-in data. If we intend to augment the management of our business with an outside-in customer perspective, then we must find a continuous process that can be improved as our organization learns and grows.

There is a lack of continuity in developing an understanding of customers' needs and how they change over time. This approach hinders the organization's ability to develop a knowledge base of the key drivers of value in the customer's business. It also limits the ability of the organization to anticipate or predict the outcome of situations faced previously.

So, when faced with the same opportunities or challenges, we re-create solutions rather than rely on sound documented history of what has or has not worked in the past. The absence of continual learning that comes from an ongoing capture of customer needs inhibits our ability to quickly adapt to changing customer needs.

Raise your hand if you enjoy surveys. Enough said. If you don't like them, then what makes you think that your customer does? I am personally not aware of a General Manager who will sit down and put an hour of serious thought in response to a survey. There are better ways and we'll touch on a couple.

We Lose Because There Is No Systematic Playbook

This simply means that the company does not have a process. All companies, large and small, need some kind of method or playbook to organize the collection, analysis, and use of outside-in customer information.

Collecting this kind of information on an ad hoc basis may work for a short period but does not stand up to the test of time.

It is critical to understand the customer's perspective. Yet when organizations only understand the customer's perspective at a point in time using an ad hoc approach, it is difficult to refresh the customer perspective as things change.

Things do change. Market conditions change. Customers' needs change. Competitors' responses change. To be effective at identifying and meeting customers' most valuable needs (from the customers' perspective) better than competitors period after period, a systematic playbook is required. This is too important to manage on an ad hoc basis.

As we explore what it takes to win with customers, we focus on how outside-in customer knowledge and its use addresses the challenges companies must overcome to win—helping customers make more money, and capturing more money in return. However, experience has taught us that the unique challenges faced by the various groups within the organization must be addressed with different solutions—all based on the application of outside-in customer knowledge.

We've taken this well beyond a process, to what many now refer to as a customer management system composed of process, tools, and people. We will build on each of these elements as we go.

Is This Book for You?

During the course of this book, we explore the perspectives of each of the functional areas of the organization in relation to these common problems that companies face in executing an outside-in customer approach. In our years of doing this work, we have also uncovered the unique challenges faced by various parts of the organization in their quest to win with customers.

If you are interested in helping improve the financial performance of your company and learning more about "how to" use a proven new business management system to win with customers, this book is for you.

Executive/management is tasked with the decision-making responsibility of selecting the growth strategies for the business, overseeing the operations, and delivering the financial results. Many executives and their teams make awfully important decisions that determine the company's success or failure without the benefit of valuable outside-in customer knowledge to inform their decision making—introducing a higher level of risk into their decision making.

If you are an executive who would like to feel more confident that your company's investment decisions will actually create value for your customers and your company—this book is for you.

Sales carries the inc\redible burden of delivering top-line growth month after month, quarter after quarter, and year after year. As organizations pursue strategies to increase customer share of wallet, transform from product to solution sales, and capture more value from every sale, sales management and their teams are increasingly challenged by customers to prove the value of their offerings versus those of competitors. The "proof" increasingly sought by many customers can only be provided by rigorous quantitative analysis and the resulting measurable value of a specific product or service when consumed by a specific customer. The increased complexity of this type of selling effort demands a set of supporting sales tools that help clearly communicate and measure value, accelerate the selling process, and help to establish the most loyal and profitable customer relationships.

If you are a sales professional who would like to have your customer heard by your company and want to sell products and services that are truly differentiated in the market—this book is for you.

Marketing is continually seeking ways to find the most attractive growth markets and segments, while developing strategies, brands, products, and plans to deliver the highest levels of sales and profit growth year after year. Despite myriad new efforts explored, the degree of meaningful differentiation among competing products and services continues to diminish. Many marketers are discovering the true basis for differentiation is found in measurable financial value delivered to customers, based on outside-in customer knowledge. However, few marketers have access to an approach, sufficiently skilled people, and the supporting tools to implement an outside-in approach cost-effectively. Although some marketing organizations have experienced success on a one-off basis, most struggle in gaining the support of other parts of the organization to implement a systematic deployment of outside-in customer knowledge to create sustained differentiation that delivers sales and profit growth.

If you are a marketer who would like to hear your organization's value proposition communicated by the sales force on a consistent basis, achieve alignment with sales on key customer needs, and develop communication that is used proficiently by the sales force in their selling efforts—this book is for you.

Research and development (R&D)/product development is challenged with the creation of a steady stream of winning technologies and products. In most organizations, the results from R&D and product development activity resemble a cycle of boom to bust—in many cases, more bust than boom. One of the greatest challenges faced by R&D is getting the needed input to focus its efforts and shape the product development portfolio planning. At the core of this challenge is finding a reliable source of real customer problems that, when solved, result in measurable economic value for the customer and attractive profits for the company. Outside-in customer knowledge and its systematic use are critical to deliver winning products from R&D and increase the return on the company's R&D and product development investment. It is also the means by which R&D and product development can effectively communicate with customers and share progress on development projects from a perspective that will gain and maintain customer interest and excitement throughout the development cycle. This critical ingredient will help organizations deliver more profitable sales from new products sooner.

If you are in product development or R&D and would like to improve the connection between your development efforts and the operational and financial success of your customers, short circuiting the process from idea to product development to successful launch—this book is for you.

Process organizations such as customer service, manufacturing, and logistics use process-based approaches and systems to support customer acquisition and retention. They rely on reliable and repeatable processes to deliver consistent, high-quality outcomes. The design of many processes and systems is based on an understanding of what brings value to the customer in support of their business operations. Organizations with limited access to outside-in customer knowledge struggle to deliver service that is most valuable to customers in general, and struggle even more to deliver truly valuable service to customers or customer segments with specific needs related to how value is created within their business. The use of outside-in customer knowledge serves as a guide to keep process organizations focused on measurable results that impact customers in ways that customers truly value.

If you work in manufacturing and would like to increase your organization's understanding of quality and its importance and value from the customer perspective and would like to know that your efforts are directly linked to the success of your customers—this book is for you.

If you work in customer service and would like to bring what customers actually care about into the center of what you do each day, feeling confident that making changes to continually improve will result in greater value for customers and more profits for your business—this book is for you.

If you work in logistics and have a desire to increase the value that your sales organization and customers place on the effort you expend to keep service programs in order and deliver what is expected, bringing innovation to your efforts that customers need and are willing to pay for—this book is for you.

Finance is responsible for managing the financial aspects of the business, including capitalization, cash flow, analysis, and reporting. The financial metrics and tools used today are great for measuring profitability (P&L statement), company value (balance sheet), and financial health (a range of financial ratios).

If you are in finance and would like to assess the business's performance based on its current and future ability to impact customer profits versus competitors— then this book is for you.

We are writing the book for each of these perspectives and more. One of the lessons we've learned is that including many functions in the journey to an outside-in approach improves the chances for success. Sure, it is important to have an executive sponsor and that strong champion and all of the rest, but real momentum occurs when a large portion of the organization sees itself through the eyes of the customer and has an organizing approach for action and measurement that becomes part of how they do work.

Throughout the course of this book, we talk about developing an outside-in customer approach from these multiple perspectives.

Why This Book Is Important

We are writing this book to share the insights gained from our experiences developed during executing our own outside-in customer approaches. We speak often to professionals in many different settings and the most common interests are: How do you do this? How do you get started? What do you do? There is really no way to answer these questions during a brief conversation. Our goal with this book is to give every business professional who is interested in using more outside-in customer knowledge in the management of his or her business a place to get information.

Improving companies through using outside-in customer information has been our career passions. Keith has spent his career working directly with companies leading the transformation to an outside-in organization. He is a true practitioner with experience using much of what we outline in the book. Jerry and his team at Valkre have seen the challenge of executing outside-in from multiple perspectives, including practitioner, service provider, and technology design and implementation. Their recent experience in leading projects and enabling results has uniquely prepared them to guide others in developing this capability.

Keith, Jerry, and their teams have experienced firsthand success and failure. Their desire in this book is for the reader to learn from these many years of experiences with the hope that an ever-increasing number of B2B companies can become proficient at driving their businesses from the customer perspective. It is our fundamental belief that in order for companies to successfully compete in today's market they must inform their decision making with outside-in customer information. Companies that are the most nimble in understanding different ways to serve customers in the face of an ever-increasing set of innovative competitors and low-cost international producers will survive. Those companies that continue to think they can survive using the status quo of what worked yesterday will continue to struggle.

What Will You Learn?

This book is primarily a how-to guide. Sure, we touch on the theory and concepts behind our approaches here and there, but the thrust of our discussions are not so much about convincing you of the theory as much as providing examples, discussing methods, allowing you to participate in exercises, and reviewing business cases from others who have experienced success.

You gain an understanding of the four real breakthroughs in thinking and practice, as well as two additional supporting aspects of this new approach to Winning with Customers.

Like most things learned, our knowledge has also been informed by those situations that did not go as planned. Our hope is that during the course of the book you will see both the successes and disappointments and be able to chart a course within your own organization that will be more successful as a result of having shared our experiences.

Our goal with this information is not to transform your organization or even to make you an expert user. The goal is simply to provide a few practical tools that can help you get started.

We hope you learn to get past the cynicism that some people have about the potential for suppliers and customers to work together for joint business performance improvement. We have been involved in thousands of breakthrough interactions between suppliers and their customers and have yet to find more than a handful of general managers who do not understand that their respective jobs require them to manage capital on both sides (customer and supplier) to maximize return. The only question really is whether you think you can do this better without the help of your supplier or your customer. If you think you can better maximize the returns on the capital you spend by working with your customers and/or your suppliers, then this book is for you. We show you how to improve.

We hope you learn that your value proposition is a big deal and understanding it deeply is the key to your success. We hope that you learn and come to agree that being able to express to your customer why your value proposition helps your customer make more money versus competitive alternatives can set you apart from competition. We hope you learn that a little bit of math and quantitative rigor can go a long way toward dispelling myths and generating true understanding of what customers value.

We hope you learn that building an outside-in customer-driven company is about "execution" and not about studies or surveys. If you get nothing else from this book, we hope that you learn this point. All of the customer insights and knowledge in the world is for nothing if it is not transformed into plans and actions that generate benefits with some *financial* value.

Is Now the Time?

A big question that many of you will likely ask is, "Is now the time to begin implementing a new business management system of this magnitude?" Well, this is a good question, and we have a good answer.

Here is the reality: There is never an ideal time. Some say that when the economy is going gangbusters, there is no time to slow down and implement a system such as this. Others say that when the economy slows and money and resources are tight, it is not the ideal time to implement a system such as this.

Based on our experience and the experience of the companies we have worked with, we argue that anytime is a good time. When you discover something of this magnitude that we believe represents a game changer in the way that you run your business, serve your customers, and leap ahead of your competitors, anytime is the right time to implement. However, we realize that some of you may wonder what a current user of this system may have to say about his decision. Here is a perspective:

> *"There is never a better time to do this . . . it is imperative to have organizational alignment on the value of the product and service investments that we make every day. That was true in 2007 when we started and is still true today in the tough economic environment we all face."*
>
> —Christian Nolte, Director of Strategic Marketing,
> Owens Corning

Owens Corning

Owens Corning has been a true partner and thought leader in our journey to help companies win with their customers for the last three years. Just as Owens Corning has learned from our experiences, its entrepreneurial spirit, focus, and thirst for being better have taught us a thing or two about how to turn something that looks great on a piece of paper into functional products that can be adopted by massive organizations. We cannot thank the company reps enough for putting up with us,

(Continued)

not being afraid to try new things, celebrating successes, and growing from failures.

Of course, that should not be much of a surprise because Owens Corning has been a leading manufacturer since 1938. Based out of Toledo, Ohio, the company pushed the envelope before by dying its insulation pink. Owens Corning's PINK insulation is well recognized and enjoys a high brand preference. I guess the question is "Why is it pink?" Common answers include:

- The company wanted to make it look like cotton candy.
- It makes you feel comfortable.
- It takes advantage of the popularity of the *Pink Panther* movies of the 1970s.

The real story is that when Owens Corning first tested All Fiber (AF) fiberglass wool insulation at the Newark, Ohio, plant, it used red dye to distinguish the product from previous white insulation. The red dye made the AF wool look pink. The new PINK insulation was tested against its predecessor with installers. However, when the new AF fiberglass insulation was put on the market, the dye was no longer used. Installers did not like it and began asking for the PINK insulation. It was then that PINK was born. They did it, and it's been a marketing sensation . . . Building materials manufacturers would die for that kind of brand recognition. On May 12, 1987, Owens Corning made legal history as the first company to trademark a single color, in this case, PINK.

Although Owens Corning is known for its PINK Insulation, it is a highly diversified manufacturer of building and composite materials. It has been a Fortune 500 company for more than 50 years, currently employs 15,000 people, does business in 30 countries, and earns about $5 billion in sales each year.

That is not to say that some of those years have not been difficult. In 2000, Owens Corning had to declare bankruptcy because of growing asbestos liability claims. And most recently, as we all know personally, the bottom fell out in the new residential housing market that is critical to the growth of any building materials manufacturer. Combining these challenges with increased activity from low-cost manufacturers and increasingly diverse and complex channels to market, Owens Corning was and is in a tremendously competitive environment. Owens Corning's customers are big-box retailers, national distributors, original equipment manufacturers, and independent contractors and dealers.

At the beginning of 2007, a critical objective was issued to the organization that all employees must be accountable for the value they create for their customers. While addressing the organization, the point was made with a simple quote:

"The fundamental reason corporations exist is to create value for its customers."

Everyone knew that Owens Corning has been creating customer value for a long time . . . It's been in business since 1938. But Owens Corning recognized the opportunity to win in the marketplace by measuring customer value and making the organization accountable for this . . . That's how improvement is made. In February 2007, we met with Christian Nolte, then the director of strategic marketing, to discuss how to turn the objective into something the organization could touch. Christian is the true definition of a Change Agent. He understood what was being requested and, with our help, began getting his organization prepared to operate from an outside-in perspective. We will never forget that first meeting with Sheree Bargabos, president of the roofing division, and being asked, "Who are you and what are you doing here?" Christian successfully gained buy-in from leadership that we needed to try something new, and we did. We interviewed more than 120 customers in about six weeks (yes, we are still recovering) and came back to the organization with a customer voice that could not be denied. To Owens Corning's credit, it listened, understood, and acted . . . obtaining a 600 percent ROI within the first year.

(Continued)

Since then, we have had the pleasure of growing and winning alongside Owens Corning. Chad Fenbert, director of building material sales, took the reins from Christian and drove the process into the sales organization. Bob Harlan, Director of Business Insights, built on Christian's and Chad's work and drove the process into the broader organization. Dave Longmuir now leads the organization from both an adoption and growth standpoint. In addition to these executives, we have been supported by strong leadership from Sheree Bargabos, Jim Drew, and other executives who now cannot imagine "not doing this." Not to be outdone, the sales organization has to be commended for learning and executing, led by early adopters such as Roger Warren and Steve Persinger. Owens Corning is a large part of the story and we will share as much as we can throughout the book without jeopardizing the advantage they have built over their competition in the past few years. You get a chance to hear the stories and lessons learned from these thought leaders throughout the book.

Summary

We recognize that a discussion on "losing" is not the most positive way to begin this book. However, we hope that by exploring the six reasons why companies lose, you can better appreciate the magnitude of the problem we and others have been working to solve for many years. The fuel that propels us forward year after year, setback after setback is the enormous size of the challenge and the immeasurable amount of financial value lost by B2B companies, their customers, and communities throughout the world.

Our belief is that the loss of value is directly related to the six issues we raised in this chapter that clearly articulate Why We Lose:

- We do not understand the customer's perspective.
- There is no systematic playbook.

- There is not enough quantitative rigor.
- The organization is not aligned or involved.
- Data collected never finds its way into planning or execution.
- There is reliance on individual surveys versus a continuous process.

Without a clear understanding of the problems companies face in their efforts to Win with Customers, we and you cannot adequately address the issues and move beyond them to a solution that works. Now we can move forward together and focus our attention on the results of our efforts—winning.

Chapter 2

Define Winning

In Chapter 1, "Why We Lose," we discussed why companies lose—what a downer! Let's move on and talk about winning. Everyone likes winning. Like sports teams, businesses that compete in markets strive to win. Winning ultimately boils down to profits and profit growth. Companies that win in one period of business operations have more profits to reinvest and, hopefully, win again. This is how successful companies are built. Win. Reinvest. Grow. Repeat.

Now for a sobering reality check. In the game of winning with customers there are others: competitors. They are also making decisions and investments to win in the same markets with the same customers. Everyone is striving for the winning strategy and the winning plays. It is not an easy game. There are smart people playing the game and the stakes are high. When you win at this game, your company grows, new people are hired, and you move up in the organization. You make more money and send your kids to college, the community prospers, new investments are made, and customers benefit from your new investments. These are the dreams and aspirations every one of us who entered business had in the beginning and hopefully still possess today.

We have developed a winning strategy and a few plays that have helped others to win. We spend the rest of the book focusing on these winning plays, so no more loser talk. We develop the plays with you through the rest of this chapter as well as Chapter 3, "The Playbook." Then we hit the field and run the plays in Chapters 4 through 8. After helping you learn to run the plays, we share some advice on forming your own team in Chapters 9 through 10.

As logic would have it, our six keys to winning, or Six Big Ideas, are generated by addressing the challenges discussed in Chapter 1, "Why We Lose." Some elements of our solution captured in the Six Big Ideas (The Big 6) are considered breakthroughs. We especially like the people who tell us this! Let's explore them and you can come to your own conclusions.

After reading this chapter you will be able to:

- Understand what is meant by Winning *with* Customers
- Define the Six Big Ideas and four breakthroughs that create the winning plays
- Understand the possible customer growth strategies enabled by this approach using the Growth Cube
- Understand the importance of knowing: "Does your customer make more money doing business with you?"
- Understand the relationship between creating value for your customers and capturing profits for yourself through a Value Exchange
- Understand the importance of achieving both cost reductions and revenue growth to win with customers . . . it is about profitability

Here we go! Why don't we start with a quick case? The hard thing about real-life cases is that they never exactly line up with the point you are trying to make. This one simply reinforces the idea that there is usually a path to winning with customers even in situations you may not think possible. The other thing about cases you will read in this book is that they are not in our voice or written by us. They are direct from the customer. So when you see the distinct improvement in writing you'll know why.

Winning with a Customer at Owens Corning

In an industry with several large customers and a product that is fairly commoditized, it is difficult to define a go-to market strategy that creates more money for our customers relative to the competition. In the past, the approach has been to paint each customer with a broad brush as the "market."

From one customer's perspective, this approach clearly was not flying. We learned that the investments that we make on behalf of our customers do not necessarily help them . . . because it did not differentiate the customers from their competition. As far as this customer was concerned, because our investment and go-to market strategy was so broad, we had commoditized ourselves into a transactional supplier. On top of that, we were dangerously close to costing them money relative to our competition because of turnover in the sales organization and increasing channel conflict. The customer suggested that "we have lost the edge we once shared together." Our challenge was to get that edge back while minimizing channel conflict with our other customers in the marketplace.

Our solution was to get clear on the value of our investments to their bottom line today and what investments could be made to improve the customer's profitability . . . with math. By being rigorous and serious with this customer, we clearly defined the specific needs for this customer, built customer-specific plans that facilitate co-creation of win–win solutions, and measured our successes and failures. This has taken the customer relationship from one that was "good" to a true partnership.

According to our customer, we have gone from a transactional supplier to a value-added partner in just over a year as a result of delivering the specific opportunities the customer identified during the Discovery Interview. We have since been updated on its needs and are currently working on doubling

(Continued)

our impact to its bottom line. As a result, we are growing with this particular customer internationally while maintaining our share and margin positions.

In parallel to winning with this customer, we sat down with more customers in this place and found that in some cases, our investments were working, and in others, they were not. We found that there were similar needs that warranted big investments, but also individual needs that we deliver on as well. It has brought clarity into how we go to market. We have found that by informing our decisions with the individual needs of our customers, we are better at segmenting our investments and reducing channel conflict.

The Big 6

Remember the six reasons we lose, as discussed in Chapter 1? Table 2.1 shows these six reasons along with their winning counterparts.

We discuss each of these six winning elements of the solution to give you a good understanding of what each means and involves. But before we do, let's examine the importance and relevance of the solution and the elements that represent breakthroughs to business success.

Table 2.1   Why We Lose

Why We Lose	The Big 6 (Why We Win)
We don't understand the customer's perspective.	We help customers make more money doing business with us.
There is not enough quantitative rigor.	We inject quantitative outside-in customer information into decision making.
Data collected never finds its way into planning or execution.	We develop and execute customer plans that deliver value (The Red Zone).
Reliance on individual surveys versus a continuous process.	We predict growth.
The organization is not aligned or involved.	We build capability and shape culture.
There is no systematic playbook.	The CVC Management System

Making major advances in the ability to win in business is no small feat—we know this all too well from experience. So let us be clear: There is no silver bullet. However, this combination of new approaches and advances in critical areas has proven to be successful. Here's why.

Amazing things happen when an organization begins to think first about how it can make its customers better off and help them make more money. Really. We know it is a tall order, and for some companies, a major change. But winning companies put their profits aside for just a moment to gain an in-depth understanding of how they are or are not creating value for customers, relative to competitors. We have found success in this area to be a true leading indicator of a sustained winning formula and profit growth. This is an idea whose time has come.

We hesitate to make the next statement, but it is true. And we could not find a better way to make the point: "You can't manage what you can't measure." We are not sure who coined the phrase, but we all know it is true. We believe it is important to apply this conviction to the customer information used to support your decision making. Winning organizations have moved beyond anecdotes and gut-feel about customers and graduated to a higher standard of quantifiable data to understand objectively how customers make money, what customers value, and what impact the company has on customer profits. Injecting this critical data into decision making results in better decisions and reduces risk—both are important contributors to winning.

If your company is like most others, you spend a lot of time developing sales plans for your customers. Winning organizations do three things differently that contribute to winning:

1. First, customer plans are developed to address the specific things that create attractive and measurable value for customers—from the customers' perspective.
2. Second, customer plans are endorsed and supported by the entire management team and backed up with committed actions and investments.
3. Third, these plans are developed, maintained, and updated by the organization—not by sales. For winning organizations, these vital

customer plans serve as the compass to keep the organization heading in the right direction to deliver what is truly important and valuable for customers. They use these valuable customer plans as a weapon to enhance execution—this sets the winners apart.

Every company, whether small, large, public, or private, would like to improve the predictability of profit growth for future periods. A key to making this happen is the ability to measure the impact of your actions and investments on individual customers. And specifically, how much more money each customer will make in future periods by doing business with you. We have developed new metrics to enable the measurement of customer value creation—one customer at a time. This, coupled with the ability to measure and forecast the incremental value you plan to capture in future periods—one customer at a time—has the potential for a major breakthrough in the predictability of profit growth. We share more later about the progress in this area.

Did we say earlier that there is no silver bullet to win with customers? Well, it bears repeating. There is no silver bullet to win with customers. There have been many different approaches pursued to help organizations be more successful. This is hard work that requires building new organizational muscles and know-how. Consultants cannot do this for you. We know because Jerry spent many years as a consultant helping companies develop the winning model. In some instances, unfortunately, the winning position eroded over time after the consultant teams moved on to the next client. True winners make a long-term commitment to build the organizational capability required to win again, and again, and again. These organizations attack the cultural inhibitors to winning with customers by systematically shaping a culture that is customer-centric, value-oriented, analytical, committed to planning and focused on profit growth.

All elements of our solution to win with customers are important and four are considered breakthroughs. However, the element we believe may be most essential is the system that brings together all the components required to deliver the winning solution. This unique combination of concepts, methods, metrics, planning tools, software, training, and certification represents the sixth big idea and a breakthrough to winning with customers.

Now, let's explore the Big 6 elements of the winning solution further:

1. *We help customers make more money doing business with us.* This is a breakthrough element of our solution. We pose the provocative question: "Do your customers make more money doing business with you?" on the cover of the book. It is no surprise that it is part of the solution. We have devised a unique, data-driven approach to understanding if "your customers make more money by doing business with you." The fundamental philosophy is that when a customer chooses a supplier, the expectation is to make more money by doing business with the selected supplier than the customer would with a competitive alternative. If this does not hold true in the customer's eyes, then sooner or later he or she will make the choice that does.

   This concept is fundamental to our approach. In business-to-business markets, economic results or profits seem to win out almost every time. Relationships are important and may keep you in the game but generating profits for your customer and for yourself are the keys to winning the game. You know the metric used for measuring your own profits. But what do you know about whether your customer is better off by doing business with you? Do customers make more money because they do business with you? There are many metrics in the business world that are positioned to tell you whether your customer is satisfied or is loyal. Our belief is that most of these measures are born out of the consumer world and then forced to fit in business-to-business. This may be in part due to the significant level of spending on marketing in the consumer world. This is a sum that dwarfs the marketing spending in the business-to-business arena. We poor business-to-business people cannot afford to come up with our own more useful measure of success with our customers.

   Our work over 15 years has resulted in the development of a breakthrough measure we call DVP, or Differential Value Proposition. It more directly measures whether your customers are better off doing business with you than any other measure we know about. This measure is genuinely business-to-business specific and has been developed with a few leading business-to-business companies. Being able to directly measure whether customers are financially better off has literally changed the management approach to working with customers. Discoveries have been made that would otherwise have gone misunderstood. A ton of money has been made by customers and suppliers that would have been left on the table had these discoveries not come to light.

We spend considerable time later in this chapter and in Chapters 3 and 4 developing this measure with you. We show you through the course of the entire book how to leverage this understanding into the management of your business and into the fabric of your organization.

2. *We inject quantitative outside-in customer information into decision making.* When it comes to understanding if your customer makes money by doing business with you, we will drive to a quantified financial understanding. Yes, we will be qualitative as well. The qualitative aspect brings color and meaning to the quantitative financial perspective. We show you how to inject this package of quantitative and qualitative outside-in customer information into your day-to-day and annual decision-making processes. You receive a massive benefit as a result of doing this. The benefit emanates from breaking the overconfidence bias that exists in your organization regarding what creates value for customers. If you do not believe that you and your organization are overconfident about what the customer wants, then we would invite you to review the work by Dr. Kahneman, who won the 2002 Nobel Memorial Prize in Economic Sciences on this topic.

Before you jump to the conclusion that we are analytic zealots, we are not. Yes, we have been derailed once or twice by going to extremes on quantitative rigor. Through the school of "hard knocks" learning, we have landed at a place that represents a level of rigor that we have successfully scaled to large organizations. What you see in the book represents the practical reality of what we have been able to achieve and sustain with great companies.

An important thing to note is that we are not going to tell you how or when to make decisions. We recognize there are many other factors that go into decision making and timing. Our goal is to provide an outside-in, data-driven approach to injecting customer needs into your decisions about how to manage your company.

3. *We develop and execute customer plans that deliver value (The Red Zone).* Achieving success in this area is a *breakthrough* for many companies and maybe not so much for others. You find in Chapter 3 that we set up the book as a playbook following a sports analogy. For all of you who do not like sports we are sorry for this, but it was the most creative organizing model we could come up with. We mention the playbook at this moment because customer planning is about executing in the Red Zone—delivering when it counts.

For those of you who do not watch football, the Red Zone is the last 20 yards a team needs to progress to score a touchdown. Up to this point, the team has invested considerable energy and effort advancing the ball down the field to get into scoring position. Now, this is a crucial time for the team when superb execution is required to score.

Likewise, customer planning is about making sure that once we have decided to invest to create value, the organization and its resources are aligned and focused to deliver value for the customer. Another key requirement of successful customer planning is that the entire sales team understands the plan and effectively communicates to customers what we are doing to create customer value.

Customer planning also clearly outlines what we should expect in return when we deliver value to the customer—how many points we should receive by getting the ball over the goal line and "scoring" with the customer. Or, in the context of winning with customers, we know how much value we should capture in return for the value we create for customers (our fair share).

So what's the breakthrough? The breakthrough in our system is that sales professionals or sales teams have plans created for them based on investments you are making rather than generating their own plans based on a top-down growth target. The initiatives within the customer plans are updated by the organization rather than the sales professional. When the sales professionals are planning for those three customer calls tomorrow, they do not have to search the vast land of e-mail to find the customer plan updates they are supposed to communicate. The organization is happy since it feels its work and words are getting directly to customers. Sales is happy because they just eliminated the hours of work required to organize all of the communication received from their organization, normally contained in long strings of e-mail. The customer plans are ready at the push of a button in real time. The customer plans are always ready and visible for executives to arm them for that customer visit without causing the sales professional to take two days out of their lives to prepare. The customer plans also create accountability with your customers because they show how you are investing in what they recommended.

The customer plans create a historical bridge that a new sales professional or business manager can use to get up to speed. These plans become the organizational history of what worked and what did not work so well in your efforts to win with customers. And these sales plans are the key to execution. They represent the Red Zone plays that turn your actions and investments into profit.

4. *We predict profit growth.* The *breakthrough* here is being able to gain more confidence in your ability to predict profit growth for the next quarter or the following year. This is done through a combination of measurement and continuous improvement. Remember what we are measuring: "Are your customers making more money by doing business with you?" If you can answer that question with some level of clarity, then try these: "Just how much more money are they making by doing business with you? Do they think they will be making more money doing business with you in the future?" If we have the answer to these questions and can see how profits follow, we begin to better understand the correlation between your investments and their impact on customers' profits. Then we gain a better understanding the following year and again the next. And over time our confidence in the ability to predict profit growth increases.

Predicting profit growth one customer at a time and for the entire business is a concept that has powerful implications. It brings a level of measurability to the financial return of investments we make in customers like never before. This measurable financial return from customer investments is captured, analyzed, and reported throughout the organization, from the sales team to the CEO.

Everyone in the business would like to be more confident in his or her ability to predict performance. We have proven it to be impactful and our goal (we are not there yet) is to have it become part of investor conversations related to business valuations as you see in the maturity model introduced in Chapter 3, "The Playbook."

5. *We build capability and shape culture.* We have seen many attempts to become more customer-centric, customer-driven, customer-informed, or whatever you want to call it fail because the organization never really engages. Organizations are like rubber bands; you can stretch them but as soon as you let go, they immediately snap back to their original form. Bill Davis, former CEO of RR Donnelley, said it this way: "Culture eats strategy for lunch." We have certainly found this to be true. We have a combined 50 years of bumps, bruises, and cuts to share from our experiences of trying to tame the organizational beast. We do not have any breakthrough advice on this topic (we wish we did), but we have learned a few things we share with you through the course of the book. Some of those things we have already teed up in the five principles we have just discussed. But there are more.

One of them is the idea of continuous improvement. Do not think for a moment that you should take everything in the book and execute it in one fell swoop. We have never implemented it that way in our own companies or with companies we have helped. We have attempted to write the book in as logical and step-wise fashion as possible. The reality is that nothing is so clear-cut when you are working in your own organization where you may already be doing some things well to win with customers. You may be doing a great job with one thing we discuss but might receive great benefit from an element of our solution you have not yet tried. You need to piece together the approach that makes the most sense for you, and then take an approach using a philosophy of continuous improvement. One thing is for sure—whatever final solution works best for your organization will require taking action, learning from your efforts, and making continuous improvements to get the results.

You know what else we need to mention at this point: process. Process and continuous improvement go together. It is difficult to continuously improve if you do not have a process. We have developed processes over the years. Most of you probably know that process and sales go together like fire and water, oil and water, or anything else involving water. Sales likes to water down processes, or, even better, wash them away!

Process matters and we have developed a few standard approaches that we are sure you will find helpful.

The other idea we should mention is building your own capability to do the work described in the book. We believe deeply that by building your own competency for the concepts and practical approaches in this book, you and your organization will be better off. Although you may benefit from the support of outsiders, you cannot hand off this work to third-party providers and expect to change your company. This is a tall order. To this end, we have put a lot of energy into building a learning academy where you have a place to learn. We call this place the CVC Institute. If you are interested, go to www.winningwithcustomers.com to find more information and resources to help you create this capability for yourself and for your organization. We also talk more about how to certify your organization in the skills necessary to accomplish things we talk about through the course of the book in chapters 9 and 10.

6. *The CVC Management System.* CVC stands for Customer Value Creation. The CVC Management System is a *breakthrough.* A big part of what has driven success is the system we have developed. In the early days it consisted of concepts and methods. Then it grew to include a little training, to "pass on the intellectual property." Admittedly, this was a challenging thing to do during the days when Jerry was leading a consulting business that used this intellectual property to help clients develop a winning formula in their businesses.

Then it grew to several methods tied together into what non–Six Sigma professionals might call a process. Then it evolved further and improved through exposure to more companies and smart people. It continued to grow and expand with time as we experienced results and received feedback—some things worked and some did not. The changing economy also had a real impact on the solution, as organizations increasingly needed to address costs, as well as revenue in the profit equation. The pace of evolution quickened dramatically in the past few years. Our customers and our own companies drove this in large measure due to the recessionary economy. Most companies were faced with the risky decisions concerning what expenses or capital investments to make or cut during these unprecedented tough times. The evolutionary bridge we crossed during this period was going from a solution that required consultants to a solution focused solely on building your own capability. One of our colleagues likes to call the CVC Management System the anti-consultant. We have nothing against consultants because much of what has been designed into the system came by way of consulting many different companies.

The two elements that have been added during the past two years are software technology and training. The software technology called Render® has been developed with leading corporations and serves as the easy button for everything you read in this book. Formalized training has been developed that will educate and certify your organization to do everything in this book on its own; we call it the CVC Institute. Render® and the CVC Institute have been the added elements that support classifying the CVC Management System as being a true system. And they have been the final and necessary elements to truly deliver a capability to your company for winning with customers.

Okay, that is all for the Six Big Ideas. We are sure that with more thought and 10,000 more debates we could reduce this list of winning ideas to four or maybe we would expand to seven, since Barbara Minto says there are seven of everything. But for now we are sticking to these six and have stories to tell about each later on.

"Conversations we have with customers are many times transactional in nature, tactical in nature. And now they have become collaborative, they have become value-oriented conversations. Nothing is more valuable

than understanding what the customer values so it does help us. This process allows us to have those types of discussions.

One of the key elements of a successful strategic account organization is enrolling your senior leadership in the discussion with customers. As simple and straight forward as that sounds, as all of us know it is a task. This process enrolls our senior leadership into the agenda for the customer. Not what we think but it allows us to share what the customer thinks. There is nothing more valuable than having a discussion with your CEO or president of a division about what the customer values. It also allows you to enable field sales to be able to obtain resources in support of the customer. Now these resources come in many forms, people resources, finances, project-oriented initiatives, but it allows you to get to the specifics very, very quickly and obtain those resources in your business.

It also drives common language and alignment in all functional areas. As we all know, to be successful with a customer, many, many process groups touch the customer. In the case of Owens Corning we have customer financial folks, logistics folks, customer service center, marketing, we have so many functional groups that touch the customer and it allows us to drive a common language across all of these process groups and allows them to get in the customer conversation and drive value.

And with all that being said, it creates speed and execution in the market. And that's what it is all about."

—Jim Drew, Vice President National Accounts,
Owens Corning

Where Does This Book Fit in the World of Profit Growth Solutions?

In our last book, *Beyond Six Sigma, Profitable Growth through Customer Value Creation* (John Wiley & Sons, 2006), we spent considerable time discussing this profitable growth cube. The cube shown in Figure 2.1 represents all of the customer dimensions that lead to profit improvement with customers.

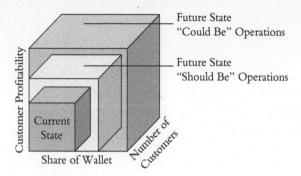

Future State
"Could Be" Operations

Future State
"Should Be" Operations

Current
State

Share of Wallet

Number of Customers

Customer Profitability

Figure 2.1   The Growth Cube

The dimensions are:

- Customer profitability
- Share of wallet
- Number of customers

The idea is that the combination of these dimensions of the cube represent all of the possible levers you can pull to increase your profits with customers. You can increase the profitability on your current business by increasing price or reducing the cost to serve your customers: customer profitability. You can increase profits by doing more business with the customers you have: share of wallet. Or you can win new customers to drive additional profits: number of customers. We had long debates on duration or the length of time you held on to customers. Duration is also an important consideration, but share of wallet over time seems to be a better measure.

We are not going to spend much time re-creating the cube in this book, but we have learned a few things that relate to the profit growth cube since 2006. Back in 2006, we talked about the three cube dimensions as being equally important. We suggested you take a close inventory of your business and then decide which dimension to pursue. The practical reality of our work with companies since then suggests there is a sequence to addressing the dimensions. Now, this may be influenced by the economy we have been in since 2006 and all sorts of other factors, but given those disclaimers, here is what we've experienced.

The share of wallet seems to be the dominant dimension in helping you win with customers. If you can command an ever-increasing share of the customer wallet, it is typically related to your ability to deliver value to your customer. Delivering value with customers you know and do business with is job #1. Customer profitability follows. If you are delivering good value and continue to seek ways to increase that value to customers, then opportunities for improving profits with the customer relative to your competitors through price or cost-to-serve reduction is enhanced. As you are figuring out how to increase share with existing customers or maximize profits, the formula for winning with new customers seems to just fall out. You will note during the book that we spend 90 percent of our time talking and working on figuring out how you create value for existing customers. But we also found that the outcome of this work yields an incredibly powerful approach to winning with new customers.

In our experience, the result of understanding the value you deliver to customers generates four benefits in this order of impact:

1. Increase share with existing customers (share of wallet)
2. Reduce cost to serve as you understand the levers that drive value (customer profitability)
3. Improve ability to win new customers (number of customers)
4. Ability to capture price as investments in new value are realized (customer profitability)

We have also found that different industries see themselves differently in the cube and in our work. Deal-based industries such as technology work differently than ongoing transaction industries such as building materials. This is not a black-and-white sort of difference, but nonetheless different. In technology, getting the big deal can make or break a year. There is tremendous focus on winning the deal, which tends to feel like the new customer dimension. In deal-based situations, there is little chance to work with a given customer to determine what is creating value and improving that value over the long term. For ongoing transactional customers, the entire health of the business is about improving value to that customer over the long term. Our focus is more on the latter than the former. The solution in this book has been built with those who have ongoing relationships with customers where gaining a deep understanding of what drives value for customers is important.

Building the Foundation: Does Your Customer Make More Money by Doing Business with You Relative to Your Competitors?

Well, it is time to start building a little more substance and understanding behind this phrase, which we have used several times already: "Do your customers make more money by doing business with you?" It is such an important concept to us and, before we are done, hopefully it will be to you as well. Here we go; put on your thinking caps.

Winning happens one customer at a time. The most successful organizations consistently develop and execute plans with precision to win customer by customer. These companies understand that each decision positively contributes to winning or it does not—there is no middle ground. You win the big contract with acceptable profit levels or you do not. You capture the target share of each customer's business or you do not. You pass through a price increase to each customer at planned levels or you do not. Each decision impacts profits and profit growth. Because winning as a business is the sum total of the ability to win one customer at a time, most companies measure profit at the customer level in the form of gross margin dollars and gross margin percent. Some companies use more sophisticated measures than others, but all are interested in analyzing this important measure of success—customer profitability.

Customer profitability comes to life in a financial report that looks something like the one shown in Table 2.2.

Table 2.2 Sample Financial Report

Customer	Sales	Gross Margin	Gross Margin %
AAA Industries	$1,321,452	$330,363	25%
Acme Distribution	11,354,768	2,043,858	18
Quality Distributors	3,943,234	1,419,564	36
Everywhere Retail	7,530,125	2,033,134	27
Giant Wholesale	32,562,903	4,884,435	15

Customer profitability has significant importance to the entire organization. For sales, customer profitability is a measure of the sales team's ability to sell the product or service at attractive pricing levels, and serves as a key determinant of sales compensation in many organizations. For marketing, customer profitability provides insights into the drivers of profitability for various customers and customer segments, thus providing an assessment of the company's true competitive advantage. For executives/management, customer profitability is the key ingredient to growing the business and its profitability—the ultimate goal of business leadership. For process organizations, such as customer service, research and development (R&D), product development, logistics, and so forth, customer profitability is how these organizations are funded. As customer profitability increases, more money is available to invest in the development of capabilities needed for these process organizations to better serve customers and create more value. The bottom line: Customer profitability is important to everyone in the company.

It is easy to understand why everyone focuses so much time on it. Billions of dollars have been invested to develop and implement Enterprise Resource Planning (ERP) systems, such as SAP, to measure profits. Even more money has been invested in Customer Resource Management (CRM) systems, such as Siebel, Oracle, and Salesforce.com, to better understand customer profitability and manage customer relationships in an effort to gain more profits from customers. Organizations look at customer profitability reports like the one above and ask questions like:

- How can we grow and sustain growth in the market?
- How can we earn more of our customers' business?
- How can we get higher prices from customers?
- How can we reduce our cost to serve these customers?

The answers to these questions typically result in decisions to develop new products, create new marketing programs, add more sales reps, increase prices, reduce manufacturing and operations costs via Six Sigma or Lean Manufacturing, and other investments to increase customer profitability. The answers to the questions above and the resulting actions are important—real money is made through successful implementation of these programs designed to increase customer profitability. There are real wins here.

However (there is always a "however," isn't there), in the highly competitive game of business, there is both winning and losing. Even if your organization is a lean, mean profit maximization machine, there may be few barriers that prevent your competition from replicating your success and moving you from winning to losing. If you are competing against low-cost suppliers from China, you know this all too well. These suppliers are proficient at reducing their costs and have the ability to kill markets by flooding them with cheap volume. If you are competing against value-added competitors, they continually explore ways to speed up innovation and their new-product development cycle. They implement CRM and ERP systems to improve customer relationships and manage customer profitability. They also continually eliminate waste in day-to-day operations to lower their costs. Of course, this is not news. However, the tools and capabilities used to compete have changed, making it easier for leading organizations to sustain their advantages while lowering the barriers for competitors to catch up quickly. In today's competitive B2B markets, the day-to-day game of survival and winning is more difficult than ever before.

The good news is that this book is not about things you most likely already know, nor is it intended to depress you with the realities of intense competitive pressure you face every day. We are writing this book to offer a solution to what we believe is one of the most critical problems that prevent companies from Winning with Customers. We believe that sometimes the best way to solve a problem is to look at it from a different perspective. In this book, we hope to provide an enlightening and valuable new perspective. Think about the discussion above and the questions organizations typically ask themselves as they compete to win. The common denominator in all of these questions is the customer. Maybe rather than asking "How can we make more money from this customer?" we ask: "Do customers make more money doing business with us?"

A favorite quote of ours from Owens Corning is:

"The fundamental reason corporations exist is to create value for its customers."

Makes sense, right? If your company is not creating value, it will not survive. In B2B markets, this boils down to whether customers are making more money doing business with your company relative to your competition. If we all agree this is a good thing, the next obvious question is why more companies are not measuring the value they create for their customers. Many companies make decisions to invest billions of dollars in new products, software, and other programs to maximize "customer profitability" without spending much time or money to understand the fundamental drivers of sustained customer profitability. We believe a greater understanding of how value is created for customers, along with the ability to measure the value, will enable your organization to improve decision making related to the improvement of customer profitability. These decisions and the resulting actions will lead to profit growth for both your customers and your business.

B2B companies that focus not only on their profitability, but also on the impact they have on customers' bottom lines, are redefining what it takes to win. We call this "Winning with Customers." As we explore how to win with customers, consider the following example. Traditionally, as we discussed above, companies measure winning along one dimension— their own profitability. In this example, we have a profitable customer that is contributing above average profitability, as shown in Figure 2.2.

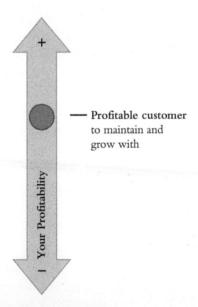

Figure 2.2 Traditional View of Profitability

However, as the company seeks opportunities to grow the business, there is some critical information not provided by this one-dimensional view. This view does not help to understand how secure the current profits may be. It does not provide insight into the specific investments the company made to achieve the current position. It does not tell you where to invest your next dollar to grow with this customer. So here is the question: Is this really a picture that measures winning?

Organizations that know how their products and services impact customers' profits relative to the competition develop a more complete picture. This picture includes an assessment of the company's impact on its customer's profitability, as shown in Figure 2.3.

This additional perspective suggests that the company's impact on the customer's bottom line is low, relative to the impact of competitors. This is not good, and indicates that the company's position with this customer is not secure. This additional view changes the company's thinking from growth to survival. Including the impact on the customer's profit creates a clearer picture of the situation and gives a more accurate assessment of whether the company is winning or losing with the customer.

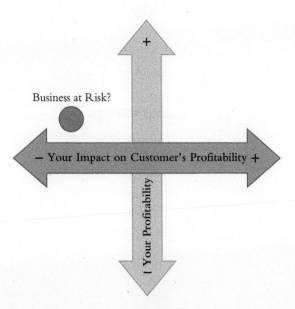

Figure 2.3 Profitability with Customer Perspective

Although the picture is clearer, it is not yet complete. Understanding customer profitability and the impact on the customer's profit are important. However, it is also important to understand two additional factors in the winning equation:

1. How to *create* value for the customer—from the customer's perspective.
2. How to *capture* your fair share of the value created for the customer.

Gaining a grasp of current customer profitability and the organization's impact on customer profits, versus competitors, provides a needed assessment of the current situation at a point in time. It is important to know where you stand with the customer.

You may be winning today. However, winning in the future requires taking the right actions during the next period of business operations, and the next, and the next. As shown in Figure 2.4, taking the right actions increases your impact on the customer's profitability.

In order to do this, it is important to know which of your actions and investments contributed most or least to the current level of customer profitability. What specific products or services, when used by the

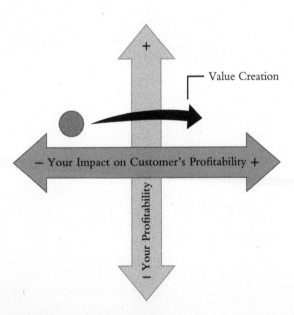

Figure 2.4   Profitability with Value Creation

customer, result in the greatest impact on their profits, as compared to those of the competition?

Gaining this understanding provides real insight into *how* value is being created for customers. Did the new initiative launched with such high expectations really deliver—from the customer's perspective? Did it have a greater impact on customer profits than other offerings you or the competition provide? Without this clarity, you do not know what to continue or discontinue—so most organizations continue to do it all.

This is much like the old advertising problem: "Half of the ads work and half of the ads don't; however, we can't determine which half actually work, so we continue all of them." In many organizations, decision making around the initiatives, programs, products, and services to help organizations win with customers is approached much the same way. As a result, organizations play the game of business hampered by the uncertainty of what really delivers value to customers. As a consequence, organizations launch new initiatives without a high degree of confidence in their ability to create more value for customers versus competition. Many organizations are timid when it comes to discontinuing products or services that do not create real value, resulting in wasted resources and distractions within the organization.

We believe a better approach is to spend the time and effort to truly understand how you are or are not creating value for customers. We have experienced organizations that have access to data and tools that provide this valuable insight and use them to separate the investments and initiatives with "most impact" from those with "least impact." We have worked with organizations that successfully used this insight to focus their efforts and resources on the activities most impactful to customer profits. These organizations possess a clear understanding of how they create value for customers—continually improving in these areas. They also understand what they are doing that does not create value for customers and put the brakes on as soon as possible—eliminating wasted resources.

Adding Value Exchange to the Picture

The picture is almost complete. There is a final view to create the most complete picture of Winning with Customers: After you have helped the customer create value, how much of the value have you captured for yourself? Have you captured your fair share?

These questions may not be top of mind for you, your colleagues, or your customers every day. But the reality is that these questions bring to light or reinforce the fundamental underpinning of business-to-business relationships. It is simple: A customer has a business need it desires to have met. The customer considers one or more alternative solutions (products or services) to purchase that will meet the need. The customer purchases one of the products or services and puts it to use within the business to meet the need and achieve the target financial result—increased sales, decreased costs or both.

If the value exchange has been successful, both parties (buyer and seller) achieve a fair share of the value created from the transaction. The buyer and seller are both continually seeking to gain a greater share of the value being exchanged. Buyers continually seek to get the same product or service for less, or more for the same price. Sellers continually seek to offer the same product at a higher price, or a less costly product at the same price. The actions by both parties are taken to extract greater value from the value exchange.

This Value Exchange occurs in business all day every day. Whether implicit or explicit, this exchange of value between buyers and sellers is at work at all times. As you attempt to help your customers make more money by doing business with you and making more for yourself in return, you must keep the value exchange front and center at all times.

We believe it is critical to know your customer's profitability, your impact on the customer's profitability, and how you create value for the customer. However, the ultimate measure of winning is how you grow your profits, reinvest, and continue to grow. For you, your colleagues, shareholders, and other stakeholders, true success is measured by whether you appropriately manage the value exchange and capture your pro-rata share (fair share) of value in each business period.

Capturing your fair share of the value you help customers create is not an easy task. This topic is a sensitive one indeed. Although some organizations are cautious about openly discussing business models and value creation strategies and profits with customers, we have found that this is a more comfortable conversation (for both parties) when using this approach to winning. It is simple: When you are consistently creating more value for customers (versus your competition), these customers value you immensely. They rely on you for their success and are usually reasonable about your profits if you are helping them to reach their financial goals. The enlightened customers certainly understand your need to reinvest to continue creating more value for them.

Okay, we recognize that not all customers are enlightened. Even when their bank accounts are overflowing from your efforts, maybe it takes a while for some customers to change the paradigm and begin to celebrate your growing profits. But here is what we absolutely love about this approach to winning: When you measure the financial impact you have on your customer's profits and continue to have an increasing impact on their profits as a result of your actions and investments, you can have a rational and logical "value-based" conversation with the customer. You can discuss how much measurable value you created for the customer and in the end you will have a pricing conversation that involves value . . . It does happen!

You see, there is and has always been an economic value exchange that occurs in business. Unfortunately, in many B2B transactions the value exchange is not quantified. The price is driven by supply and demand with an underlying assumption that all of the products and services offered by competitors are the same—providing the same *value* to the customer. In reality, the impact on customer profits usually varies from competitor to competitor. However, the traditional approach to winning does not include insight into how various competitors create value uniquely, nor does it include an economic measure of the relative impact on customer profit. Ultimately this leads to commoditization, which is not good for anyone. Less profit for suppliers and customers, fewer investments, and eventually a business that no one wants to be a part of (see Figure 2.5).

Consider this: If you are creating more value for customers—having a greater impact on their profits—whose responsibility is it to prove it? How can you prove it without quantifiable economic measures developed with customers from their perspective? When you prove that you provide more value, will customers share the value appropriately? Is it easier to have the value conversation with customers when you can quantify and measure the value exchange?

A senior executive at Owens Corning put it best: "Creating value for customers is great, but let's talk about what we get in return."

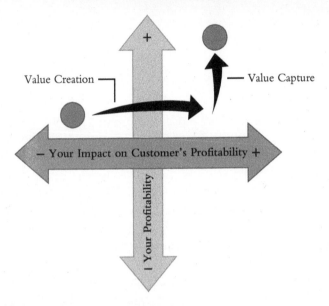

Figure 2.5 Profitability with Value Capture

The completed picture shows how the additional actions and investments created more value for customers, resulting in additional value capture and increased customer profitability for the company. This completes the winning cycle and demonstrates how to create endless opportunities for sustainable profit growth by helping your customers make more money doing business with you and making more money yourself in return.

To truly Win with Customers, your organization must do four key things to provide a complete picture of current customer profitability and develop the actions required to increase and sustain profits:

1. Analyze the profitability of the business you currently enjoy with your customers.
2. Understand the impact you have on your customers' profitability, relative to the impact your competitors have on the same customer's profitability.
3. Measure how value is created for your customers (from the customer's perspective).
4. Capture a fair share of the value you create for your customers.

Using this approach to business management will equip your organization with keen customer insight to make better decisions—one customer at a time and with the entire customer set—to improve customer profitability and Win with Customers.

We do hope that when we say "Do your customers make more money doing business with you?" you are starting to understand what we mean. As we mentioned, this is foundational. You might be thinking now, "Yes, but how do you measure this?" We introduce you to our measures in Chapter 4, "Winning Metrics."

Revenue, Cost, and Profits

Before we leave Chapter 2, there is one more point we need to make in this chapter about winning. Winning with Customers is not just about revenue and revenue growth. It seems that whenever you start discussing creating value for customers, many people start thinking you are talking about increased revenue as the focus path for increasing profit. Nothing could be further from the truth. In our work, understanding the drivers of customer value becomes as much about eliminating activities and investments that do not create value as it is about creating new investments. Let's face it, we would not likely be around to write this book if this were not the case. The past couple of years, we have been focused on delineating investment that is creating value and eliminating or refocusing investments that are not. There is a massive amount of waste associated with companies' activities and investments intended to drive customer value. By understanding how that value is received by the customer, you are in a much better position to drive revenue growth or eliminate waste and cost. Either way you improve profits.

Summary

Remember those six learning objectives? Here they are again:

1. Understand what is meant by Winning *with* Customers.
2. Define the Six Big Ideas and four breakthroughs that create the winning plays.

3. Understand the possible customer growth strategies enabled by this approach using the Growth Cube.

4. Understand the importance of knowing: "Does your customer make more money doing business with you?"

5. Understand the relationship between creating value for your customers and capturing profits for yourself through a Value Exchange.

6. Understand the importance of achieving both cost reductions and revenue growth to win with customers . . . It is about profitability.

Our aim in this chapter is to give you a sense for where we are going with the book and what you can get out of it. If you cannot tell by now, we think understanding whether your customers make more money doing business with you relative to competitors they might choose is a big deal. We have started talking about some of the big ideas we have developed over a long time that have worked for us. Finally, it is not just about revenue. Somehow, whenever someone uses the word "customer," everyone thinks revenue; it is just as much about cost and the ultimate goal is profitable growth.

Chapter 3, "The Playbook," sets up the field of winning plays to help you Win *with* Customers.

Chapter 3

The Playbook

As we have worked with companies over the years, our philosophy has evolved. In the early stages we were focused on projects. We would work our tails off to find people and businesses that got it. "Got it" means someone who fundamentally believed that injecting a rigorous customer perspective into his or her business would yield meaningful business results. There were plenty of professionals who wanted to have the dialogue but not nearly as many who were willing to take on the real work of incorporating the customer's view beyond a survey, or something else that did not take much time. This was true for practitioners and service providers alike—even for some who were considered thought leaders. Imagine that.

As a practitioner and thought leader, Keith Pigues has gone through the school of hard knocks in his career pursuit to lead companies through the painstaking process to become a more customer-focused organization. Jerry Alderman's career has been half and half. He developed his passion for the power of customer focus as a practitioner and for the past 10-plus years has worked to help companies as a thought leader and solution provider.

Through these experiences (the good, the bad, and the ugly) we have come to a common place in a "Playbook" that represents our best insights into what it takes to "Win with Customers" and maximize your profits. This is a playbook developed for serious players who want to win and win big.

After reading this chapter you will be able to:

- Understand where and how the Big Six Ideas and four breakthroughs are integrated into the playbook.
- Become familiar with the winning plays: Discover; Analyze; Execute; Measure; Certify; and CVC Management System.
- Understand why management decision making is not in the playbook.
- Understand the key philosophies that shaped the playbook's design.
- Understand the Winning with Customers maturity model and how to use it to guide the efforts in your organization.

Okay, let's get to it.

Defining the Playbook

Our playbook has six plays, which are listed in Table 3.1. On the left are the Big Six Ideas (Why We Win). We discussed these earlier. On the right are the plays that address each of the six requirements to Win with Customers. We use this framework throughout the book (referring to it often) to help you learn the plays and select the right play at the right time to be successful.

Before we move on, there is one little nuance about the playbook we would like to point out. There are six plays listed in Table 3.1: Discover, Analyze, Execute, Measure, Certify, and CVC Management System. The first five are discreet plays—the things you do on an ongoing basis to overcome the challenges you face. Each of these plays is designed for a specific challenge, and we show you when and how to run these plays.

The sixth play, CVC Management, is not a discreet play. It is a system of technology, tools, processes, and people required to make the

Table 3.1 Why We Win Playbook

The Big 6	The Playbook
We help customers make more money doing business with us.★	**Discover** Chapter 4: "Winning Metrics" Chapter 5: "What Does Your Customer Think?"
We inject quantitative outside-in customer information into decision making.	**Analyze** Chapter 6: "Informing Decisions"
We develop and execute customer plans that deliver value (the Red Zone).★	**Execute** Chapter 7: "Executing Value Creation and Value Capture"
We predict profit growth.★	**Measure** Chapter 8: "The Scorecard"
We build capability and shape culture.	**Certify** Chapter 9: "Getting Started" Chapter 10: "Sustaining and Scaling: The Maturity Model"
The CVC Management System.★	**CVC Management System** "Afterword"

★Breakthrough.

plays work as designed. You might call the sixth play a support play. After reviewing the first five plays, we discuss how to use the support play to achieve and sustain results.

If you happen to be the CEO, COO, CIO, business unit or division president, HR leader or manager, training leader, or other professional supporting the team, you can think of Play 6, the CVC Management System, as your play. This is the play that never makes the highlight real, but plays a huge role in why we win. You cannot win without it.

One additional point: We are not teaching the actual plays at this point in the book. Our goal in this chapter is to help you understand the nature, goal, and intended outcome of each play. We devote a significant portion of the book in later chapters to individual play development.

When we talk to organizations about this approach to winning with customers, we have found that it works better if we begin by discussing what you get from the approach—the deliverables. So as we introduce the plays, we show some of the deliverables—pictures are always good.

You may not fully understand the deliverables immediately, but do not worry. You get a chance to see them develop in much more detail later.

Play 1: Discover

We once had a CEO say, "If you are not interested in understanding how you deliver value to your customers then you probably should not be in business." Delivering value to the customer is what business is all about. You make investments in people, products, manufacturing facilities, service centers, logistics, technology, information technology, infrastructure, marketing, and everything else for the sole purpose of delivering value to customers. If you are not delivering value to your customer, then you will not be in business long. The first play, Discover, measures this value. This is where it all begins.

What Is Discover?

Discover is designed to help you capture your customer's perspective on value—what a great place to start. This play has three key components: Prepare, Conduct Interviews, and Capture Data. Prepare includes things like figuring out how much money you think the customer makes by doing business with you (your internal hypothesis), determining which customers to include in the initial discussions, and developing structured documents to guide the discussions. Conducting Interviews is self-explanatory. However, the approach to customer interviews may be quite different from your previous experiences. We thought you might also find it interesting that these two components of the Discover play will be accomplished during the normal course of business by your people (not by outside consultants). This creates a deeper conversation with your customer and really helps to keep costs down.

Capturing data happens after the interviews are completed. This component of the play involves putting data into a system in an organized way to support analysis and insight generation. It documents and preserves what you have learned about how you create value for customers, and it captures the data you use to calculate customer value.

What Do You Get?

Figure 3.1 shows a deliverable that results from the preparation portion of Discover (your internal hypothesis). This is a representation of the kind of homework done before ever talking to a customer. As you learn, this preparation is worth its weight in gold when it comes to having a robust customer conversation. Do not try to understand all of the numbers you will learn about in Chapter 4, "Winning Metrics." For the moment just note the following:

- On the far left is your value proposition. In this case, the *Attributes* of value that we believe create differential value for this customer are our product line, customer service, brand, sales force, and loyalty programs. This represents the results of investments that we have made to create differential value for this customer—value above and beyond what our competitors provide. As you see, the value attributes total 100. We force trade-offs among the value attributes to reflect their relative value to the customer.
- The bar just to the right represents where these attributes directly impact the customer's financials. In this case, the *Drivers* are to reduce the customer's operating cost and increase the customer's profit per unit.
- See that number near the top of the chart? *DVP: 1.9 percent or $19,000 for every $1,000,000 purchased*. This represents an estimate of how much money the customer makes by doing business with you. This number is the internal hypothesis of your Differential Value Proposition, or DVP. In this case, the customer makes $19,000 for every $1,000,000 of purchases, as a result of the value attributes that you provide and their impact on the customer's financials. In other words, if the customer stopped doing business with you, it would lose $19,000 for every $1,000,000 it is purchasing from you. Would you not like to know this number for each of your customers? Of course you would. That's why we're writing this book. Half the business books ever written talk about this number in some form. (We have figured out how to calculate it and help you use it to win with your customers.) The DVP is an important and powerful number. And for companies that are using it to win, it has proven to be an incredibly useful number to know

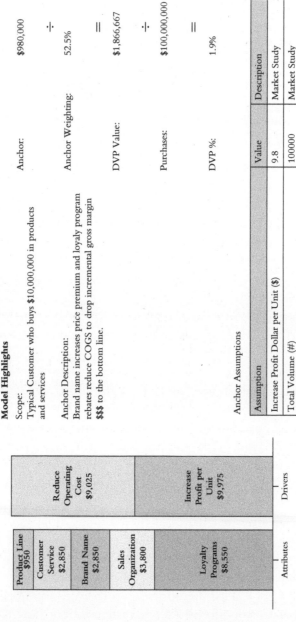

Figure 3.1 DVP Hypothesis Quantification

and manage. It is one of the ideas we consider to be a *Breakthrough*! We develop this measure and the science behind it in Chapter 4, "Winning Metrics."

- Over on the right-hand side box you can see math under the labels Model Highlights and Anchor Assumptions. This information summarizes the math behind the development of the DVP of 1.9 percent.

You have completed the Prepare component of Discover Prepare provided your internal hypothesis of how you create differential value for the customer, its impact on the customer's financials, and a measure of your differential value versus competitors. The result—*a quantification of your competitive advantage.*

Now, let's move on to the second component of the Discover play—Conduct Interviews. This is where you test the hypothesis with the customer. This involves in-depth interviews or structured discussions with various people throughout the customer's organization—getting their perspective on the value you create for them versus competitors. The results are robust—both qualitative and quantitative—and provide a reality check of your true position with the customer. We get into the details of the customer interview approach later. For now, let's examine the deliverable that results from the customer interview shown in Figure 3.2.

Here is how you interpret the interview results:

- The far left bar is the customer's *current* view of differential value you create. The customer's current view is compared to your internal view (internal hypothesis) developed earlier in Prepare. This comparison provides a powerful dose of customer feedback. As you might imagine, if you had the results of these types of interviews from 10, 20, or even 50 different customers, you would learn a lot about how customers view your position with them, as compared to your own views. This is a big opportunity to identify things that are and are not creating value for the customer and adjust your actions and investments to better align with what the customers value.
- The next bar is the *future* view of differential value the customer believes you should provide. This represents how the customer thinks the differential value proposition should change to help them make more money. It answers the question: How would the customer spend

Differential Value Summary
AAA Industries: Widget Contractor

VALKRE

Differential Value Proposition

| DVP = 1.9% | DVP = 2% | DVP = 6% | DVP = 4% |

Internal	Current	Future	Opportunity
Product Line 5%	Product Differentiation 20%	Training 5%	Training 14%
Brand Name 15%		Marketing Materials 25%	
Customer Service 15%	Product Line 10%	Product Differentiation 10%	Marketing Materials 71%
		Product Line 5%	
Sales Organization 20%	Brand Name 25%	Brand Name 15%	
		Customer Service 20%	
Loyalty Programs 45%	Customer Service 25%		
		Sales Organization 15%	Sales Organization 14%
	Sales Organization 10%		
	Loyalty Programs 10%	Loyalty Programs 5%	

Value Creation Opportunities

Marketing Materials
• With the economy slowing down, need the necessary materials to close a customer when the opportunity arises.

Sales organization
• Starting to become respectable. Maybe time to take a strategic approach to down channel selling, rather that a mass market approach.

Training
• Could use some technical training on your products. Would help us sell through the value.

Figure 3.2   Sample Interview Results

your investment dollars to create more value for them? Talk about customer intimacy. Can you imagine a more intimate relationship between you and your customer than making joint decisions about how to spend your investment dollars to make you both better off?

- The final bar represents the *opportunity*—the change between the customer's current and future view of your differential value. It is obvious in this example that the big opportunity from this customer's perspective is to improve marketing materials.

- On the far right is a *summary of opportunities* for improvement that includes each value attribute and the corresponding actions to deliver the value.

- Along the top of the stacked bars is the DVP% again. The current DVP is 2 percent and the future DVP is 6 percent, resulting in a 4 percent improvement opportunity. The change in DVP percent represents the amount of additional financial impact the customer believes is possible. If this were a $10 million customer, this 4 percent improvement opportunity would suggest that the customer believes there is an opportunity for you to improve their bottom line by $400,000 (4 percent of $10 million). We call this the *customer road map*. Understanding the quantitative and qualitative road map for improvement from your customer's perspective is powerful information. It maps out how you can help the customer make more money in the future.

A few key points on play 1, Discover:

- *Quantitative rigor.* Being able to talk with your customer about how you can help them to make money is a powerful conversation. The more you can do this by using real dollars and cents, the better. In our own experiences we have found that many people attempt to explain a value proposition with words and fail to show the math. Now, this happens for a variety of reasons. Some think that doing the math is too hard. Some do not feel equipped to talk in this level of detail with the customer for fear they will be wrong. Others do not believe that the customer will understand the financial math. The reason we like best is that this type of discussion with customers might reveal some kind of confidential information. Think about that for a moment. As you consider the relationship between a supplier and customer, the one thing that should not be a secret is the value proposition. After all, it is the basis for a supplier and customer to do business together.

Half the business books ever written talk about the need for a differentiated value proposition. By clearly articulating and quantifying the value proposition and creating the DVP% we are bringing much needed clarity to the impact of value propositions on customers. This clarity will help you get on the path to pursue measured improvement in your customer's business. This is the path to winning.

- *Use your own sales force.* You count on your sales force day in and day out to deliver the value message to your customers and close sales. You can also count on them to understand what is valuable to customers. If you have ever been a sales professional you understand how much information is pushed to you with the intent of increasing sales and profits. But as a sales professional, trying to get the people in your company to listen to the customer in a way that causes your company to change its behavior . . . It is tough duty! A key to making customer discovery work is to empower and equip your most highly leveraged face to the customer—the sales force. Make discovering customer value part of how they do business.

- *Engage your customer organization.* Too many times the focus of discovering what is valuable to customers happens only at the transactional level, resulting in customer feedback like "Your price is too high," "Your shipment was late last week," and so forth. This is normal everyday stuff between purchasing and sales professionals. However, they are both better off if their respective organizations spend time together exploring the key attributes that truly create value for the customer. The purchasing professional is better off if suppliers are making investments that will improve the value delivered to their organization. The challenge here is that no one individual in the customer's organization knows the whole value creation story. To do this well requires getting a variety of people in your customer's organization engaged. In addition to purchasing, you need the perspective of sales, marketing, operations, and general management. The people with these responsibilities understand the concepts of managing budgets, making investments, and delivering value. Getting

them engaged in this more meaningful discussion is a requirement
to create more value for customers.

- *Prepare.* Like many things, the effort you put into understanding customer value is correlated to what you get in return. Collectively,
we have been in and around thousands of discovery sessions between
customers and their suppliers. The key to making this work well is to
be prepared. There is a basic element of human interactions at play
here known as reciprocity—if I provide something to you, then you
feel compelled to provide something in return. If you send your customer a survey, they are not compelled to reciprocate with anything
of significant value, like their time. If, on the other hand, you take
the time to visit them in person with a well-structured approach to
understanding value you will be amazed at their participation. We
have seen this time and time again. What was planned as a one-hour
meeting stretches into two because of your readiness and preparedness to have a meaningful conversation.

Hopefully, this discussion of the first play, Discover, has helped you
connect with the big picture of Winning with Customers. How do
you measure whether your customers are making money doing business with you? You begin by developing your own internal view. Then
you gain the customer's current view of how well you are doing and
the company's future view with specific improvement opportunities.

It is okay if you did not understand all the numbers we introduced
in this chapter, how to get them, who to speak with within your customer's organization, which customers to interview, how to train people
in your organization to do this, how to manage the data, and any other
unanswered questions. We spend considerable time in Chapter 4,
"Winning Metrics," and Chapter 5, "What Do Your Customers Think?"
addressing these issues in detail.

Now that you have an understanding of the first play, let's move to
play 2, Analyze.

Play 2: Analyze

Let us begin by taking another look at the playbook and the Big Six
Ideas presented in Table 3.1.

What Is Analyze?

Analyze is the play that ensures customer data is delivered to management and other decision makers in a way that enables them to make decisions augmented with customer knowledge. We recognize that customer knowledge is not the only input into your decisions. Your knowledge of macro-market forces, R&D efforts and technologies, competitive intelligence, organizational constraints and capabilities, and other types of information are used in decision making. This play is about augmenting that information and knowledge with an outside-in perspective of the customer. If you think about it, the customer represents two important sources of data and information. Customers know what would help them make more money and they know the value of your competitors' offerings.

As you might imagine, during the Analyze play we look at the customer data from a variety of perspectives. You approach Analyze differently, depending on your role in the organization and what you are trying to accomplish. If you are a sales professional who wants to look at your accounts, or a marketer who is interested in bringing greater clarity to the value proposition, or maybe an executive who wants to better understand common customer problems and the capital requirements to solve them during capital planning. Whatever your interest happens to be there is an application of this play to help you get meaningful quantifiable customer data to help make the decisions. There are currently manufacturing organizations that start their quality meetings by looking at the data received from their Winning with Customers work!

So what is Analyze? It is simply taking the outside-in customer data and turning it into information to be used in decision making. By using this type of information in the decision-making process, you bring greater objectivity to mitigate your own overconfidence biases about what is valuable.

What Do You Get?

There are many different types of analyses that can be performed, but the single most coveted output from Analyze is "The List" shown in Figure 3.3.

The List contains the top opportunities identified by your customers to help them make more money. The List contains the top 3, 5, 10,

Value Attribute	Source Analysis	Initiatives	Value Creation
Product Differentiation	Attribute Segments	Upgrade existing low end products to provide an offering for price-sensitive buyers	$3,082,000
Product Line	Attribute Segments	Fill gap in product line by offering a High End Option that provides is a natural upsell to mainstream products	$1,843,000
Loyalty Programs	Attribute Segments	Simplify the paperwork required to participate in Loyalty Program	$1,645,000
Sales Organization	Attribute Segments	Increase focus down channel to drive demand with our customer's customers	$2,071,000
Marketing Materials	Attribute Segments	Upgraded materials required to help close the sale with our customer's customers. The materials need to be simplified and widely available in all branches.	$5,401,000

Initiative Summary — VALKRE — Planning Period: 2009 · Level: Business Unit · Scope: Widgets · Country: USA

Figure 3.3 The List

or whatever number of significant ideas your customer has suggested would create significant differential value for them. The list shows the value attribute that needs improvement, a short description about the nature of improvement, and the potential dollar impact to the customer's bottom line. Pretty cool! Everyone in business should have a List.

The List is a way to inform executives who are making resource allocation decisions with data and information to understand quantitatively what is valuable to customers. Instead of having only one source of information to make decisions, now the executive will have two sources.

The first source of information is the traditional inside-out knowledge such as historical financials and macroeconomic forecasts. This information exists in the company and is used to make operational and capital planning decisions.

The List represents an additional source of data and information to help improve these decisions. It provides the customers' perspectives on what will create value for them (Value Attributes and Initiatives). It also provides the amount of differential value that can be created for the customer from each initiative. Yes, the List provides what customers believe is most valuable (in dollars and cents). This is something you want to keep locked in the vault—maybe it is your source of true competitive advantage. However, the items on the list should be woven deeply into the decision making and execution of the company at all levels. The List is as valuable as pure gold.

It is important to reiterate that the customer perspective comes through a filter of what your customer knows about the competitive landscape and your direct competitors. The List also provides data and information to help you measure potential value creation opportunities relative to your competitors. Again, this is worth keeping in the vault. And it provides great insight into the opportunities to continually grow your sales and profits with specific customer initiatives and their associated contribution.

The List is available to executives as an additional set of data and information to consider along with other sources to augment their decision making. You have just added a fact-based and quantitative outside-in customer perspective. This is powerful stuff that works. When you inform operational and capital planning with a well-structured customer perspective, you are now starting to align the operations, marketing, customer service, sales, product development, and other parts of the company with the customer. Not many companies do this well.

Chapter 6, "Informing Decisions," is the place to go if you want to get into the nitty-gritty of Analyze. Have fun there!

Management Decisions: The Missing Play

You may recall from the learning objectives for this chapter that we want you to understand what is and is not in the playbook. The playbook includes the Six Plays to help you win with customers. We have discussed two of the plays: Discover and Analyze. Before we move on to discuss the other four plays, this is a good time to discuss what is not in the playbook—Management Decisions.

Management decisions are the determinants of a company's success or failure. Yes, we get how important they are. Some would argue, and we agree, that management gets paid to make good decisions. So why do we not include Management Decisions in the playbook? The answer is that we do not have any new insights to add to management decision making. There are many good tools in use today, including Stage Gate; elements of Six Sigma; portfolio management; options; product management; scenario analysis; and the list goes on.

Our goal is to "feed the decision-making process" with a healthy dose of outside-in customer data and information to improve the outcomes or your chosen decision-making processes. We have focused our energy on providing teams with customer data and information to improve decisions without reengineering the decision-making process itself. We know this area well and we are sticking to our knitting. We also thought you would appreciate this.

Before we discuss the third winning play, this is also a good time to introduce the field of play. This is the place where all of the plays come together with customers, competitors, and a host of other market

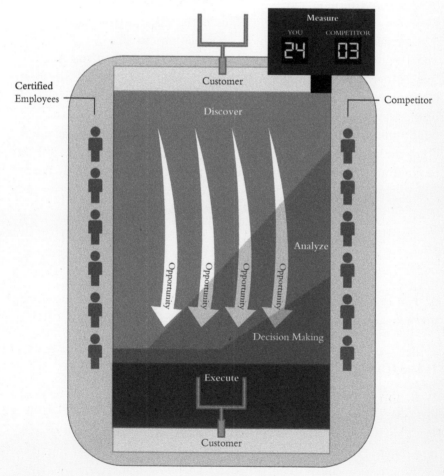

Figure 3.4 CVC Stadium

forces. The place you enter every day to compete and, hopefully, win with customers. We call the field of play the CVC Stadium as shown in Figure 3.4—how fitting.

As you examine the CVC Stadium, you notice the two plays we have already discussed and their position on the field. Play 1: Discover, is to generate opportunities to help customers make more money. Play 2: Analyze, is used to further examine some of the opportunities generated by Discover. Depending on the nature of the opportunities, some require additional analysis before determining whether to pursue them. Others are quick wins that can be pursued without in-depth analysis.

As you continue moving down the field of play, you arrive at Management Decision Making. This is the place on the field where management must decide which opportunities to pursue and which opportunities not to pursue. The work done with Discover and Analyze (where needed) will improve decision making and produce the best opportunities to move forward with. These opportunities are moved further down the field of play into the next area where you have the opportunity to turn the efforts into real results. Yes, the place where it is do or die, put up or shut up, or _____. (Insert your favorite phrase to communicate that it's time to deliver what the customer really needs and values.) Yes, this is it! Hearts pounding, palms sweating—you get the picture.

Play 3: Execute

As you review the Big Six Ideas shown in Table 3.1 again, you notice that Execute is the play where you move into action.

What Is Execute?

Well, this is the biggie! Think about where we are on the field of play. We are in scoring position.

This is the time to get focused and aligned to turn opportunities into results. A team's performance in this critical area of the playing field determines how many points it scores and how many games it wins. This is where the winners truly outperform the competition.

Likewise, in business, an organization's ability to execute customer plans that puts more profits in the customer's bank and more profits in its bank is a requirement for success. Yes, both must happen to win. Your organization's ability to run this play successfully will determine its success at winning with customers. Yes, it all boils down to execution of customer plans.

So, what are these customer plans? Well, there are two parts of the Customer Plan. The first is focused on value created for the customer and is shared with both the customer and the internal organization. It is used to manage customer value creation activity and communicate progress and results. The second part of the Customer Plan is focused on the value captured in return. It is the ultimate success for the organization. If you create value for the customer, yet are unable to capture your fair share of the value you helped to create, that is not winning. We do not need to tell you this, but we wanted to ensure that we are on the same page.

Let's take a look at the first part of Customer Plans that includes the actions and investments, resulting from management decisions, which improves the differential value you create for customers. For example, changing a service program, launching a new product, increasing sales force coverage or sales call frequency, creating a new customer promotion, enhancing the logistics and delivery network, and so forth. You are probably thinking that these are the kinds of things we do today to serve customers. And you are probably right. The question is this: "Can you say with confidence that the decisions you've made result in the actions and investments that help your customers make more money and result in meaningful differentiation from your competitors?" Good question, right? And another question which is equally important: "Why are you confident that your actions and investments will help the customer make more money doing business with you versus your competitors?"

The first part of Customer Plans focused on customer value creation provides the specifics of how to plan and measure success. This is an essential component of Play 3, Execute, and provides several tools and deliverables we think you find valuable. The tools and deliverables also serve another important purpose—to help get your entire organization involved (working together) to deliver results.

What Do You Get?

In short, the customer value creation portion of the Customer Plan shows the specific actions—the things you do to create value for customers. The plan also includes the required investments to deliver the value, along with the estimated financial impact on the customer. It also shows the direct link between the actions and the value attributes provided by the customer. The plan closes the loop with the customer—we cannot over-emphasize the importance of providing feedback to customers about your plans and commitments based on their input. The plan clearly communicates what you will do, when it should be completed, who is responsible, and so forth. And it helps to organize and align your resources to deliver the results—focusing resources throughout the organization squarely on the goal of delivering value for the customer, as the customer has out-lined. This is a requirement for success that is not easily achievable. This tool has been invaluable in helping companies overcome this obstacle.

Let us examine this play by looking at the portion of the plan that would be shared with a customer. Let us assume that this is a Customer Plan for one of your customers.

The Customer Plan begins with a restatement of the customer's perspective on the opportunities in the first section of the plan labeled "Customer Needs," as shown in Figure 3.5. You may remember that this is a summary of the picture we saw in Play 1, Discover. On the far left, the stacked bar represents the three opportunities for improvement based on customer value attributes. In this case, the customer estimates that the three opportunities are worth a total of 4 percent of differential value (a DVP of 4 percent). This means that for every $1 million the customer purchases from you, there is an opportunity to improve their bottom line by $40,000. Not bad!

The table to the right shows each of the value attributes and the resulting opportunities. As you move right, you find qualitative descriptions of the opportunities and the specific members of the customer's organization who provided the information for each opportunity. All of this information becomes important as you manage the execution, report progress, and update the plans as things change over time.

Let's continue to explore the Customer Plan and the next deliverable—Discovery Initiatives. Here you find a description of the initiatives you will pursue to deliver the results.

Customer Needs

VALKRE

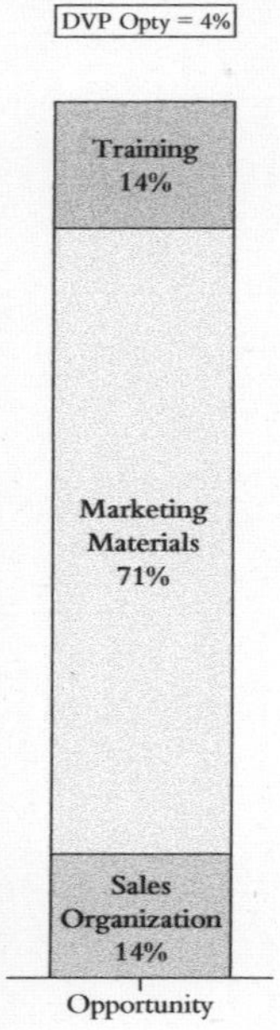

Value Attribute	Opportunity	Contact(s)
Marketing Materials	With the economy slowing down, need the necessary materials to close a customer when the opportunity arises	Bob Jackson & Sally Jones
Sales Organization	Starting to become respectable. Maybe time to take a strategic approach to down channel selling, rather that a mass market approach.	Bob Jackson & Sally Jones
Training	Could use some technical training on your products. Would help us sell through the value.	Bob Jackson & Sally Jones

DVP Opty = 4%

Training
14%

Marketing
Materials
71%

Sales
Organization
14%

Opportunity

Figure 3.5   Customer Needs

69

As shown in Figure 3.6, Discovery Initiatives provides the details of the total opportunity to improve your customer's profits and the associated initiatives to get this done. In this case, you see that the customer currently purchases $160 million. Based on the additional value creation opportunity of 4 percent, the total value creation in incremental profit dollars totals $6.4 million (4 percent of $160 million). Your organization put plans in place to create only $5.485 million of additional value for the customer. Through analysis and management decision making your company decided not to take action on the full $6.4 million of opportunity. (This happens: Not all opportunities are created equal. Some fall within your organizations capabilities, while others may not. Some represent significant value creation for the customer, while others may not. Some represent an opportunity for greater competitive differentiation than others.) The Discovery Initiatives section of the Customer Plan includes only the initiatives you have decided to pursue and shows how they are aligned with the customer's input on value creation. This makes for a valuable conversation with the customers about their business, your business, and how you can help them be more successful. A conversation shaped by value—how refreshing.

This deliverable also includes the team within your organization that is leading each initiative and the specific person who is responsible. The current approval status of the initiative is also included. So everyone knows where each initiative stands at all times.

Discovery Initiatives		Purchases: $160,000,000 Value Creation Opty: $6,400,000 Value Creation Plan: $5,485,000	Business Unit: Widgets Customer Type: Contractor Market Type: Residential			
DVD Plan $	**Value Attribute**	**Initiative**		**Team**	**Owner**	**Status**
$914,000	Sales Organization	Increase focus down channel to drive demand with our customer's customers		Sales	Maria Burud	Approved
$4,571,000	Marketing Materials	Upgraded materials required to help close the sale with our customer's customers. The materials need to be simplified and widely available in all branches.		Marketing	Brian Kiep	In Progress

Figure 3.6   Discovery Initiatives

Other Initiatives				
Value Attribute	**Initiative**	**Team**	**Owner**	**Status**
Loyalty Programs	Implementing Loyalty Program Website to simplify management of account and rewards	Marketing	Jeff Navach	In Progress

Figures 3.7   Other Initiatives

The next two deliverables (shown in Figures 3.7 and 3.8) are Other Initiatives and Opportunities Not in Plan. Other Initiatives are those that were not developed as a result of customer input from Discovery but have the potential to create additional value for the customer. Opportunities Not in Plan lists those opportunities the customer identified that you decided not to execute in this planning period. Some opportunities may not be appropriate to pursue (based on management decisions) for one of several reasons, as we discussed previously.

The final deliverable from this portion of the Customer Plan is Initiative Detail, shown in Figure 3.9. It provides a snapshot of the plan to help manage the execution and track progress. It provides you with a lot of detail, including a description of the initiative, actions taken, initiative owner, status update, start date, and percentage completion along with additional notes. This is an incredibly valuable tool to help people throughout your company and the customer organization stay connected to what's happening with the execution of the plan. These activities are critical, and your success in getting them done according

Opportunities Not In Plan
VALKRE

Value Attribute	Opportunity	DVD Opty $	Reasoning	Contact (s)
Training	Could use some technical training on your products. Would help us sell through the value.	914000	Would require 3rd Party Training Curriculum Development. Will consider at future time due to size of investments.	Bob Jackson & Sally Jones

Figure 3.8 Opportunities Not in Plan

Initiative Detail for Upgraded materials required to help close the sale with our customer's. The materials need to be simplified and widely available in all branches.
VALKRE

Owner	Team	Status	Value Drivers		
Brian Kiep	Marketing	In Progress			

Action	Team	Owner	Status	Start Date	% Complete
Focus Group to define material requirements	Marketing	Maria Burud	Completed	1/1/2009	100%
Designs created and submitted to graphics firm	Marketing	Jeff Navach	In Progress	3/1/2009	0%
Materials produced and distributed to customers	Sales	Bill Hass	Not Started	10/1/2009	0%
Customer Focus Group to determine effectiveness	Marketing	Maria Burud	Not Started	1/1/2010	0%

Note	Date Added	From
We've approved basic concepts for new marketing materials. Expect to see samples by 6/1/09.	10/19/2009	Brian Kiep
Focus Group Completed on 1/1/2009. Results were fantastic as we were able to design 10 new potential marketing assets that are simple and effective. Next steps include working with graphical design firms for mock-ups.	10/19/2009	Brian Kiep

Figure 3.9 Initiative Detail

to plan determines whether customer value is created, whether your customer makes more money, whether you outperform the competition. This tool helps the entire organization keep abreast of the status of each activity and measure progress in delivering value to the customer. And equally important, this is a tool to help you provide regular and accurate feedback to the customers on the things they believe are most important and valuable. Can you imagine the impact this will have on your customer relationships?

We have given you an overview of the first portion of the Customer Plan. The Customer Plan, with its supporting deliverables, is designed to share with customers. It helps you develop an effective plan to manage the activities that lead to value creation, and communicate the plan to customers and your organization. Here are five things that Customer Plans enable your organization to do well. We believe each of these five points is important to execute your plans with precision and help your customers make more money.

1. *Customer follow-up.* You may be amazed how often companies ask for their customer's input and never follow up. Most companies do not follow up to tell the customer what, if anything, they are going to do differently. Some companies follow up when there is a major problem with the customer that represents a potential threat to the current business. Follow-up rarely happens as a part of the way a company does business. So the first objective of Execute is to communicate back to the customer—reinforcing what was shared during Discovery. We accomplish this in the plan by showing the customer their recommendations and linking those opportunities directly to initiatives. The customer follow-up also includes actions you decided to forgo, as well as those you decided to pursue.

2. *Customer accountability.* It is critical to make the linkage between what the customer said and your initiatives because this creates accountability. We cannot overemphasize the power of making this connection. The accountability generated on both sides of the table helps improve execution. To the extent customers have had input and see you are following up, they will feel guilty if they do not help you to be successful. There is nothing sneaky here; it

is just the way it is—it is a human thing. Do not forget that your customer is better off if you invest money in a way that will improve their business. We have found that customers typically make a significant commitment to help you deliver results when their success depends on it.

3. *Make customer planning easy for sales.* This one is subtle, but it makes a big difference in the results you get. An important role of the salesperson in winning with customers is to make sure the organization understands the opportunities to create customer value, which are created in Play 1: Discover. Customer plans are generated for the sales professionals based on where the company decides to invest. And it is the responsibility of the salesperson to communicate these investments and supporting customer plans to the customer. Sales professionals love this. They love feeling their company is truly considering what the customer wants and they love selling the plan. And most of all they love not having to create the plans. Step back from this a moment. Is it not better to have those who are making the investment decisions create the customer plan? It is not the sales professionals' role to make these investment decisions for customer value creation. The sales professionals want to have their say in the process and then sell the resulting decision like crazy. Seeing this at work is something special.

4. *Getting everyone on the same page.* It is difficult to get everyone on the same page within any organization. Even when they are on the same page, the outbound communication to customers can be all over the map. We have made significant progress toward solving these challenges by creating customer plans that are consistently generated based on the process we have discussed. And we have developed training to help communicate the plans effectively and confidently. It is great to wake up in the morning feeling confident that your investments are being communicated to customers in an accurate and consistent manner.

5. *Leveraging the sales force.* Most sales professionals are fundamentally wired to beat their competition by doing a better job of understanding what the customer needs and then positioning their companies as being the right fit. You should see what happens to the attitude of the sales force when the companies they work for actually become

an organized partner in support of their effort. The energy goes off the chart, as do the sales results.

Everything we have shown so far in customer planning is intended to be shared with the customer. And a lot of time, energy, and resources have been devoted to developing and executing plans that create value for the customer. Now we turn our attention to how this makes you better off. You must get an acceptable return on your investment to create value for the customer, or this whole effort becomes a charity case. Let us be clear, CVC Management and this book have a single goal—helping you increase profits for your business.

Let's take a look at a deliverable included in Play 3, Execute, related to capturing value for your company. It is also included in the Customer Plan and is called the "Value Summary." This is an important deliverable as you will see. The picture in Figure 3.10 is a sample of what is included in the Value Summary.

On the left is a summary of value creation for the customer. On the right is a summary of value capture for you. Continuing with the same customer example we used earlier in this chapter, you can see the value creation opportunity for the customer is $6.4 million. The value capture opportunity is measured by the change in gross margin dollars from the prior period to the plan period. In this case, your value capture opportunity is $5 million (in gross margin) or 13 percent growth.

This is your value capture opportunity for one customer. Imagine how the opportunity grows as you create value for additional customers. As you create value for more customers across districts, regions, market segments, business units, divisions, and throughout your entire company, your value capture opportunities and profits will continue to grow. This is Winning with Customers.

There is much, much more to share on Play 3, Execute, including more deliverables and more details about how to create and use Customer Plans in your business. Our goal in this chapter is to position this play in the field of play, share how it can be used to help you win by executing with precision, and to give you a glimpse of the tools we have developed to help you. You find the real meat in Chapter 7, "Executing Value Creation and Value Capture," which is all about customer planning.

Value Summary

Value Creation

	Current	Future	Opportunity
%	2%	6%	4%
$	$3,200,000	$9,600,000	$6,400,000

Value Capture

	Prior	Plan	Change vs. Prior
Sales	$160,000,000	$180,000,000	13%
GM %	25%	25%	0%
GM$	$40,000,000	$45,000,000	13%

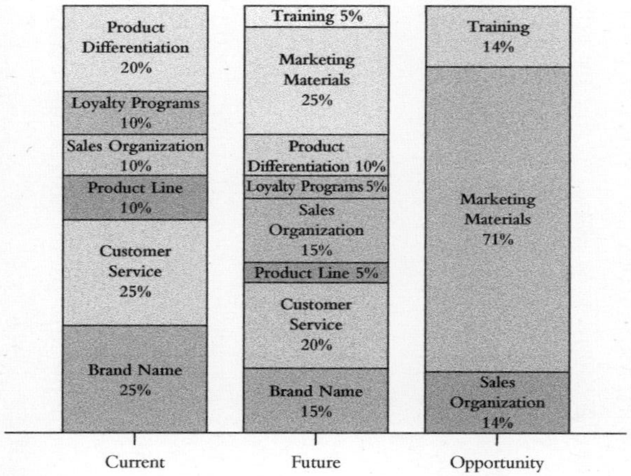

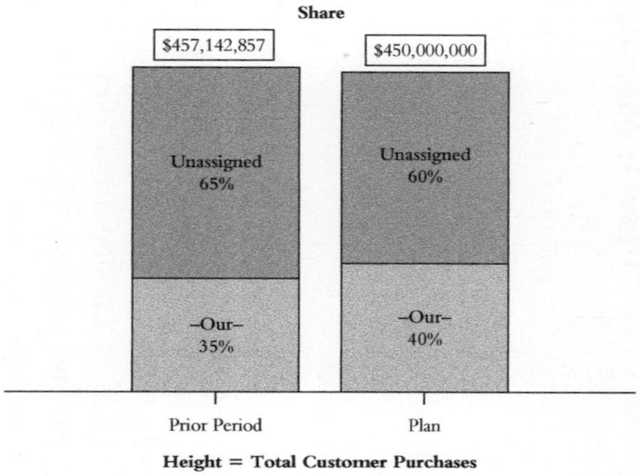

Share

$457,142,857

$450,000,000

Unassigned 65%

Unassigned 60%

—Our— 35%

—Our— 40%

Prior Period

Plan

Height = Total Customer Purchases

Current:
Product Differentiation 20%
Loyalty Programs 10%
Sales Organization 10%
Product Line 10%
Customer Service 25%
Brand Name 25%

Future:
Training 5%
Marketing Materials 25%
Product Differentiation 10%
Loyalty Programs 5%
Sales Organization 15%
Product Line 5%
Customer Service 20%
Brand Name 15%

Opportunity:
Training 14%
Marketing Materials 71%
Sales Organization 14%

Current   Future   Opportunity

Figure 3.10 Value Summary

VALKRE

75

Play 4: Measure

The Big Six Ideas and playbook tell us this has something to do with predicting profit growth. It does, and being able to better predict profit growth is truly a *breakthrough*. Would you like to have more confidence in predicting the trajectory of your profits? Of course you would.

What Is Measure

Before we get too deep into examples, the concept here is really quite straightforward. Simply add the elements of time and continuous improvement to things we have already discussed. If you measure both value creation for the customer and value capture over time you can begin to see the relationship between the two. You get better at under-standing what investments work, how the impact of your value propo-sition changes in good economic times and bad, the lag time between investment and return, and more.

As you learn more from the experience and results of using the CVC Management System, you improve the outcome of your next decision, and the next and the next. And the relationship between investment, value creation, and value capture tightens. This is no different than the feedback loop for any other process.

This is like investing in your house. There is good information available to help you determine the return on investment for a kitchen remodel as compared to a bathroom remodel or pool addition. You develop the data to help you make decisions about investments to create value for customers. As you make investments to create more value for customers—selecting opportunities to pursue, developing and exe-cuting customer plans, capturing your share of value, and reinvesting again—you develop increasingly deeper knowledge about the invest-ments that yield a greater return than others. You have greater confidence in the investments and their impact on profits in the immediate period and over time.

Embedding this capability into your organization helps you pre-dict profit growth—for a customer, for groups of customers, and for the entire business. Based on the experience of those using the CVC Management System, we believe this has the potential to impact earnings projections and support business valuations. We spend more time on this topic in Chapter 8, "Scoreboard."

Let's position Play 4, Measure, on the field of play using the CVC Stadium diagram shown once again in Figure 3.11.

As we indicated earlier, you can think of Measure as the scoreboard. The scoreboard shows you the current score at any point during the game, as well as the game statistics to help you understand how teams are performing in a variety of areas that impact their performance and

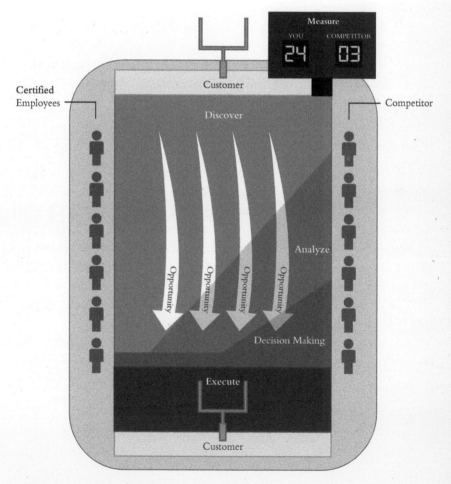

Figure 3.11 CVC Stadium

ultimately their ability to win. And the scoreboard also provides historical information and statistics from previous games, previous seasons, and even over the life of the team.

Before we show you some of the deliverables, let's take a view from the top of the stadium and get a "bird's-eye view" of this game—Winning with Customers. This helps to connect the deliverables with key activities in the game and the material we have covered thus far. Before the game begins, you prepare. When the game officially starts, you begin working with customers to discover ways to outperform the competition. You identify opportunities to win with the customer and begin moving the best opportunities down the field—analyzing and making decisions along the way. After working to advance customer plans, you move in position to score. It is time to execute—get the results—create value for the customer and capture value in return—score—put points on the scoreboard. The scoreboard captures each score, along with all of the key statistics for the game.

What Do You Get?

Well, as we explore the scoreboard, let's assume that this is your company's scoreboard for Winning with Customers. Let's take a look at how you have faired in the game with one customer during 2007 to 2009. We use a variety of measures of success.

We begin with one of the more basic and often-used measures of success that companies rely on to view progress in a given year and over time. This is the Differential Value Proposition over Time.

The chart in Figure 3.12 is organized in pairs of bar charts. A pair for each year you have been keeping score (2007–2009).

The upper section of the chart: The first bar in the pair shows the customer's current view of your differential value proposition (Current), along with the Differential Value Proposition Percentage (DVP%) and the relative value attributes the customer believes contribute to your current DVP%. The second bar in the pair shows the customer's view of how it would like your Differential Value Proposition to change (Opportunity), along with an estimate of the Differential Value Proposition improvement opportunity (Oppty%) and the change in value attributes that will cause the improvement.

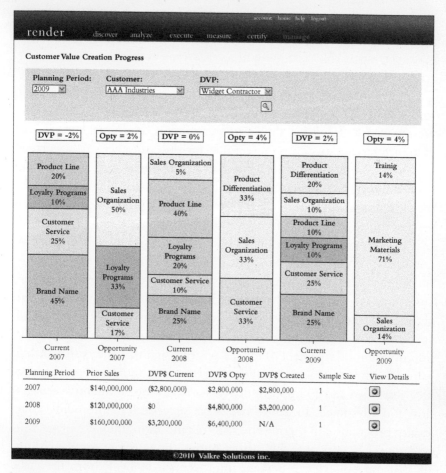

Figure 3.12 Differential Value Proposition over Time

The lower section of the chart: It includes the key stats used to measure success with the customer during each planning period, including prior year sales (Prior Sales), the amount of value currently delivered to the customer (DVP$ Current), the opportunity to create more value for the customer (DVP$ Oppty), and finally the actual value created for the customer (DVP$ Created). Now that we have a handle on what's captured on the scoreboard, let's see what it means. How have you faired in creating value for this customer over the period?

In 2007, you had a Differential Value Proposition of negative 2 percent. This means that for every $1 million the customer purchased from you, the company was losing $20,000 to its bottom line relative to a competitive alternative. Not good! I think it is fair to say that this customer was at risk. The good news, however, is that the customer saw a value creation road map to improve the DVP by 2 percent effectively getting you to DVP of 0 percent (competitive parity). This is not a great road map. The value attributes included in the Opportunity indicates that you needed to work on the sales organization, customer loyalty, and customer service to create more value for this customer. Your current sales were $140 million, your DVP was negative $2.8 million, and your DVP improvement opportunity was also $2.8 million. If you only had the current sales data, and maybe even the current profit or profit margin percent you were receiving from sales to this customer, it would be impossible to assess your true position. Although the data on the scoreboard was not positive, it did provide a road map for improvement and success.

After a year of working to increase the value you created for the customer, let's see what happened in 2008. You were successful at getting back to competitive parity with a DVP% equal to zero. The customer has also given you a road map to achieve another DVP improvement of 4 percent. This is a positive sign that the customer has gained confidence in your ability to create even more value. This is a nice road map and an opportunity to start creating competitive separation and advantage. In 2007, you were successful at improving your loyalty programs and getting the sales organization onto the map. You will note, however, you fell further behind in customer service. All in all, you did achieve a 2 percent improvement in DVP from the customer's perspective—meeting the customer's expectation. In 2008, the customer gave you additional opportunities to continue creating future value, including improving customer service, continuing to work on the sales organization, and adding a dimension of product differentiation to your value proposition.

In 2009, you moved into a winning position, achieving a positive DVP of 2 percent. This represents a measurable competitive advantage over your competitors. You also continued to achieve a robust improvement in the DVP road map, as the customer believed you could further improve the DVP by an additional 4 percent.

The Scoreboard shows the key metrics of success in your efforts to win with customers. It also provides an improvement path to move you into a winning position. You can see how after multiple periods, it is possible to see trends, begin understanding the connection between your investments and return, as well as the impact of your evolving value proposition on the customer's profit.

It also helps to capture the story behind your success to share with your board of directors, investors, and employees. The story and the learning are also valuable tools to help focus and align the entire organization on a path of success. The Scorecard is more than just numbers.

Now for the "Value Capture" side of the equation—how much of the value have you captured for yourself?

We perform a simplistic assessment of value capture at this stage to help you understand how the scoreboard is used to measure your ultimate success at winning with customers. In Chapter 8, "The Scoreboard," we get into much more detail to analyze the financial success.

For this example we use the gross margin dollars (GM$) Trend chart shown in Figure 3.13. The chart shows your financial results from this customer in GM$ for each of the three years (2007–2009), comparing the planned level of GM$ and actual GM$ captured during the period.

Note: The plan GM$ carries all macro-market growth factors to remove the growth that resulted from general market conditions versus investments you made to improve performance.

Figure 3.13 also includes the change in your DVP% each year as a reference for the impact you had on the customer's profit each year.

In 2007, you achieved $25M in gross margin from the customer versus a plan of $22M, resulting in a $3M value capture. During the same period, you created $2.8M of value for the customer. In 2008, your value capture was $8M ($40M–$32M) relative to customer value creation of $3.2M. From 2007 to 2008, the actions and investments you made to create more customer value (improving your DVP by 2 percent) resulted in 266 percent value capture improvement ($8M/$3M). Your efforts during the period (2008–2009) resulted in a 163 percent ($13M/$8M) value capture improvement.

Your efforts in creating more value for the customer and gaining a competitive advantage also resulted in attractive value capture for your business. This is a picture of winning.

You can begin to see how to connect value creation for the customer to value capture for you. This is a basic set of data. We explore this area in

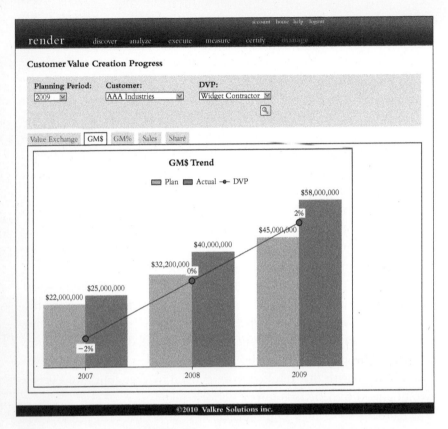

Figure 3.13 Gross Margin Trend

more detail later in the book. One of the areas we examine is the change in value attributes that directly impact the customer's operations and profits—leading to a change in the DVP and increased gross margin dollar capture. Another is the financial impact of multiple customers, and yet another is an examination of differing investment portfolios that can help to predict future value capture and profit growth, in relation to value creation opportunities.

A Few Additional Insights

- Consider for a moment if you had the data and scoreboard through good markets and bad. You would be able to see how your customers value your products and services differently depending on market conditions. We have certainly seen this during the past few years. What if you could anticipate the shifting needs of customers and stay ahead of the changing demand and competitors by changing your value proposition to meet new market conditions? We believe this may be possible.

- You can see the need for a philosophy of continuous improvement. Whether you are working with patient outcomes or athletic feats, a necessary ingredient for improvement is the visibility and tracking of those measures over time. In order to improve, you must measure over time and strive for continuous improvement.

- One customer at a time is at work. Sure, we are going to measure at all levels, by sales rep, by division, by region, by business unit, and at the company level. But execution happens one customer at a time. Being able to understand and communicate what is happening with value creation and value capture at the customer level is fundamental to our playbook and the CVC Management System.

- When it comes to managing the business, executives are always seeking to better understand how their investments and strategies create tangible value for customers, while delivering financial improvement for the business.

- For sales professionals who are always tasked with explaining the change in profit contribution for individual customers, they now have a measure to explain from the customer's viewpoint.

- Being able to correlate and measure value creation and value capture has implications for an organization that are far reaching.

Play 5: Certify

As we have said before, we believe that a critical capability for companies to have is the ability to gather, analyze, execute, and measure value delivered from the customer perspective. Creating this kind of capability does not happen overnight. The Certify play in our playbook is focused on the details necessary to help organizations put together a combination of skill-building activities necessary to create such a capability.

The People

If we consider the CVC Stadium (the field), certification is about the players, coaches, staff, and front office. We all need to understand the Playbook and how each play is going to be run. By understanding the plays, the coaches and staff can get the right players. By knowing the plays the players will understand their field assignments. Let's spend some time thinking through a few of the perspectives.

The sales professional. We would like the sales professional to have the capability to collect the customer's understanding on the question "Does your customer make more money doing business with you?" We want the sales professional to be confident in this conversation and come across to the customer as genuinely interested in understanding how the customer makes money as a result of using their products and services. From our professional experience, sales professionals love this stuff. They love having their own companies being organized around understanding how their customers make money. They love being equipped to have the conversation with their customer. They love having their customers tell them that this is the first time in the history of their relationship that they have taken the time to really understand the business economics from the customers' perspectives. They love doing something different that every other sales professional walking in behind them is neglecting or not doing as well.

There are other considerations with the sales professional. We also want the sales professional to follow up with the customer to make sure that we have captured in writing what the customer really meant to say. This might seem kind of obvious but it is critical. You see, salespeople are really good at telling people why they should buy, but often are not as skilled at listening and still worse at taking the time to organize what they heard into a document. We need to make sure they can do this well as a first step in making customers feel they've been heard. For customers to see their own voices in a nice organized document that is obviously being readied to share with executives accomplishes the mission of getting started on the right foot.

We also want sales professionals to be equipped to communicate back to customers what the company is doing to address their inputs. How have capital plans, operational plans, and other strategies been changed? We want sales professionals equipped to communicate to customers, with confidence, how we are progressing on our effort to increase the value delivered to our customers.

With the sales professionals, we need to get all of this done against the highly skeptical sales backdrop of "Here we go again with another program that is going to add to my work and make me look foolish in the eyes of my customer." Maybe they are not this skeptical, but do not lose the point. History is replete with examples of getting customer input that never resulted in anything of value to the customer. History is also replete with new programs that heap a ton of work on the sales professional. Most of the time it seems like the new work is all for the purpose of providing management information, which does not help salespeople sell. Some might be thinking, "Oh, cry me a river," or may be striking the air violin pose, or some other little quip meaning "Stop crying you big baby and get on to doing what I told you to do." The reality is that for any effort to sustain there has to be something in it for everyone. A quick way to kill any effort in winning with customers is to heap a load of work on salespeople so daunting that the effort comes to a screeching halt as soon as it starts.

We might be rambling here, but this point is important. We depend on the sales force as the leverage point for information communicated to our customers. If we are successful in leveraging them to bring into the organization what is important to customers we have achieved a huge win. A key to "Winning with Customers" is to get the sales organization involved and committed to understanding how customers make money by using your products and services. This is really tricky and requires a well-thought-out approach to ensure that the sales force sees this kind of work as part of their jobs. The insights on this point that will be developed through the course of the book are among our most important to pass along to you.

The marketing organization. We need marketing to serve as the glue between functional elements of the organization. In organizations we deal with, marketing normally maintains overall ownership for developing a "Winning with Customers" capability. Though marketing may have overall ownership, in the early stages it works well to pass this responsibility around within the organization as the capability is being built. Marketing may be the first owner as initial tests and pilots are conducted to get the organization off the ground. This allows marketing to ensure that they are providing the right level of information to the sales organization to facilitate getting the customer perspective. Afterward, it is powerful to have sales take ownership. A good time to switch to sales ownership is at that point when you are transitioning from small-scale tests to building capability with larger swaths of the sales team. Giving sales ownership during this time allows them to fine-tune the process to meet their particular needs. More important, this transition of ownership develops buy-in as the sales organization fashions the approach to ensure that it will help them to be more effective in their jobs and with their customers. After sales, it works well to pass ownership on to Operations. Operations in this sense means customer service, pricing, planning, logistics, and so on. The Operations personnel are usually better at embedding this capability into the fabric of organizations, processes and procedures.

Beyond serving as the glue, a key role for marketing is turning data into information and ultimately into knowledge. Marketing takes the valuable data from customers and develops it into knowledge of what customers value and why. Marketing should develop knowledge about segments of customers, opportunities for investment, opportunities to divest, changes in the differential value proposition, and on and on. We need the marketing organization to possess the analytical skills necessary to turn data into knowledge and the communication skills necessary to disseminate this knowledge internally and externally. Establishing these analytical and communication skills is essential to augmenting the business with an outside-in customer perspective.

All of that said, let's step into the world of a B2B marketer. Marketing within B2B companies is not often present at the CEO's table. B2B is traditionally a world organized around manufacturing and selling. If you do not have sales and manufacturing in your background then you are not destined to be a general manager—this is a common mind-set in the world of B2B today. We see leading companies significantly changing this mind-set and we would not bother writing this book if we did not. However, when you walk the halls of a B2B company you find marketing organizations that are still working their way out of this long held mind-set. So what? Well, B2B marketing is normally lacking in analytic skills, lacking in their connection to the sales force, do not have a strong connection to customers, are not critically listened to during capital planning, and do not have a voice in the real meeting where decisions are made.

Winning with Customers requires marketing to play a significant role. A key, we have found, is not to replicate the marketing function of a business-to-consumer (B2C) organization. This can be a deadly and career-limiting mistake. The costs, culture, and work to be done are just too different between B2B and B2C to make the direct connection. The key to success has been to build a system of tools, methods, and processes that can be deployed at a cost consistent with the budget framework of a B2B company. To this end, our book is dedicated to you, the B2B marketer.

The management organization. As authors, we have both run sales and marketing organizations and have held management and executive roles as well. We understand the executive and management perspectives. In terms of capability, we want management to use outside-in customer knowledge in making their resource decisions. Decisions about staffing, capital, product development, service level commitments, solution development, and more. We want executives to be able to invest in and manage their DVPs in a context beyond the pure product dimension. Does my sales force create value, how about logistics and customer service, or those services we are or should be providing? To accomplish this objective, management will need to be able to understand, interpret, and balance the knowledge delivered from customers alongside the knowledge they already have about their business. Ultimately, we want management to have the capability to see how their investments in value creation for customers generate returns via value capture for their company. We also want management to have the capability to learn from past decisions by studying the trends of value creation and value capture over time. We have not come across many management teams that have these capabilities. We have found few management teams that do not want them. So what is the rub?

To understand the rub we need to step into the shoes of an executive. Executives are inundated with data on a daily, weekly, monthly, yearly, and historical basis. From all of this data they make decisions on investments that will, in their view, minimize risks and maximize returns. There have been a ton of books written about the art and science of how this is done well. One part of the large equation at play is the customer dimension: What are my customers saying? What are they saying about my current performance? What are they saying about areas for improvement? How much is it worth to them? How much is it worth to me? Will they really buy this if I build it or develop it? Is this riskier than getting that next 10 percent of efficiency from my manufacturing plant or development staff? The rub for an executive is that the business case supporting the customer perspective is not presented well. It is not organized or quantitative. Most of the time the customer case is carried by a few loud greasy wheels and his or her own personal interactions with customers, which serve to establish dangerous biases. Biases driven by limited data and unorganized decision-making frameworks inevitably lead to poor quality decisions that depend more on luck and intuition than data. For the executive, we aim to inject customer input into your decision making utilizing science and rigor as a method for reducing risk and maximizing returns. As managers we have both been asked by the CFO what the return will be on a specific customer investment. We provide you a path for answering the question with confidence.

The R&D and product development organization. At any given time, these organizations are working on new or existing products and services intended to improve the performance of the business. The processes for managing the development of these products and services is a science unto itself . . . Stage Gate, Portfolio Management, Decision Quality, Workflow Software, Ideation, Real Options, and the like. When it comes to capability, Winning with Customers requires a tighter connection between these activities and the customer. We want R&D to see how their portfolios of projects are aligning with what customers see as opportunities for value creation. We want R&D to be able to communicate product and service development updates to the sales force in a manner that allows customers to feel they are part of the process.

This is not easy for R&D to do well. If you are an R&D professional it is hard to get your message heard. You likely have two or three projects and do not have a great context for which customers might really value what you are developing. You probably over-communicate to sales and rarely hear anything back. You fight for the value of your projects, since it is your job, but get little real-time market feedback that might allow you to adjust and adapt. The connection between R&D and customers is not tight. In "Winning with Customers," we talk about tightening this link. How does R&D really know which customers will value the products and services being created? How can R&D ensure that sales is communicating the development status to those customers and getting feedback?

Customer service organization, manufacturing, and the rest. Winning with Customers is an organizational effort! We want customer service and manufacturing to see themselves through the eyes of the customer. How does our quality and service stack up versus competitors'? We would like these functional parts of our organization to be able to answer these questions. We want them to have the information available necessary to continuously improve and understand how their work is contributing to customer success.

Well, if you are in customer service or manufacturing you know this kind of information is hard to come by. You are always offering to go see customers, be more involved. The reality is that for cost, time, and plain logistical reasons the number of direct experiences you have is limited. You need a way to essentially bring the customer into your meetings and help your team feel like it's part of the value creation and capture process.

What Do You Get?

Getting your people on the same page relative to the concepts and ideas in this book in relation to skill levels, awareness, and capability is not a small endeavor, as you already know. We understand. To this end, we provide our insights on how to create teams, get started, and scale this work in your organization in Chapters 9 and 10.

For the companies we have been involved with, we have created a learning Academy (see Figure 3.14). The Academy includes a combination of computer-based courses and a two-day training course.

In addition to the Academy, which tends to be specific to a particular company initiative, we along with others have formed the CVC Management Institute. You can reach the institute at www .winningwithcustomers.com. Here, you can collaborate with others who are doing this type of work, talk to thought leaders, find out where this

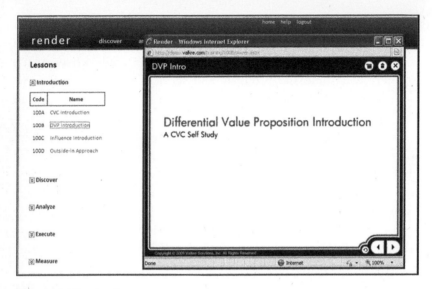

Figure 3.14   Academy

subject is being discussed at upcoming conferences, gain access to the Academy, or talk to us. Our goal with this book and these resources is to provide you with a path to your continual learning and success. If you do not see the path for you then contact us and we will help you find one.

Do you know the most powerful thing about Play 5, Certify? Do not teach the other team your playbook! Some of them do not even know how to play the game! This play gives you a real sustainable competitive advantage.

Play 6: CVC Management System

This is the final play in the Big Six Ideas and playbook shown in Table 3.1.

What Is the CVC Management System

The CVC Management System, Figure 3.15, is a combination of Technology, Tools, Process, and People. It represents our complete solution to Winning with Customers and brings everything we have

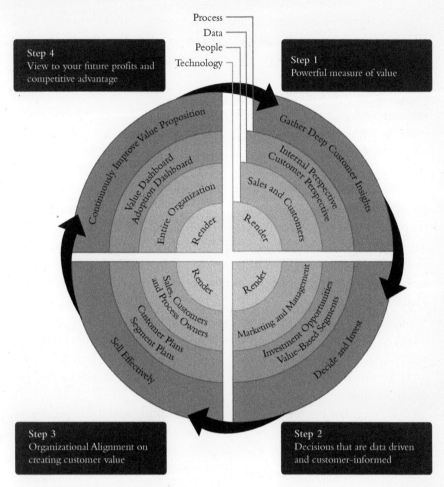

Figure 3.15 CVC System Image

discussed together into one picture. If you refer back to the CVC Stadium, Figure 3.11, the CVC Management System is the Field.

At the core of the system are the standard blocks of Technology, Data, Process and People. We now introduce a picture to show you how technology, data, process, and people are integrated into the system.

We help you understand the picture by talking through the technology, data, process, and people layers.

Technology. Technology is a big deal and is really what enables you to do the work in this book in a cost-effective manner. We like to think of Technology as what makes Winning with Customers easy! We make a point of discussing technology and how it can be used to help in your endeavor to win with customers as we progress from chapter to chapter.

Data. This is the "What you get" layer. As we mentioned earlier, you get a measure on how your customers make more money doing business with you, you get initiatives for cost reduction, revenue generation, and profit growth, which have been informed by customers, customer plans, and a scorecard.

The next layer is Data, customer data. The system helps you to collect, analyze, store, and input customer data into your organizations' processes and decision making. We tend to think of this layer as turning data into understanding and finally into understanding what drives competitive advantage. This is the origin of the Render® name—taking complex data sets and turning it into information and understanding: Rendering the data.

Process. On the process layer, the system includes Discover, Analyze, Execute, and Measure. We have already pointed out that Decisions are part of this layer, which we do not cover. These four processes make up the core organization of the book when it comes to day-to-day work flow.

The next layer is process. Here, we are talking about the process of using customer data and understanding to inform organization process and management decisions. Capital allocation decisions, organizational design, customer planning, operational planning, new product development, innovation, strategy, and everything else you can imagine where rigorous customer understanding has impact.

People. This layer is where we introduce how to go about creating organization capability and momentum. We introduce and discuss the tools to get this done in the certify section.

The final layer is culture and organization. The CVC Management System organizes change management through learning and certification programs that helps people to integrate customers into their daily work. This may be the single most important layer because it allows you to leverage one of your biggest assets, your people.

It is a system that has been a long time in the making. We are looking forward to sharing it with you throughout the rest of the book and beyond. Before we get to the how-to chapters, a couple more points are worthy of mention—Key Philosophies, Technology, and the Maturity Model.

Key Philosophies

You might also think of these as key success factors. They are not really part of any one play. Instead they make up a few key philosophies that have played a role in system design, how we do work, and how we generate success as shown in Table 3.2.

Until the customer understands what's in it for them, any effort is hard to sustain. Play 1, Discover, and Play 3, Execution, are most influenced by this philosophy. If we listen to the customers and then show them we are executing against their input, they will be better off and we will be rewarded. It works! We think that what many miss is execution. We listen to the customer and the input goes into a black hole that is never resurfaced in a way that creates the link back to the customer. There is some magic that happens here that has something to do with ownership and commitment. If you execute against what the customers suggest, they will feel orders of magnitude more ownership and commitment than if you came in with only your own ideas. That is not to say you should not have ideas of your own. When you do not show how you are directly executing against their ideas, the ownership is lost and it turns into a skeptical "If you would just do what I suggested" attitude.

The organization needs to be engaged and understand its role. This is critical in all the plays but turns out to be so important that we have created an individual play, Play 5, Certify, to reinforce the philosophy.

Table 3.2 Key Philosophies of Building the Playbook

Until the customer understands what's in it for them any effort is hard to sustain.

The organization needs to be engaged and understand its role.

The organization needs to see the benefit.

Execution happens one customer at a time.

Continuous improvement is key.

We have seen organizations rely on any number of service providers to tell them how customers value their products and services. We are here to tell you that there is no substitute for digging in and developing your own capability. In order to develop this capability, you need to understand what is expected of you. Sometimes you do not see yourself as being part of this game, Winning with Customers. For those, we always go back to our favorite CEO quote, "If you are not interested in understanding how you deliver value to your customers then you probably should not be in business."

The organization needs to see the benefit. Play 2, Analyze, and Play 4, Measure, are heavily influenced by this philosophy. Play 2, Analyze, establishes a rigorous quantitative perspective that sets up our ability to measure progress over time. Play 4, Measure, measures how we improve our value creation to customers and compares it to how our own value capture is improving. Or when our customers make more money do we make more money? Incorporating the quantitative rigor and resulting financial ROI is the required antidote for failed attempts at building this sort of capability you may have experienced in the past.

Execution happens one customer at a time. Play 1, Discover, and Play 3, Execution, incorporate this important philosophy. One thing that separates a broad market study and Winning with Customers is that we are executing with one company and its respective sales professional at a time . . . Getting input one customer at a time, writing plans one customer at a time, communicating back one at a time, measuring one at a time. Sure, we would like to find overarching solution themes that span multiple customers, geographies, businesses, and such to leverage investment and activity. But the key capability is built to help the organization execute one customer at a time.

Continuous improvement is key. And finally, continuous improvement. This philosophy runs through each and every play. There is real power and benefit in running each play with a customer in a given year or planning period. But you should see what happens when you run the same plays the following year! It is not only the fact that the customer is more convinced that you are serious about your game; it is that you are better at running the plays.

You see these philosophies threaded through everything we discuss in the balance of the book.

The Role of Technology

If our five key philosophies have shaped and informed each play in the playbook, then we would be remiss not to mention that technology serves a key role in executing the playbook. To take the game metaphor a bit further, consider the playing field upon which your organization will run its plays. Would you rather play on a sloppy, torn-up field or one that is modern and well-kept? Sure, your team can play in poor conditions, but which playing surface gives you the best chance to ultimately "Win" with your customer? In case that was not too obvious, technology gives the best playing field available. With the proper technology in place, your team can focus on running its plays and be less distracted by the "field conditions."

For instance, we previously mentioned the goal to avoid having customer input drift into a black hole, but instead being linked to that specific customer. We need to execute one customer at a time, yet to leverage investments and solutions across multiple customers. This combination of macro-analysis and micro-execution can be best achieved with proper software and tools. With pen, paper, spreadsheets, and sheer manpower, it becomes much more difficult and time-consuming.

When it comes to supporting our philosophy of continuous improvement, technology again serves as a great enabler. Each play we run for a customer occurs within a single year or planning period. But these plays do not exist in a vacuum. We should be able to look at the degree of success or failure of these plays over time and identify ways to run the play better each year. Consider this the "film room" that technology provides for adopting and maintaining an organizational culture of continuous improvement.

Throughout the upcoming chapters, we discuss the underlying role of technology as it contributes to the successful execution of the Playbook. We believe technology is a force multiplier.

The Maturity Model

Through our years of experience and practical application, we have found that the concept of Winning with Customers makes common sense. It is a sound concept that people at all levels of an organization understand and intuitively believe can result in true competitive advantage and sustained profit growth for their companies.

Even though you may think the plays make sense, we guarantee that you will not master them in one game or one practice. You need to practice them over time and improve. We have found the maturity model in Table 3.3 to be helpful to guide the journey.

Along the x-axis are the stages of maturity: Reactive, Discrete, Pervasive, and Predictive. Along the y-axis are our old friends, the Big Six Ideas. In the grid boxes are short descriptions that follow the logic of "You know you are here when."

Let's discuss the x-axis a moment. *Reactive* generally means that you are reacting to your environment. Maybe there is a big customer blowup or you find yourself losing share and need to determine why. The *Discrete* suggests there are pockets of activity but they are not well coordinated into an overall system or process that has any kind of cadence or continuous flow. *Pervasive* suggests the entire organization is engaged and employees know the playbook and when the plays are being called. *Predictive* results after having run the plays over and over and you can start to predict the outcomes, which ones are we good at. Predictive is being able to understand how your investment will generate customer value and be able to predict with more and more certainty how and when profits will follow.

We use the Big Six Ideas down the y-axis as we have found these to be the key determinants of success in winning with customers. As you go through each of the chapters and learn more about each of the Big Six Ideas, you can identify where your organization resides within the maturity model map.

Amazingly, or maybe not so amazingly, nearly all of the organizations in our experience believe in this concept of Winning with Customers and want to achieve the results that are possible from this approach to business management. We have experienced companies that excel at collecting data and developing plans; however, some of these same companies are unable to put what they learn into action to truly manage value. A major reason companies are unable to put the learning into action is due to the significant cultural and behavioral challenges they face.

Table 3.3 Maturity Model

Level of CVC Maturity	Reactive	Discrete	Pervasive	Predictive
Understand Value of Products and Services	No documented understanding	Known for select customers	Known for 80% of revenues	Known for 80% of revenues and key influencers
Make Customer-Informed Decisions	Sales decisions	Marketing and management decisions impacted	Organizational decisions impacted	Customer-informed strategic planning
Create Value and Capture Fair Share	No customer planning	Sales creates customer plans	Organizational aligned and accountable	Customer-informed organizational planning
Measure and Improve Value Proposition	Market value proposition established	Segment value proposition established	Integration of value creation and value capture	Value management dashboards
Build Capability-to Sustain CVC	Employees have hands-on experience	Ability to collect data established	Ability to analyze and get into action	CVC integrated in job description and supported with training
Enable CVC System to Scale and Speed	Render® software implemented	CVC processes defined	CVC processes integrated with business processes	Render® software integrated into IT strategy

Sales personnel are accustomed to communicating with customers about volume and pricing—not value. Marketing regularly makes decisions about new products, marketing programs, and the like without much (if any) meaningful research with customers related to customer value creation. In cases where research is used to include the customer perspective in decision making, there is not a clear and measurable linkage between the company's actions and investments, and their impact on customer profitability versus competition. Finance analyzes and measures the profit made from customers, while there is no analysis or measurement of how the value is created versus competition. Additionally, functions within the organization traditionally work independently to deliver value to customers. Their efforts are not aligned and integrated to create maximum value for the customer. Cultural and behavioral barriers represent implementation challenges in nearly every part and every level of the organization.

This is a new way of doing business that requires different thinking and different leadership. Importantly, it requires an attitude of continuous improvement. Fundamentally, continuous improvement is fraught with peril. Culturally, people like things to be completed now! I want my rewards now! Unfortunately, you will not change your organization overnight. Thinking about change through some sort of maturity model is critical. The reason it is critical is so that you can recognize wins along the way and will not be left wanting only for the end.

To put the opportunities and challenges of adopting and sustaining this approach to business management in context, consider manufacturing best practices before and after Toyota moved to the now state-of-the-art management system. Other manufacturing companies throughout the world believed in the concept of the Toyota Management System; however, Toyota was arguably one of the first to move beyond belief in the concept and used it to deliver significant business results. Toyota was willing and able to do what was required to implement and sustain the improved management system, and deliver measurable results.

Toyota and other leading manufacturing companies reaped the rewards of the improved management system in the form of improved operational and financial measures that contributed to growth of the company. As hundreds of thousands of organizations around the world now employ these manufacturing best practices, many of the early adopters continue to benefit financially from their willingness and ability to adopt and sustain these practices.

When you consider the "before and after" picture of manufacturing best practices, the real difference between then and now is management—the processes, tools, and metrics that were available for manufacturers to effectively assess their operations, identify opportunities to eliminate waste, develop and execute plans, measure progress, continue to learn, and improve. Each part of the management system is important to deliver the business results, but clearly the operational and financial metrics that served as the bottom-line proof of success led to adoption and continued use of the new management system.

Likewise, many B2B companies believe in the concept of Winning with Customers. But the availability and use of the management system to help companies like yours *analyze customer profitability, understand your impact on customer profitability (versus competition), measure how value is created for customers, and capture your fair share of the value created* is vital for success.

Summary

In this section we used four key pictures that are used to reinforce concepts and understanding throughout the book. The Big 6—Playbook Map, the Field (CVC Stadium), the CVC Management System, and the Maturity Model.

You should now be able to:

1. *Understand where and how the Big Six Ideas and four breakthroughs are integrated into the playbook.* The Big 6—Playbook Map (see Table 3.1) is the best way to keep these organized and reinforced as you continue to read the book.
2. *Describe the plays.* Discover; Analyze; Execute; Measure; Certify; and CVC Management System, particularly noting breakthroughs, use the CVC Stadium picture and the CVC Management System pictures shown in Figure 3.16 to help here. The CVC Stadium is intuitive and easy. The CVC Management System diagram reminds you that it is a system that includes Technology, Data, Process, and People.

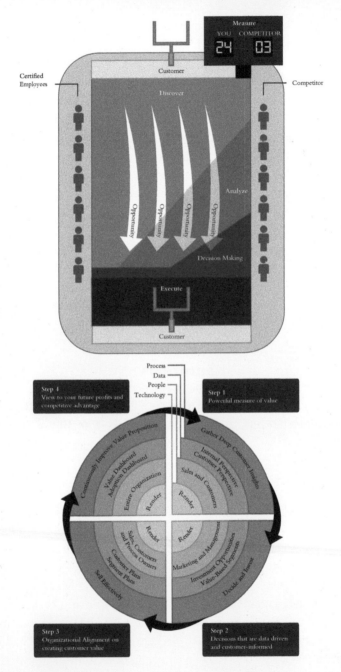

Figure 3.16   CVC Stadium and CVC Management System

3. Define the key philosophies behind the playbook design as shown in Table 3.2.
4. Discuss the maturity model shown in Table 3.3 and how to guide and monitor your progress of winning with customers.

Chapter 3, "The Playbook," is a setup for the rest of the book. For the most part, all we have done so far is to set up the playing field and described the game. In the sections to follow, we start to actually play the game. We try to keep the game simple for now.

Case Study: Health-Care Products

The fascination with the concept of Winning with Customers— helping companies create more value for customers and capturing more value in return—began for Keith more than 15 years ago. One of the earliest applications was in the health-care products industry and represents one of the most powerful examples. The experience and learning gained from this early application became the foundation for future learning and development of the approach.

Restoring Financial Health in Health-Care Products

As a newly minted MBA from the University of North Carolina Kenan-Flagler Business School in 1993, I took on an assignment as a market manager in a large global health-care products and services company. The task was to help build a new business to address the rapidly changing health-care landscape and the resulting financial pressures on the business. The ultimate goal: launch a new business that would accelerate profitable growth of the $300M U.S. surgical kits business unit.

Armed with the results of a consulting study from a major management consulting firm and a high-level business plan, we set out to address the anticipated negative impact on the business due to changes in the health-care system. Our goal was to turn

(Continued)

the bleak industry outlook into a sound business that would deliver profitable growth. This was a tall order.

As health-care insurers (insurance companies and self-insured companies) sought ways to battle rapidly increasing costs, they began shifting the financial risk of providing health care from insurers to health-care providers (hospitals, surgical centers, etc.). In 1993, health-care providers were in no way prepared for such a rapid shift in risk, as they had managed their business on a cost-plus basis forever—taking whatever costs they incurred in performing medical procedures and marking them up, on the order of 20 percent to 30 percent to arrive at a price they passed on to insurers. The thought of having to manage their business lines, or individual medical procedures, on a profit-and-loss basis was daunting. Providers could not identify the specific costs for individual surgical procedures or take specific actions to manage or reduce these costs to determine the profitable and unprofitable procedures.

With the consulting study in hand, we set out to understand the industry challenges and develop a strategy to win with our customers (U.S. hospitals and surgical centers). The study suggested that in the early 1990s, people and people-related expenses in U.S. hospitals represented more than 60 percent of their total costs. Total people costs were growing at a rate of 9 percent per year—three times the rate of inflation. One of the most significant areas of growth in people costs across all hospital operations was in the area of inventory management. This included handling of the health-care products by hospital staff, from receipt of bulk shipments at the receiving dock, consolidation of multiple products throughout the hospital, final packaging and kitting of all products used for a single procedure delivered to the operating room suite and disposal of waste from the surgical procedure. This category of people costs was growing rapidly at 9 percent annually.

Costs were spiraling out of control, driven by people costs, and these costs were being passed on to insurers. This created a major backlash from insurers as their businesses began to suffer, due in large part to their inability to control health-care costs. Insurers changed the rules of engagement and began requiring hospitals to bid on large multiyear health-care contracts with price guarantees. This change in the market resulted in significant downward pressure on the prices hospitals could charge for their services and resulted in rapid deterioration of hospitals' profits.

As the consulting study and our internal management assessment indicated, U.S. hospitals (our customers) faced two major challenges:

The first challenge. Hospitals were invited to bid on large contracts of surgical procedures consisting of many different types of surgical procedures without knowing their costs on a procedure basis. There was limited and insufficient knowledge of the costs and drivers of costs for each surgical procedure, and no data was being captured on a procedure basis.

The second challenge. Hospitals were not equipped with skills, experience, or viable plans to reduce costs and achieve suitable profit levels. After many years of simply marking up their costs and passing them on to insurers, managing profitability of a surgical procedure (or product line) was a foreign concept.

These were serious challenges for our customers. In some instances, hospitals were forced by insurers to take all of their surgical procedures or none at all. For hospitals in a dire financial situation, this was a "bet your business" decision. If they were successful in securing the contract, profitability was not certain immediately or over the life of the contract. If they elected not to bid on these contracts, which represented significant volumes of surgical procedures, the loss of market share

(Continued)

could make their challenging financial situation even worse. It is fair to say, these were challenging times for our customers.

And, as with any business, challenging times for customers translates directly into challenging times for the suppliers. We certainly recognized that our business would never be the same, and our customers reminded us daily. Many hospitals, in a reactionary move to stem the tide of their rapidly eroding profits, turned to health-care product manufacturers seeking price reductions of up to 30 percent. We, and our competitors, who had not been able to secure price increases in years, and who spent the previous several years reducing operating costs to maintain profitability, were beginning to question if survival was possible with a 30 percent price reduction.

As our team worked to assess what all of this really meant for our $300 million surgical products kits business tucked away within this multibillion dollar global health-care products manufacturer, we knew that every aspect of our business had to be examined in an attempt to find a solution. We began by taking a hard look at the fundamentals of our business and business model—what did we do for our customers and why it was important to them?

We knew that what we provided was important to our customers and to the patients they served. The kits and individual products our people manufactured and distributed every day were used to perform a range of surgical procedures—ranging from open-heart surgery to a knee arthroscopy procedure, from a gall bladder removal to a tonsillectomy. Some kits contained up to 200 items for an individual patient's surgical procedure— items that must be present for the surgery to be performed as planned and to create satisfied customers (surgeons, nursing staff, hospital administration staff, and purchasing team).

As we considered the industry-leading capabilities developed over the years to meet the needs of a customer one procedure at a time, we reflected on the precision with which we manufactured products and assembled and distributed kits to hospitals in urban and rural cities and towns throughout the country. We also thought about the unmatched service we provided to help hospitals determine the most cost-effective products for each procedure kit, develop economic order quantities, and plan delivery schedules.

We also reexamined many of the significant investments made over decades to continually improve the manufacturing and distribution of surgical products for hospitals. These investments resulted in hospitals being able to increasingly focus on their competence of delivering health care, while relying on us to get the right supplies to the hospital when and where they are needed, at the most attractive prices.

We concluded that the real success of our business had been driven by the ability to take costs out of the surgical products value chain shown below in Figure 3.17. Our efforts were focused on three key areas of the value chain: Product Manufacturing; Product Sterilization; and Product Distribution.

As we considered the current situation, a major area of focus was the path that had led to the formation of the company. We asked, over and over, did this now make sense? The company's formation was the result of a leading medical products manufacturer's acquisition of a leading stand-alone health-care products distributor. These two companies had been successful as independent organizations for decades. Given the challenges faced by the industry, was the recent combination now a blessing or a curse?

So as we took inventory of the successes of the combined entity and the value it contributed to the industry and customers, we concluded that much value had been created by the combination of the businesses. The company had introduced

Figure 3.17 Surgical Products Value Chain

(Continued)

significant efficiencies and cost savings through the use of technology to improve distribution—developed state-of-the art information systems, distribution and sorting centers, truck routing optimizations methods, and so forth.

Its services to hospitals had evolved by continually incorporating innovations to improve its offerings and value proposition, including:

- Manufacturing of a branded line of leading surgical and ancillary products, providing a broad range of products for use in health-care procedures.
- Packaging of individual nonsterile surgical products and delivering them in kits to hospitals, reducing product acquisition and distribution costs for the hospital.
- Packaging of individual sterile surgical products and delivering them in kits to hospitals, including moving product sterilization operations in-house and sterilizing entire kits of products simultaneously to reduce sterilization costs.
- Packaging and shipping kits of combined sterile and nonsterile products in large quantities to hospitals, further reducing product acquisition and distribution costs.

In short, much had been done to create value for our customers over the years. However, the value was not measurable for customers. As a result, as customers began demanding significant price decreases, we did not have the ability to justify our pricing in a way that was objective, quantitative, and measurable. The rapid change in market conditions called the true value of our offerings into question. This was a wake-up moment.

Why We Lose

We lose when we fail to truly understand the measurable value of what we provide to customers. Each customer purchase transaction represents exchange of value—customers spend money to buy a product or service for use in their business in return for increased sales, decreased costs (or both) that result in increased profits. The customer determines if the purchase has a positive impact on profits, and the relative impact from various competitive products.

When we lose sight of this value exchange and do not ensure that our products truly create measurable value for customers, our business becomes more vulnerable to the latest change in the economy, changing market conditions, or the low-price competitor. We do not have a defensible position when asked to make major price concessions.

We recognized that the company made many investments over the years to bring innovation into the marketplace and meet the needs of customers. However, we did not bring innovation to the process of determining how to bring the most value to the customer. We did not innovate the system to measure the value we created for customers, rather than leaving it to interpretation or chance. And, finally we did not innovate the way we measured the value we received in return for the investments we made in customers—we did not know if we received a fair share of the customers' winnings that we helped to create.

We had no way to measure or prove that our products and services provided more value to our customers, versus competition. We concluded that until this changed we could not win.

The Playbook

Our team comprised sales, marketing, finance, operations, and general management. We set out to do something that (to our knowledge) had not been done in the health-care products industry—determine how our customers could make more money doing business with us. We recognized that the consulting study we inherited was insufficient to answer this question. Although it provided a good understanding of the market forces and their impact on our customers (generally), it did not identify specific areas where we could add value to individual

(Continued)

customers or customer segments in a way that was superior to the competition. This was critical to ensure we focused our actions and investments on the areas that mattered to customers and could give us a real competitive edge.

To answer this question, we enlisted the support of a former hospital financial and operations executive. His knowledge of the customers' strategies, operations, and cost structures combined with his access to key customer contacts in all functional areas and at all levels within the organization was essential. Our previous contact within the customer organization had been limited primarily to the nursing staff and purchasing organization. As a consequence, we had a limited view of the customer's business and received a narrow perspective of how we could really add value. And we thought we knew our customers—we were in for a big surprise.

Talking Value

One of our first observations was that the narrow perspective of hospital nursing and purchasing staff led us to focus our efforts almost exclusively on two things—product quality and price. And we had continually addressed both year after year. As we began having conversations with finance executives, administrative staff, surgeons, inventory management, and others, it was as though scales were being removed from our eyes. We began to see the hospital's business from a completely different perspective and realized that we did not really know our customers. As a result of these in-depth discussions with customers, we developed keen insight about customers and where we could create real value that mattered. This expanded our understanding beyond what was captured in the initial consulting study and helped to identify the customer's major business problem and needs—something actionable to guide our efforts in developing a winning strategy.

Here is a summary of what we learned.

Key Drivers of Hospital Economics:

- 60 percent to 65 percent of annual expenses for people expenses.
- People expenses growing at 9 percent per year (inflation 3 percent).

Insight From In-Depth Value Discussions with Hospitals:

- Hospital major business/operational problem: Inventory Management and Handling of Surgical Supplies.
- Major customer need: To *identify* and *reduce* total costs of surgical procedures (both people and surgical product costs on a procedure basis).

This insight gave us hope. Maybe there was an opportunity to create real value for customers that would shift customers' focus from the 30 percent price reduction mandate. Maybe there was an opportunity to change the conversation to a value-based conversation.

Our discussions with a wide range of hospitals, including large and small hospitals, urban and rural hospitals, teaching and nonteaching hospitals, as well as those focused primarily on surgical procedures and those focused primarily on nonsurgical procedures, helped us to gain a broad view of the market and specific knowledge of the needs of different types of customers.

This approach enabled us to develop an assessment of the potential impact of the industry changes on various types or segments of customers. And, even more important, we identified what each customer type or segment valued—what would have an impact on their business. As a result, we knew more about how our hospital customers could make money than ever before.

(*Continued*)

The customers helped us to identify three specific areas of opportunity where we could create real value:

1. Identification and reduction of costs for surgical product components, on a procedure basis.
2. Reduction of inventory and inventory costs (carrying and handling costs).
3. Reduction of costs for disposal of waste from surgical procedures.

Although these three areas of opportunity to create value for customers were identical for all customers, the relative value of each of these three changed significantly by customer segment. We identified three distinct "value based" segments that would require different solutions to meet their needs.

The chart in Figure 3.18 shows the unique customer segments and what they valued.

At this stage, we were confident that there was an opportunity to deliver real value to customers that could result in the creation of $1billion of additional value by reducing people, inventory, and waste disposal costs. If we could capture 30 percent of this incremental value, we could double the size of the business from $300 million to $600 million.

We had solid targets from our work with customers to understand their business. We also realized that we had raised customer expectations during the process that included in-depth discussions with people throughout the organization, including

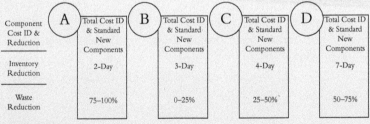

Figure 3.18   Customer Segments

the senior executives we had gained an audience with for the first time. Now, if we did not deliver, our situation would be worse. We had to demonstrate to customers that we listened and were willing to take actions and make investments to help them make more money doing business with us. Given that this had never been done in our industry, to say that customers were skeptical would be a gross understatement. We had a real challenge ahead.

Despite the significant challenge, we were excited and encouraged by the valuable new customer insight and new relationships at all levels of the organization. We knew that if we could help hospitals identify their costs on a procedure-by-procedure basis, they would be able to make sound decisions about what bids to pursue or not to pursue, based on profitability. Each time they won profitable business or walked away from unprofitable business, the impact on their profits could be directly attributed to our efforts.

Second, we knew that if we could help hospitals reduce costs, both people and product costs, we would enable them to manage costs and increase their profitability—we could directly impact their operations and impact profits in a way our competitors could not.

Third, we believed strongly that we could begin to measure and quantify the value created for customers. This would shift the discussion with the customer from price to value, giving us a real shot at capturing our fair share of the value we helped to create and grow our profits. This was a stark contrast to the views held by our senior management team at the outset of this effort.

These were three huge learnings that shaped all of our efforts going forward as we began to work with individual customers to develop solutions and plans that included making investments and taking actions to address their problems. In addition, as a result of the insight gained from meeting

(Continued)

with multiple people within the hospitals, we had a deep understanding of specific needs to address in various parts of the hospital, along with knowledge of hospital operations and financial measurement systems. These were critical to deliver value to the hospital in a measurable way. Now it was time to make it happen systematically throughout our organization— getting everyone aligned and integrated to deliver what the customer valued.

Scaling

I was given the responsibility to lead the initial 17 hospital trials where I would begin to develop and implement the new value proposition and solutions with customers. I traveled the country working with these hospitals to co-develop their unique solutions working with our sales, operations, finance, and customer service organizations.

As we worked to develop the solutions (products and services) for customers, we focused on four things—shaped by the work we had done previously: (1) meet the identified customer needs; (2) develop the best solution; (3) link each element of the solution to customer needs; and (4) refine the initial customer value estimates as we learned from working with the customer to develop and implement the solutions.

- We worked with the marketing, product development, and IT organization to focus all our efforts on meeting the needs that were identified with customers.
  - Identify the cost of surgical components and supplies on a procedure basis.
  - Reduce the cost of surgical components and supplies on each procedure.
  - Reduce the inventory levels and associated costs for surgical components and supplies within the hospital.
  - Reduce waste related to surgical components and supplies used within the hospital.

This clarity of valuable customer needs enabled each of the functions within the company to focus and work collaboratively like never before.

The executive team had a clear picture of the business proposition that could result in a doubling of the size of the business by addressing four valuable needs generated by customers—worth an estimated $300 million in additional sales with attractive margins.

The marketing team clearly understood the value proposition that would be most attractive to customers, as well as how it differed by customer segment.

The sales organization was eager to sell a solution that was truly valuable to customers—one that represented an opportunity for significant competitive advantage.

The operations team knew that any changes in the operations and associated investments would be driven by the goal of meeting the customer needs and delivering products and services with the quality required to help our customers win.

The finance team had greater insight into how we could monetize customer needs and begin to measure how much our competitive advantage was truly worth in dollars and cents.

- The product development group made a commitment to develop the "best" solution. The best solution was defined as the solution that met the customer needs and delivered the most value to the customer. Yes, the solution that had the greatest impact on the customer's profits. A different definition of the best solution than the product development group had used in the past.
  - As a result of this new definition of the best solution, several changes occurred. The search for solutions began with the customer's needs in mind, rather than the latest new technology idea we were trying to find a home for. The team actually searched for solutions outside of the

(Continued)

organization—ones that met the needs. The source of the technologies was irrelevant. The solution development team was broadened to include other areas that possessed expertise that would be relevant, such as IT, logistics experts, and operating room nurses.

- The operational and financial teams worked closely together to ensure that each element of the solution was linked directly to a need. This was important to close the loop with the customer and enable us to show the operational and financial impact of the solution from the customer's perspective, using their language. This is where the initial discovery work with a variety of customers and players throughout the customer organizations really paid off.

- As we worked with the 17 customers included in the trial, the initial estimates of $1 billion of value creation and $300 million of value capture were continually refined using insights from real customers—one customer at a time. Although specific customer situations represented more or less value creation and capture than originally estimated, we found our initial estimates to be directionally correct and the business proposition

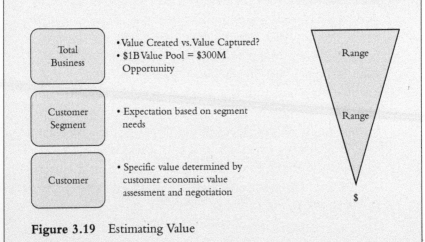

Figure 3.19 Estimating Value

was realized. Figure 3.19 shows how the process works to move from an initial estimate of value for the entire market, to a refined estimate based on development of distinct customer segments within the market, to individual estimates customer by customer. This approach helped to determine if the initial value estimates were consistent with the actual results as we worked with real customers.

The most significant and consistent feedback we received from customers over and over again during the trial centered on their disbelief that we listened to their input and did something about it. Although you cannot put a monetary figure on this feedback, it set the tone for a new level of engagement and trust with customers. And although we certainly had some miscues during the trials, as with any new business venture, customers were forgiving. This was due in large part to the increased level of trust and the customers' belief that we were in this together. After six to nine months working with the 17 customers in the trial, we expanded the offering across the entire business unit.

Planning

We were now poised to aggressively launch the new value proposition into the market with all customers, confident that we were able to meet their needs and provide measurable financial benefit superior to our competitors. The value proposition was supported by an impressive lineup of new products and services that were developed and refined during the trial.

The new products and services included enhancements to existing products offered by the business, as well as new products and services that broadened the offering—positioning the business to capture a greater share of the customers spend and capture higher margin services business. Each of these elements of the solution were linked directly to customer needs and created measurable value for the customer.

(Continued)

Figure 3.20 shows the set of products and services that were launched to create value for customers.

The final chapter in the success of this venture is getting a fair share of the value created from all of the actions and investments to create value for customers. We were able to use value-based pricing to capture maximum value from the product and services solutions. This was enabled by the "heavy lifting" that was accomplished early in the process with customers to quantify the value of their needs—gaining a keen understanding of the operational and financial benefits to the customer by implementing the solutions.

We initially estimated that 30 percent of the value we created could be captured through value-based pricing, with the

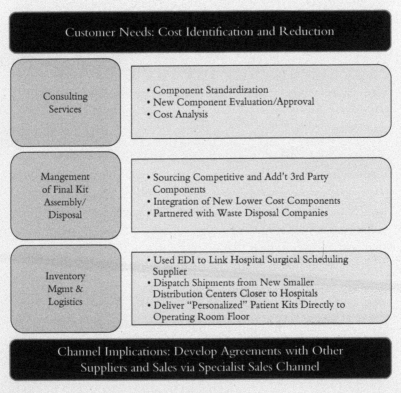

Figure 3.20   Products and Service Solutions

customer retaining 70 percent of the value. These initial estimates were obtained using benchmarking data for similar offerings from other businesses. We found our final value capture percentage to be consistent with the initial estimates.

However, as competitors began to enter the picture, we had to continually prove the value of our solution. As competitors arrived, many of them used similar descriptions of their value propositions. However, our early mover advantage, deep knowledge of the customers' business, value measurement tools, and strong customer relationships allowed us to continually provide solutions that were superior in creating more value for customers.

The value estimation and measurement system, as well as the value-based pricing tools, were used by marketing and sales to estimate value and develop appropriate pricing on a customer-by-customer basis. Figure 3.21 shows the Value Estimation Tool we used to justify the value of our solutions versus competitors.

Figure 3.22 shows the Value-based Pricing approach we used to capture our fair share of the value we helped to create.

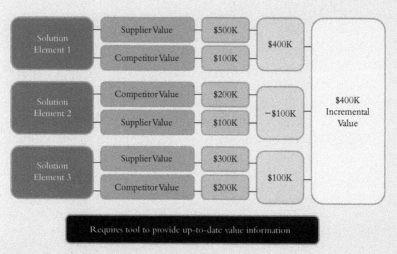

Figure 3.21 Capturing Your Fair Share

(*Continued*)

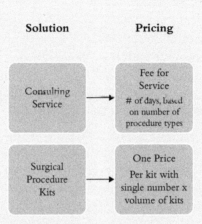

Figure 3.22   Value-Based Pricing

This early example of using outside-in customer information to drive profitable growth in a business was a huge success. This business delivered consistent revenue and profit growth for over a decade and continues to be used as a model for Customer Value Creation at its best.

Since the launch of this business, many new developments have taken place in the area of Customer Value Creation as we have continued to learn and make the process easier for organizations to implement and sustain. Software has been developed to capture and update customer information. New metrics have been developed to quantify competitive advantage. New tools have been developed to plan, execute, and manage these activities with customers systematically. All of these developments are now a part of the CVC Management System as we know it today. With this new and improved system, it is easier to achieve what we achieved in this business more than 15 years ago. It is now easier for organizations to adopt and implement this proven approach to win in the marketplace.

Chapter 4

Winning Metrics

This is a surprise chapter. When we created the book outline, this chapter was nowhere to be found. We had originally planned to cover this part of our story in Chapter 2, "Define Winning." But during these past six months there has been a growing interest in the discussion of our metrics. So we thought, given the interest, we should isolate the discussion into its own chapter. You see, somewhere along our journey of work in Winning with Customers something surprising happened. The metrics we use as a necessary evil to organize our work have taken on a life of their own. We are surprised at the interest because the metrics have always flowed from our work. Our work did not flow or follow from the metrics.

After reading this chapter you will be able to:

- Understand the foundation of all metrics we introduce in the next chapters, the "how to" chapters.
- Understand the characteristics of a good metric.
- Understand the evolution in metrics from Loyalty and Customer Satisfaction.

119

- Define the metric for Winning with Customers: The differential value proposition.
- Understand how the metric segments your customers according to value creation and capture.

Owens Corning

This is a story that begins a couple years ago. When we look back at 2005 and 2006, we were enjoying a robust building economy. Then, like the rest of the United States, we started to see the market soften. Now Owens Corning as an organization has gotten pretty good over the years as a process-based organization. We have done a lot of work with Lean and Six-Sigma. We know how to operate in a disciplined fashion. When we looked at the challenge of a softening economy, we started to ask ourselves a different question. We started to ask ourselves how we regard our customers. Traditionally, Owens Corning, like many companies, has regarded our customers through the lens of what we see and what we know. So we had some good customers based on their profitability, and our share. And we had some great customers. But as the economy softened we knew that was not enough, we needed to leverage our experience of operating a process and get to know our customers differently.

So at the beginning of 2007 the company defined a goal for itself that was simply concise and meaningful. In 2007, we were going to understand the value we deliver to customers and determine a means to measure it. And the operative word in the goal is *measure!* So we set out to find a measure. We looked at many of the available measurement schemes in the market. We talked to Gallup, we talked to Bain, JD Powers, and we talked to many different people. We found many of those schemes were not going to achieve our goal. They were largely retrospective; they were largely based on things like satisfaction and loyalty and engagement but they really did not help us understand our value. We really wanted to get to the universal standard of

---

value—money. So we challenged ourselves with the question "Do we know if our customers are making more money doing business with us versus the other guy?" And as we challenged ourselves with that question, we really thought that this has the ability to crack the code. If we could answer this question, we could move our company, in terms of having our customers make more money doing business with us than with the competition, that our ability to capture some of that value would be increased as well. And it would be truly what we had established as the mantra Winning with Customers.

We set our sights on how to measure the value of Owens Corning through the lens of making money with our customers. As we looked around, we found a scheme that we thought made a lot of sense. It was brought to us by the Valkre team and it encompassed a phenomenon called "differential value." At Owens Corning today, if you were to walk around the hallway or sit in any of our meetings you would likely hear the citation of differential value. It has become, in 2009, the way that we talk about how we operate with our customers. It is prevalent and it is the language of differential value. Differential value is really a simply defined phenomenon. Are we making a difference and do our customers make more money doing business with us than with the other guy?

—Bob Harlan, Owens Corning, Director of Business Insights

The History of Our Metrics

As we mentioned before, our work has spanned the range from individual customer projects through company transformation. In the early days, our work focused primarily on projects with a relatively small set of customers. In most cases, we worked with customers for which we were directly accountable. We did not have any metrics per se. We engaged with those customers to understand how their business worked for the sole purpose of positioning our own products and services. We did not change the investment footprint of our companies, and we did not come away with a metric that was communicated up and down the organization. We were being good sales and marketing employees. We had a bit of a methodology that was influenced by our business schools and a few consultants, and not much more.

Fast-forward to today. The balance of work has shifted toward the transformational end of the scale. Part of the reason is because we have gotten older, more experienced, and that is what is expected. But we have also gotten better with each project. As we have gotten better at this, we have had the opportunity to communicate with broader and broader audiences with increasingly higher expectations. By the way, this is a good thing. As a result, we could no longer take our own small teams and muscle our way through a few customers and deliver the results our companies expected. They expected scale and leverage across the organization. Metrics are required to achieve scale and understanding across the organization. They are essential ingredients of success.

So the metrics we use for winning with customers have evolved. Here are a few things we have learned over the years that have shaped our metrics and that we build on in this chapter. And, we must say, of all the lessons we have learned along this journey thus far, one of the greatest lessons is that metrics matter.

- *Metrics matter to the customer.* This is the single most important point. The customers need to see themselves in the metric. You cannot win with customers if you are not measuring what is most important to them . . . the performance of their business. This is not a bashing session for existing Satisfaction or Loyalty measures, but we do think there is significant opportunity for improvement of these measures by adding an element of a customer's success. In examining these measures, it begs the question: What's in it for the customer?
- *Metrics matter to the sales organization.* The metric needs to be one that can be used directly by sales in the day-to-day management of their sales activities with customers. Sales have a difficult time dealing with large macro measures that seem a million miles away

from their daily lives. And they really get annoyed when that same measure, the one they do not understand, is used to judge their performance! They want a measure that makes sense to them and their customers, that is accepted by their corporate leaders, and has practical application to achieving their sales targets.

- *Metrics matter to people throughout the customers' organization.* The metric needs to be relevant to people throughout customers' businesses, so you can organize your work around improving the score. It needs to be a metric they will take the time to help you understand from their perspective. If a general manager is not willing to sit down and discuss the metric for an hour, then it is not the right metric.
- *Metrics matter to you.* The metric needs to be one that if improved will generate results for you and your company.
- *Different metrics are required in B2B versus B2C.* Decisions in the B2B world are heavily influenced by economics rather than attitudes. Attitudes tend to shift with individual personalities. You do not want to win one day and lose the next because personalities changed on the other side of the table. That is hard to explain to your CEO! You need metrics that link directly to the economics of B2B.
- *Metrics should be forward looking.* You need a metric that can help you to look around corners and develop a road map for future success. Measuring last year's performance is nice, but anticipating next year's is even better.
- *Metrics must be understandable.* If your sales professionals cannot explain to their customers how it works, then it is no good. If you need a Rosetta Stone to help people understand how the metric is linked to improved profits for them and for you, then you will struggle to get the results you want. A simple rule for metrics: Keep it simple.
- *Metrics must scale up, down, and sideways.* You need a metric that scales up to the business level, down to the customer level, and across business and customer types. The measure must allow you to aggregate information for decision making but also disseminate information for execution.

People like metrics because metrics provide an objective way to monitor progress and evaluate success. And the results-oriented folks in business (hopefully everyone) cannot live without metrics. With that said, metrics will influence people's behavior. So we better use the right metrics—the ones that get everyone working toward the result we want to achieve. Metrics matter.

Developing the Metrics

As we explore metrics, let's begin with the Winning with Customers framework discussed earlier (shown in Figure 4.1). Rather than measuring success on a single dimension—your own profitability—success must be measured by both your profitability *and* the impact you have on your customer's profitability (relative to competitors).

For most organizations, the first opportunity to adopt the Winning with Customers Management system is developing a metric that measures the organization's impact on customer profitability. This metric is important to gain a more complete picture of true success with customers, and answers the *critical question*: Are your customers making more money doing business with you relative to your competitors?

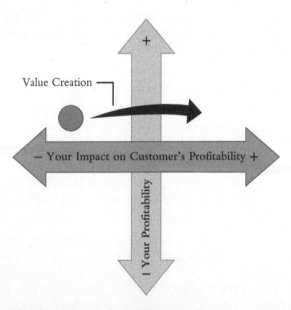

Figure 4.1   Winning with Customer's Framework

Several methodologies and approaches are in use today as a proxy for this measure, such as Customer Satisfaction or Customer Loyalty measurement programs. These programs typically come in the form of surveys or structured interviews that are akin to "vacuum cleaner" sessions in which information is sucked out of the customer for the benefit of your organization. Often driven by a marketing function, customer feedback programs are designed to help marketing and are rarely seen by sales or the customer again. The end result is a number of reports or binders that allows someone to check a box that they are a customer-focused company.

These programs were designed with good intentions. Customer Satisfaction surveys can be great tools for identifying "dissatisfied" customers, or alerting management of situations in which their profits are at risk. Unfortunately, that is really where the value ends. It has been found that Satisfied Customers still switch suppliers . . . leaving organizations with blind spots in their customer feedback programs. The defection of satisfied customers is especially troubling given that you count on those satisfied customers for growth.

In an effort to get a better grasp of how to grow with satisfied customers, B2B marketers have begun using Customer Loyalty measurement programs. Customer Loyalty is about understanding how likely a customer is to refer a product or service to a member of their "network" (as a proxy for their loyalty). The thought is that if the customer is willing to stick its neck out and refer a company, product, or service, it is likely to continue as a customer. And these companies might be great prospects to buy even more. In recent years, Customer Loyalty measurement has taken hold as a replacement to Customer Satisfaction surveys because of these incremental improvements.

In B2C markets, Customer Loyalty makes real sense . . . The more people out there talking positively about a company, product, or service; the more likely others will buy. There are numerous case studies of restaurants or personal electronics manufacturers that have seen real financial benefit by increasing the number of customers loyal to them. Its application in B2B, however, leaves plenty to be desired. Some common pitfalls to implementation of Customer Loyalty programs in B2B are shown in Table 4.1.

Table 4.1   Common Customer Loyalty Pitfalls

Pitfall	Outcome
B2B decision makers don't answer surveys.	Insights being directed by people who can't reward you for your work.
Insights are reactive.	Always fighting fires rather than staying ahead of competition.
Attitudes have to be taken at face value.	Insights can be gamed to increase leverage in negotiation.
Attitudes disappear with customer turnover.	Have to start from scratch with new decision makers.
Sales is not involved.	When it comes time to execute on the insights, there is resistance or disagreement on the action.
Factors/questions are static when they vary based on changes in markets, strategies, and competitive responses.	Wasteful investments are made in an area that isn't important to the customer at the time.

In our work with companies, we have encountered numerous failed attempts to implement Customer Satisfaction and Loyalty management systems designed to improve Winning with Customers because of their inability to truly measure competitive advantage. This lack of confidence in metrics to assess the impact on a customer's profitability has been the single greatest barrier to success. People at all levels of the organization believe in the approach, but the ability to gain management support and successfully implement the system falls apart in the absence of an appropriate metric to determine if the impact on customer profitability is truly superior; that is, whether there is truly a measurable competitive advantage that you can take to the bank.

We have found that to truly measure the value customers receive from a company's offerings, relative to those of a competing company, the metric must demonstrate a direct and measurable relationship between a company's investments to improve customer profitability and the financial impact of those investments on the customer's business operations. A suitable metric must measure the value to customers in dollars and cents that show up on the customer's profit-and-loss statement and balance sheet. Although Customer Satisfaction and Customer Loyalty measurement programs may provide value for other decisions or business performance assessments, they do not help to understand why customers do or do not make more money doing business with your company versus your competition.

"When we look at loyalty programs and we've done them as well, it is our operating theory that the thing that drives loyalty as strong as or stronger than anything else is the ability for us to help our customers make money. Where there are many schemes for measuring loyalty, we rather think the most powerful way to engage our customers in this kind of conversation is better served by talking to them about their ability to make money."

—Bob Harlan, Director of Business Insights, Owens Corning

We have also found that measuring the differential impact a company has on a customer's bottom line has to be simple. When we started this work, there were deep complex financial models designed to simulate how much profit could be delivered to a customer from a given investment. These models were incredibly successful for a few highly analytical customers, but they were impossible to scale because of their complexity and rigidity. The only people who understood them were the people who built them . . . notably absent were acceptance and comprehension by sales and the customer. This work continues today by various consultancies in the form of projects referred to as Customer Value Analysis or similar names. These efforts are highly recommended for the three to five most strategic customers, but they are almost impossible to implement on a systemic, far-reaching basis.

Finally, we have found that the metrics need to be relative to competition, but should not focus on the competition. Metrics should focus on assessing how you help the customer succeed. Additionally, the metric must quantify your competitive advantage. There is a time and place for competitive SWOT analyses (i.e., a strategic planning method used to evaluate the Strengths, Weaknesses, Opportunities, and Threats) to enhance your decision making, but focusing solely on the competition can cause your organization to follow competitors down a rat hole of commoditization. Winning with Customers is about focusing on what you can do to create competitive advantage, not simply reacting and

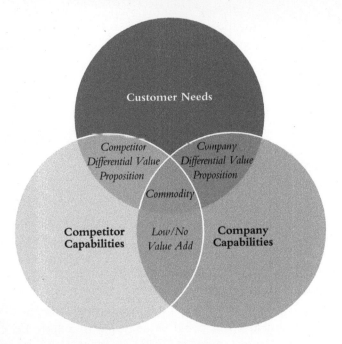

Figure 4.2   Focus of Winning with Customers

mimicking the competition. The Venn diagram in Figure 4.2 makes the point. The focus is on understanding your competitive differentiation.

The Winning with Customer Metric

You are surely thinking to yourself by now, "So what is the metric already?" The metric we have found that meets the criteria and has been successfully adopted by leading organizations is something we call a *Differential Value Proposition*, or *DVP*. Sometimes when we reveal this as the magic metric, we get some confused looks. "A Value Proposition is not a metric," they say. Our response, "It is now." If you agree that the primary basis of competition in B2B markets is to make your customers more money (aka creating value), what better way to understand where you stand than by measuring it directly? A Differential Value Proposition (DVP) is typically a piece of sales or marketing collateral that depicts the investments you make and the impact it has

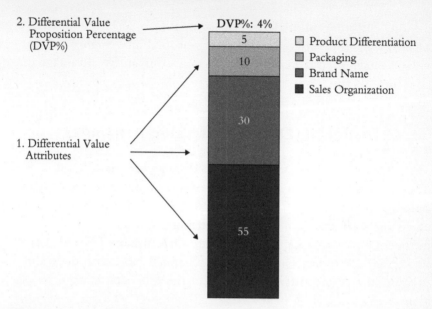

Figure 4.3 The Differential Value Proposition

on a customer's bottom line relative to your competitors. All we are suggesting is to measure it.

As a metric, your DVP has two critical parts (as shown in Figure 4.3) that, when combined, create powerful insights into the core of your business:

1. *Differential Value Attributes:* The investments a company makes that create value for a customer and are unmatched by competition.
2. *Differential Value Proposition Percentage (DVP%):* The impact of company investments on a customer's profitability, DVP%.

In essence, the DVP is a measure of a company's competitive advantage in measurable financial terms.

The DVP is depicted as a simple chart that is easily understood and communicated at all levels of the company and customer organization—simple language and a simple chart to communicate the output of a rigorous and powerful metric. The Value Attributes are depicted as a stacked bar chart that is constrained to 100 points where the DVP% is shown as a percentage on top of the stacked bar chart. This simple graphic quickly summarizes which of your investments created value for the customer (unmatched by competition) *and* the impact of company investments on a customer's profitability. Figure 4.3 provides a much-needed measure of company competitive advantage one customer at a time.

Exploring Differential Value Attributes

Value Attributes are factors that impact your customer's bottom line. They can be thought of as categories of investments that your organization makes to create competitive advantage. In our experience, companies may have as many as 30 attributes in their arsenals and can include investments such as the Sales Organization, Brand Name, Packaging, or Product Differentiation . . . much more than the features of a product. Value Attributes represent the full value of your investments to a customer.

Your organization may have 30 different areas of investment to create value for customers. However, it is unlikely that a customer will find differential value in each of these areas of investment. For a given customer, there may only be four or five Value Attributes that make up your DVP. To show the relative value and impact of each Value Attribute, the Value Attributes are shown in a simple stacked bar chart that adds up to 100 points or 100 percent. In this example, Brand Name would be considered three times more valuable to the customer's bottom line than Packaging.

Value Attributes displayed as a stacked bar chart, as in Figure 4.4, provides a simple and powerful view of the differential value you provide to each customer. In a single simple chart, it sums up the net impact of your investments, relative to your competitors.

Consider this: Allocating a significant portion of your operating budget to customer service does not mean that every customer sees differential value from that investment. The value of the investment may be different based on your customer's strategy. For example, Customer (A) who competes on operational efficiencies and waste elimination (lower costs), receives significant value from your customer service investments that directly reduces inventory and operations costs.

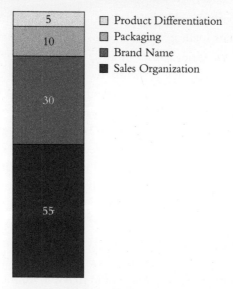

Figure 4.4   The Differential Value Attributes

Another, Customer (B), places far less value on your customer service investment because this customer competes on demand generation and sales conversion through intense sales and marketing efforts. For this company, it sees customer service as doing a good job, but not a key driver of its profitability. Only through measuring Value Attributes do you begin to understand the nuances of your DVP customer by customer. And without this understanding, you might continue to invest in customer service, advertise your customer service differentiation, and wonder why you are only successful with a portion of your customers and prospective customers. In this instance, your value proposition resonates with one customer, while another customer sees less value in it.

The other important view is whether the value created from your investment in customer service for Customer (A) provides competitive advantage. Does the investment deliver a greater or lesser impact on this customer's profitability as compared to the investments made by competitors? If the answer is yes, then you have created differential value for the customer and a competitive advantage. However, if your competitor has made similar investments, you have not created differential value or a competitive advantage. And your current profitability with this customer is not secure.

As you can imagine, understanding the DVP for each customer is a daunting task without a means to measure and communicate it effectively. To make matters more complex, your DVP varies among the decision makers and influencers within an individual customer's organization. The Purchasing Agent or Buyer has insights into some of the value you provide, but not all. People in your customer's sales, marketing, and operations organizations all have other insights into the value you provide. In fact, as you talk to different people within the customer organization, you will likely develop differing DVPs, as shown in Figure 4.5.

Understanding these differences is critical to investing appropriately. If your decision making was heavily biased by the perspective of a Purchasing Agent or Buyer, you would make investments primarily in

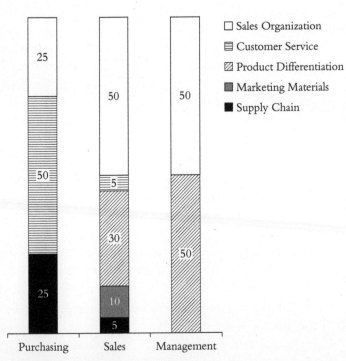

Figure 4.5 Value Attributes by Customer Function

customer service to gain a competitive advantage. Alternatively, if your decision making is driven by the perspective of Sales or Management within your customer, you would likely make investments in different areas to create value for this customer.

To further explore the DVP for a given customer, consider the multiple levels of decision makers and influencers within an organization. For example, a larger customer may have a corporate office, several regional offices, and many stores, branches, or distribution centers. At each of these locations, the impact of your investments and customer needs will likely be different.

The various elements of your value proposition may differ in value for each of these groups, resulting in differing perspectives of your DVP. For example, at big-box retailers, the executives may value Partnership and Product Differentiation, the regional managers may value Training and the Sales Organization, while the individual stores may value Supply Chain and Customer Service, providing you with multiple perspectives of the DVP, as shown in Figure 4.6.

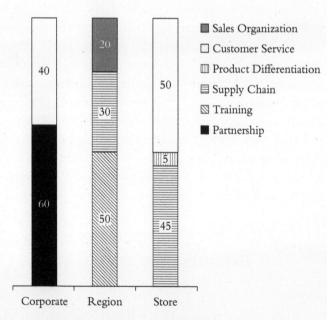

Figure 4.6   Value Attributes by Customer Level

One final perspective of the DVP to consider is time. As a result of the ever-changing marketplace, the attributes in your DVP are always changing even if your investments remain the same. This happens because of changes in your customers' needs and competitors' investments. Your customers' needs may change based on their changing strategy or market conditions. To put this in perspective, think about what your customer needs in good markets versus times of economic recession like those of 2008 and 2009? In times of growth, customer strategies are typically focused on growth and they are primarily looking for value in areas such as sales and marketing support. In declining markets, your customer's strategy changes to one of cost reduction and liquidity, where survival and cash is king. During these times, the company's needs may shift to reducing inventory with a more flexible supply chain, or other areas of cost reduction and cash management.

By introducing the element of time, you might be worried that your organization's DVP has changed in the time you spent reading this chapter. The good news, however, is that your DVPs do not change on an hourly, daily, or even monthly basis. In our experience, an understanding of your DVP typically has a shelf life of about a year unless the marketplace dramatically changes.

The point of covering these complexities is not to cause you to lose sleep at night, but rather to present an opportunity. By better understanding the complexities and nuances of the investments that create differential value for each customer, different functions within a customer and across the many levels within a customer's organization on a continuous basis, organizations are armed with an ability to invest smarter and faster to create competitive advantage and win with customers. This is made much easier with the ability to *measure* the differential value you provide for customers, and this simple stacked bar chart of Value Attributes has worked well for leading outside-in B2B companies.

Exploring the DVP%

It is important to understand the Value Attributes that make up your DVP. They tell how you have created competitive advantage.

However, the question remains: How much value have you created versus competition?

Say, for example, you sell raw materials to an original equipment manufacturer and your primary competition is a low-cost supplier from China. You may have proven through market studies or customer research that you have the best product, supply chain, and sales organization. In effect, you have identified the attributes that make up your DVP. However, you continue to lose market share to your Chinese competition. A likely reason is that your customers are making more money doing business with your competition despite your advantages in product, supply chain, and the sales organization.

The additional information you need to fully understand your DVP is how much money ($) you put into your customer's bank account using your DVP. Now, you could take a few accountants, financial gurus, and some marketers, put them in a conference room for a few days, and build models that may help you understand if your customers make more money doing business with you. However, there is a challenge with this approach. We have learned from experience that it results in a complicated model built on internal data and assumptions. Measuring how much value you create in this fashion has a few deficiencies:

- *It is hard.* Building Value Creation models require lots of time and very well educated (and expensive) resources to pull together the data to build them.
- *The scope is limited.* It is nearly impossible to model customer value creation for every customer, given how different your DVP may be for each customer.
- *The results are complex.* Anyone well schooled in change management knows that one of the keys to gain adoption of new concepts and tools by an organization and its customers is simplicity. The results of the analysis must be simple to understand and communicate. Complex spreadsheets and databases are usually considered cool only by the people that build them.

What organizations really need is a metric that can be calculated on the back of an envelope that simply and clearly shows how much customer value is being created. We have developed a metric called the Differential Value Proposition Percentage (DVP%) that fits the bill. A DVP% is a simple ratio that can be easily explained and communicated both internally and with customers. DVP% is calculated as:

$$DVP\% = \frac{\text{Differential Profits to Customer}}{\text{Cost of Your Products/Services that Customer Buys/Uses}}$$

Said another way, the DVP% represents the amount of differential operating margin dollars created for a customer for each dollar of goods and services they purchase from you. As an example, if your DVP% is 3 percent for a customer, and they buy $1 million worth of goods, your DVP is worth $30,000 to their bottom line.

The DVP% metric is of interest to both you and your customers and it gets to the essence of business. Your customers decided to do business with you because they believed you could help them make more money, relative to alternative choices. You do business with your customers because you believe you provide them a superior alternative that provides you with an attractive profit. We are measuring the intersection of truth between these perspectives. The DVP is a rigorous measure that is founded in economics that can be backed up with data that creates clarity on where you stand. If your DVP% is 0 percent, that means you are a commodity and slight fluctuations in price may drive a customer to switch. If your DVP% is negative, that customer is making more money doing business with your competition and any business you have can be considered at risk. The interesting part of this is the relationship between DVP% and pricing. It is hard to pass through a price increase when you are considered a commodity. If your DVP is up to 6 percent to 8 percent though, you stand a better chance of increasing prices or gaining share relative to competitors.

Let's put this metric into some context by looking at some actual DVP% calculations from real companies, as shown in Figures 4.7 to 4.9. These examples of DVP% demonstrate how the impact on customer profitability can vary from customer to customer.

For a distributor that buys $32 million in product, our Brand
Name and Marketing Efforts bring in 5% more Sales a Year.

This volume lift amounts to an increase in $500K in
incremental profits for our customer.

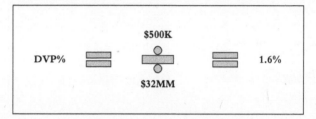

$500K

DVP%   ═══   ═══   1.6%

$32MM

Figure 4.7   Creating a DVP% with Volume Growth

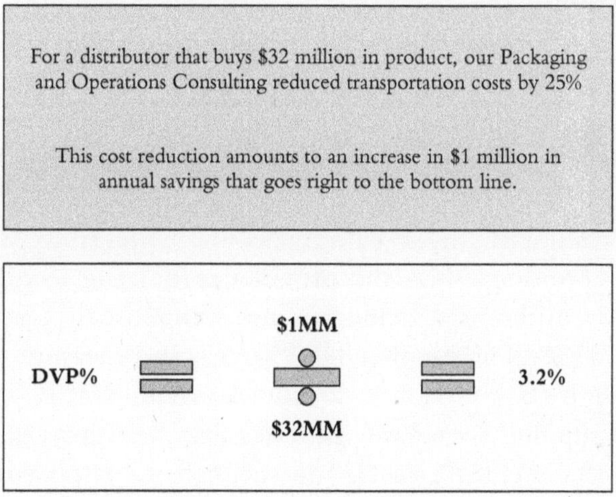

For a distributor that buys $32 million in product, our Packaging
and Operations Consulting reduced transportation costs by 25%

This cost reduction amounts to an increase in $1 million in
annual savings that goes right to the bottom line.

$1MM

DVP%   ═══   ═══   3.2%

$32MM

Figure 4.8   Creating a DVP% with Cost Reduction

These examples of DVP% and how they are calculated demonstrate
the power of its soundness economically, as well as its simplicity for ease
of communication and use.

The numerator in the DVP% (Differential Profits to Customers) is
important to understand. We spend much of the remaining chapters helping you learn how to create and measure differential value and profits.

For a distributor that buys $32 million in product, our Just In Time Supply Chain reduced inventory levels in half.

This improvement freed up $5 MM in working capital. At a cost of capital of 15%, $750K in incremental profits is recognized.

$$\text{DVP\%} \quad \frac{\$750K}{\$32MM} \quad 2.3\%$$

Figure 4.9   Creating a DVP% by Freeing Working Capital

Understanding the DVP% from a customer's perspective is easier than you think. It is simple. The higher the number, the better off they are. Customers want to make more money doing business with you. The DVP% metric allows them to objectively understand and track changes in the value they receive. Some of your customers may feel confident in their ability to understand how much differential value you create. Others are less confident. For those who are confident, the DVP% takes away the faulty assumptions of an overconfidence bias and provides real clarity to the attributes that deliver differential value among competitors. Some customers know what their supplier DVP%'s are and measure them every day, although they probably do not call them "DVP." They build their own supplier scorecards and measure their gross margins, volume growth, operating costs, and so forth, to assess you and your competitors.

Customers are interested in the DVP% and spend time measuring it because it is critical to their profitability. It is the customers' job to pick the right supplier to help them make more money. If they do not, the person who picked that supplier gets fired. Customers who pick the right suppliers all the time will be more profitable than those who make the wrong decisions time and time again. Said another way, if a customer is doing business with a supplier that provides a strong DVP and then that supplier goes away the next day that customer's profitability will drop.

> *"They know how we are performing today and can assign a number to that, frequently they ask us to look at their numbers with them. And I think this was a bit of a surprise to many of our folks that customers would be that open. But we found that there was real magic in talking to people about how they make money and how they can make more money. And that's a conversation that everybody wants to have and it really opens up the channel of communication which allows us to be very candid and allows the customers to be very candid."*

> —Bob Harlan, Director of Business
> Insights, Owens Corning

For a customer, the DVP% is more than just a number. The DVP% essentially represents the strength of your competitive advantage in financial terms:

- If your DVP% is negative, that means your customers are making more money doing business with your competitors. Obviously not a good position.
- If your DVP% is zero, customers consider your DVP to be a commodity. They make just as much money doing business with you as they do with your competition.
- If the DVP% is positive, your actions and investments are positively contributing to the value customers receive versus the competition. You have measurable competitive advantage and are positively impacting the customer's bottom line.

Without the Value Attributes and DVP% (simple yet powerful metrics of differential customer value creation), it is impossible to have a meaningful, fact-based discussion with customers about the value you help them create versus your competitors. These critical metrics enable B2B companies to assess where they stand versus competitors, identify the specific actions, and investments that create value and measurable competitive advantage. We believe this metric provides a simple way to measure competitive advantage and answer the question "Do your customers make more money doing business with you?"

The Different Snapshots of Your DVP

Up to this point, the DVP may come across as a static metric that measures what is valuable to customers at a point in time. While true, we like to measure it at three different points in time:

- Internal Perspective: What your organization thinks the DVP is at a point in time
- Current Customer Perspective: What your customers think your DVP is at a point in time
- Future Customer Perspective: What would customers think your DVP can be in 18 to 24 months

Each of these DVP perspectives add obvious insights by themselves . . . but looking at the differences between the three snapshots is where the real learning begins. Comparing what you think and what your customers think aligns your organization in terms of what really is valuable. Even more valuable is comparing what the customer thinks of you now and where they think your DVP can go. This difference is what defines the opportunity to make customers more money. A future DVP% of 5 and a current DVP% of 2 means the customer believes you can add $30,000 for each $1 million they purchase from you . . . simply by doing the things they requested. Not to get ahead of ourselves, but one of the most powerful indicators of success that we've found isn't the Current Customer Perspective or the Future Customer Perspective, it is the difference between the two.

We will cover much more of this in upcoming chapters but didn't want to lose this point as the metric is being explained in the first place. In the next section, we'll start introducing some of the management views that can be created when the DVP is measured in these ways.

Using DVP% on an Aggregated Business Level

So far we have developed the DVP% at the customer level. Taking a broader or portfolio view of groups of customers, using these two metrics allows you to see how you are doing with value creation and capture across the business. When you consider these two measures

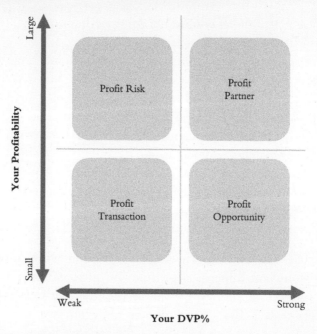

Figure 4.10 DVP% Starting Point

together across groups of customers, it provides insight into the current status of the relationships between you and your customers—whether they are secure or at risk.

We have developed a way to view these groups of customers using what we call the *Starting Point*, as shown in the diagram in Figure 4.10. Performing this analysis for your top 10 customers, or top 20 percent of your customers, will provide meaningful insight.

1. *Profit Partner.* This is the upper-right corner. In this situation, both you and your customer are enjoying a mutually rewarding relationship. It is always nice to have 50 percent or more of your customers in this quadrant but that is seldom the case.
2. *Profit Risk.* This is the upper-left quadrant. You enjoy healthy value capture at the expense of your customer's income statement. This business could be considered at risk. This is the business that corporate says, "Do not lose this customer," while the customer says, "If you do not improve I am going to be forced to go elsewhere." It is powerful to measure this. At any given time there always seems to

be those voices of "If you do not improve I am going elsewhere," but it is hard to separate the rhetoric from the reality.

3. *Profit Opportunity.* This is the lower-right quadrant. Your customer sees strong value in the investments you make, but your organization is not being rewarded for it. This is the quadrant where you may be looking to fire your customers only to find they do not want to be fired. Rather than firing, the necessary work is to rebalance the exchange of value.

4. *Profit Transaction.* This is the lower-left quadrant. Your customer is not making much money doing business with you and the business could be considered at risk. This may be okay with you as you have a weak financial position with them as well.

In Figure 4.10, we are viewing our position with customers in the now or current dimension of time. In other words, do our customers make more money by doing business with us relative to competitors today? But, as we discussed earlier, we also focus on whether the customer sees a road map for improvement.

As we have mentioned before, we are not only interested in how we are helping our customers make money today, but we are also collecting their perspective on the future. Do they see an opportunity for improvement, how much, what attributes need to be changed and how? We call the future perspective "The Road Map" as shown in Figure 4.11.

In the Figure 4.11 road map, you still have the common axis of how the customer views you in today's terms, the DVP Current percent. In addition, the future dimension of the DVP Opportunity percent has been added. The DVP Opportunity percent tells us if the customer sees a road map for improvement with our business and how attractive that road map is. This is a powerful picture. Customers who see you as providing little DVP% today, but who see significant room for improvement, are fundamentally different than those customers who see you providing little DVP% today and also do not see a significant improvement road map. Before we move on, let us describe the four quadrants of the DVP% road map shown in Figure 4.11.

1. *Value Creation Partner.* In the upper-right quadrant are those customers who see strong value today and also believe there is significant room for improvement. They see an attractive road ahead or road map for improvement.

2. *Value Creation Maintenance.* In the lower-right quadrant, we have customers who are receiving above average value from us, but do not see significant room for improving the situation.
3. *Value Creation Opportunity.* In the upper-left quadrant, we have customers who believe they are receiving below average value from you, but do see significant opportunity for improvement.
4. *Transactional.* In the lower-left quadrant, you have customers who are receiving below average value from you today and do not see a road map for improvement.

Now think about Figures 4.10 and 4.11. Figure 4.10 is about today's profits that result from transacting business between you and your customer. Figure 4.11 focuses on the opportunity for value creation your customer sees in the future.

Start with the *Profit Partner* quadrant on the Figure 4.10. This set of customers is making good money by doing business with us and we are receiving above average profitability in return. Not all of these customers see the same road map for improvement, however. If you consider Figure 4.11, it is possible that some of the customers in this

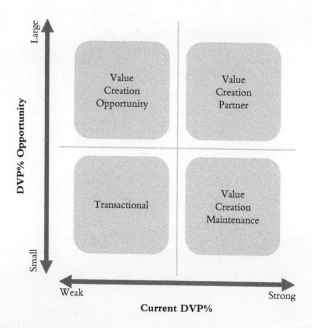

Figure 4.11   DVP% Road Map

quadrant see significant road maps for improvement and some do not see much room for improvement. Would you not like to know what those customers are thinking who represent excellent profits currently, are making good money from the relationship with you, and also see significant room for improvement? We call this subgroup "Pathfinders." Of course, there is also the group in this quadrant that represents excellent profits for you, are making good money from the relationship with you, and do not see significant room for improvement. It would sure be nice to know what this group does not see that the pathfinders do.

Think about the *Profit Risk* quadrant. In this quadrant we have customers who represent excellent profits for you but are not making, in their view, more money by doing business with you. If you look at the road map picture, we know these customers must fall into one or two customer quadrants, either *CVC Opportunity* or *CVC Transaction*. The group that is *Profit Risk-CVC Opportunity* represents excellent profits to you. The customer does not receive significant value, but does see a strong road map for improvement. This customer is different from the other who is *Profit Risk-CVC Transaction*. In this case, you receive excellent profits; the customer does not receive significant value and does not see a road map. We will just tell you straight away, your chances of retaining the *Profit Risk-CVC Opportunity* customer are much more probable than the *Profit Risk-CVC Transaction* customer. We hope you are beginning to see that this is not only about how much money your customer makes with you today. It is equally important to understand how they view the road map for improvement. The road map for improvement is Customer Value Creation. We do not continue to examine all of the quadrants at this point. We leave that to Chapter 6, "Informing Decisions."

Summary

Business is about making money. We need to measure it. Metrics matter.

You know it. We know it. Your customers know it. In business-to-business markets, companies work each and every day to make money. As a supplier of goods and services, you invest to differentiate from your competition. As a customer buying goods and services, companies choose suppliers that give them the best chance to beat their competition. In either scenario, management teams of these companies are counted on to make investment or supplier decisions that maximize financial performance. If they consistently make the wrong choices, they get fired or go out of business. It's really as simple as that.

Given the importance of making money, it is no surprise that companies have invested far and wide in accountants and software to measure how much money they are making. Measurement provides a mechanism to understand the progress made, whether good or bad. But you know as well as we do that all of the accountants in the world cannot show us the whole picture. We also need to know what the customer is thinking.

Knowing where you stand with the customer is a big deal because it tells you how secure your profits are today, as well as your future outlook for profits with that customer. Measuring customer feedback has been perfected to a statistical science in B2C markets like consumer-packaged goods, but translating these methodologies to B2B has not been as successful. What is the reason? B2B customers make supplier decisions based on how much money that supplier makes them (economics). This is quite different from when a consumer makes a decision to buy cereal at a grocery store.

In other words, understanding a customer's perspective on where you stand needs to be based on what is important to them, not to you. In B2B, it is about suppliers and customers making money—our metrics should reflect that.

Value Attribute White Paper—Gbenga Babarinde
There is more to these value attributes than meets the eye. Here is a research paper that goes deeper.

Effective and Efficient Data Collection for B2B Companies

B2B companies require deep and accurate customer understanding for strategic decision making and development of customer operating plans. Knowing customers needs begins with collecting the right information, using the right metrics, and sustaining the effort. This paper highlights the critical issues to consider when deciding the type of customer information to collect.

(Continued)

Primary or Secondary Data Collection?

There are several issues to consider in deciding how the B2B company wants to collect data from the market. One is the option of using primary or secondary data collection. Primary data collection involves making direct contact with customers, suppliers, and other influencers in the market to collect information. Examples of primary methods include focus groups, mail-in questionnaires, structured interviews, and open-ended interviews. Secondary data collection involves acquiring market reports and statistics from third-party providers. Examples include industry reports, market research reports, and government statistics.

Between primary and secondary data collection approaches, it is generally preferable to use primary methods to collect specific information and also those the company wishes to control or influence. Using primary methods here has potential to yield deep insights. Secondary approaches are used when the goal is to collect general information and situations where other parties might be more efficient at collecting information with less bias. Secondary data is useful for understanding demography trends, industry trends, sociopolitical impacts, economic trends, and so forth. Secondary data is usually obtained faster, cheaper, and more easily than primary data, but it is unable to provide competitive advantage because it is available to everyone. Most companies combine the use of primary and secondary data collection in their portfolio of approaches.

Qualitative or Quantitative Data Collection?

Another consideration in data collection is the level of qualitative and quantitative information. Primary data collection methods (see Figure 4.12) like focus groups can be wholly qualitative while mail-in questionnaires can be largely quantitative. Others like structured interviews might be a mix of qualitative and quantitative data. Similarly, secondary methods like public statistics are mainly quantitative while industry reports tend to be a mix of quantitative and qualitative.

In general, the level of quantitative data required in data collection is correlated with the level of clarity in what the variables of interest should be. So at early market research stages—hypothesis development—when little is known, highly qualitative methods such as focus groups and company hypothesis sessions are used. As uncertainty reduces, and the company seeks actual values for the variables of interest—hypothesis confirmation—more quantitative methods, such as mail-in questionnaires and structured interviews are used. Last, as the interest shifts to experimenting how variables affect desired market results, data collection becomes even more quantitative in causal relationships testing stage.

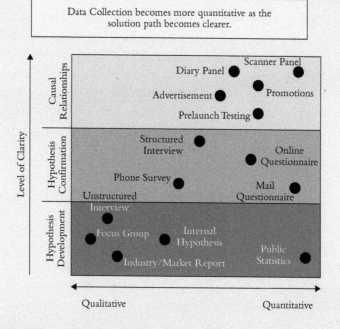

Data Collection becomes more quantitative as the solution path becomes clearer.

Figure 4.12　B2B Data Collection Choices

(Continued)

In summary, effective data collection should have sufficient quantitative data on the variables of interest as direction for market research becomes clearer because quantitative data is more powerful in analysis for definite answers.

Metrics for Quantitative Data Collection

As B2B companies seek to collect quantitative customer data to drive specific insights, it is important to determine appropriate metrics for customer survey. There are several customer satisfaction surveys out there, but the critical issue is to identify the right metrics that will lead to reliable and actionable customer insights.

Most B2B firms have used traditional customer satisfaction surveys in the past. These surveys use arbitrary numeric scores (e.g., 1–10) as metrics, which have no meaning in absolute terms. Respondents are not forced to trade off as they assign scores in the surveys, potentially making the data unreliable.

Recognize that economic value is the metric business customers really understand and speak. It is therefore necessary to figure out the appropriate financial ratios or measures that represent economic value to the customers, as opposed to arbitrary numbers. It is such metrics that business customers really care about, and the only ones that can lead to deep customer understanding for decision making in B2B firms.

Quantitative Data Collection Design

Having chosen the right metrics, the design of the quantitative data collection is also critical to ensuring ease of use, accuracy, and cost-effectiveness. There are mainly two ways of designing quantitative data collection: Attribute Rating and Conjoint. Each of these has its own advantage over the other. Henrik Sattler and Sussane Hensel-Borner effectively compare both design methods in their paper titled "A Comparison of Conjoint Measurement with Self-Explicated Approaches."

Overall, the Attribute Ranking design option is less costly to design, execute, and analyze compared with the Conjoint design. Also, the Attribute Ranking is actually easier to work with, has greater ability to handle large numbers of attributes, and causes less strain on respondents.

However, the Conjoint design has greater resemblance to real choice situations, has a higher chance of detecting actual importance weights, has less likelihood of double counting, and has a better chance of detecting nonlinear relationships.

Going by these theoretical comparisons, Conjoint seems to have better predictive validity over Attribute Ranking. However, empirical studies of both survey designs do not support the superiority of Conjoint. Most empirical studies have found either no difference or higher predictive validity for Attribute Ranking. B2B firms seeking to efficiently collect customer data, in a cost-effective way, should consider Attribute Ranking designs.

Using Attribute Ranking Design

To use Attribute Ranking effectively, the appropriate metrics need to be identified and should be driven by what the B2B firm is trying to achieve. The metrics should not be arbitrary numbers but tangible metrics that customers care about and can relate to. Therefore, for business customers whose main purchase decision driver is economic value, an effective metric will be financial ratio or absolute financial measure. So a typical B2B company survey will ask about variables and by what amount the variables create economic value for customers using the appropriate metrics. Rather than ask for an arbitrary number score (e.g., 1–10) to indicate level of satisfaction in a customer satisfaction survey, for example, the survey will ask for the amount of economic value each variable being measured adds to the customer's business.

Furthermore, it is highly effective to use percentages to show how individual parts make up a whole. This means respondents can show how the economic impact of a variable breaks down into components with percentage scores. Doing this forces the

(Continued)

respondent to trade off, as the total has to be equal to 100 percent, thereby increasing the accuracy of the feedback.

A similar approach to the one described above can be applied to other things the customer cares about, apart from economic value. These could be market factors such as supplier/buyer power, market share trends, new-entrant impact, and so forth. Overall, creating effective Attribute Ranking data collection design will depend largely on the ingenuity of the B2B firm in using what the customers really care about to get the information they need for various analysis.

Selecting Data Collection Approach

Customer information drives various analyses, including market segmentation, pricing, customer analysis, demand forecasting, customer planning, new product screening and prioritization, competitor analysis, and optimal marketing mix, to mention a few. And these analyses support strategic decision making and development of customer operating plans.

As mentioned earlier, there are several data collection methods available to B2B companies, and the challenge often comes down to deciding the appropriate method for various analyses.

B2B companies need to adopt a strategic approach to sourcing customer information. An approach that ensures effective and efficient data collection, not only as a one-time effort, but also for continuous tracking. This paper has reviewed critical considerations in selecting data collection methods to provide a frame for B2B companies to determine and develop the right approach for data collection.

In addition to effectiveness and efficiency considerations elaborated in this paper, B2B firms should assess the cost versus the strategic value of the data collection method options. Cost can be assessed using total annual expenditure or cost per respondent for data collection method. Using cost per respondent, mail questionnaires and phone surveys will typically turn out less costly compared to structured interviews and focus groups.

Assess the strategic value of a data collection method, using the collected data's potential to produce deep and specific insights about customers and markets. This characteristic is largely informed by the metrics used in data collection and the type of analysis executed. Figure 4.13 shows on a relative basis how the various data collection methods differ in cost and strategic value.

—Gbenga Babarinde, University of Chicago, graduate school of business,
May 2008

> Data Collection for strategic use through less costly
> methods should be the goal of any B2B company.

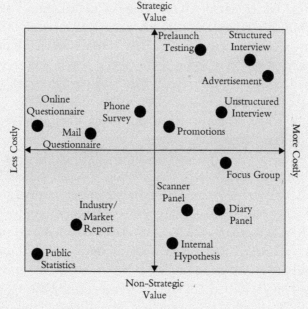

Figure 4.13   Cost versus Strategic Value

Gbenga wrote this paper for us in the summer of 2008. You would have to know Gbenga to really appreciate the short paper. Gbenga is a stickler for detail and is not capable of analyzing anything in a manner less than robust. Gbenga wrote the paper to provide insights into the value attribute trade-off methods for those who saw the value attributes as a simple stacked bar chart. We think the beauty is that the stacked bar is easy to understand and yet the methods and insights gained through the forced trade-offs can drive powerful insights.

The other thing this paper led us to consider more carefully is the structured interview. The structured interview is a great way to get both qualitative and quantitative data but is also the most costly. We needed a way to use the power of the structured interview but drive the cost down. The solution has been to certify an organization's own people to do these structured interviews during the course of their normal business routine.

Another interesting thing we found has to do with Figure 4.12, where Gbenga discusses the need for clarity as you progress through Hypothesis Development, Hypothesis Confirmation, and Causal Relationships. We found the data sets developed through our approach have allowed organization to progress through each of these stages quite nicely. The key has been to take a continuous improvement approach. Do not get the wrong idea and start thinking our methods replace all other research needs, because they do not. They have brought tons of focus, however, to the questions needed to be answered through additional research. Now, instead of figuring out that packaging is a problem for our customers through focus groups, then determining what variations or factors of design need addressing through surveys, and then testing designs through conjoint analysis, we are able to jump the curve. Through our routine structured interview, we can find out how important packaging is relative to other attributes, quantitatively understand the opportunity for improvement, qualitatively understand the levers being suggested by customers, and jump straight to a design and test methodology. The benefit is about six months of research time, decreased risk that you would have found out late relative to your competitors because you only do broad market survey periodically rather than continuously, and you have used the power of your own organization to find the opportunity rather than outside research assistance.

We write about all of these points throughout the book. We thought this paper might cause you to step back just a moment and reflect on a bit of the science and motivations for our approach.

Chapter 5

What Does Your Customer Think?

W
e are now ready to shift gears from the theory of how to win to understanding the detailed plays necessary to win with your customers.

After reading this chapter you should be able to:

- Learn the basic elements of the "Discover Play": Prepare, Conduct Interview, and Capture Data.
- Understand what it means to Prepare and why it is critical to achieving a successful outcome.
- Develop your own qualitative and quantitative differential value proposition.
- Develop a sense for the balance between the qualitative and quantitative nature of Winning with Customers.
- Achieve a general knowledge for how in-person interviews are conducted.
- Think critically for a moment about how to capture and manage data.

Get on the Field

Are you ready to get on field? I said, *Are you ready to get on the field??* Let me hear ya! 1, 2, 3, *win with customers!* HOORAAAAAA!

Okay, enough of that. The point is that it is now time to move into action. Just in case you are nervous about getting on the field, remember that is natural and everyone has a few butterflies before the game. You are ready because in Chapter 1, "Why We Lose," we talked about losing and teed up the challenges we all face. In Chapter 2, "Define Winning," we introduced a few approaches that have helped us and others to win. In Chapter 3, "The Playbook," we described and positioned those winning approaches as plays in a game—okay, an American football game. We acknowledge the pain using a football metaphor may be creating for you, but as we said, we are not creative enough to come up with anything else! Chapter 4, "Winning Metrics," was dedicated to metrics and established our method for keeping score. Now, here is Chapter 5—you are going to get on the field and play the game.

Do you remember the CVC Stadium? (See Figure 5.1.) This is the field. As you can see, our first field play is going to be "Discover." The whole purpose of Discover is to find out from our customers how we can help them to make more money by doing business with us. We are looking for their perspective on what opportunities they see in the market for a company like ours to create differential value relative to competition.

Just in case we did not make this clear before, the guys on the other sidelines in this picture are your competitors . . . not your customers! Sometimes it is easy to forget this in the daily grind. So the idea is to run each of these plays better than your competitor. Having the customer on your side as much as possible is generally a good way to run a better play. Some have tried to win this game by ignoring the customer . . . sometimes it works for a time, but never for long. This is akin to not understanding where the end zone is located. We will let you in on a little secret. When you see your customer hanging on the opposite sidelines with your competitor, *you are in trouble!* Your job is to keep the customer on your side and stay focused on running the plays better than your competitors. If you do, you are off to a good start.

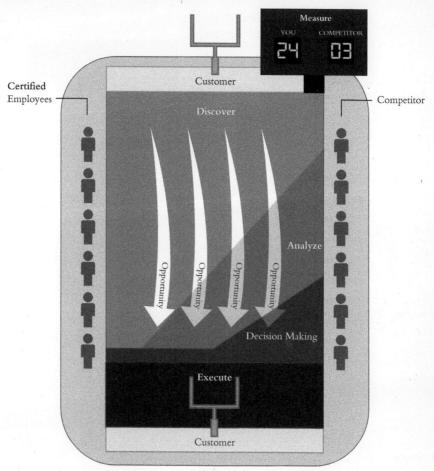

Figure 5.1 CVC Stadium

The Discover Play

Take a look at the CVC Management System in Figure 5.2.

During this play we are going to gather the customer insights using the metrics discussed in Chapter 4, "Winning Metrics." We are going to do this from an internal and external (customer) perspective using your own sales force. You are also going to include the customer. The Discover play has three main parts: Prepare, Conduct Interviews,

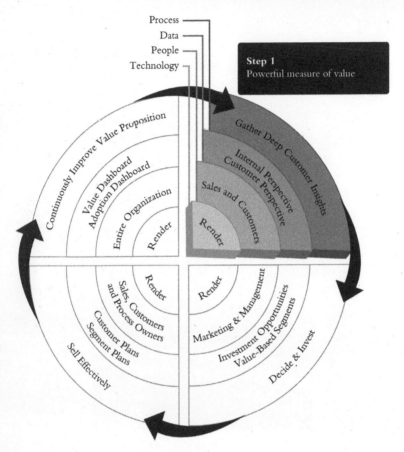

Figure 5.2   CVC Management System

and Capture Data. During these three parts we focus on delivering the following outputs that sum up the entire chapter.

Prepare

First "Prepare." There are two basic pictures for Prepare that we need to fill in. They are Figure 5.3, "DVP Hypothesis: Value Attributes," and Figure 5.4, "DVP Hypothesis: Quantification." These figures represent an internal view on your differential value proposition. We like to say, put your value proposition on one wall and your customers

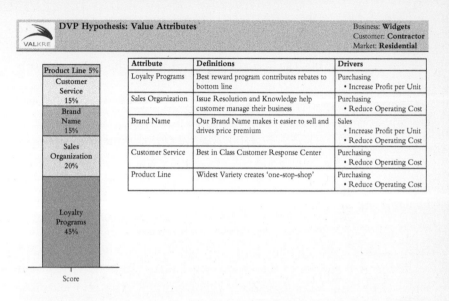

Figure 5.3 DVP Hypothesis: Value Attributes

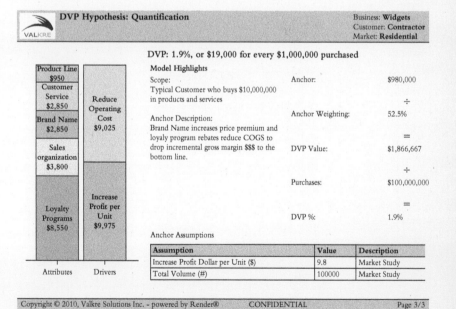

Figure 5.4 DVP Hypothesis: Quantification

financial statements on the other and make them connect. The Value Attributes figure paints the word story (qualitative) of your differential value prop while the Quantification figure paints the financial math picture.

These two figures, taken together, form the internal hypothesis. Do not worry about the content in these figures right at the moment. We cover it in detail soon enough. Now we take the internal hypothesis and create our interview guide.

Conduct the Interview

To conduct the interview we need an interview guide. The interview guide comes directly from the internal hypothesis views and is shown in Figure 5.5, "How Do We Create Value for You," and Figure 5.6, "Top Value Creation Opportunities." This is an example of a guide we might use in an in-person session. There are differing guides for other data collection methods. We focus on this one for the book.

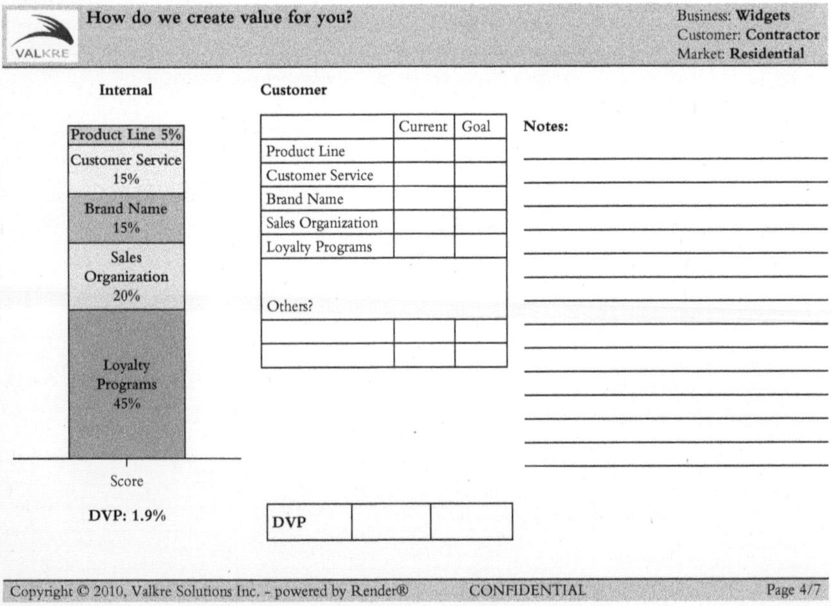

Figure 5.5   How Do We Create Value for You

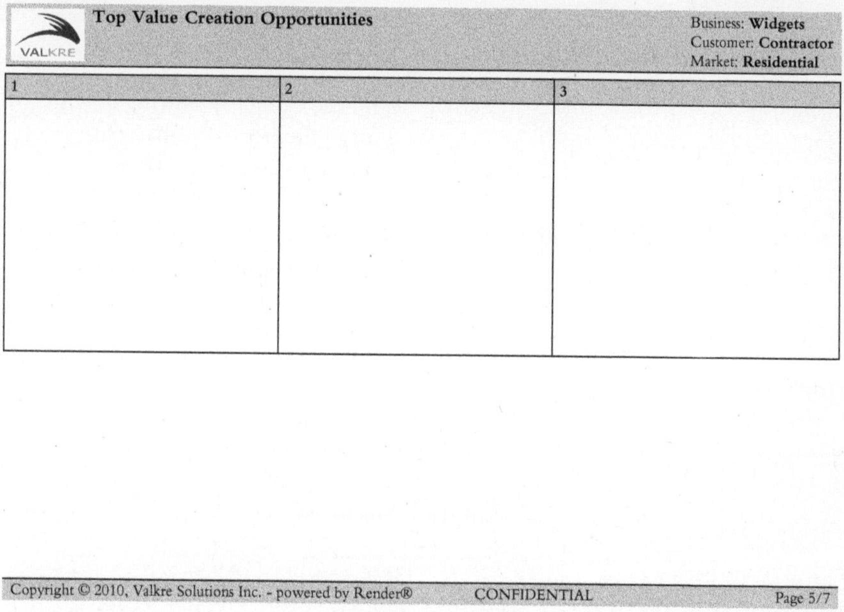

Figure 5.6 Top Value Creation Opportunities

You probably notice the interview guide is relatively simple. Your eyes are not failing you. The guide is nothing more than a depiction of your internal hypothesis created in a format for you to take copious notes. Do not let it fool you; however, there is much more behind it that you will know after we finish this chapter. Using the guide effectively is part art, part science, and part a belief that getting your customers input matters to your business and that of your customers.

Capture Data

After the interview is completed, we will Capture the Data. The next series of figures outlines the data from a given Interview. In Table 5.1, "Top Value Creation Opportunities," we capture the top three or four things the customer believes we can do to create more value for their business. The opportunities are described qualitatively.

In Figure 5.7, "Value Perspective," there are a number of things going on. Do you see the four bars? The four stacked bars represent

Table 5.1   Top Value Creation Opportunities

Business Unit	Value Attribute	Opportunity
Widgets	Marketing materials	With the economy slowing down, need the necessary materials to close a customer when the opportunity arises.
	Sales organization	Starting to become respectable. Maybe time to take a strategic approach to down channel selling rather than a mass market approach.
	Training	Could use some technical training on your products. Would help us sell through the value.

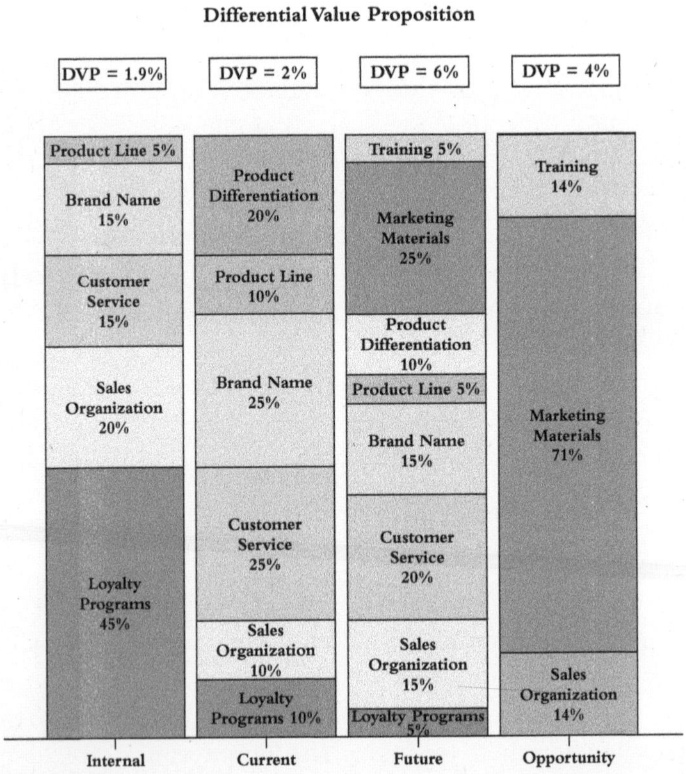

Figure 5.7   Value Perspective

from left to right: (1) What we think our value proposition is; (2) What our customer thinks currently; (3) What our customer believes it can be in 18 to 24 months; and (4) The opportunity for improvement. Each of these bars is using a value attribute trade-off approach that we discussed in Chapter 4. At the top of each of the bars is the DVP% metric depicting whether you are creating more value than your competition. The real trick with data capture is organizing all of this so that you can get 10, 20, 50, 100, 500 customer interviews together and learn—learn what individual customers, groups of customers, regions, and all matter of combinations are saying. Also to learn what they are saying from one year to the next, during good markets, and during tough markets. And to be able to do this without spending a billion hours each time you seek an insight. We provide some insight on how to do this later in the chapter.

Value Creation Notes are the qualitative commentary captured within the interview. They provide more color to each of the value attributes identified in Table 5.2.

So this chapter is really simple. All we need to do is talk about filling in the pictures and why.

Do My Customers Care . . . Will They Talk?

Now, before we go further we need to take a short segue. Somewhere about here you might be thinking, "Are my customers really going to talk to me about this stuff, do they even care?"

Table 5.2 Value Creation Notes

Value Attribute	Note
Brand Name	Remains the cornerstone of your value proposition.
Product Differentiation	Great job on the new product. I asked and you delivered.

How about this quote from Bob Harlan at Owens Corning:

"We have across 500 interviews experienced customers of all sizes. Direct transactional customers and down the value stream customers. We've had great conversations with all types. We have had one example out of 500 where the customer was not so forthcoming, 1 out of 500 is not bad."

Odds are your customers, at least quite a few of them, would jump at the chance to talk to you in a more rigorous way about how you can make more money together! They are just people trying to run the plays like you.

In our tenure as executives within companies and business partners with others, we have been involved in more than 1,000 structured investment conversations of the nature discussed in this book. And you know what? Business is still about people running the plays, the people at your customers, and the people within your own company. It would be fun to write a book just on this topic. The book would be interesting because it is about people. People of all different types, people with amazing financial acumen who can tell you exactly how much money they make doing business with you, others who have no clue, people from large corporations and small businesses, people with strong dominating personalities and those who aim to please, people who are skeptical and those who are engaged, people who are eager to learn and those who already know the answers, people who look at you crossways and others whose eyes tell you they really care, people who are looking for business help and others who see you as part of a great evil business conspiracy, just people—and most of them are good. This is a little set up to let you know that every conversation is not the same. We try to share several cases in this chapter to show you that they are not the same. That said, the key to having a good dialogue with most people is to focus on the investment nature of what you seek. You see, there are few business people who do not understand that at the end of the day business is about a series of investments: investments of time, capital, resources, and so on. If we can align investments with how you make money we will all be better off. And people like to talk about money and how they can make more of it!

It is time for us to get back to the game starting with the part of the Discover play that is Prepare.

The Discover Process: Prepare

As we mentioned earlier, during Prepare you are going to get your differential value proposition down on a piece of paper or on a hard drive, whichever you prefer. It should represent your organization's best thinking on the value you are selling—why you expect a customer to buy from you. You are going to use this work to conduct customer interviews and learn where you have potential disconnects between your thinking and that of your customers. It also provides the customer with a broader basis from which to recommend improvement. It might open their eyes to the investments made to create value beyond the day-to-day travails of price.

Do I Really Have To?

Let's start off this section with voices of people who have complained about having to prepare and then reflected later after having done their fair share of customer interviews. Believe us, we have heard all the excuses on why you do not have to do your homework! It is amazing how none of us likes to do homework even after all these years. That is why we have changed the name from homework to Prepare!

> *"You know I hated going through that exercise of Preparing our Internal Hypothesis. I was skeptical and was thinking to myself, 'Let's just go talk to our customers.' Now maybe that is because I am a sales executive and don't have the patience. But you know what—I realized the value of the preparation when I was the one on the hook for conducting the interview. By having gone through the preparation I was ready to listen. If I had not done the homework there is no way I could have conducted the interview and really listened to what the customer had to say. I would have been busy building my own hypothesis of value on the spot!"*
>
> —Owens Corning sales executive

And another short story:

> *"This is a very interesting exercise. There are a lot of opinions in the room, we try to make it as fact based and data based as possible and it*

demonstrates within the four walls of our company, to our executives, to everybody that was in the room having these conversations that we have such diversity of opinion that we really had to force some consensus. It was an interesting exercise and necessary because it challenged us to really put down on a page what we thought and that is just a very compelling place to start."

—Owens Corning marketing executive

Exactly! You heard the marketer suggest that it was compelling to get people on the same page on "just what the heck" is our value proposition. The sales executive acknowledges that it helped him to prepare for "listening" to the customer's opinion. Let's process these thoughts.

- *It's like taking a test.* Here is the amazing thing—if you do not write down your value proposition on a page before getting the customer's input you will be surprised at how many people will say in retrospect, "Well, of course that is our value proposition." Now, customers may have been right or they may have been wrong, but you will never know. You have just lost a learning opportunity. By getting your organization to commit to its value proposition and then finding the right answer from customers allows you an opportunity to understand where you do not have it quite right and to learn. If customers do not value the things you are selling and investing in, then maybe you need to assess and redirect your communications and investment approach.
- *Building a sense of anticipation.* The other thing about taking a test is that people tend to anticipate getting back their scores and finding out the right answers. It is irritating when the professor does not get them graded in a timely manner. A ton of learning occurs during the preparation for the test and feedback from taking the test. Same thing here—if you do not have the organization prepare and take the test before getting the answers, then it learns less and is less anxious for the results.
- *The basis for discussion and the interview guide.* Yes, you are going to show the customers your perspective on your differential value proposition and then get their input. You would not believe how many market researchers have told us, "But doesn't that bias the customer?" We suppose it does but think about this for a minute.

Dum da dum da dum da dum, dum da dum da dum, da da da da da, dum da dum da dum da dum, dum, da dum da, dum, dum, dum, daaaaa dum. Well, if you do not watch *Jeopardy* you likely did not translate the jingle. Even if you do watch, you probably did not. Anyway, continuing on the *Jeopardy* theme. We are in the category of "Business for $1,000." And the answer is "This age-old business axiom is the single most important thing you want to ensure every customer understands about your business." And the question is "What is a value proposition?" You got it!!! It is still your board. So let's get back to the market researcher question "But doesn't that bias the customer?" The answer is yes and that is good. Your value proposition was not supposed to be a secret in the first place and you would like your customers to know and be biased by your value proposition. But are they, and does it create value for them even if they knew what it was? Can they even see a road map to improvement based on the path we are on? That is what we are after. Remember, this is the reason you are in business.

- *Getting this all done in 90 minutes.* By going in with your value proposition on a piece of paper it gives the customer something much easier to start from and you are better able to get at the points of disagreement. Ninety minutes goes by quickly and you will not get anywhere on this conversation if you do not start with your point of view. Been there, tried it.
- *Preparing to listen.* You heard the sales executive suggest that by having prepared the internal perspective on the differential value proposition that he was prepared to listen. This is so true. Really listening is not an easy thing to do for most of us. My hand is raised . . . guilty! If you go into your customer without having taken the test and having not put your answers on paper, we will absolutely guarantee that you will not be listening to the customer, but instead you will be processing your ideas on the answers. In all likelihood, you will start to process your ideas with the customer as you are developing them on the spot and at that moment you have failed. You have failed because you are not using the valuable time to let your customer talk. And you have failed because the conversation has just become between you and the customer and not between the customer and your organization's view on the differentiated

value proposition. Your aim is to get the customer's perspective on the things your company invests and believes in, not versus your opinions.

- *Showing commitment to understanding the customer's business.* How many times in your life have you had a customer or supplier or whomever ask you for feedback? How many executives or general managers do you know who take the time to respond to surveys? In any of your survey experiences, did you feel you were having a serious discussion about the essence of someone's business? The very soul of why that person invests? The hopes and dreams of their employees, their families, their communities? What was your answer? Would you not like to think your business is important enough to get considered feedback? If you take the time and give serious thought to your differential value proposition for the purpose of expressing it to your customer, you will get the feedback you seek because it demonstrates commitment by you to understand your customers business in the context of what you do. When you are in front of someone seeking their feedback, they can tell in about a nanosecond your true desires and commitment based on how well you have prepared. You give someone a list of questions and have them scored 1 to 10 and you get about as much time and considered thought as it took me to write and think about this sentence. In addition to your 10 questions, you also have a couple open-ended questions to fill in and they'll think, "Crap, I have to come up with something to fill this blank." Now this might work to provide feedback at a conference but not to get feedback on your value proposition. When you go to your customer with a well-considered perspective with numbers to back it up you will be 70 percent of the way to having a great conversation with your customer. The other 30 percent is being alert and present and the rest. Just like taking a test.

My Short Story

I was working with a company and we were getting ready to see one of their largest customers . . . really large. When this customer sneezed, the company I was working with would catch a cold kind of large. One of the people we were going to see was a big-time senior vice president. The counsel I received was not to be worried or embarrassed when the senior vice president excused himself after 5 or 10 minutes and left his staff to finish the interview, as this was his custom. So we made a friendly bet and the over/under was 15 minutes. The company I was working with took the under and I had the over. To make a long story slightly shorter, after an hour and a half, the senior vice president was still in the room. The room had been booked by another meeting, so we actually continued the meeting in his office for another half hour. At the end, the senior executive said he had never had someone come in really prepared to have a discussion on how and why he made money in the context of the supplier's value proposition.

Do I really have to Prepare? The answer is yes and it matters a great deal. Okay, now it is time to move on and discuss what and how you prepare for the conversation.

Let's Prepare

As we enter this portion of the book it becomes somewhat tactical at times, so we offer a couple of pointers for ease of your reading consumption. The first is this swim lane process chart that you see in Figure 5.8.

We use the process diagrams in the next few chapters to help you to keep track of what is going on from a tactical perspective. The second pointer is for all of you who do not want to wade through tactics. You should skip ahead right now! You will not miss a thing relative to the concepts. You might consider skimming through the paragraph headers, read what is interesting, take in the summary, and then proceed to the next chapter. Each time you see the process flow chart in the next few chapters you might consider following a similar strategy. The dreaded process flow chart can be your warning: Boring stuff to follow! Now, for those of you who may be on the hook to actually implement, you should hang in there. I was only kidding on the boring thing.

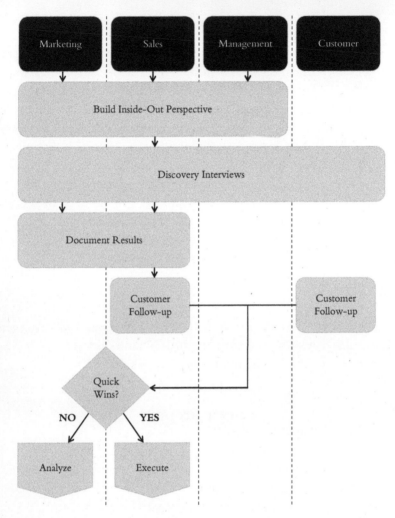

Figure 5.8 Discover Process Flow

Now it is time to build the internal perspective on your differential value proposition (DVP), aka the internal hypothesis. Refer to Figure 5.8, which shows the Discover Process Flow. The first block suggests that we build the inside-out perspective. That is what we are doing right now. You can see it points out that sales, marketing, and management are involved.

The first step to building the internal hypothesis is getting a cross-functional group in the room or on a webinar that has significant input to your DVP. We like to get five or six people together. Normally this includes marketing, sales, general management, logistics, operations, and finance. There could be more or less depending on how your organization operates. You get the idea. You want to get a team together that can credibly represent and create your company's DVP and that will also learn from the results. You need people who can legitimately take the test and will be anxious for the results. Some of the team members should also be those you will depend on to lead and participate in interviews.

Once you have a team, you can start building the DVP. We have done this with some teams in an hour, and with others it has taken as many as five or six hours. It really just depends on how well your organization is currently managing the DVP and how much data you have to support your claims. This is not meant to be hard. Whenever I get into one of these sessions I always suggest that if you already have a detailed DVP then just give it to me so we can get out to the market. So far, no one has ever just handed it over!

You will need to decide at what level to construct the DVP—at a product level, market level, business level, company level, channel, and so on. We suggest that you create the DVP at whatever level you sell to the customer. With this said, a good place to start is by picking a customer. Not the largest, not the smallest, not the one with all the problems or the one who cannot live without you. Just pick an average customer and start to create what you believe to be your DVP for that customer. You may find in the end that you need to break apart the DVP into lines of product, but that will become apparent to you as you go through the process. A word from experience—the marketers normally want to break the DVP down into tiny little chunks, whereas sales professionals like to level it up to a place they would normally communicate and sell. Neither is right or wrong. You just want to gain agreement on how you communicate your DVP to the market and at what level you think it reasonable to get the customer's perspective.

Building the Word Story

Now refer back to Figure 5.3, "DVP Hypothesis: Value Attributes." You are about to put together a word story of your DVP. To get started, identify the value attributes that separate your organization from its competition. Think about these value attributes as investments you make to create value for your customers. Everything you do to create products and services and deliver them to your customer requires investment. You make investments in people, systems, processes, tools, R&D, technology, market knowledge, capabilities, and much more. You cannot be better than your competition on every dimension. What you are looking for right now are those attributes where you do make a positive difference to your customer because you are better than the competition—the reasons a customer does and should buy from you. Something customers get from you that is different from others, which will allow them to make money by doing business with you.

What are the items that make you different and better than your competition? Is it your brand? Is it your supply chain? Take a moment and write down the attributes that you think make your company unique. Let us take an example. Let us assume the team identified six things that make you unique: the Sales Organization, Customer Service, Packaging, Product Differentiation, our Product Line, and our Marketing Programs. For each of the six you will also write a short word story on why you are unique on these dimensions. Something similar to what you would expect a sales professional to say when selling the competitive advantage.

Now that you have identified the attributes, you rank them by distributing 100 points. This is the whole value attribute trade-off thing we discussed in Chapter 4. I am always amazed at how much discussion and debate this creates among the team. The reason the debate happens here is because up to this point the team was not faced with thinking critically about what is really driving the DVP. Instead, the team members were contributing their own points of view on why customers buy, and you know what, everyone has an opinion. At this point you are going to work toward deciphering the most important, the next, and the next. And you will assign weightings. As you work through this process, which was initially a debate, it often turns into a small breakthrough. The team starts to realize the list cannot be so long and gets critical on the dominant few. The team members start to realize that while they can agree on a long list of things that do contribute some differential value, they have differing opinions on which are the most differential in nature to the customer: What are the value attributes that really set us apart from competition and how would you describe that difference in a couple sentences? Trade-offs are indeed made and the teams are driven to conclusion because they know that they should be able to communicate what they are about to the customer in a succinct manner. Getting this succinct perspective down on paper can be a small breakthrough for some. In fact, we frequently find that value attributes that are on the original list fall off throughout the conversation. That is okay because it means that you are getting at the heart of the value proposition.

In our example shown in Figure 5.9, we have completed the weightings and put the remaining value attributes in a stacked bar chart.

In our stacked bar chart, we have identified the Sales Organization as one of the big components of our DVP. The reason we believe this is that our sales organization provides more training support to the distributor as well as invests more of their time identifying and closing leads for the distributor. We weighed Packaging, Customer, Service, and the Sales Organization equally—each carrying about one-fourth of our overall value proposition. What this means is that we believe

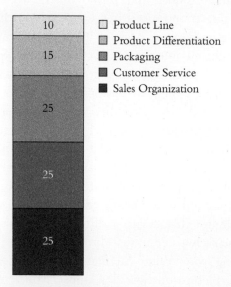

Figure 5.9 Value Attribute Weighting

the investments that we make in each of these categories have the same financial impact on our customer's bottom line. Simply stated, these three attributes are the primary drivers of our value proposition in the marketplace. In this case, we not only believe that our packaging is unique but that it creates significant value for the distributors. This could be because they are able to get more products on a single truck, or because it stacks better in their warehouses, decreasing the amount of space required for our products. We believe that these unique traits, whatever they may be, are not available from our competitors.

In our initial list of value attributes, we also identified Marketing Programs as an attribute. In Figure 5.9, you notice that it is no longer part of our DVP. This may be because we did not think our Marketing Programs created any differential value for the distributor, or we simply thought that the marketing programs were table stakes—which we needed to provide to the customer simply to be even considered for the business. An item that scores a zero when comparing your value proposition against your competition indicates that you are not creating differential value with it—that your competitor is as good, or better, than you are on that dimension.

In addition to these three attributes, we have identified product differentiation and product line as the other two components that make up our value proposition, but we weighted these slightly less. The weighting is important, because it indicates how significant the role is that the value attributes plays in creating value for our customer.

To complete the word story, you now connect each value attribute to the financial drivers on your customer's financials. Does the value attribute uniquely help the customer drive increased volume, additional customers, higher prices, reduced selling cost, reduced inventory, and so forth. Having someone on the team from finance will really help out here. Remember when we said earlier this was like putting your value proposition on one wall and your customer's financial statements on the other and then making them connect? Well, connecting your value attributes that create a difference to the drivers of your customer's financials is a step in that direction.

By translating your Value Attributes into financials drivers, you can paint a nice picture on how you impact your customer's bottom line. For example, if Sales Organization, Product Line, and Product

Differentiation were about bringing in new customers, while Customer Service and Packaging were about reducing operating costs, we can build a "Value Driver" summary. In Figure 5.10, you can see that 50 percent of your DVP aims to bring in more customers, while 50 percent of your DVP reduces your customer's costs. Once you have this picture, you are now ready to start quantifying that difference.

Building the Quantitative Story

Now that we have identified and weighted the attributes and drivers that make up our internal perspective, we need to think about how much differential value these items collectively make for the distributor. In other words, what is the DVP% created by our value proposition?

Before we go there, however, let's just review a little bit from what you learned in Chapter 4 on winning metrics. Remember, the whole key is to determine if your customers are better off by doing business with you: Do they make more money doing business with you than with a competitive alternative? Well, most businesses need to

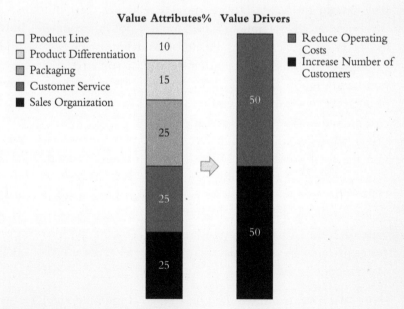

Figure 5.10 Value Driver Weighting

make approximately 15 percent operating margin. With a 15 percent operating margin, companies can generally cover their cost of capital (financial charges), overhead expenses, and the rest necessary to drop some money down to the take-home line. This book is not intended to be a study on finance, so just give us the 15 percent operating margin number for the purpose of getting at a concept. The 15 percent operating margin the customer makes is partially driven by you! Do you believe that? It can actually be positively driven or negatively driven! It is positively driven if you are truly offering differentiated value to help your customer's business and negatively if the customer has better competitive alternatives. As we mentioned in Chapter 4, "Winning Metrics," a positive 4 percent value proposition is a strong DVP in many industries. This means that for every $1 million the customer buys from you, their operating income would increase by $40,000. What is your DVP%?

- Start with the known entities: For the average distributor that you selected, how much do they purchase from you? Let's assume $1 million. Remember, this is the denominator in our DVP% ratio.
- Pick one of the Value Drivers such as reducing costs and answer the question "How much?" For million-dollar customers, how much do you save them by virtue of your Customer Service and Packaging? In some cases, you have the data you need right there in a handy report. In other cases, you might need to make a few phone calls to get the data you need. Let's say, in this case, the total cost reduction was $20,000 a year.
- Using your quantified Value Driver ($20,000 in this case), back into the total profits your DVP delivers to your customer. In this case, we determined that Reducing Costs was 50 percent of the DVP. That means the other 50 percent must be worth $20,000 as well . . . totaling $40,000.
- Calculate the DVP% by dividing the $40,000 by how much your customer buys. In this case, $40,000/$1 million give a DVP of 4 percent.

Once you have quantified the DVP, conduct a simple, smell test— does the figure make sense? Use this simple scale—for a customer that makes a 15 percent operating margin across its entire business. Remember, you are just a part of its business so the margin on the portion in which you participate could be higher or lower. In our experience, the 95 percent of the bell curve is captured between a range of −5 percent and +10 percent.

- A DVP of −5 percent = you are in trouble. The customer is losing money by doing business with you relative to competitive alternatives.
- A DVP of 0 percent = indicates that you have no differential impact on the customer's operating margin and your products are a commodity or the same as competitors.
- A DVP of 2 percent = indicates that you have a weak impact on their bottom line.
- A DVP of 4 percent = indicates that you have a solid impact on their bottom line.
- A DVP of 6 percent to 10 percent = you have a significant impact on their bottom line.

In much of the work we have done, a strong, healthy differential value proposition is about 4 percent. There are all sorts of factors and variances going on here that would require a whole separate chapter on statistics, but for a good rule of thumb, 4 percent is not bad.

In Figure 5.11, we identified a DVP% of 4 percent. What this means is that we believe that our overall value proposition creates $40,000 of incremental value to our distributor's bottom line that would disappear instantly if it did not do business with us on a million dollars of purchases. It also means that 25 percent, or $10,000, of our DVP is driven by our Sales Organization. Once you have identified the DVP% and the value attributes, review what you have on paper. Does it make sense for the distributor that you used to model it? Does it make sense for other distributors in your marketplace? If it does not, adjust it accordingly.

With this stacked bar chart and the DVP%, we have the data that we need to conduct an interview. We have done our prep work and now need to build our interview guides and line up the customers that we are going to go interview.

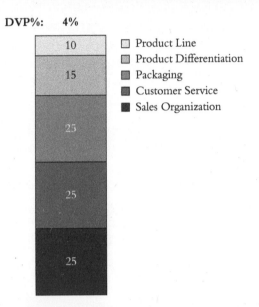

DVP%:   4%

- ☐ Product Line
- ☐ Product Differentiation
- ☐ Packaging
- ☐ Customer Service
- ☐ Sales Organization

Figure 5.11   Quantifying the DVP

Building the Interview Guide

When you first get started with companies, everyone wants to know what the interview guide looks like. What questions are you going to ask the customer? The simple answer is that the Interview Guide is created around your internal perspective on your differential value proposition. That is it. It is not meant to be tricky or sneaky. It is about facilitating a conversation on the investments you make and how that is working with your customer's bottom line.

To build it, combine the internal DVP hypothesis picture with an area to capture the customer's perspective on the Value Attributes and DVP% both today and in the future. Leave plenty of room for qualitative detail, you will need it.

Who Should You Interview?

Your customers. Seems simple at first glance, but there are many different positions within your customer's organization that may provide differing perspectives.

The answer to this question is mostly captured in the following interview by Owens Corning during a webinar we did with the Strategic Account Management Association (SAMA).

Q: *How do you get past purchasing?*

A: Jim Drew, Owens Corning Sales VP: *"We don't, we include purchasing but also include others and that's the neat part about this. We do everything from the warehouse logistics manager, to purchasing, to the buyer, to the vice president, all the way up to their senior leadership. There are multiple interviews that you can do so you don't have to exclude or bypass purchasing, you can include them and do others as well. And they are receptive to that just to give you some feedback."*

Owens Corning, marketing executive: *"We look at this through a very practical conversation with our customers and the important thing about these conversations is that we are talking to the P&L owner, the general manager; we are talking to the person who really knows, and believe me they know! It is a very interesting engagement when we sit down with our customers. They can tell us in about a 90-minute conversation what it is they value about Owens Corning today, what it is they would like to see Owens Corning to in the next 12 to 18 months so that we can increase the value that they realize."*

As you can see from the quotes, the answer is that you want to get multiple perspectives within your customer's organization. You would like perspectives from people in purchasing, marketing, general management, operations, corporate, regions, locations, and maybe more, depending on your business. It is truly remarkable how these perspectives are different, and the learning that results for you and your customer by putting them together. Corporate wants this and the location wants that. Sometimes the magic that happens in this process is getting the customer on the same page about what is valuable. And whose job is that? You guessed it, yours.

The Value Chain

The only other thing we add here is the value chain perspective. This means generating an understanding beyond just those customers where you have a direct exchange of goods and services. We like to create what we call an influence map. The influence map provides a good picture on whom else beyond your direct customers you should consider including in your approach to Winning with Customers. If someone in the value chain has great influence on the demand for your products and services then you certainly should understand how your value proposition impacts that person's business or life.

Here is a short primer on creating an influence map. Similar to measuring a Differential Value Proportion (DVP), we measure influence in a way that is simple to understand and communicate. First, start by identifying the participants in the value chain up until the point of consumption. A simple example is shown in Figure 5.12. Next, allocate 100 points to the value chain participants based on their ability to influence demand.

In this particular case you see that the contractor has the greatest influence at 65, the distributor 25, and the consumer 10. Assuming that the distributor is our direct customer, then we should definitely have a strategy for also understanding how our products and services are creating value for the contractor.

In some cases it makes a whole lot of sense to generate these influence curves on more than the dimension of influencing general demand. Often the curve looks different if we look at the players in the chain and their ability to influence demand for product versus brand. Take product, for example. The contractor, installer, and consumer will likely have more to say about the product to be used than the

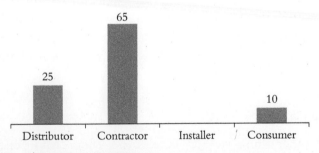

Figure 5.12   Value Chain Participants

particular brand of product. As an example, consumers may want a particular insulation kit in their homes to reduce energy consumption and to help with the greening of the earth, but will likely have less concern or knowledge of who actually makes the insulation. On the other end of the chain, the distributor probably has little impact on the product decisions. But once the product type decision is made, the distributors have significant influence on the demand as they educate others on the various brands they carry and why one is better or different from the rest. This is important stuff to understand if you are launching a new product where you are trying to generate demand. You have to get your value proposition understood by those who influence demand given the business situation that you are trying to influence.

There is a ton more we could write on this subject but we leave it for another book for now and move on.

Who Conducts the Interview?

We recommend in the beginning to have a minimum of two individuals at each interview to fulfill two different roles. The first role, the Interview Lead, is responsible for making sure that necessary data is collected in the interaction. This person acts as the primary voice from your company and is focused on making sure the conversation stays focused on value and investments. The interview lead should not be the salesperson responsible for the account. The primary reason for this is to decrease the possibility of bias. Additionally, the salesperson who calls on the customer may make assumptions that do not accurately portray what the customer is saying. Remember, a successful interview requires that you are able to listen effectively to your customer, to understand what investments you are making impact his or her business. Frequently, we have found, the account representative is prone to either defend actions, or include his or her own opinion on what benefits the customer. By having an unbiased interview lead, you are able to decrease the potential bias substantially.

The second individual, frequently played by the sales representative responsible for the account, plays multiple roles. The sales representative is responsible for getting the customer engaged in the conversation. The rep has the relationship with the customer and is able to put the customer at ease with the conversation by participating. This conversation is new to your customer and you want him or her to feel comfortable opening up. Customers find it refreshing once they understand it, but they can be a bit apprehensive at the beginning.

The sales representative is also responsible for taking notes and capturing what the customer says. The benefit to the sales representative is that he or she can get into action quickly and hear what the customer has to say directly, without a filter. Having two people at the interview also ensures that bias is kept to a minimum. After the meeting you have two people who can validate with one another what they heard the customer say. From a practical perspective, if the conversation is flowing smoothly, you want to avoid the interview lead from having to stop the conversation to make sure that person accurately captured the customer's sentiment.

Tired of preparation yet? Okay, then . . .

The Discover Process: Conduct the Interview

Finally the fun stuff! More than anything else we have discussed, we enjoy this element of winning with customers. Maybe we have been warped over the years and have an odd sense of fun. We have been told that by a few people by the way. No matter, we still enjoy this part because it is at this point we get to hear from our customers about how we are doing and what can be done better. We mean "better" in the context of making them more money and making more for ourselves in return. We like conducting these interviews knowing the rigor of our preparation, the knowledge that better management decisions will follow, and knowing full well we will have the opportunity to come back to the customer with our plan. Nobody does this as well as you are about to.

If you take a quick look at Figure 5.8, "Discover Process Flow," you see that we are in the second box, discovery interviews. This step involves sales, marketing, management, and the customer.

Before moving on here is a little primer:

"Once we determined what we thought we hit the road. Along with some assistance from the Valkre team in 2007 we talked to 50, 60, 70 customers and we started to develop a point of view that in some cases was close to what we thought and in some cases was very different. But for the first time at Owens Corning we could start to say that we really knew. We could start to say that with a different conversation we were having with our customers we had an informed point of view on how we were performing in the interest of their ability to make money."

—Owens Corning, marketing executive

Interview Guidelines

"When we have these conversations it is us talking for 5 percent of the time and the customer talking for 95 percent. It's all about how they make money. And we are clear that making money is not just a margin or revenue conversation, we consider the universe of value. So we ask them to regard their relationship with Owens Corning and think today about how we are performing in the interest of their working capital, their cash position, their waste elimination, their cost position and their revenue position. So we really try to open it up as wide as possible in terms of their business results and how we are helping those business results."

—Bob Harlan, Director of Business Insights,
Owens Corning

The number one guideline as just suggested is that you need to go listen! Here are three more:

1. *No selling.* The goal of this conversation is to hear what the customer has to say. There is plenty of time to sell later after the meeting. Do not confuse the goal here. Though it is nice to sell product and services, we are taking a step back to have a conversation about value.
2. *No solving.* In our experience, trying to solve an issue that the customer has is one of the harder things to avoid doing. As sales individuals, we want to make sure that our customers are happy.

When customers identify an issue, we want to solve it. It is human nature. In this instance, however, it can derail the conversation. Rather than discussing opportunities and what the customer values, the interview time can be spent trying to solve an issue that may not be the crux of the problem. Discovery Interviews are focused on uncovering opportunities. The decision on how to solve problems happens once this data has been collected. Sometimes the solution to the problem can best be solved at a higher level than by a single customer; a single customer may just see the symptom of something.

3. *No justifying.* You are not there to tell the customer what you think. You are there to listen. Justifying actions tells the customer that you do not believe there is an opportunity in a particular area. Instead of explaining why the company has done something, listen to what the customer has to say about it. How did the decision impact them? Did it help? Did it make their life more difficult? Why?

We put these rules in place to keep the conversation focused on the customer. If you start to sell, solve, or justify, it can send the message that you are not listening to your customer. There is ample time to develop a cohesive plan once you hear your customer's perspective.

The Interview

For this portion, there is no amount of words to describe experience. We focus on having some real life stories do most of the talking.

Q: *Can you provide a specific example of the question you ask customers in order to quantify the value improvement target and did you start with quantitative metrics before you developed the questions.*

A: Bob Harlan, Director of Business Insights, Owens Corning: "*In these conversations we start with more of a qualitative conversation. What are the areas the customer values about our company today, what are the areas they would like us to invest more in the future? We force them to make trade-offs by using the stacked ranked attributes so it's not just a wish list. And then we simply ask what* *that's worth to your business. As they start to talk about what it's worth, it's not so much about the specific questions, it's more about the dialogue, asking the Five Whys, and probing with the customer. Not probing because we are nosy but instead to help them with their thinking. Helping them process the conversation so that it becomes very real to them in terms of dollars. So a customer may say I need some help with my inventory management, I've got too much material in the yard, what can you do about that, can you reduce the minimum order quantities. That's a conversation we have, yes, from what to what. Well, today it is truckload; I would sure appreciate it if we could get that down to one quarter truckload. Okay, what would that mean to you? Well, it would help me to reduce my inventory. Well, how much, if you have $2 million of inventory today, what would it be with this new program? So we keep talking about modeling different scenarios. We are trying to get a finite view from the customer's perspective in terms of what it would be worth to them."*

There is a lot of good stuff in there from Bob Harlan. He is a true pro. Now rather than talk about an interview we thought it might be helpful simply to walk through one that went well and then to view more situations for additional color. Before you start reading, go back and look at the interview guide examples in Figures 5.5 and 5.6. Imagine that you have filled out your own internal hypothesis on your differential value proposition and are having a conversation with one your important customers.

A Good Interview from Start to Finish

We were in the early stages of working with a chemical manufacturing company. We were about to interview one of their largest customers who also happens to be one of the largest auto chain retailers in the country. The team from our side consisted of Jim, VP of sales, Paul, a manufacturer's rep from the

(Continued)

chemical manufacturer's agency, and me. The interview was
with the customer's corporate team and included Gene, SVP
of merchandising, Bill, VP of purchasing, and Cindy, category captain for our products. The mix of people was okay.
Three people from our side and three from theirs. It might
have been better if we could have had fewer on our side but as
usual, everyone wanted to attend and witness the discussion. Jim
did a nice job of describing why we were there: "We want to
understand how you make money by doing business with us and
where we should invest to improve from your perspective," and
kicked it over to me. Good! We were off to a fast start. No one
felt compelled to spend 15 minutes discussing the weather and
last night's game.

As always, I started by describing differential value and the
ideas of helping the customer to make more money by having
the chemical manufacturer better align investments with those
things most important to the customer. Ten minutes in we
are on track. I was nervous. You never know what is going to
happen. You never know what tone the conversation will take.
It is like public speaking on a new subject. When the audience
is good, you can have a really good time. When it is bad, it can
be torture. But part of getting the audience involved is to be
"on" yourself. I turned to the first of our two working pages,
the influence curve picture *(Note: In this example we are discussing a Value Chain Influence Curve similar to one shown in Figure
5.12. Including these types of pictures in your interview guide can
be a great way to enter a strategic customer discussion. The discussion
described next talks at a high level how these conversations might go,
but is not a required step nor a focus of this book.)* I was focused on
the objectives: get the customer talking, get their perspective
on how the value chain works, and understand if the customer
sees emerging industry change that would change the picture,
and find out where within the value chain the chemical manufacturer should be spending its time. Gene, the SVP, took the
lead in responding to the questions. He liked the picture and

as it turned out he had been considering the value chain in his own strategies and positioning and he had a lot to say. *Sweet!* We are off to the races. Then Gene said something negative about how the industry worked, something like, "This industries' packaging is in the dark ages and manufacturers need to take more ownership." Paul, the manufacturer's rep from our team, jumped in like a cat after its prey: "Well, you probably are not aware of this and how about that and this and, oh, by the way, Cindy, the category captain and I were planning to update you on this and that next week." Now Paul, the manufacturer's rep, only had the opportunity to be in a meeting with Gene, the SVP, maybe once a year at best. He was bound and determined to make sure everyone—the customer team and chemical manufacturer—knew he was on top of anything and everything. He represented a manufacturing rep company that was paid by the chemical manufacturer whose job it was to represent the chemical manufacturer and he was determined out of the gate to not let anything surface that may look like new information. Then Jim, the chemical manufacturer sales VP, chimed in. Jim got caught in the same quagmire as the rep. "Yes," Jim says. "We are doing this, that, and the other." I could see the customer team starting to lose interest; you could tell they were wondering if they were going to get in another word or not! In an awkward moment, I interrupted and redirected back to Gene, the SVP, to elaborate on his point. Crap! Now we were 25 minutes in and the customer was wondering if we were here to really explore and understand their point of view or make a sales call! Bill, the purchasing agent, started talking. Bill had 20 years' experience in auto appearance chemicals and at this point launched into the history of the business. Now, I knew we were not exactly on point, but at least the customer was talking. At this point, I started to get nervous about the interview. On our side of the team we have a defensive manufacturer's rep, Jim, the sales VP, is trying to keep everyone

(Continued)

happy; Bill, the customer purchasing agent, is showing everyone how well he knows the business; Cindy, the customer category manager, has not said a word; and Gene, the customer SVP, hasn't got a word in edgewise since his first bit of constructive feedback. We needed to get back on track. I politely thanked Jim and Paul, our guys, for their input and restated to the group that we were really here to hear what Gene, Bill, and Cindy had to say. All the while I was thinking to myself, "This is going to be a tough session, one piece of negative feedback and my team launches into a full court defensive press. I'll be less polite the next time and cut them off before they can get started."

I redirected back to Gene, the SVP. "Gene, I am not really sure I captured your full thought on the potential for improving packaging."

Learning Comment: No matter how much you prepare, getting your team to avoid defending their positions or solving the problem when confronted with something that may seem negative is tough. It takes practice.

Gene finished his thought on packaging and went on to talk for the next 10 minutes. He discussed his perspective on each player in the value chain. He discussed the strengths and weaknesses of each and went on to point out how he thought the value chain would look in the future. He had a lot to say. Then Cindy, the category manager, chimed in and added a nice layer of input. Now I'm thinking to myself, "Okay, now they are talking, good." Now my challenge is that we are 35 minutes in and we are still on the influence page. Further, we have had a nice qualitative discussion, but have yet to get into any sort of quantitative detail. It is time to press and see how this team deals with numbers. "Okay," I said. "I think we've got the qualitative picture. Now, let's spend a few minutes putting some numbers together with the story."

Learning Comment: The vast majority of people are much more comfortable starting in the qualitative spectrum before moving into quantitative. In most cases, you will be well served by letting people just talk for a while before pressing them on numbers.

Cindy, the category manager, took the lead on giving her perspective on the influence numbers. As she was talking, you could see both Gene and Bill start to squirm in their chairs. As soon as Cindy was done, Bill suggested he had a slightly different point of view. Cindy thought the majority influence holder was the consumer and had assigned this consumer 50 of 100 points, 30 points to themselves as the auto chain distributor, and the rest to other players in the chain. Bill thought the consumer and the auto chain distributor should be reversed. His perspective was that consumers bought what they carried. And then Gene interjected with yet a different perspective; he thought the manufacturer should have more points than themselves as the distributor. All the while I am thinking to myself, "Now we are going!" Gene, Bill, and Cindy processed their perspectives for a bit and came to a conclusion that was closer to Gene, the SVP's, perspective. Learning was happening right before our eyes. Cindy thought the consumer had all of the power because her job was to understand the consumer and position the category to serve its needs. Bill thought the auto chain distributor had the power because he used the power on a daily basis to negotiate deals. Gene saw the picture as a group of companies that made investments. We had just developed a view that encompassed each of their qualitative and quantitative perspectives that could be built on and referenced for years to come. They would not have put the picture together without us and we could not have put the picture together without them. We had just finished the first page of our discovery, "Influence."

Learning comment: There is something magical about numbers. In this case, like so many others, the team talked and listened qualitatively for 15 minutes, each seeming to agree with the others comments. But when you asked them to paint their story with numbers, a whole new conversation begins. Numbers have a way of bringing the trade-offs you make between choosing this or that into stark relief.

(Continued)

Learning comment: One of the great things about having multiple customer perspectives at the table is because these debates happen. The customers realize they do not have a consensus of their own and they learn through the process. Through this learning, they will start to look to you to guide them to new and higher levels of understanding.

Learning comment: The Influence discussion serves as a nice ice-breaker. It allows the team to start talking in qualitative and quantitative terms about something that is not directly between us. It is a picture that reinforces to the entire group that together we are just two companies in a system of other companies and that we need to be smarter than the rest about our investments.

Well, at this point, I am 50 minutes into a session planned for one-and-a-half hours. I tell the team we are going to have to pick up the pace if we are going to finish on time. Gene jumps in and suggests that we not worry about the time.

We turn the page to Value. You can imagine this page looks similar to Figure 5.11, but with lots of space to capture the Customer's perspective on the DVP today and in the future . . . and even more white space to take notes! "Okay," I say, "this is the fun part. How do we help you make money? We have put our hypothesis together on how the chemical manufacturer believes it creates differential value for you." I go on to spend a few minutes explaining each of the elements of the value proposition and provide our thinking on how the chemical manufacturer believes it is creating differential value for them. Now the question for you, Gene, Bob, and Cindy is "What is your perspective?" Bob had a clarifying question about one of the value attributes. Jim, from the chemical manufacturer, jumped right in and answered it succinctly without justifying or defending. I think Jim had reflected on our earlier side-track, reflected on what we had talked about going into the session, and was now with the game plan. The manufacturer's rep started to add additional clarification and Jim politely cut him off and redirected back to the customer. Perfect! Nice work, Jim! During our discussion on influence, Gene, Bob, and Cindy had each mentioned a point or two regarding what was important to them and things needing improvement in the industry. I had made note of their comments and used them at this time to get the conversation going. "Gene, you mentioned packaging earlier; as you can see, the chemical manufacturer believes that is one of the elements of its differential value proposition. Is the chemical manufacturer helping you to make money with its packaging?" This was clearly a hot button for Gene and he took the opportunity and ran. After he talked for a while, I asked him what the number one thing the chemical manufacturer provided that helped his business to make money. And then Cindy jumped in and then Bob. The conversation was flowing freely at this point. The session challenge now had nothing to do with getting the customer to talk and everything to do with keeping the conversation going on a focused track. Before long we had a good prioritized list of things that the auto chain distributor valued about the chemical manufacturer. Just like in the Influence conversation, we had been talking on a qualitative basis up to this point. I now asked them to assign weightings to each value attribute. Even though we had prioritized them it was still hard to tell if they thought the top attribute was worth much more than the next or if they were all relatively the same. We went through the list and distributed the 100 points. As before, the number weighting brought out some debate. During the whole conversation I could not help but pick up through their explanations that a couple of the attributes were important, but not really differential to competition. I asked them, "I understand these attributes are important to your business but is the chemical manufacturer delivering on these attributes better that the competition in a way that allows you to make more money by doing business with them than other alternatives?"

Gene thought about my question for a moment. Then he admitted that although important, the chemical manufacturer

(Continued)

was not providing differential value relative to its competitors in the current state. So we assigned those attributes a big fat zero.

As is normal, the whole conversation was a little mixed between what the auto chain customer valued about the chemical manufacturer and what it really wanted in the future. I worked hard to not to cut off the comments about how the future should look while at the same time capturing a good picture of the value being delivered today. I had a good enough picture. "Okay," I said to the team. "We have a good picture of what the chemical manufacturer is doing to help you make money today, now where should they invest to create value in the future?" I asked the question I love to ask at this point: "If you had a million dollars, where would you have the chemical manufacturer invest that money to help your business?" "Packaging, more people to work with you, shorter lead times, new products, future innovations." *Learning Comment/Long Diatribe: Now, I like to keep the "future" defined as to no more than two or so years. I do not think this kind of conversation takes the place of deep R&D at a company whose purpose is to see out in the five-year horizon. You can, however, discover excellent ideas from the conversation to feed into your strategic innovation pipeline. I tend to think of this conversation as supporting tactical innovation. These are the innovations and improvements that the customer can see right in front of their noses. Things they are confronted with day in and day out in the operation of their businesses. Things their customers are requesting, complaints they are receiving from their location, ideas bubbled up from their organization. Powerful ideas. People love to answer this question on where they would spend a million dollars. People like to have input. Sometimes at this point I reinforce the serious nature of the question depending on the group. The reality is that the chemical manufacturer spends far more than $1 million in its annual budget in its quest to create value for customers. The reality is that in their hearts and minds they desire nothing more than for you to receive this value to improve your business and get a fair return in exchange. The reality is that the chemical manufacturer understands that business is about investing money and generating value for you. The* *reality is that if those investments are in alignment with strategies and tactics that improve your business economics you will be better off. You do the same in your business. Where would you invest a million dollars? Now, I do not do this in a stern lecturing voice that probably just surfaced, but I am serious about the point. This is real money; we are talking about real money. Companies all around the world spend gazillions of dollars every year in hopes of creating value for their customers. I have no idea about the efficacy of those investments. I do know there is a canyon of room for improvement. If you do not fundamentally believe in the idea of making sure your investment portfolio is aligned with things your customers value and will pay for, then stop reading immediately because this book and this interview is fundamentally about getting to the core of this idea. Anyway, back to the story—I got on my soapbox there for a minute, sorry!*

"Gene, how would you spend $1 million?" Gene was thinking hard. He understood the question. The fact of the matter was in two hours he was going into his own budgeting meeting with his CEO to allocate capital dollars. He wished he was more confident in how his customers would answer the same question. Gene brought up two specific ideas. One was packaging, of course, and the other had to do with both companies needing to do a better job with local marketing, which he went on to explain in detail. Cindy added a couple of ideas important to her world, and Bob did the same. We spent time getting into details on each. Then we rank ordered them: how much of the $1 million would we allocate to each. We then focused on getting the future differential value proposition that the auto chain retailer desired to receive from the chemical manufacturer. "Packaging is currently worth 10 percent of the total of what should it be in the future, 15 percent, 20 percent, more? We did this for each of the value attributes and a couple more the auto chain had added to our list. In the end, we had a clear picture on the desired future state, how our value proposition should change, and the trade-offs one of our largest customers would make to get there.

(Continued)

Now the capstone question: What is this worth to your business? Are we creating any differential value today and will the improvements we have discussed have an impact? I told the auto chain retailer, in our hypothesis, we had calculated differential value as being a little over 2 percent, not great but something. We discussed a bit what the number meant. Well, our philosophy is that you should make more money doing business with us than with our competitors. Two percent means that for every $1 million you purchase from us you are able to increase your operating margin dollars by $20,000, or 2 percent. I went on to explain that a 0 percent would mean we were basically a commodity. You could replace our business tomorrow with a competitor and not have your operating income change. The number could be negative, meaning there is a better competitive alternative. A strong healthy differential value proposition is about 4 percent, I told them. Six percent to 8 percent typically means you could not imagine a world without the chemical manufacturer in it. We talked about the idea of the number for a couple of minutes. I told the rep that the chemical manufacturer's business depended on delivering a differential value proposition to them. In my experience, I've seen differential value propositions range from -10 percent to +10 percent. The extremes do not seem to last long. At the negative extreme, the customer is losing $100,000 for every $1 million in purchases from that supplier relative to a better competitive alternative. This kind of situation normally does not last long as the customer switches to the alternative. In the case of +10 percent, the situation is normally characterized by a new breakthrough product or the manufacturer's pricing in such a manner as to drive penetration of a market. This situation does not tend to last forever as the product matures or competitive forces come to bear on pricing. All in all, a nice healthy position is 4 percent. During this time, I was talking on purpose as I could tell Gene and his team were thinking. I wanted to give the customer that time to think and not respond to quickly.

I finished and looked to Gene. Gene looked at each member of our team and said, "I don't know the answer to your question but I wish I did." I wish I knew the answer for every supplier we have! At this point I was not sure if Gene was avoiding the question and just being nice or if he really meant what he said. I gave him the range option: "Well, is it in the 2 percent to 4 percent range or more in the more in the 0 percent to 2 percent range?" Gene looked at me and said, "I really don't know, but I would like to know." Jim, from our team, stepped in and suggested that if they were willing, the team could work to calculate it within a week or two. We would need the data on our products and that of our competitors. Some conversation ensued about how they could provide that information in a way that was comfortable for them. The team went into problem-solving mode for a bit until Gene stopped the dialogue by stating he wanted to know the answer and directed his team to work with the chemical manufacturer to find the answer. Gene went on to suggest that once the baseline answer was calculated he would commit to having a conference call to discuss how much the number could be improved by the opportunities he and his team had suggested.

Postscript: All of this did happen and the baseline number was calculated to be 3.2 percent and the team felt the chemical manufacturer could get to 5 percent based on what had been discussed.

Learning comment: Plenty of professionals shy away from having this discussion about whether the customer makes money by doing business with them. Sometimes I think it is because they are not comfortable with finance. Sometimes I think it is because they are afraid of the answer. Sometimes I think people believe this is all an elaborate scheme to talk about pricing. Price does play a big role because you can price yourself right out of a healthy value proposition. The conversation is really about simply understanding the value proposition in a deeper, quantitative way. I bet that more than half of the business books ever written talk about the need to have a differentiated value proposition. But

(Continued)

what is it? People try to measure it in all manner of obscure ways . . . customer satisfaction, and so forth.

How about just measuring and talking about it straight away. Ninety-five percent of the time it turns out to be a refreshing and enlightening conversation. The other 5 percent are part of the great business conspiracy where everyone is out to cheat everyone else. Life is too short to do business this way! Anyone who does this kind of work as a way to raise prices will lose the trust of their customers and never again be allowed the opportunity for true discovery. Value pricing is something that happens after you discover what is valuable to your customer and are able to use that discovery to ensure that your customer makes more money by doing business with you.

Learning comment: Here is a conversation about this case where the overall value goes from 3.2 percent to 5 percent. We like to call this along with the specific opportunities and the relative changes in the value attribute scoring the "road map." Does the customer see a road map to improvement? It tells you a lot about how the customer is thinking about you. In this case, the customers provided clear improvement opportunities; they have given us a clear picture on how they would change the value attribute weightings; and they have told us how much the improvements could be worth to their businesses, 3.2 percent to 5 percent of purchases. Assuming you had a $10 million customer, that would mean they see an opportunity to improve their bottom line by as much as (1.8 percent times $10 million) $180,000. This is a pretty good road map. I think the road map your customer sees is often more important than its perspective on the current value proposition. A dangerous situation is when the customer sees a low current value proposition and is not able to express any real future opportunity. I'll personally take a customer who sees the current value as 0 percent but sees a road map to 4 percent over a customer who sees current value as 2 percent and cannot see a road map past 2 percent. The former holds a bright outlook while the latter sees a future that is gray. We talk much more about this elsewhere in the book.

We were wrapping up the session when a real breakthrough occurred. You see, we had also been trying to get into see a few region managers and stores as well, with mixed results. At this point, Gene offered that he absolutely wanted the perspectives of his region managers and stores included and would make whatever calls necessary to make those meetings happen. He went on to ensure that we had particular regions and stores on the list for input bases on where he was doing well with the category and others where he was not. We went on to conduct those sessions.

Three weeks later we came back to Gene, Bill, and Cindy. We shared the results of the stores and the regions that had gone through the same process as Gene, Bill, and Wendy. The regions and stores had some similar ideas but also had a few different ideas. Gene was fascinated by the mosaic that was created and there was a joint discussion around how hard it was to get everyone on the same page.

After sharing the results of the regions and locations, the chemical manufacturer shared their plans for investments. They were not able to tackle all of the opportunities but made a solid dent in the list. After the plan had been presented, Gene told the group he appreciated the first conversation relative to what his company valued about the chemical manufacturer. He went on to admit his expectation was that he would likely never hear another word. He was blown away when the chemical manufacturer followed up and had a real plan with real investment aligned with the opportunities for improvement that had been discussed. He was also bullish on the idea they had a way to measure improvement. Gene turned to Cindy, the category manager, and told her that one of her objectives for the year was to work the plan with the chemical manufacturer!

More postscript and comment: This was a good interview and a good session. We share plenty of others but may well focus more on the differences and spare you the long detail. We are not going to share the results of this case for confidentiality reasons you probably understand. We share results from other cases but split them from the interview detail. Sorry, but there are competitive advantages

(Continued)

being built. I will say one more thing about this case that I have found to be true time and time again and that is the difference in perspective between headquarters and the field of those customers you are serving. Many of us sit back and are frustrated by the fact that corporate wants one thing and the location want another. We struggle to get credit from corporate for the work we do at the locations and from the locations for the work we do at corporate. We wonder why corporate cannot get the locations to fall into line and why the locations do not communicate more to corporate about how valuable we are. Whose job is it to make this happen? I think it is yours. It is your job to manage your outcomes with the customer. Your customer is likely dealing with many, many, maybe thousands of suppliers. You'll probably be better off by taking a rigorous approach to exposing the differing perspectives yourself and managing value at all levels of the corporation.

The following stories are real examples that are not complete, but do provide some great color. Remember this is about people and some of what you will find is truly hilarious and some of it is a little somber.

Customers with ADD

Every organization has them: Customers we love but that have serious Attention Deficit Disorder. The challenge with these folks is how to take the precious time you have with them and turn it into a productive conversation that drives results. If you walk in with a blank piece of paper and ask, "How can we do better?" you are wasting your time. You will end up with three hours of your life that you will never get back, carpal tunnel syndrome from trying to keep up with the notes, and a more confused outlook on how to work with this customer. One of our favorite stories has to do with a religious customer who repeatedly turned a value conversation into one on his personal beliefs on faith. Now, we are not trying to suggest these types of conversations are not important, but this customer was one of the largest customers in a strategic location. A road map to create customer value was critical to growing in this market. Unless supporting his local church was going to positively impact his business's bottom line, this conversation was destined to be unproductive. This is where having an agenda and a rigorous discussion on money helps keep customers like this focused. By using interview guides, pictures, and metrics based on their money, you can keep customers like this on track by continuously asking if the subject of their story will make them more money. Also, if the customer is really fired up about a subject, he may ramble on and on for a good 15 minutes before coming back to earth. This is when paraphrasing back what you have heard in a few bullet points really ensures that you understand what the customer is trying to tell you. Get those bullet points written down on the interview guide and move on to the next subject.

Do Not Be Fooled by Seemingly Unsophisticated Customers

Every once in a while, you run into a customer who causes you to think, "No way is this going to work." Usually, this is because in the first five minutes on an interview, it becomes apparent that while the customer has run a successful business for years, he or she doesn't typically use words like "Value Proposition" or "Value Chain." One of our favorite quotes during a training session came from a sales rep working the middle part of the United States when he said, "There is no such thing as a 'hypothesis' in Arkansas." Still makes us laugh . . . because it is true at some customers. The thing you learn and

(Continued)

are humbled by when you meet with these "unsophisticated" customers is the ingenuity and work ethic that drives their successes. You also learn that no matter how much formal business training they have received, they understand how you impact their bottom line.

A great story from a few years back is when we walked into a customer's office that you could tell used to be a dentist's office. It even had the sliding door that separated the receptionist from the waiting room. Except, in the office today, the chairs and magazine racks had been replaced by a large birdcage occupied by a feisty parrot. Standing there with our interview guides and pressed shirts, the parrot turned upside down, cocked his head, and said, "Assholes." Talk about being caught off guard. Then two minutes later, we met the parrot's owner and found out where he learned his language. Undaunted, we stuck to our guns and got through the conversation. What started off as a swearing rampage on the continuity of the sales organization ended with the insights that because we had changed the size of their samples, they did not fit in this customer's home-made display. This meant that the newest products being released were not being pushed to prospective customers. After that understanding, the delivery of some new samples and some adjustments to the lighting, the value proposition was on full display . . . as long as the our customer's customers got past that parrot.

Skeptics

You know them when you see them: Customers who are skeptical of anything that smells like a consulting project. These customers see a few guys from corporate come into their office with some fancy interview guides and immediately think that the next 90 minutes of their life is going to be a waste of time.

Once, a customer saw the picture of the stacked bar chart in the interview guide and said, "Time out. When you proposed to your wife, did you need a stacked-bar chart to get her to say yes?" "Of course," the interview lead said. "It was made up from the fact that I went to college, have a job, decent car, and can be funny sometimes." It was a riot. The key with customers skeptical of the conversation is to be humble and get through it. Do not waste your time trying to convince them that this conversation is the greatest thing since sliced bread in the meeting . . . It will feel hollow and desperate. Instead, be humble, thank the customer for putting up with you, and get into action. The minute we went back to this customer with a plan on how we were going to operate differently, the attitude changed to one of collaboration.

There really is not much more to say on Conducting the Interview. You have got to have fun with this stuff. Being able to conduct a good interview takes practice. You will not learn to be good at this by reading a book. A little humor and sense of humility goes a long way.

Method of Collecting Customer Data

Q: *Do you conduct surveys over the phone?*

A: Bob Harlan, Director of Business Insights, Owens Corning: *"We never do them over the phone. This is a dialogue we feel requires an across the table, face-to-face meeting. Because this is the basis of our future, the basis of our plan, the basis of working together. We want to show that we are investing from the outset. Visiting them, sitting at their desk, and having this conversation."*

And

Roger Warren, Owens Corning sales executive: *"I would like to start by touching on the interview process. It is a simple 90-minute interview. We've held it with key stakeholders in the organization.*

I wanted to touch on that because being a sales professional it's important to keep it simple, it's important for the process to be clear and understood to the customer and, most important, it has to be measurable."

Well said. We do think the best method is in person. The trick here is to get this done in the normal course of business to reduce the expense. We have noted before that a big secret is developing your own capability. This is where the rubber meets the road. If you develop your own capability then this can be done in person during the normal course of business at little incremental expense for time and travel that normally makes in-person methods costly. In this book, we continue to focus on the in-person method.

All of this said, we continue to develop, with the help of technology, alternative methods such as interactive online collaboration. This has proven beneficial for participants down the value chain and as the number of customers gets larger. Using online methods has helped us to round out data sets where getting enough in-person interviews done over a particular time is not enough to provide good data into management decisions. Online methods also work as a way to get companies started while they are getting their own data collection force certified. What we have found is that doing an online collaboration with a customer who has been through the process in person once before is effective. This has come in handy for cases when a sales professional is just too swamped or maybe there has been a change in sales coverage and you would really like a couple more ears in on a conversation but cannot swing the travel.

How Often Should Customers Be Interviewed?

Q: *With the changing dynamics of the economy, how do you continue to validate data that was gathered in 2007?*

A: Steve Persinger, Owens Corning sales executive: *"We did generate data in 2007. However, we do the Customer Discovery process with each major customer a minimum of once a year and sometimes twice a year. So our data is being refreshed on a 12-month moving total or a 6-month moving total depending on the customers. That helps us to keep our data and our successes in tune and in line with real-time business. One of the great learnings through all of this has been that your value proposition is not a static object. If you think back to 2007 to today and you look at customers who have been involved, their wants, their needs, and what they value has significantly changed. It has been a fascinating journey to watch the dynamics of those changes and to see how quickly it changes. We are all still learning how quickly you need to readdress your value proposition, how fluid and dynamic you need to be at changing messages and investments in the marketplace.*"

Steve suggests that he conducts interviews once or twice per year. That's about right. This has actually been a fascinating area of learning for us, especially in the past few years. The learning has been around just how frequently your value proposition needs to change. What is your value proposition in a good market versus a bad one? Are there just these two states or are there states in between. How do you manage all of this and is it important enough to manage? We will let this hang and it will become good fodder for our next book or the next time we see you. The short answer is that the differential value proposition is in part driven by the environment. Your ability to keep your differential value proposition fresh relative to the market has big rewards.

On to the third main component of the Discover Process, which is capturing the data in a useable format.

The Discover Process: Capture Data

"As we built more and more interviews and more and more perspectives it was necessary for us to house it someplace so we established a system."

—Bob Harlan, Director of Business Insights,
Owens Corning

Take a quick peek at the Discover Process Flow diagram in Figure 5.8. We cover the rest of the process flow in this section. The next step in the process diagram is to Document Results.

The most important thing about documenting results is to actually do it. It is important to have the conversation, but if you do not document the conversation within a few days using a method that allows you to compare this conversation with others then you will realize about 1/1,000,000 of the potential value from having the conversation. Not documenting the conversation is akin to not listening in the first place.

What to Capture During an Interview

Refer to the figures presented during the interview case study. The data you want to capture are:

- How does the customer view our differential value proposition today relative to our internal hypothesis perspective? You will want to capture:
  - How the customer would change the stacked bar or value attribute trade-offs. Maybe they added whole new value attributes.
  - The qualitative story on why they made the changes they did.
  - The overall value (DVP%).
- What is the opportunity for improving the current situation over the next 18 to 24 months? This is the future bar, or as we like to say the "road map." If the customer had a million dollars, how would they spend it?
  - What is the future stacked bar? What trade-offs does the customer make when it comes to investing time and money in things that would improve their business?
  - The qualitative story on why they made the changes they did.
  - The potential improvement in overall value (DVP%).
- The top two or three opportunities to improved differential value.

For us, the no-brainer answer to do this well is to let technology help you. The following few paragraphs are written by Matthew Cobb, a chief technologist, who has helped us drive the adoption of technology with several companies.

The Discover Process: Customer Follow-Up

The final steps in our process flow diagram in Figure 5.8 are "Customer Follow-Up" and "Quick Wins." First, let us discuss Customer Follow-up.

After you have organized the notes and captured the quantitative data, you should share the completed document with the customer. Send it via e-mail or review it on your next sales visit. This will be your first step toward differentiating yourself from your competitors. Customers are not used to anyone actually following up on this stuff. We guarantee that by sending the customer a quality document that reflects the conversation, you will automatically be elevated to elite status in the field of listening. It is much easier to keep the customer on your side if you actually solicit and use their feedback in your efforts to win the game. If you happen to mention them in the after-game press conference, even better!

Sending a follow-up document is also the next step in generating accountability. You have been accountable in capturing the data in a manner that can be used to improve management decisions. The customer is going to be held accountable to having given you an accurate portrayal of their business. You will see that we continue to reinforce accountability as we continue through to execution. Accountability will be reinforced when we come back to them with an action plan based on their input in three to four months. It will be reinforced when we communicate updates on our investment/project progress during the course of the year. The ultimate accountability will occur when we repeat the interview in a year, maybe less, and discover whether we have made any improvement. Holding yourself and your customer accountable in this is a big deal. A lot like holding up your end of the bargain. If both sides are holding up their end of the bargain and improvements are made then great . . . you have been successful at the fundamental essence of business. If the two companies are holding up their ends of the bargain and are not successful, then maybe there needs to be a redirect. Either way, accountability is key.

The Discover Process: Quick Wins

Take one more look at Figure 5.1, "CVC Stadium." Do you notice how some portions of Discover move into Analyze and others move directly to Decision Making? Well, those portions of Discover that move into Decision Making are the quick wins. Not everything you are going to discover requires analysis, senior executive eyeballs, or capital. They can be simple and even powerful improvements carried out at the local level. There is no reason to wait three or four months for investment decisions for the process to continue before moving into action. Move into action now and surprise everyone! Nothing like a quick score to set competitors on their heels.

You Will Go Broke Doing What the Customer Says

Before we conclude this chapter, there is one last thing we would like to cover and that is the notion that you somehow believe we are proponents for doing everything the customer says. We are not and you should not be either. You cannot be all things to all customers and that is possibly the most concrete fact written in this book so far. You will go broke trying to achieve the goal of satisfying everyone on every dimension they can conjure up to make more money. But do not let those who will tell you that you will go broke by doing what the customer says deters you from getting your customer's input to help you to win the game of business. Those people who tell you that you will go broke by doing everything the customer says have not won with many customers . . . guaranteed!

The aim of this book is about balancing your decision making with an outside-in customer perspective and getting the results of those decisions executed in the market. No more and no less. The challenge for most of us is that we are so overconfident in our beliefs that we struggle to balance our thinking and decision making with the customer's point of view. This is a difficult thing to do and we would again invite you to study the Nobel Prize–winning work by Dr. Kahneman or Richard Thaler on Improving Decisions.

So we do not subscribe to the notion that you should do everything the customer says, nor do we subscribe to the idea that you will go broke by doing what the customer says. What we do know from experience is that you will make more money if you find a balance that tempers the overconfidence of your boardroom and executive team with the reality of the customer's point of view. And the reality of the customer's point of view is not going to find its way into the boardroom from anything that looks like a survey, third-party exercises completely divorced from the fabric of your organization, or from occasional dinners.

Sorry for the rant.

How Technology Can Help

Whoa. As you read through this chapter, your brain may have started to think about all the tasks your organization would need to undertake in order to begin the Discovery process. And if so, then your brain may have experienced a feeling similar to the classic head explosion in the movie *Scanners*.

It can be daunting to implement a management system that provides the organizational structure to formulate Internal Hypotheses, produce Interview preparation materials and guides, standardize the collection of Interview notes and customer insights, and follow up with all your customers in an organized manner.

Investing in the software and tools to facilitate these tasks will give your organization the best chance of successful Discovery. Whether you purchase the tools or custom build them on your own, they will be instrumental in the Interview process and beyond. Employee efficiency is of great importance, and any time you can automate a significant amount of manual, repetitive labor with technology, your entire organization wins.

Interview preparation materials can take serious time to put together. Wouldn't it be great if you had the tools to automate this? Comparing your internal beliefs to your customers' perspectives to identify opportunities can all be done on paper, but where does it go from here? Ultimately, you will need to conduct customer trend analyses across all the customer insights gathered, factoring in the multiple layers of perspectives within your customer base.

Essentially, you don't want your employees to be experts in quantitative statistical analysis or be slide presentation savants. You want them to be experts in Discovery with your customers. A management system supported by software and tools will allow for such focus.

Summary

This chapter was dedicated to the first on-the-field play of Discovering "What Do Your Customers Think." In the grand scheme of the CVC Management System, we just covered "Step 1," as shown in Figure 5.13. We spent considerable time discussing how you should prepare, and we pressed the point that preparation is key to successfully gaining the customer perspective. Through preparation, we built an interview guide that is suited for in-person interviews. Instead of trying to write about how you should conduct interviews, we focused more on

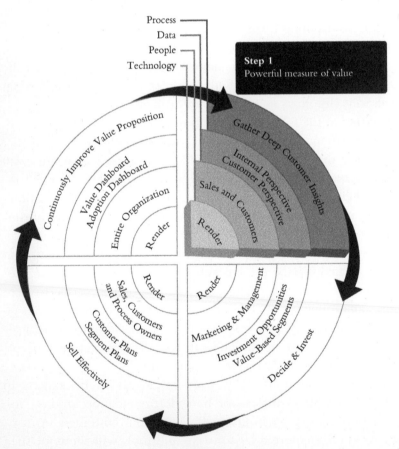

Figure 5.13   Step 1 of the CVC Management System

a few real examples. Hopefully you gained some sense for the ebb and flow of a typical interview session by reading these. Toward the end of the chapter we teased out data capture and strongly suggested that you enable yourself with some kind of technology.

In Chapter 6, "Informing Decisions," we show you how we generate insights from the data. But before we leave this chapter, how about one last case example from a senior sales professional who has been around the block more than once.

Steve Persinger: Building Materials Distributor

I had quite a learning experience with a building materials distributor. As you can imagine, most of my conversations with this distributor were about buying and selling my products in the marketplace. During a customer discovery interview, the distributor made obvious to me another great value opportunity and that was to support it in expanding its warehouse services and logistics business—a departure from the buy-sell product conversation. We were able to jointly develop a new ordering process to expand this customer's asset utilization, resulting in improved profitability and cash flow for them. In return, we exceeded our sales plan by 50 percent in a tough market. Additionally, the solution for this customer raised our service levels to other customers, creating more customer value as a result. It has all been a real success. Without the discover process, I would probably have never engaged in this specific activity.

Chapter 6

Informing Decisions

T his chapter is all about generating insights from the data that you have collected from customers to help you make better decisions.

Let's face it, at this point, you have spent time and resources engaging the customers and setting an expectation that you are going to act on what they told you. If you do not follow through, you will create a serious customer relationship problem. Even if you had a less than desirable situation with customers before preparing and conducting interviews, it will get even worse if you do not use their valuable input in your decision-making process and close the loop with the customer.

It is time to make decisions—customer-informed and data-driven decisions. Management has to decide what opportunities to pursue and what investments to make that will help customers make more money. And while there may be a tendency to resist the use of fact-based customer data to make decisions, capturing and analyzing customer data helps to keep the organization honest in its decision making.

Once you have made these decisions, the organization will have a portfolio of the best investment opportunities to win with customers. Successfully managing these opportunities becomes the priority of the organization and represents the drivers of profitable growth. This will set the organization on a course to create more value for customers, outmaneuver the competition, and grow profits.

There is also another important point to consider. As the organization looks ahead to execute plans that help customers make more money, it is also important to make it as simple as possible to put these plans into action. One of the ways to do this is to create value-based customer segments. Okay, in plain language this means forming groups of customers (based on the results of your analysis) who value the same elements within your value proposition. By grouping customers in this way, you can meet their needs and create differential value for them with the same or a similar solution. It is obvious that this approach helps you to meet the needs of more customers sooner, as opposed to developing and rolling out the solutions that only meet the needs of a single customer. And this helps to grow your profits faster.

In this chapter we discuss how best to consolidate the data collected through the "Discover" process, analyze it to help your organization make better investment decisions, and accelerate execution using value-based customer segments.

After reading this chapter you will be able to:

- Identify the required inside-out and outside-in data to conduct the necessary analysis.
- Identify the questions to answer to fully understand your current differential value proposition.
- Understand how to identify investments that may be underperforming, or not valued by your customers.
- Determine if you are being rewarded for the value you create and what levers can be used to gain your fair share of value.
- How to take data from Discover (Customer Interviews) and turn it into valuable customer projects and plans.

Silencing the Loudest Voice with the List of Initiatives at Owens Corning

You know your organization is operating outside-in when the loudest voice in the room can be silenced with data. More times than not, when executives are asked a question, they will have an answer, even if they do not know the answer. This is how bias and subjectivity can cloud and alter critical decisions. No one likes to answer "I don't know." At a recent sales leadership team meeting, you could see the shift from loud subjective voices dominating the conversation to one that was founded in customer data. In this meeting, there were several investments being evaluated on their progress and direction. One executive in the room repeatedly went off subject and suggested what customers need. To their credit, the sales and marketing leaders in the room were aligned and presented the data that backed up the actions that were taken. It was cool. What was even cooler was that when it came time to discuss this executive's customer value creation actions, he had none. His organization had no data to support the investments he was making. It became apparent to all in the room that there is nothing more powerful than the quantified customer voice. It is difficult to dismiss and, therefore, causes objective decision making to occur.

What Is Analyze?

Informing decisions with outside-in customer data sounds simple. We like to think that our customers impact our decision making daily. However, to make this a reality, we must get the right data in the right form to be used effectively in day-to-day decision making. Let us take another look at the sequence of plays in our playbook, shown again in Table 6.1.

With Discover, you have collected a significant amount of data that is not necessarily in a format that your management team can immediately act on. We have introduced the metric to measure if your customers are making more money doing business with you versus

Table 6.1   Why We Win Playbook

The Big 6	The Playbook
We help customers make more money doing business with us.★	**Discover** Chapter 4: "Winning Metrics" Chapter 5: "What Does Your Customer Think?"
We inject quantitative outside-in customer information into decision making.	**Analyze** Chapter 6: "Informing Decisions"
We develop and execute customer plans that deliver value (the Red Zone).★	**Execute** Chapter 7: "Executing Value Creation and Value Capture"
We predict profit growth.★	**Measure** Chapter 8: "The Scorecard"
We build capability and shape culture.	**Certify** Chapter 9: "Getting Started" Chapter 10: "Sustaining and Scaling: The Maturity Model"
The CVC Management System★	**CVC Management System** "Afterword"

★Breakthrough

competitors (the DVP). You have gone to the market and collected significant outside-in data that tells specifically what you can do for each customer to create value for them. You are now ready to inject that knowledge into your decision-making process. And we are ready to help you do this with the next play in the Winning with Customers' playbook. We call this play—Analyze.

What You Get

As we mentioned in Chapter 3, "The Playbook," one of the cool outcomes from Analyze is what we call "the List," shown in Figure 6.1. Based on the data you collect from your customers, the List identifies the top items your customers suggested would create value for them. It shows the specific attributes that need improvement, a short description of the attribute, and the potential value created for your customers' bottom lines. This is powerful stuff! It is only through analysis that you will be able to create such a powerful tool.

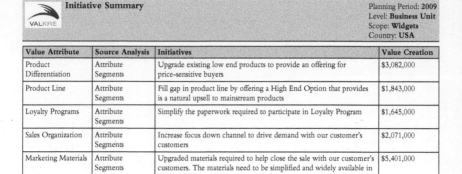

Value Attribute	Source Analysis	Initiatives	Value Creation
Product Differentiation	Attribute Segments	Upgrade existing low end products to provide an offering for price-sensitive buyers	$3,082,000
Product Line	Attribute Segments	Fill gap in product line by offering a High End Option that provides is a natural upsell to mainstream products	$1,843,000
Loyalty Programs	Attribute Segments	Simplify the paperwork required to participate in Loyalty Program	$1,645,000
Sales Organization	Attribute Segments	Increase focus down channel to drive demand with our customer's customers	$2,071,000
Marketing Materials	Attribute Segments	Upgraded materials required to help close the sale with our customer's customers. The materials need to be simplified and widely available in all branches.	$5,401,000

Figure 6.1 The List

"The List" can be developed for an individual customer, as well as a group of customers across a district, region, business unit, or division, by aggregating the data you collected. Here is a perspective from someone who has used the List to prioritize investments across a business unit.

Bob Harlan, Director of Business Insights, Owens Corning: Using Analyze to Aggregate Data and Create the List

I mentioned before the ability for us to aggregate all of the data and to be able to see themes across multiple customers. What this generates for us is a prioritized list across an entire business in terms of identifying what is the number one thing, the number two thing, the number three thing that we can invest in ... to make the biggest difference for our customers in aggregate. Like (some) of you, Owens Corning has hundreds of large customers and thousands of customers who are a little smaller. To be able to understand the landscape across hundreds of different customers and address what is the number one thing we can do to improve their business's condition is huge. And is something we can say in a fact-based way. We can say it with the depth of knowledge that includes the customers who told us, and what they told us it was worth. This

(Continued)

allows us to get our customers engaged; it allows us to get our corporation engaged at all different levels—all of the different process organizations—with clarity and speed. It just takes the debate out of the conversation. No longer is it the loudest voice in the room. Now that we have a fact-based approach, we know what to invest in to help our customers.

Yes, indeed everyone loves the List. We find executives carrying around the list from meeting to meeting. It truly serves as a guidepost for them to respond to the question "What do our customers want?" This is a tough question to answer with any kind of rigor. Now they can!

But the list is not the only thing you get from the information we have just collected. Here is a cut at a few more things you are going to get and see during this chapter.

- *Hypothesis vs. current.* We compare the internal DVP perspective you generated versus that of the customer's Current DVP (how customers believe you are creating differential value today).
  - *For individual customers.* At the individual customer level, the focus is to better align the customer and the individual sales professional on what is important and differentially valuable. This creates a basis from which your sales professionals can plan, interact, and improve your companies standing.
  - *By combining multiple customers.* At the multiple customer level, the focus is to better align the market of customers with your entire company organization. You see if the market agrees with your differential value proposition. Where it does, you can reinforce your commitment, and where it does not, you need to assess your positioning. The right answer may be to reduce costs on this dimension and spend the money on something that is or could deliver differential value.
- *Current vs. goal.* We compare the Current DVP versus the Goal DVP (do customers see a road map for you to improve differential value in the next 18 to 24 months?).
  - *For individual customers.* This serves as the basis of an improvement plan with them . . . The customer has just handed you a road

map. There may be ideas in here that your sales professionals can execute immediately without capital or approval—quick wins. If this is a $200 million customer, there may be financial justification to invest in these improvements just for this customer. In all cases, we come back to this customer and tell them what we can and cannot do relative to their improvement road map.

- *By combining multiple customers.* Now, this may be your entire customer base or it may be segments of customers. Here, you are trying to find groups of customers who have common views on what could enhance the differential value you deliver. If there is common perspective with enough customers, there may well be a business case for investment. This is where the List comes from.

Now, if you think hard at all, you can come up with all manner of different views and reports you would like to see from these data sets. We cover several in this chapter.

Generating Actionable Insights

Up to this point, we have focused on the outputs produced by a few simple analyses to help your organization inform its decisions with an outside-in customer perspective. We have shown you some of the deliverables that provide a glimpse of what is possible. If you are like most people we have shared these with, these cool outcomes have probably piqued your interest. You have likely reached the point of asking, "How do we get these deliverables or tools for our business?" Well, that is exactly what we lead you through for the remainder of this chapter—focusing on the "who's" and "how's" and the process to get everyone aligned to execute with precision. And, as you probably expect, there is an awful lot of work required to get these simple and yet powerful deliverables to help improve your decision making. But the powerful results are well worth the effort.

We have the capability now where we can aggregate all data up. So let's say for a particular business in a particular distribution channel, we have completed 80 different interviews that we can roll that up and see what those distributors have in common. What are the top three or four themes that those customers are looking for us to improve on in order for them to make more money?

The process of developing insights such as this begins when the Discovery Interviews are complete—once you have the customer's input on what creates differential value for them. Again, we emphasize that the objective is to augment your existing decision-making processes with an outside-in perspective, not to replace it.

Figure 6.2 shows the process used to ensure the customer data is analyzed sufficiently to inform your investment decisions. We will use

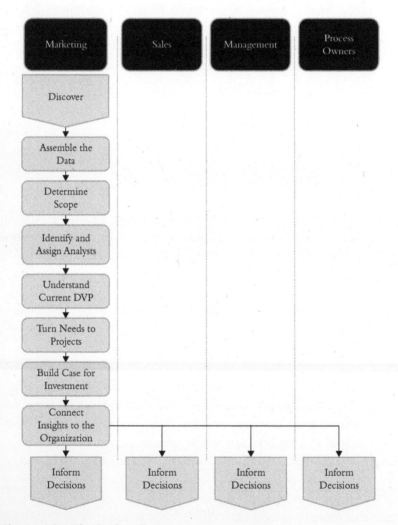

Figure 6.2   The Analyze Process

this as a guide to help you apply this approach within your company and we will use it to organize this chapter.

This process outlines what is required to effectively analyze data collected from Discovery. It includes: Assembling the Data, Determining the Scope, and Identifying and Assigning Analysts. Our experience in working with organizations that have done this well suggests these are the critical steps to perform successful analysis. Otherwise, the valuable data you collect from customers will be ignored, as it will not be organized in a way that can be acted on by the organization. Having the data is not enough. It is also your responsibility to get the data in shape to truly impact decision making. The marketing organization within your business is likely best suited to lead this process with considerable help from others.

Interpret One Interview

Before we march down the path to analyzing loads of data, let's take a minute just to look at one interview. If you can understand one interview, then interpreting tons of data is much easier.

Let's work from this finished interview shown in Figure 6.3. There are not too many moving parts on this particular interview so it works well for explaining the basics.

Overall DVP%

In your hypothesis you thought you were creating a healthy 4 percent DVP (the customer was making $40,000 of operating income on every million purchased from you). In this case, the customer is not receiving 4 percent but something closer to 2 percent. So you thought your differential value proposition was strong and the customer sees it as reasonably weak at 2 percent. A big key in this particular interview is that the customer sees an opportunity to get to 5 percent. That is big. I cannot emphasize enough that in my experience the predictor of potential profitable growth is more correlated to the change in current to future than it is in the absolute value being created today. Let's say this customer had seen the Current DVP as -2 percent but still saw a

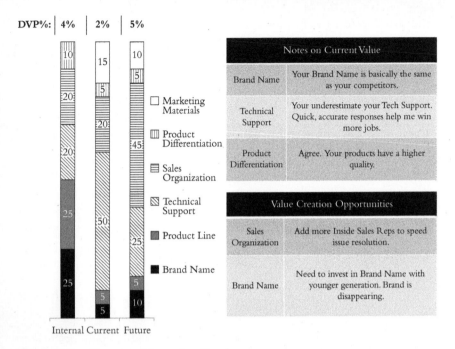

Figure 6.3 Completed Interview Results

road map to 5 percent in the future. The difference between 2 percent and 5 percent versus a −2 percent and 5 percent is time. In the case where your Current DVP% is negative, you better get on your horse and start making improvements right away!

Now, think about this customer who said the situation was 2 percent today and potentially 5 percent in the future versus another customer who was buying similar products and services from you who says the current is 2 percent and the future is 2 percent as well. Both of these customers think similarly about the value you are creating today but have different ideas about future prospects for improvement. We will tell you flat-out that these two customers are fundamentally different relative to your opportunity to achieve profitable growth. If you pay attention and use the concept we are stressing here you will be successful. Find those customers who see a road map to improvement, understand who they are and what they are asking for, and get back to them on what you plan to do. We explore putting these DVPs together from many customers later in this chapter and interrupting the nuances. Just as a heads-up: If you add the variables of your profits and time to the picture, you are on your way to a level of understanding few on the planet have.

When we say adding the variable of time we mean what this same customer will say next year or in six months when we conduct a Discovery Interview with them again. They thought we could go from 2 percent to 5 percent. Well, what happened? Did we make it to 4 percent, all the way to 5 percent? Or did we stay flat and not perform? Talk about getting an organization's attention. Take a group of 50 customers who have given you an improvement road map from 2 percent to 5 percent, operate for a year and find out you did not improve at all from their perspective. Be faced with the data that you did not actually execute anything and also set this in the context of reduced profits for yourself. Seen it! Now, unless your organization is comatose, you will likely find that people start getting a bit more serious.

Adding the variable of your profits starts advancing you down the path of value creation versus value capture. Mapping your profits together with the customer DVP over time provides a clear picture of your ability to create value for customers and then capture a fair share for yourself. If you get into a pattern of creating incremental differential value for your customers on a year-over-year basis, you will be amazed at how much easier pricing discussions become. We explore this more later in this chapter and in Chapter 8, "The Scoreboard."

Value Attributes Interpretation

Let's break apart Figure 6.3. Remember, the far left stacked bar is our original DVP internal hypothesis. The middle bar is the differential value your customers see currently. The right bar is the customer's perspective on what can be achieved in 18 to 24 months. The notes on the far right provide qualitative color.

We just like to start at the bottom and work our way up to the top.

Brand Name We missed the boat here. We thought brand name was driving 25 percent of our current value and the customer said 5 percent. Now, if the customer said the value of brand name should continue to be no more than 5 percent in the future then this might be a place where we should consider reducing or redirecting investment. Instead, the customer said brand name needed to be a slightly higher portion of the future DVP, up from 5 percent to 10 percent. Analysis rule of thumb: We see a positive change from current to future of 5 percent as being noteworthy and an increase of 10 percent as being very significant. Now, there are all sorts of statistics and correlations that you can use to determine statistical significance but a quick rule from experience is 5 percent is noteworthy and 10 percent is significant. These 5 and 10 percent changes become particularly relevant when you start looking at many customers together and are trying to determine the "so what." In the case of brand name, this particular customer would like to see some improvement in brand name and we can see in the qualitative notes detail that they would like us to do a better job of making younger generations more aware of our company. This may be solvable for this customer. However, if the reality is that many customers have this same concern, then we better figure it out. Do you start to get the picture? It might be the case that the local sales professional could hook up this customer with some local marketing activity and move this point into the category of quick wins. If the sales professional cannot, then it may be that many customers have the same concern and a larger initiative will result that may require investment from corporate.

One more thing while we are on the brand-name example. Let's say this customer purchases $5 million from us and in our make-believe book world that makes them a relatively small customer, one of hundreds who are just like them. With a little math, we can determine the value of this brand name improvement to our customer. Disclaimer: The math I am about to show you is a quick way to get at the approximate value for a given customer. There are some more sophisticated things that happen if you want to get really serious.

- The difference in DVP% from Current to Future is 3%. For a $5 million customer, this is an improvement opportunity of $150,000.
- Driving the value creation effort seems to be improvements in Brand Name and Sales Organization as they are the Value Attributes that increase from current to future

- Brand Name moves up 5 points, while Sales Organization moves up 25 points. This suggests that Brand Name is 16 percent (5 points) for Brand Name divided by 30 (25 + 5) total opportunity points of the value creation opportunity.
- 16 percent of a $150,000 opportunity is ~$25,000.

We may not be able to invest in Brand Name for one customer. But if 75 out of these 100 smaller customers all have the same problem, then this is worth 75 times $25,000 for a total of ~$1.875 million of customer value creation. All of a sudden that seems like a darn meaningful number—a number you would like to know as you are deciding in the boardroom where money is going to be allocated to improve business performance.

Do you see how the numbers are working? We ask the customer to use the forced attribute trade-offs to prioritize what is important today and where improvements need to be made in the future. The overall DVP% then allows you to translate the trade-offs into real dollars and cents.

Product Line This one almost fell of the chart completely. Whatever we thought was creating differential value is not. You need to look at this closely. Do you need to reduce investment or maintain? Maybe this will require further investigation. Here is something that you and your organization had thought made up 25 percent of your differential value proposition and it is barely even on the list! Take note!

Technical Support We thought our tech support group created 20 percent of the Current DVP of 4 percent. This comes from that internal hypothesis work you did in Chapter 4: 25 percent of 4 is 0.8 percent. You can see that the customer views the tech support as creating 50 percent of the differential value it is currently receiving but the DVP dropped from 4 percent to 2 percent. A little quick math: 50 percent of 2 is 1 percent. Looks like we had the differential value of our technical support close. As you look to the future, you see the customer has reduced tech support from 50 percent to 25 percent. Now, in this case this does not mean we should reduce our investment or emphasis on what we are doing with sales. Twenty-five percent of the future DVP of 5 percent is 1.25 percent. Tech support is still significant. What this is telling us is that we need to better balance our future DVP with other value adding attributes.

Sales Organization Wow, this one is significant. Here is a Value Attribute the customer increases significantly in the future relative to the current situation. They need more inside sales support to handle issues and it is worth the remaining 84% of the $150,000 opportunity ($125,000).

Product Differentiation This is similar to "Product Line." Maybe this customer does not see products as the clear path to increased profitability?

Marketing Materials This comes out of nowhere. It was not on our list to start and the customer says it should make up 10 percent of our future value proposition.

Moving on to Multiple Customers

Well, we thought it was important to take the time to interpret one interview. What we just went through is the level of detail that your sales organization would need to understand. At this point it has told the organization what is important to its respective customers. The organization has also put itself in a position of better under-standing what is important to its customers. Good stuff to know as you plan your sales strategies and tactics. As a sales organization, the company may be able to move forward on a few quick wins. Always nice! What sales is really looking forward to knowing is: What did everybody else's customer want. And what is corporate going to do about it?

Step into salespeople's shoes just for a second. Their chosen pro-fession is to convince customers that they should buy your goods and services. They know deep down that in order to do this really well they need something to offer that adds a dimension of value to the customer that is better than the next guy. They have some idea on what those things are and probably have a beverage now and again with the customer talking about what it could be. But somehow the information never seems to reach corporate in a way that causes anyone to act. That is all about to change as we are going to start putting all of those individual customer voices together!

Assemble the Data

Turning Discovery Interviews into actionable insights requires two types of data: outside-in and inside-out. When these two types of data are combined, you are able to paint a clear picture of what the customer values and what we expect to capture from the investments we make. Let's take a closer look at both types of data.

Outside-In Data

As discussed in Chapter 4, "Winning Metrics," a critical part of outside-in data is your Differential Value Proposition (DVP) that measures your customer's perspective on the differential value you provide today and in the future. When many customer interviews are conducted, you will compile a database of three pieces of outside-in data: DVP%'s Value Attribute Scores, and Influencer Scores. This database provides the outside-in portion of the data set required to better inform your decision making.

To prepare the outside-in data set for use in decision making across the business, the three pieces of data are combined in a straightforward operation. The DVP%, Value Attribute Scores, and Influencer Scores were all collected in identical fashion across the business. Combining the data to get a DVP% Value Attribute Scores, and Influencer Scores for the entire business is done simply by averaging the individual customer data collected during the customer interviews. The finished product looks just like the results of an individual interview, but it provides insight into the business as a whole. See Figure 6.4.

As you can see from this example, your internal hypothesis developed during "Prepare" resulted in an estimated DVP of 4 percent.

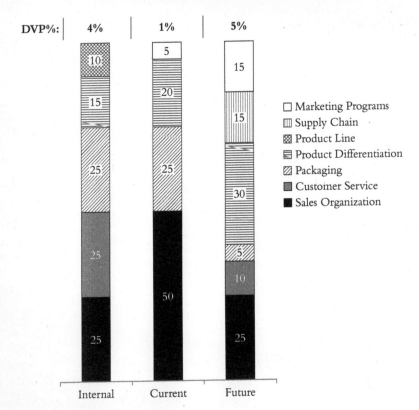

Figure 6.4 Average DVP Results

This is an average of all of the estimated DVPs for individual customers included in the interviews. So your organization felt really good about the differential value proposition and the economic value your business creates for your customers. This equates to an average estimated operating profit of $40,000 for each customer per $1 million in purchases, over and above the value provided to customers by your competitors.

However, the Current DVP suggests that customers are not as positive about the differential value you provide. The average DVP from all customers interviewed during Discover is 1 percent. This suggests that customers are not as positive about the incremental value you provide. And competitors may be nipping at your heels without your being aware.

The future bar, sometimes called the goal, which reflects customers' collective perspectives of future differential value you can create over the next 18 to 24 months, is positive. The Future DVP% of 5 percent suggests that your customers in total feel good about the future prospects of your business. The data suggests there is an opportunity to significantly outmaneuver the competition by providing $40,000 of additional operating profit for each customer for each $1 million of purchases.

The differences in Value Attributes and their relative scores from Hypothesis to Current to Goal also tell an interesting story. Your internal hypothesis suggests that your Sales Organization, Customer Service, and Packaging each represents 25 percent of your differential value. The customers' current views suggest that 50 percent of your differential value is delivered by your Sales Organization. Further, customers believe that 60 percent of the future DVP opportunity could be delivered by Product Differentiation, Supply Chain, and Marketing Programs. Supply Chain and Marketing programs represent two new Value Attributes not included in the internal hypothesis or current customer view, suggesting that you have work to do to further develop these two elements of your value proposition.

To summarize the outside-in data: Directionally, this data suggests that the management team may be overconfident in assessing its competitive advantage as compared to the perspective of customers. There is currently a disconnect. The good news is that customers believe strongly in your capability to create significantly more value for them in the future. Working with the customer, you have developed a clear road map of value attribute changes to deliver the expected future value.

There is unbelievable power gained by capturing and analyzing this outside-in data—power that can be unleashed to create more value for customers by improving decision making at all levels. The insights gained here will result in better connections between the entire organization and the customer, and provide specific plans to that show how each part of the organization can create more value for the customer.

Inside-Out Data

We have made references to inside-out data in the book. Let's spend some time examining this source of data in greater detail and discussing

> ### Bob Harlan: Using Analyze to Align the Entire Organization around Creating Customer Value
>
> As we put all of that data together we can start to see themes that cut across multiple customers and it gives us the opportunity to inform our company and inform all of the process owners in our organization, supply chain, R&D, human resources, law, marketing, about how the people of Owens Corning marshal our considerable resources in the interest of our customers. And this is really what this is all about. And I will tell you, it is a compelling conversation. Employees want to know in an organization that their work is meaningful. They want to know that their work is making a difference for customers. There are many opinions about whether that is true, but for the first time as we started this process we had data. And we could really exercise the power of Owens Corning for our customers.

how it can be used in conjunction with outside-in data in the decision-making process. Inside-out data includes the internal financial data that resides in your Customer Relationship Management (CRM) and Enterprise Resource Planning (ERP) systems. And in many cases this data also resides in the heads (or on the hard drives) of your employees. Do not worry—this is not about to become a conversation about data integration, data management, or a major project to manage your business intelligence. The effort to capture and analyze inside-out data will not require a major software system implementation. In fact, you only need a few basic pieces of information at the customer and macro levels. You will need sales, gross margin $, and share data. That is it.

You likely have a company financial reporting tool that regularly provides sales and gross margin metrics with a few clicks. For many businesses, market share data is not usually stored in a readily accessible place. If you do not have ready access to this data, the next best source to seek for this data is the people who know your customers best—your Sales Organization.

The sales data is easily accessed for those customers who buy directly from your company. It is likely stored in a central database or ERP system.

For indirect customers, or businesses that you do not directly invoice, accessing sales data may not be as straightforward. Here is an approach to get the data for this type of customer. The sales metric for indirect customers is a measure of the dollar value of what the customer buys from you (just as it is for a direct customer), but it is stated in terms of the indirect customer's financials. For example, let us look at a retailer (indirect customer) that buys lightbulbs from a distributor to whom you sell product directly (direct customer). You sell $1,000 worth of lightbulbs to the distributor; the distributor marks it up, and sells those same lightbulbs to a retailer for $1,500. The sales metric for the distributor would be $1,000 and $1,500 for the retailer. By keeping the sales metric in terms of your specific customer's financials, it is easier to engage in a discussion about value creation each type of customer.

For indirect customers, the amount that they spend on your products and services may not be available in a database because you do not directly invoice them. Access to this information is gained through one of the following methods. Your direct customers share their point-of-sale data with you directly or you utilize a mechanism with these customers to collect invoices that capture the sales data. Sometimes this is done with rebates or marketing programs that require indirect customers to share their invoices (sales data) in order to receive the rebate or other marketing program credit.

If this type of data is not available for your indirect customers, the next best data source is, again, your Sales Organization. The Sales Professionals in your organization should have a good idea of how much product an indirect customer purchases, as well as the purchase price. In cases with limited data, the best approach is to get an estimate from the Sales Professional and store it someplace. This starting point of data collection provides an Anchor from which to begin your measures. We discuss this Anchor concept at length in Chapter 7, "Executing Value Creation and Value Capture."

Share, of course, represents the percentage of a customer's total purchases enjoyed by your company relative to the customer's purchases enjoyed by your competitors. Calculating Share requires two inputs, the total sales of goods and services customers buy from you and the *total* amount they spend among you and all of your competitors. Knowing the sales metric discussed earlier provides half the story, but knowing how much in *total* a customer (direct or indirect) purchases across competitors can be a bit trickier.

Again, in our experience, the best source of this information is your Sales Organization. At times, your Sales Organization will know your exact share position with a customer. However, it is important to note that your market share position with an individual customer can change regularly. If your market share is not known exactly, the best approach to get an estimate is triangulation—using the data you have (preferably a couple of sources) and common sense. Here is a method for estimating your share for a customer:

- Estimate what you think your share position is qualitatively. For instance, if you think you have half their business, put down 50 percent.
- Distribute 100 points across your competitors to represent the percentage of business each competitor has that *you do not have.*
  - Competitor 1 has 50 percent of the business you don't have.
  - Competitor 2 has 40 percent of the business you don't have.
  - Competitor 3 has 10 percent of the business you don't have.
- Combine the assumptions you just made with your sales metrics and build a complete picture of the competitive situation with this customer.
- Customer buys $1,000 from you.
  - If you have 50 percent of the business, then the customer must buy $2,000 total.
- Each competitor then must sell:
  - Competitor 1: $2,000 × 50 percent × 50 percent = $500
  - Competitor 2: $2,000 × 50 percent × 40 percent = $400
  - Competitor 3: $2,000 × 50 percent × 10 percent = $100
- Use common sense:
  - Do you really sell twice as much than Competitor 1?
  - Does Competitor 3 really only sell $100 worth of stuff?
  - Adjust accordingly until you feel comfortable with the picture created.

Now, as you can tell, this is based on assumptions being made by an informed Sales Organization, but it is a start and provides your organization with an anchor from which to measure progress.

The final piece of inside-out data required is your gross margin for the customer. This data usually is stored in a database or system somewhere in your organization, and represents your profitability from sales to the customer. This is easily obtained for direct customers.

For indirect customers, analyzing gross margin is a little different. Although the gross margin for an indirect customer impacts your direct customer's bottom line, changes in your indirect customer's gross margin may not have an impact on your profits. Take the lightbulb example from before. If the retailer bought those same lightbulbs for $2,000 instead of $1,500, your bottom line stays the same. You get $1,000 in sales from the distributor, independent of the sales price received by the retailer. In this case, instead of focusing on your indirect customer's gross margin, it is best to focus your efforts on getting the indirect customers to buy more from your direct customers. This would represent the best profit opportunity for your business.

When you have collected and assembled these forms of inside-out data, you will have the following inside-out data set for customers, as shown in Table 6.2, to help make decisions to maximize the share of value you are able to capture.

Once outside-in data is assembled, turning Discovery Interviews into customer insights and real opportunities to help customers make more money is simple and straightforward. The added financial data in the inside-out data set will help you develop a quantitative assessment of the value you can capture in return from helping customers make money. The combination provides a solid business case to help decide

Table 6.2   Sample Inside-Out Data

Metric	Our Distributor	Average Customer
Sales	$10,000,000	$2,500,000
Gross Margin %	18%	25%
Gross Margin $	$1,800,000	$625,000
Share %	50%	25%
Average Customer Purchases	$20,000,000	$10,000,000

which opportunities to pursue and not pursue. This data truly helps to inform your decision making.

Later on in this chapter we talk a bit about the role that technology plays in making the assembly and analysis of this data set easier. Automating the capture and analysis of this data is important to ensure the data is up-to-date to support ongoing decisions as a normal part of doing business. Before we do this, however, let us continue to discuss the basic requirements to effectively analyze the data captured from customers.

Determining Scope

It is important to know what decisions you are trying to make and the appropriate scope of data you need to help inform those decisions.

The examples that we have covered so far have used a summarized data set, meaning that Discovery Interviews from more than one customer were used as an input. Anyone who has designed data analyses knows there is more than one way to slice and dice a data set . . . each with different desired outcomes. For example, compiling and analyzing Discovery Interview data at a Regional View is going to produce different results than a view of the data for the entire country. In order to make the best use of time and resources devoted to analyzing Discovery Interview data, you must decide what to and what not to analyze. Otherwise, you may begin venturing down the slippery slope of analysis paralysis—collecting mounds of data that hinder rather than help decision making. The first step is to determine the level of data analysis that is most appropriate. Table 6.3 shows some levels of analysis to consider.

At first glance, you may be thinking that it is valuable for your organization to analyze the data at all levels. This may be true; however, it is also important to assess the varying degrees of analysis at each level—we call this Scope of Analysis. For example, it may be of value to perform the analysis at the customer Level for some of your larger customers, but not all of them. To determine the most valuable analysis to perform, it is important to define the Scope of analysis within each large customer. This effort of sorting and prioritizing results in a list of the most valuable analysis, and estimating the effort required

Table 6.3 Sample Levels of Analysis

Level	Contains Data From . . .
Customer	The corporate, regional, and store interviews with one customer organization
Sales Team/Region	Interviews collected from a sales team
Value Proposition	Interviews for a given business unit and customer type
Customer Type	Interviews for a customer type across many business units
Business Unit	Interviews for a business unit that spans across all customers types
Business	All interviews conducted

Table 6.4 Sample Analysis Plan

Level	Scope	No.
Customer	AAA Distribution	4
	Morgan & Sons	
	Ready Distribution	
	Pacific Northwest	
Sales Team/Region	All	6
Value Proposition	All 5 Propositions	5
Customer Type	None	0
Business Unit	All	2
Business	All	1
	TOTAL	18

to analyze the data is important. This prevents the organization from getting lost in the data and analysis and results in an "Analysis Plan." Table 6.4 shows a sample Analysis Plan organized by Level and Scope of analysis.

In this example, we have identified a total of 18 potential ways to look at the data set. The goal is to minimize the number of analyses that are required to achieve your organization's objectives. By spending time developing an Analysis Plan before jumping into the analysis, your organization is able to quickly and effectively take the data collected in Discover, make decisions, and move into execution.

The Bob Harlan example shows how analysis at the customer Level for a large customer, with a Scope that includes multiple parts of the customer organization (headquarters, regions, and branches), generated new insight into how to be successful.

Bob Harlan: Using Analysis to Develop an Integrated View of Customer Value for a Large Account
It also created a way for us with our larger customers to understand them at different levels and with greater depth. To the extent that we have large national customers we have an executive team at their corporate headquarters, they may have a number of different regions, and within those they may have a number of different stores or branches. Those perspectives are going to differ. Within a single-customer company, you get different points of view, which are held by different constituencies in terms of what Owens Corning is doing for them and in terms of what they would like Owens Corning to do for them. This creates an interesting phenomenon where we can go back and educate the customer executive team members about what their company values, not just on the executive level, but at a store and regional level as well. The perspectives are going to be different, the value demands and the needs for the future are going to be different, and it is important for us to exercise energy around satisfying all of those.

Identify and Assign Analysts

Once the Analysis Plan is developed, you might find that there are many Analyses required for your data set. This is where we are compelled to offer a little coaching. Before getting all worked up, take a deep breath, take a yoga class (just kidding), and consider the skills required to perform the analyses we discussed in this chapter. It is simple and straightforward analysis and math. There is no complex statistic or sophisticated financial modeling required.

One of the powerful and refreshing things about the CVC Management System is that the Analysis can be performed within your organization by your current staff without the dependency of highly skilled statisticians or consultants. You think your sales leaders want to wait around for numbers being crunched before getting into action around the insights? Hardly. This is about getting people in your organization to adopt and do this work on their own, and moving as quickly as possible to help the organization create more value for customers. Here's what they need to be able to do:

- Work in spreadsheets
- Understand basic income statement drivers
- Create charts using spreadsheet or presentation software

That's it. The beauty of having a repeatable, measurable conversation with your customers is that the analysis is simple and repeatable. That said, you will have to decide "who" will do the analysis. In the process flow shown earlier, in Figure 6.3, Analysis was labeled as a marketing task. This suggests that the best analysts are people in the marketing function who possess analytical skills. However, you may be surprised, as some other users of this system have been, that people with the required analytical skills may be found throughout marketing, sales, business analysis, and other parts of the organization. Table 6.5 offers some suggestions for the analysts that are the best match for the various types of analysis you will need to perform.

You will likely want to look at the data set from a number of perspectives. So it is valuable to have a variety of resources across the organization available to perform the analysis. This will help to

Table 6.5 Scope and Suggested Analysts

Scope	Analysts
Customer	National Account Managers
Sales Team/Region	Regional Sales Leaders
Value Proposition	Business Managers
Customer Type	Marketers
Business Unit	Marketers
Business	Marketers

spread the workload across the organization—a real plus to prevent overloading any single group. Another benefit of delegating analytic tasks to resources outside of marketing is that it directly connects people responsible for action to the data source. For example, when conducting an analysis at the customer level, where you may be looking at corporate, regional, and local results, it makes sense to have the individuals closest to the account conduct the analysis. As with our recommendation to include Sales Professionals in the Discovery Interviews, we will trade off some objectivity in performing the analysis for the ability to get into action quickly any day. And to be quite honest, objectivity is less of an issue with analysis, as potential bias is generally limited because of the linear, simplistic nature of the analysis. There is not much room for interpretation in evaluating the results of the analysis performed here. So select your analysis team and get on to making sense of the data and take action!

Understanding Your Current Differential Value Proposition

Now that data is assembled and a team of analysts is raring to go, it is time to set them lose and turn the data set into knowledge. The first task is to assess your Current DVP. This data analysis allows you to establish a baseline from which to generate organizational learning and develop improvement plans. To guide your efforts and keep focused on the things that really matter, we have boiled down the objectives of this analysis to a set of critical questions to answer. It is valuable for the analysis team to refer back to these questions often to ensure they are only performing the analysis required to answer the critical questions. Their task—help the organizations answer these questions as soon as possible and get on to execution. Here are the critical questions:

- What is your current Differential Value Proposition (DVP)?
- Which current Investments are underperforming, or may be wasteful?
- How does your DVP vary among the traditional customer segments?

- How are customers segmented based on value?
- Are we being rewarded fairly for the value we create?
- What is our value capture risk in the future?

Let's spend some time working through the process of answering each of these questions.

What Is Your Current Differential Value Proposition?

This is a question for the ages, right? In most company annual reports, there is typically a blurb on "How We Compete" and it will say things like "Best-in-Class Customer Service" or "Innovative Products" or "International Distribution." Unfortunately, there is not much additional information to translate these lofty claims into a demonstration of true competitive advantage from customers' perspectives with quantitative metrics to show the financial impact on the customer's profits. And there is no clear connection between the investments in these specific areas and the impact on the company's financials (sales, share growth, and margins) for previous and future periods. Would this not be a great addition?

The CVC Management System focuses squarely on the DVP—the lifeblood of a company. This first bit of analysis focuses on assessing the health of your DVP. The results help to address the issues above and enable the organization to move from general claims to specific understanding and measurable proof of your competitive advantage. Why is this important? It is the company's competitive advantage that creates clarity on which investments make your customers more money. Additionally, clarity of your competitive advantage is valuable to all parts of your organization to help align resources around customer value creation. Understanding your Current DVP helps key parts of your organization in the following ways:

- Prepares sales to better understand the sales pitch and focus on the aspects of the value proposition that truly create more value for the customer.
- Enables management to assess the strength or health of the competitive advantage.

- Provides management guidance in deciding what to cut and what not to cut, and prevents the temptation to engage in potentially dangerous across-the-board cuts.
- Demonstrates to the organization which investments have been successful, as well as those that have not.
- Provides marketers crystal clear direction in positioning the company, its brands and offerings—enabling the development of marketing messages that truly resonate with customers (based on value).

To understand what you are doing today to create differential value for your customer, you need only look at the average of the stacked bar charts collected during the Discovery Interview as depicted in Figure 6.5.

In this case, you can see that your Current DVP consists primarily of three areas where you have made investments: Sales Organization, Product Differentiation, and Packaging. These represent the areas where you are winning, not just competing. If management decides

Figure 6.5   Average Stacked Bar Chart

to reduce investments in packaging, given your Current DVP, it will decrease your customer's profits and you can expect some unhappy customers. Similarly, if you experience a turnover in sales, it would likely cost your customers money and negatively affect your competitive advantage.

While this analysis of the Current DVP provides a quantitative understanding of where you stand today with customers, it is also important to include a qualitative understanding of how each Value Attribute provides differential value to the customer. Using the information from both the Internal Hypothesis exercise and Discovery Interviews, the quantitative measure can be augmented with qualitative support. For each attribute, you will have a deliverable like this to bring your value proposition to life: *Our packaging, which represents 25 percent of our competitive advantage, reduces our customers' operational costs by 25 percent each time we make a delivery. This customer value is a direct result of the investments we have made in our logistics systems that make it easier for customers to handle our deliveries versus competitors.* If your Discovery Interviews were done correctly, you will have comparable quantitative and qualitative details to bring your value proposition to life in the marketplace—clearly demonstrating where you provide differential value and how it makes your customers more money.

Discovery Analysis and Focus Groups

Old habits are heard to break sometime. Despite having a database full of direct customer insights, there will be some inertia to change how your marketing organization collects customer data to inform their decisions. On one recent example, more than 100 Discovery Interviews were conducted and a major theme that arose was a specific addition was needed to the product line. By doing so, it would provide an upsell opportunity for customers to improve their profitability. Less than two weeks later, a focus group was organized, complete with attendee recruitment and two-way glass. The result of that focus group: the same insight found during Discovery Interviews. As the research team

(Continued)

reflected on this, it was easy to see that a focus group designed to identify the attributes of this new product would have been more productive than another "white space" conversation. What's more, the research team already had the names and addresses of the customers who saw value in this new product. Getting those guys in a room together for a few hours would have provided R&D with the data they needed to get started quicker and cheaper.

Which Investments Are Underperforming or Wasteful?

The analysis of your Current DVP helps to identify the things you are doing that create value for customers. Equally important, it also helps to identify the things that are not creating value—the investments and actions that are wasteful.

Jim Drew and Bob Harlan on Using Analysis to Assess Investment Opportunities and Identify Waste

Q: *When your customers buy on an annual basis but suggest you need to invest capital to maintain the relationship, how do you capture enough value to justify a project like that?*

A: Bob Harlan: *"Well the reality is we may not. If what that individual customer is asking for is unique, it may be that there is not enough of a business case for investment. As I said before, when we have these interviews, as we go through this dialogue with customers, we make it clear that this is a discovery process. We are not walking out the door with any kind of guarantee that we are going to be able to act on everything they've asked for. If we see there is a customer that is asking for something that requires capital investment and other customers are asking for something similar, we have the means now because of the interview; because we can aggregate the data, we are able to support*

> business cases on some of these opportunities more so than we
> have before."
>
> A: Jim Drew: "I'll build on that point. There have been a number of
> projects we have been investing in for years that had no value to
> our customers. So I'll go to the opposite end of the spectrum. We
> thought it was a great idea. Unfortunately, our customers never
> saw any value in it, and for whatever reason we never had the con-
> versation with them and so we continued to do these projects that
> cost us significant money that were bringing no value. So there
> were a number of projects that we eliminated and saved our com-
> pany a lot of money and our customers were helpful in pointing
> that out to us."

We will point out again that increasing your profits is the result of growing revenues at attractive margins and reducing costs (including waste elimination). Analyzing your DVP enables you to understand opportunities for both.

To sort out wasteful investments, you compare your Current DVP to a couple of other perspectives to assess the performance of the investments you are making today. This will help you understand what is valuable to your customers and what is not. It also creates a learning opportunity to better understand which investments are underperforming or maybe even wasteful (see Figure 6.6).

To make this assessment, you need your Internal Hypothesis (a view of what your organization thought internally prior to conducting Customer Interviews), as well as the customer's perspective of your Current DVP and DVP Goal (or customer's future estimate). In situations where the customer's current value of a Value Attribute is lower than what you thought internally, but that customer sees an opportunity for you to improve in the future, this may indicate an underperforming investment. In this example, Customer Service may be an underperforming investment, as it has a score of 25 internally (suggesting differential investment), a current score of 0 (suggesting no differentiation),

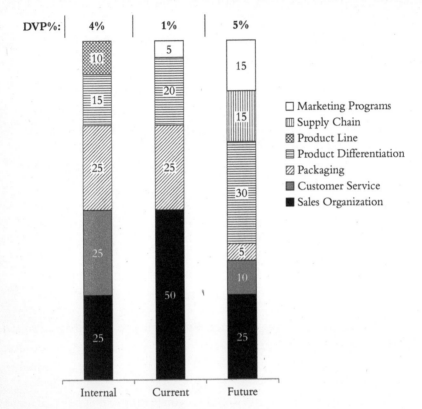

Figure 6.6 Comparison Analysis Chart

and a future score of 10 (suggesting that you can get where you thought you were).

Opportunities to eliminate waste in your operations can be identified by looking for Value Attributes that, from your customers' perspectives, are not as valuable as you thought and are not considered an opportunity for future growth. In this example, investments in Product Line may represent an opportunity to eliminate waste. This suggests that if you are investing to create differential value in Product Line, it may be difficult to earn an acceptable ROI because customers do not assign a differential value to this Value Attribute. From an organizational learning perspective, this picture can be huge. It provides a clear picture of your competitive advantage—what it is and what it is not. Any project you are currently pursuing or planning to initiate related to Value

Attributes that do not appear in the Current or Goal (future DVP) pictures from the customer perspective, should be seriously reconsidered. And, if you are counting on these projects to deliver significant profit growth, these projections should be reevaluated.

How Does Your DVP Vary among Traditional Customer Segments?

Beware of averages. Any marketer worth his or her salt knows this— there is no average customer. Marketing to the average customer results in marketing ineffectively to all customers. That is why customer segmentation is important.

For the nonmarketers out there, segmentation is a practice that seeks to create distinct groups of customers, who based on some things they have in common, can for all marketing intents and purposes be considered the same. Strategies and investments are tailored to these distinct groups and help the organization to break the "one size fits all" differential value proposition. By the way, this is a fallacy—there is no-one-size-fits-all differential value, although many companies treat customers as such. The most important benefit of a customer segment strategy is that it yields better returns by creating differential value that is relevant to each of the customer segments—maximizing value and eliminating waste.

Now, there are all sorts of segmentation schemes that marketers apply. Some are demographic, such as customer region, size, and so forth. Some other attempts include attitudinal schemes that classify customers according to how satisfied or loyal they are. Some companies use behavioral segmentation as well to understand how their customers operate their business based on the type of business models used to compete in the market. Whatever segmentation scheme is currently used within your organization, it is a good idea to line up your quantified DVP next to them to gain some insights.

This is easy to do. As long as you can classify the customers you interviewed according to a segmentation scheme, you can aggregate the DVP data by customer segment and look for similarities or differences. One form of analysis that we highly recommend is to segment the DVP data based on your own profitability. In this instance, you may segment your customers using quartiles of profitability to determine how your

DVP is similar or different along the spectrum of customer profitability levels. If, for example, you find that Brand Name is much more valuable to the customers that provide you healthy margins than your more transactional customers, you can infer that you are being rewarded for the value you create with your Brand Name. In contrast, if your lower-margin customers overwhelmingly value training, it might suggest that you are not being rewarded for those investments—maybe you are giving away valuable training that represents an opportunity for differentiation and profit growth. Other classic demographic DVP segmentations you may want to consider are Regional segmentation to determine how your DVP varies across the country, or Customer Size segmentation to determine if larger customers value different investments than smaller ones.

Segmenting your DVP along behaviors (or business model) is interesting as well, as it helps to determine if customer value differs based on how much your value proposition delivers to customers with different operating models or business strategies. For instance, you might find that a customer who subcontracts out all of their employees versus having full-time resources values your investments differently. The same can be said for a customer who competes on personal relationships versus being a low-cost provider. The difficulty in doing this type of segmentation, however, is that it is difficult to segment a customer base behaviorally . . . more on this later.

Finally, segmenting customers based on attitudes is recommended to reinforce the validity of existing customer satisfaction or loyalty surveys in your organization. You know by now that we believe (from experience) that understanding your DVP is a far superior metric to data collected using surveys. However, if you have existing studies that classify customers based on their attitude toward your company, it may be a valuable learning exercise to determine if there is a correlation between customers' attitudes and your DVP. This will help identify customers who say they are "loyal" or "satisfied" but are not making money doing business with you. These are the customers to watch out for, as they could represent the surprise detractors. Although they may give you the highest loyalty score, or identify themselves as one of your greatest promoters, they may also represent customers that put your profits at risk.

There are numerous customer segmentation approaches. However, we believe, and our experience has shown, that the most effective and valuable customer segmentation is Value-Based Segmentation.

We firmly believe that the best way to segment your customers is to group them according to how you make them more money. Any segmentation that falls short of accomplishing this is not valuable in helping you Win with Customers. Value-Based Segmentation is much more powerful than traditional methods of segmentation because your investments are directly aligned with your customer's bottom line. A picture that shows how your DVP is different by region is a nice view of the world, but unless your DVP is really different by region, it is kind of useless. That is why there are so many segmentation schemes out there. Marketers and statisticians slice and dice data along many factors until they find the dimensions that create truly distinct groups of customers. There are all sorts of statistical packages out there that crunch data to take the individual customer data and develop meaningful segments. In the end, the most effective segmentation is one that creates segments based on what customers value similarly.

So why not just start there? We think this is a great and cost-effective idea. With the data set gathered as a result of the Discovery Interviews, you can begin by grouping customers based on the Value Attributes customers value more. By virtue of the stacked bar chart constraints, customers have to prioritize what makes them the most money. By grouping these customers together, you know exactly what makes up your competitive advantage with this group of customers. And once these customers are grouped together, it is easy to pull in all of the other traditional segmentation schemes to develop a customer profile of the ones who, for example, who see Sales Organization, or Brand as the primary driver of value. This profile might include a distribution of customer size, your profitability, and the measure of customer loyalty. You can pool together the total Gross Margin and Sales dollars that these customers account for and assess what would happen to your bottom line if you made cuts or underperformed in the Value Attributes that are so valuable to them. What is so powerful about this approach to customer segmentation is that it is much easier (and less costly) to do than trying to back into what traditional customer segments value. It requires one segmentation scheme based on Value Attribute scores with data that is readily available by virtue of the Discovery Interviews, and is regularly updated as a normal part of doing business. This just makes sense to us and the organizations that have done this. It further reinforces the power of understanding how your customer makes more money doing business with you. It serves as the most effective organizing principle for your business—your investments, your planning, and your customer segmentation.

Using a simplistic approach, you can create value-based customer segmentation by looking for Value Attributes that make up a significant amount of their stacked bar chart. We place significant in quotes, as this can vary depending on the degree of statistical relevance you want to achieve. Significant can mean attributes with a score of 20 or higher, or ones who are in the Top 3 attributes in a given scheme. When the results of these two approaches are compared, the resulting segmentations will vary depending on the variance of the data set.

The more complex approach to create value-based customer segments includes factor analysis techniques. These techniques can be used to statistically evaluate Value Attribute independence and come up with value-based segments that are based on multiple value attributes. One of the potential benefits of this approach is that factor analysis can identify if multiple Value Attributes are always valuable in combination (e.g., Sales Organization and Training). The two Value Attributes would then be collapsed into one. This makes it easier for your organization to manage customer segments, as it is easier to keep track of three or four distinct customer segments rather than one for each Value Attribute in your DVP.

Are We Being Rewarded for the Value We Create?

Okay, if segmentation does not get you fired up, then this section will. How do you know if you are getting your fair share of value? It is important for you to create value for customers—help them make more money. But the end game is to grow your profits. If you are helping to drop significant profits to the customer's bottom line, you should be getting rewarded for it—getting your fair share. That is the final measure of Winning with Customers.

The analysis required to determine if you are being rewarded for the value is simply building the Starting Point picture discussed in Chapter 4. The Starting Point takes a broader or portfolio view of groups of customers and plots the DVP % against your Gross Margins to see how you are doing with value creation and capture across the business. When you consider these two measures together across groups of customers, it provides insight into the current status of the relationships between you and your customers—whether they are secure or at risk. The Starting Point framework is shown again below in Figure 6.7.

Stepping back as someone in charge of managing a portfolio of customers, this view can show the status of each relationship. We like to think of each customer fitting into one of four groups: Profit Partner, Profit Risk, Profit Opportunity, and Profit Transaction.

- *Profit Partner.* This is the upper-right corner. In this situation, both you and your customer are enjoying a mutually beneficiary relationship. It is always nice to have 50 percent or more of your customers in this quadrant, but that is seldom the case.
- *Profit Risk.* This is the upper-left quadrant. You enjoy healthy value capture at the expense of your customer's income statement. This business could be considered at risk. This is the business that corporate says, "Do not lose this customer," while the customer says,

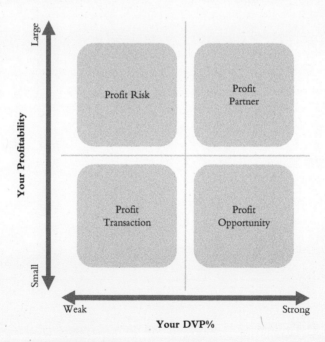

Figure 6.7 Initial Framework

"If you do not improve I am going to be forced to go elsewhere." It is powerful to measure this. At any given time there always seems to be those voices of, "If you do not improve I am going elsewhere," but it is hard to separate the rhetoric from the reality.

- *Profit Opportunity.* This is the lower-right quadrant. Your customer sees strong value in the investments you make, but your organization is not being rewarded for it. This is the quadrant where you may be looking to fire your customers only to find they do not want to be fired. Rather than firing, the necessary work is to rebalance the exchange of value.

- *Profit Transaction.* This is the lower-left quadrant. Your customer is not making much money doing business with you and the business could be considered at risk. This may be okay with you, as you have a weak financial position with them as well.

The actual deliverable might look something like Figure 6.8.

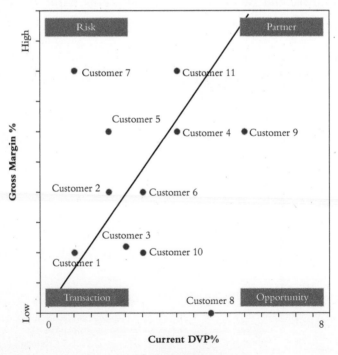

Figure 6.8   Gross Margin versus Current DVP% Chart

After plotting the data, you can simply observe the plot looking for a trend. If a trend is present, it will be easily observable. And if there is a linear or nonlinear trend present with the plot, a statistical software package is not required to find the correlation.

The stronger the trend (the greater the relationship between GM percent and DVP%) the greater the likelihood that you are actively managing value creation and value capture. If you observe a strong trend, this is a good sign.

Whether there is a strong trend, an examination of each customer on the plot will provide insight into your current position with that customer and provide some clues on how to improve your position. For example, Customers 7 and 8 are not a part of the trend. Let's examine each of them to assess the findings of the analysis.

Customer 7 on the scatterplot reveals something interesting. You are enjoying high GM$ from this customer with a relatively low DVP% in other words, strong profits with low differentiation. This combination suggests that your business with this customer may be at risk. If you would like to maintain the attractive Gross Margin $, it's a good idea to look at the value creation opportunities on the List from the Discovery Interview. They represent the priority and high-impact investments and actions that can strengthen your position with this customer.

Moving to Customer 8. In this case, you are not being rewarded for the value you are creating for this customer—as evidenced by the relatively high DVP% and corresponding low GM percent. You are making investments and creating value, but not being paid for it. This is not good. You should take a look at the results of the Discovery Interviews to determine why this is the case and determine if there is an opportunity to change your position. If not, this is a customer you might consider transitioning to your competitor.

For the customers who fit the trendline, like customers 1, 2, 6, 5, and 11, the objective is to move all of these customers up and to the right by continuing to create more value and capturing your fair share. Again, the List of prioritized value creation opportunities and DVP Goal with Value Attributes provides the road map to make these continuous improvements over time. As you create these specific customer plans, you continually improve your position with these customers and improve the financial results of the business overall.

No matter where each customer lands when comparing your profits, your ability to do something about the picture needs additional insights—again, as discussed in Chapter 4, "Winning Metrics." By taking those same customers and plotting the Current DVP% against the opportunity to create more value, you can begin to get a sense of whether there is a road map to winning with these customers. We call this the DVP% road map, as shown in Figure 6.9.

Now, think about combining these two pictures. The first, Figure 6.8, (GM% vs. DVP%), is about today's profits that result from transacting business between you and your customer. The second focuses on the opportunity for value creation your customer sees in the future. Comparing Figures 6.8 and 6.9, you can see that Customer 1 sees a transactional world today and provides little road map to create value. Winning with this customer is going to be a little like skiing up hill. In contrast, Customer 7 has provided a great road map to create value

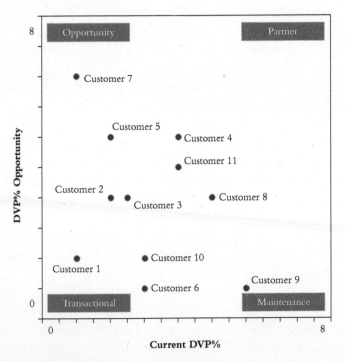

Figure 6.9   DVP% Road Map

and if you are able to deliver, you will have the basis to save your sales and profits with this customer.

We hope you are beginning to see that this is not only about how much money your customer makes with you today. It is equally important to understand how they view the road map for improvement. The road map for improvement is Customer Value Creation.

What Is Our Value Capture Risk Going Forward?

Looking at the correlation between your bottom line and your DVP% helps frame strategic thinking on how to manage customers one at a time, but it does not do a great job of helping you see the big picture for the entire business. It is also important for management to understand the strength of your competitive advantage by understanding the risk associated with your Sales and Gross Margin dollars. Are they at risk or are they secure?

A simple way to perform this risk assessment is to group your internal financials by customer based on the customers' assessment of your DVP as in Figure 6.10.

In this case, by creating DVP% tiers (less than 0, 0 to 3, and greater than or equal to 4) you can determine what percentage of your business is at risk. This analysis provides a powerful and insightful "bird's-eye view" of the condition of your business and future impact on your financials.

This example suggests that half of the organization's sales are currently to customers where there is a strong differential value proposition. However, 20 percent of current sales are considered at risk due to a weak value proposition. This analysis identifies the segment of customers where your value proposition is strong, as well as the segment where your value proposition is weak. In a world of limited budgets and resources, this analysis helps management prioritize their investments to continually improve overall performance of the business.

Another way to assess the risk inherent in your business based on your competitiveness is by examining the strength of your DVP% with your direct customer base and the distribution channel as in Figure 6.11.

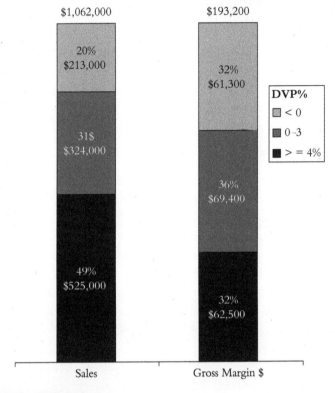

Figure 6.10   DVP Risk Assessment

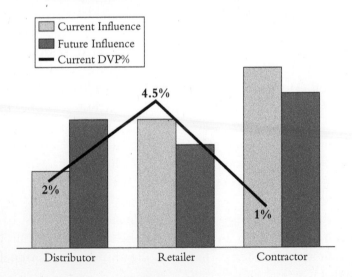

Figure 6.11   Influence versus DVP%

By averaging the DVP% by Customer Type and the Influencer Scores gathered during the Discovery Interviews, you can build a simple but powerful picture of what is happening across the Value Chain. As we mentioned before, it is critical to have a strong DVP% with businesses in the value chain that control the demand for your product and service. By plotting Influence and DVP% together, you can see the strength of your Value Proposition in various parts of the value chain. And you can also determine if your DVP% is strong with key influencers in the value chain. Both of these are key indicators of your future success.

In this example, Contractors have more influence in the channel than Retailers, yet your DVP% is stronger with Retailers. You would prefer to have a stronger DVP% with contractors—the player in the value chain with greater influence on the demand for your products. Additionally, the Distributor is projected to gain greater Influence in the future, but your DVP% is relatively weak with the Distributor. If the Influence of the Distributor continues to increase and your DVP% does not improve, your competitive position in this value chain will weaken. This is serious cause for concern about the long-term competitiveness of your business.

These analyses help you to see beyond the current situation with individual customers and provide management with insight into the future competitiveness of the business. Insight that may otherwise be invisible, were it not for the customer-informed, fact-based data you captured to understand where are you are winning and losing with customers. This is powerful data to help make decisions for the long-term success of the business.

Turning Customer Needs into Potential Projects

Once you have a firm understanding of your current differential value proposition, it is time to think about how to improve your current situation. This is done by gaining a forward-looking perspective from the customer that was revealed during the Discovery Interviews. The specific data used for this purpose is the DVP Goal Stacked Bar Chart and the qualitative Value Creation Opportunity details. This data may appear to be basic on the surface, but it allows you to answer three powerful questions to improve your decision making:

1. What is the Value Creation Opportunity worth to the Customer's bottom line?
2. What are the Top 10 investments you can make to build competitive advantage?
3. How can customers be segmented according to their needs?

Here is how it works:

What is the Opportunity worth to the customer?

As you know by now, the Winning with Customers conversation begins with the current DVP. However, it is also important to uncover ways to make the customer more money in the future. For a specific customer, the answer to this question is found in a prioritized list of opportunities. The qualitative detail is captured directly from customer input during the interviews. And the prioritization of Opportunities is determined by the degree of change in attributes from the Current state to the Goal.

For example, if you look at the stacked bars shown in Figure 6.12, you see that Supply Chain and Product Differentiation are the investments that will create the most value. They both increase by 15 points from Current to Goal. Customer Service is a smaller value creation opportunity, as it increases only 5 points. To make this analysis really simple, we created an Opportunity stacked bar chart that clearly spells out the difference between the Current and Goal bars. This is done by calculating the difference in scores for each Value Attribute and determining the relative importance of each by allocating 100 points the Customer was asked to make this trade-off during the quantitative portion of the Discovery Interview. In this case, Supply Chain and Product Differentiation increase by 15 points, while Customer Service increases by 5 points, resulting in a total change of 35 points (15 + 15 + 5). This means that Supply Chain and Product Differentiation are estimated to contribute ~43 percent of the Total Opportunity and Customer Service is estimated to contribute ~14 percent. The stacked bar graph clear communicates the opportunity.

It is a good thing to have a pretty picture that details what the customer wants—pretty pictures are nice. However, without knowing

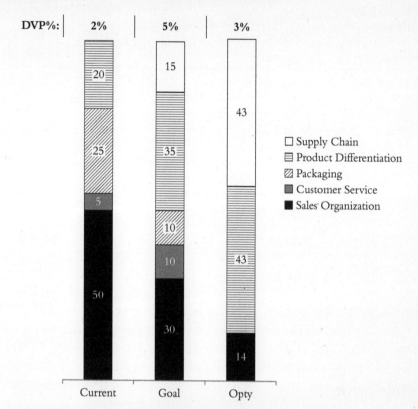

Figure 6.12 Discovery Interview: Opportunity Bar

how much money can be created if your organization acts on the customer needs, the picture leaves much to be desired. The good news is that this data can be easily calculated using the Discovery Interview data and some basic Customer Financials.

Customers have communicated how much value can be created during the DVP% portion of the conversation. In this example, the current DVP% is 2 percent and the Goal is 5 percent. The Opportunity to create value is 3 percent. We call this the "Oppty DVP" percent. Also, it is simple to translate the Opportunity into value creation dollars by multiplying the Oppty DVP% by the amount of customer purchases. The Value Creation Opportunities are shown in Table 6.6.

Table 6.6 Value Creation Opportunities

Value Attribute	Opportunity	Percent of Oppty	DVP Oppty$
Supply Chain	If you were to reduce your lead tie 3 days, I could eliminate half of my inventory.	43%	$129,000
Product Differentiation	Need a product that meets the latest energy efficient codes. Without it both you and I are going to be left out.	43%	$129,000
Customer Service	I don't like the automatic phone. Can I have the direct number to the same customer service rep?	14%	$42,000
	TOTAL	**100%**	**$300,000**

There is a $10 million customer with an Opportunity DVP% of 3 percent. This suggests the value creation opportunity for this customer is $300,000 (3 percent of $10 million). We call this the "DVP Oppty$." Or, the money that is available for your customer if you deliver on what the customer values. You might also think of it as a measurable amount of additional value to create for your customer.

Once we know the total value that can be created, we can allocate the appropriate amount to each of the individual opportunities, based on their relative priority. The Supply Chain represents 43 percent of the $300,000 value creation opportunity, so the Supply Chain Opportunity is worth ~$129,000 to the customer's bottom line. The Sales Organization is also worth $129,000 (43 percent of $300,000). The Customer Service is worth $42,000 (14 percent of $300,000).

What Are the Top 10 Investments to Make?

Now that you have quantified the value creation opportunity, it is important to understand how to prioritize the investments to capture as much of the future value as possible. Sometimes an opportunity can be overlooked or ignored unless the particular customer is not large or influential. Yes, it is easy to ignore the needs of one small- or

Table 6.7   Total DVP Opportunity ($)

Customer	DVP Current Percent	DVP Future Percent	DVP Oppty Percent	Sales (000s)	DVP Oppty$ (000s)
1	1	4	3	1,000	30
2	−2	2	4	12,000	480
3	0	1	1	400	4
4	4	6	2	1,600	32
5	2	2	0	11,000	0
6	−1	5	6	2,100	126
7	3	4	1	23,000	230
8	1	6	5	1,500	75
9	3	4	1	31,000	310
10	0	2	2	1,800	36
TOTAL			1.5	85,400	1,323

medium-size customer. But the beauty of quantifying the customer voice is that you can take the input from multiple customers and add them together, as shown in Table 6.7.

If there are 10 customers interviewed, the total opportunity is the sum of the opportunity identified by each customer, regardless of their size. And it is important to include the input from all customers to gain a comprehensive understanding of customer opportunities.

To illustrate how this works, consider the following example using the Total DVP Opportunity $ chart. Ten customers were interviewed that purchased a total of $85 million in sales. By calculating their DVP Opportunity $ individually and adding them up, a total DVP Opportunity $ of $1.3 million is identified. This represents an average DVP Opportunity percent of 1.5 percent (1.3/85).

That is great info, but similar to an individual customer, the magic is breaking down this $1.3 million value creation opportunity across the specific "To Do's" outlined during the Discovery Interview.

It is typical to expect the 10 interviews conducted to generate a list of 30 to 40 quantified opportunities. If you have 100 customers, that list could balloon to 300-plus opportunities. Do you think that an executive is going to read and effectively use all of those details to make better decisions? I don't think so. They want a Top 10 list of things to do to make improvements. The challenge is to create a compelling list

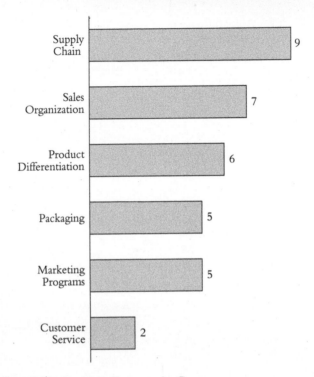

Figure 6.13   Value Creation Opportunity Pareto

of opportunities to create customer value that the organization can rally around.

The good news is that because each opportunity is quantified and categorized by Value Attribute, processing this information to create the Top 10 is straightforward. We like to start with a Pareto chart of value creation opportunities to get an idea of how much qualitative information is out there by Value Attribute. (See Figure 6.13.)

Now it is valuable to read specific opportunities and summarize them into a "project" that can be executed by your organization. We call these value creation initiatives, as shown in Figure 6.14.

Each Initiative is simply made up of similar customer value creation opportunities. The value of the Initiative to the customer's bottom line is the sum of all of the opportunities that make up the Initiative. In this case, customers see incremental value creation by reducing lead times on the top selling products:

Initiative	Increase Plant Inventory Levels for Top 3 SKUs	
Value Creation Opportunities		
Customer	Opportunity	DVP Opty$ (000's)
1	Takes too long to get your standard products.	15
3	There are too many times when I lose orders because you are out of stock. Need to have shorter, consistent lead times.	2
4	Lead times are too long. Maybe you should increase your inventory levels so I can reduce mine.	20
9	I could reduce my inventory by 50% if you built up stock levels of your top products.	200
10	Three times in the past month I have missed orders because your leads times are inconsistent. Need to maybe increase your stocking levels to reduce the variability.	30
	Total	267

Figure 6.14   Initiative Opportunities

By reviewing each value attribute and transforming individual customer needs into Initiatives, you can create a list of the top projects your organization could execute on behalf of your customer's bottom line. When summarizing, it is powerful to spell out the Total Value Creation Opportunity, how that opportunity is broken down by Initiative, and the percentage of Customers interviewed that informed that opportunity, as shown in Table 6.8.

When creating this list, remember that you are identifying projects that are bigger than an individual customer relationship. This means that not every Opportunity will be included in an initiative. In addition to summarizing the Value Creation Initiatives, it is also important to keep track of the Value Creation Opportunities that are not part of an Initiative as shown in Figure 6.15.

Table 6.8 Value Creation Initiatives

Value Attribute	Initiative	DVP Oppty $ (000s)	Percent of Customers Included
Product Differentiation	Introduce high-end product that provides upsell opportunity	513	60 percent
Supply Chain	Increase plant inventory levels for top SKUs	267	50 percent
Sales Organization	Increased focus on selling to our customer's customers	150	40 percent
Packaging	Bundle pack our products to make them easier to handle in the warehouse	75	30 percent
	TOTAL	**1,005**	**90 percent**

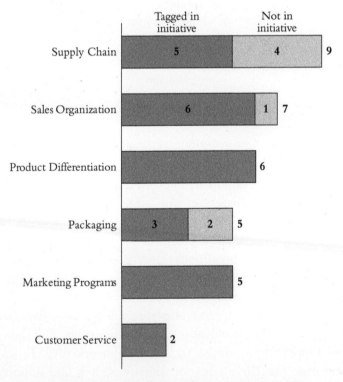

Figure 6.15 Value Creation Opportunity Pareto—Not in Scope

This provides some perspective on the amount of opportunities that you are leaving to the Sales Professional and their customer to execute on their own. Do not lose sight of these opportunities, as they need to be managed and reviewed as well.

How Can Customers Be Segmented According to Their Needs?

For those of you who are tracking with us, you know that we've already answered that question. For others of you, we are checking to see if you are awake. With the exercise you just completed—reviewing and combining similar Value Creation Opportunities to create your Top 10 List—you have defined your needs-based-segmentation scheme. That is right, it is done. Each item in the Top 10 List represents a needs-based customer segment that is actionable with specific to-do's identified. And what makes this segmentation really powerful is that the customers segmented themselves by prioritizing how they would spend the next million bucks you have available to invest. Again, this data was obtained from customers during the quantitative portion of the Discovery Interviews.

Now there is a little work left to do to fully understand the new segmentation scheme. That is because the segmentation you have in hand is based only on the customers you interviewed, not the entire population of customers. A logical next step is to build a profile of the customers that informed the potential investment for value attributes addressed by each of Top 10 opportunities. This is important to better understand the customers in the segment who are making the request. This allows you to "predict" the types of customers who also would be interested, and who were not included in the interviews.

Tactically speaking, this involves gaining a better understanding of the customers who were included in the interviews by using various segmentation schemes mentioned earlier. These include organizing customers based on their size, profitability, location, and any behavioral or attitudinal segmentation factors you have available. By doing so, you should have the data necessary to build a customer profile for each opportunity, which allows you to include customers that were not interviewed but can benefit from the improvements.

Turning Initiatives into Investment Decisions

In some organizations, simply putting together the list of quantified initiatives is enough to get the organization into action. For most organizations, however, a project or Initiative of this magnitude requires a rigorous business case to gain management approval. Any good business case addresses two critical areas: return on investment (ROI) and risk. When you are building business cases for Value Creation Initiatives, getting comfortable with ROI and Risk is easier because the data comes from customers using a reliable fact-based method. This data is less likely to be internally biased and is founded in rigorous economics.

Let's take a look at how to build a rigorous business case for one of the value creation initiatives identified earlier: "Bundle pack our products to make them easier to handle in our warehouse."

Building Out Value Creation Initiatives The Value Creation Initiatives that are created through Analysis are more than a prioritized list of the things customers want you to do. Initiatives are the backbone of your organization's effort to create customer value. To that end, there is much more to an Initiative than a simple description. In fact, Initiatives should look and feel more like a project. As you know by now, we like to keep things functional while driving accountability. Therefore, for each Initiative, a few details should be clarified:

- *Description*. Name/Description of the Project being executed.
- *Value attribute*. The part of your DVP in which you are investing.
- *Value creation drivers*. How the Initiative will impact a customer's bottom line: reduce costs, improve margins, win more customers, and so forth.
- *Team*. Part of the organization that is responsible, such as a Sales Team, Manufacturing Plant, or Customer Service Team.
- *Owner*. Specific person in your organization that is accountable for the execution of the Initiative.
- *Status*. Clearly communicates if the Initiative is in Progress, Completed, Canceled, and so forth.

Now, some Initiatives may are more complex than others. For example, coordinating a $10 million marketing and merchandising initiative will be more complex than providing a direct contact in Customer Service. For the more complex Initiative, it might make sense to add more detail to fully communicate what is being done for the customer. Your organization probably has its own way of structuring the projects. You might have dedicated Project Managers or Special Assignment Teams that create detailed project plans. Before going off the project management "deep end," we recommend keeping the details limited to a simple list of actions or milestones. Think about what customers and executives have in common when it comes to their preferred method of communication. For these and other sane people, the famous one-pager is probably a good place to start. Getting the key information on one sheet of paper makes it easy for people to understand your points quickly. There is always time to dig deeper if needed on a particular subject.

The same is true when creating a Value Creation Initiative. For a Training Initiative, you may want to list all of the training events included in the plan. For a Marketing Initiative, you may want to list the specific advertisements, point of purchase displays, and sample materials included in the plan. To keep things functional, we like to list these high-level activities as Actions to better communicate both internally and externally what you plan to do as a result of the customer's input. For each Action, it is a good idea to have the following characteristics:

- *Description*. Name/Description of the Action or Milestone being executed.
- *Team*. Part of the organization that is responsible, such as a Sales Team, Manufacturing Plant, or Customer Service team.
- *Owner*. Specific person in your organization that is accountable for the execution of the Action.
- *Status*. Clearly communicates if the Action is in Progress, Completed, Canceled, and so forth.
- *Start Date*. When the Action Started.
- *End Date*. Expected time of completion.
- *Percent Complete*. Estimate of how much progress has been made on the Action.

Figure 6.16 shows an updated look of the Initiative with some actions and milestones included . . . It still fits on one piece of paper!

Initiative	Increase Plant Inventory Levels for Top 3 SKUs		
Status	In Progress		
Value Attribute	Supply Chain and Logistics	Team	Manufacturing Leadership
Value Creation Drivers	Free Working Capital	Owner	Bob Smith

Actions						
Description	Team	Owner	Status	Start Date	End Date	% Complete
East Plant Raise Inventory Levels	Mftg East	Joe Johnson	In Progress	1/1/09	3/1/09	75%
West Plant Raise Inventory Levels	Mftg East	Jerry Monacelli	Not Started	3/1/09	5/1/09	0%

Figure 6.16   Updated Initiative Plan

Setting Value Creation Goals

The Value Creation Initiatives developed thus far are grounded in customer data and quantified from the customer's perspective. However, the metric used (DVP Oppty$) may be foreign to your organization. You have to turn the DVP Oppty$ into a metric your organization can grasp, one that is familiar. In our experience, this is best done with some quick back-of-the-envelope calculations that translate the DVP Oppty$ into metrics that both you and your customer traditionally measure.

Well, let's begin by reviewing what the DVP Oppty$ represents: "Incremental Operating Income" that will be created for a specific customer. The quantitative value is also accompanied by a qualitative

Metric	Value	
Sales to Customers Impacted	$30,000,000	
Sales per Delivery	$10,000	
Number of Deliveries in a Year	**3000**	
Projected Operating Costs Saved	$75,000	
Cost per Hour to Handle Packaging	$25	
Projected Hours Saved	**3000**	
Projected Hours Saved per Delivery	**1**	

Figure 6.17   Calculating DVP Cost Savings

description of *how* the opportunity will impact the customer's income statement: Will it Reduce Costs? Improve Sales? Increase Margins? Reduce Inventory? Take our example about bundling packages of products so that they are easier to handle. In this case, the customers suggest easier to handle packaging reduces their costs by making their employees more efficient. It might be helpful to translate the $75,000 in cost savings to a metric that is more easily measured, such as time saved. Figure 6.17 is a simple example of translating DVP Oppty$ into hours saved as a result of improving packaging:

As you can see, a fairly simple translation of DVP Oppty$ turns $75,000 in savings to a corresponding operational improvement goal of one hour's time savings for every delivery as a result of the Packaging Improvement Initiative. The DVP metric is now expressed in a form that is easily understood by people across your organization and by the customer. This same approach can be used to translate the DVP Oppty$ for all opportunities surfaced by the customer.

Estimating Investment Required

You understand what the customer is looking for, have set value creation goals, and mapped out the actions required to deliver more value to

Metric		Value
New Bundler		$10,000
Investment per Delivery	$20	
	✕	**➕**
Number of Deliveries	3000	
Total Expense	**=**	$60,000
Total Investment		$70,000

Figure 6.18   Estimating Investment

the customer. Now it is time to determine what level of investment is needed to deliver the value. We do not go into much detail here, but it is important to point out that all required investments should be considered, including capital, expenses, and resources. Once you determine the total expense, sometimes it helps to allocate the investment to the specific customers involved—those customers you included in the model used to determine your value capture goals.

In our Packaging example, Figure 6.18, after a little investigation it was determined that improving packaging required a new shrink-wrap machine that costs $10,000, and the materials to do the bundling cost $100 per delivery. Using these costs and aligning them with our value creation model, we estimate the total investment is $70,000.

Setting Value Capture Goals

Okay, now the fun part. Most of the analysis covered so far has been focused on understanding how you impact your customers' income statements today and in the future. Yes, the first requirement to win with customers is to help the customer make more money. But Winning with Customers is not philanthropy. The second requirement to win is capturing your fair share. As we walk through the approach to set value capture goals for your business, the processes and tactics we share will

likely not be new for your business. We review some of them to reinforce the concepts.

The first step to understand how to capture your fair share of a
value creation opportunity is to identify the value capture driver.
The value capture driver is the financial lever that directly impacts
your own income statement. Examples include: Increasing Volume,
Improving Gross Margin percent, Growing Share Position, or Reducing
Costs. Choosing the right Value Driver is critical to building a case
for investment and successfully winning with customers. To select a
value driver, we use two basic rules of thumb. First, the Value Capture
Driver should align with your current financial position with the customer. Let's say, for example, you have a 75 percent share position
with a customer; it may be difficult to capture your fair share of the
value you create for the customer by winning more of the customer's business. In this instance, growing share is probably not the best
value driver.

The second rule of thumb: The Value Capture Driver should not
conflict with how you are making the customer money. For instance,
helping a customer win more business will improve your volume. In
contrast, saving your customer money may not increase volume, but
you may be able to increase your gross margins or share position.

In the case of our Packaging Initiative, Table 6.9, let's take a look
at the profile of customers included in the Initiative as compared to an
Average Customer.

The metric that stands out for potential growth is Share, as you
have five points lower share with Initiative Customers than you do
with your Average Customer. Given that the main Value Creation
Driver is reducing these customers' costs, it seems appropriate that you

Table 6.9 Initiative Customers versus Average Customers

Metric	Initiative Customers	Average Customer
Sales	$10,000,000	$2,500,000
Gross Margin %	30%	25%
Gross Margin $	$3,000,000	$625,000
Share %	20%	25%
Total Customer Purchases	$50,000,000	$10,000,000

could capture a fair share of those savings by asking for more of the customer's business.

Now that the value capture driver is established as a share increase, we can set some goals. To get started, we like to establish what the necessary share gain would be to break even on our investment of $70,000 in equipment and materials.

Using available data, we made a few calculations and found that by gaining just 0.5 percent in share, we would generate an additional $233,000 in sales at a 30 percent gross margin. That would cover our $70,000 investment. Breakeven calculations are a quick way to help understand the riskiness of the investment. Figure 6.19 shows a sample breakeven calculation.

Breakeven calculations make you feel good, but they do not get you excited. What you get excited about is the money you can make and the attractive return on your investment. Figure 6.20 shows the financial estimates.

Metric	Value	
Value Creation Estimate		$75,000
Total Investment	$70,000	
	÷	
Existing Gross Margin %	30%	
	=	
Incremental Sales to Breakeven	$233,333	
	+	
Total Existing Sales to Customers	$10,000,000	
	=	
Breakeven Sales to Customers	$10,233,333	
	÷	
Total Existing Purchased by Customers	$50,000,000	
	=	
Share Required to Breakeven	20.5%	
	−	
Existing Share	20%	
Incremental Share to Breakeven	=	0.5%

Figure 6.19   Sample Breakeven Calculation

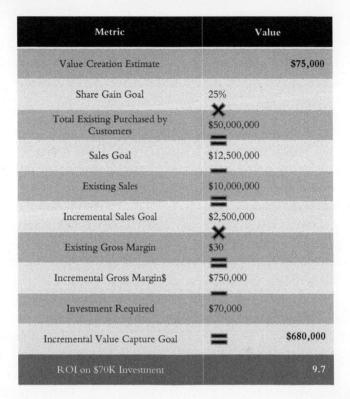

Metric	Value
Value Creation Estimate	**$75,000**
Share Gain Goal	25% ✕
Total Existing Purchased by Customers	$50,000,000 ═
Sales Goal	$12,500,000 ▬
Existing Sales	$10,000,000 ═
Incremental Sales Goal	$2,500,000 ✕
Existing Gross Margin	$30 ═
Incremental Gross Margin$	$750,000 ▬
Investment Required	$70,000
Incremental Value Capture Goal	═ **$680,000**
ROI on $70K Investment	9.7

Figure 6.20   Sample ROI Calculation

To show the potential return, it helps to project what you expect to get as a result of executing the Initiative. In this case, let's say the goal is to gain a 25 percent share position. With some simple calculations, it looks like that might deliver an incremental $680,000 of profit improvement and an ROI of 9.7.

To put this in perspective, think about customer planning. Instead of declaring that your goal is to have a 25 percent share position, you can say that "a Share position of 25 percent is expected because of the cost savings the customer will realize as a result of your packaging improvements." That is a statement your customers might buy before you invest a penny.

One final metric to consider when building business cases for Value Creation Initiatives is the Value Capture Ratio. A Value Capture Ratio is a measure of the dollars you expect to capture for each dollar you create for your customers.

Continuing with the same example, the Value Capture Ratio is $680,000 (value captured) divided by $75,000 (value created), or approximately $9 captured for every dollar created. This is a quick and important measure of how the value you created for customers is being shared between you and the customer.

Initiatives to Investment Portfolio

As a result of building business cases for Value Creation Initiatives, your organization will be in a position to make better decisions by understanding the entire value story, not just your own. Think about all of the new projects, products, or programs in which your organization has made investments over the years. Each project that was approved likely had some form of a business case that projected an attractive return on investment. Some of these investments did not deliver the value that was projected. Why? The value creation for customers was not realized. That is how manufacturers end up with warehouses full of products that seemed like a good idea but were not a commercial success. By understanding both the Value Creation Potential *and* your return on investment, your organization will be in a better position to make smarter decisions.

You can help facilitate decision making by plotting Initiatives on a 2x2 that includes the Value Creation Opportunity on one axis and your ROI on the other. This Initiative Portfolio provides a view of all initiatives and their relative value. This can be used as a decision-making tool to help management prioritize initiatives to pursue.

Let's take a closer look at the framework in Figure 6.21.

Let's begin with the "Risky" quadrant. On paper, these initiatives appear to have an attractive ROI, but based on the low DVP Oppty percent, your customer is not confident in the initiative's ability to deliver a differential impact to their bottom line. This does not mean the investment should not be made, but it does mean that you should be prepared to clearly communicate the initiative's impact on the customer's income statement. Similarly, ideas in the "Philanthropy" quadrant should not be automatically tossed out. If there is significant customer value to be created, there might be an opportunity to work with the

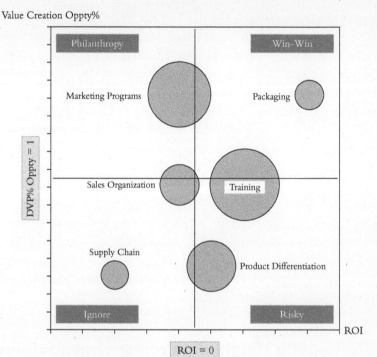

Figure 6.21 Initiative Portfolio

customer on an arrangement that makes sense for both parties that yields greater value capture for your organization. The "Ignore" quadrant represents initiatives that, no matter how exciting they may appear (to you or the customer), you should avoid. They do not make money for you or the customer and represent waste of valuable resources. Finally, the "Win-Win" quadrant contains initiatives that help you win. They provide the greatest impact on the customer's profit and allow you to capture an attractive return.

Insights to Decisions

At the beginning of this book, we stressed that Winning with Customers is not about changing how you make decisions but about being better informed when you make them. A key to informing these decisions is the process used to get knowledge from an analyst's head into the broader organization. Without this conduit, your organization will create binders of data that sit on a few people's desks, but you will not get this data into the hands of your people throughout the organization to make decisions from an outside-in customer perspective.

We have seen organizations successfully integrate this valuable information into their decision-making processes. The approach generally includes three key steps. First, there is a presentation of the data, or a "read out," to a broader audience—creating awareness and fueling constructive debate. Second, they inject the insights into all organization decision making. And they create a clear definition of the next steps that result in decisions and actions. This step is the one we have found to be most challenging—moving the data into the center of decisions and actions. Here is where we provide some guidance to help you perform this step well.

Connecting Insights to Process Organizations

Critical to moving the data into the center of decisions and actions is getting insights outside of Sales, Marketing, and Management and into the hands of Process organizations such as Supply Chain, Customer Service, R&D, and Manufacturing. These resources are rarely included in value proposition discussions and absolutely love this type of data. After all, their work contributes to your DVP every day . . . They should be able to see what customers are saying about them.

We like to supply these organizations with slimmed-down versions of the insights that are tailored to their part of the organization. By virtue of categorizing insights by Value Attributes, this is really easy. On a regular basis, make sure these groups have what customers are saying about their organization today and what customers are looking for from them in the future. A regular dosage of outside-in insights goes a long way to inspiring new ideas and continuous improvement.

Another way to get the broader organization involved is combining customer insights on a regular basis with other data that comes in to the central marketing and finance organizations such as competitor and macroeconomic information. If you have already got a balanced score-card developed that contains this type of information, add the customer perspective as well. The more information the easier it is to inject it into everyday decision making.

Bring the Customer into Every Meeting

At Owens Corning, the customer is at every meeting. They discuss standard reports organized by Value Attribute that highlight new insights into their value proposition and cus-tomer needs on a regular basis. These discussions generate next steps that vary from simple organizational communications to new investments. In the case of New-Product Development, the Initiatives that are identified during Analysis are directly fed into the Product Development Lifecycle Management stage gate process.

Encourage Ad Hoc Analysis

We have presented a number of analyses to better understand Dis-covery Interview data and use it in decision making. It is actually an amazing phenomenon to see. Although these analyses are power-ful, your organization will surely want to further analyze the data to bring even greater insight and value to your business. Trust us, they will have lots of new ideas. Your initial reaction may be to create a standard process to handle all requests to prevent overloading your analysts. Some may even consider using Six Sigma to improve the process and streamline operations. Please resist this temptation, at least in the beginning. Holding back data and insights from the organization can generate frustration that is difficult to reverse. We recommend that you make the resources available to meet the demand from your organization and work to build process and struc-ture over time.

Empower Resources to Become Analysts

A dangerous situation that can develop is a dependency on one or two people who know everything because they process all of the data for everyone else. If you have not noticed by now, analyzing Discovery Data is relatively straightforward by design such that resources that are not considered analysts can perform data analysis also. Not only does this help you scale and process more information, but it creates more subject matter experts in your organization that are firmly aligned with the customer's perspective. You begin to notice that the analysts become the most powerful people in the room because they have irrefutable evidence on what the market is asking for. The more analysts you have, the more likely the insights will be injected into everyday decision making.

Benefits of Technology

Over the course of this chapter, we have seen plenty of charts, numbers, and notes gathered from the Customer Discovery process. As the number of interviews conducted continues to grow, the enormity of the size of the customer data set becomes readily apparent. Likewise, the amount of time and effort required to process this data set grows rapidly. So you have two choices.

You throw more bodies at the work and attempt to manually organize, process, and analyze a large and growing data set. Or you can enable the discovery process with software and technology. The ultimate decision is up to your organization and will likely be based on its values for human resource allocation.

By making the first choice, you might consider using something called a spreadsheet. This spreadsheet will contain numerous worksheets with pretty little squares filled with numbers. It will contain macros and mathematical algorithms to analyze all your customers and identify key opportunities. Over time, its file size will grow exponentially as will its importance to your colleagues. Eventually, someone will jokingly refer to this morbidly obese file as the Mother-of-All-Spreadsheets. And henceforth, it will forever be referred to as the MOAS. Some may feel the need to e-mail it to others, instantly leaving a wake of destroyed inboxes in its path.

Unless this spreadsheet is kept and maintained by a single owner, the integrity of the spreadsheet will be in question. It is nearly impossible to keep the spreadsheet synchronized among hundreds of users and all it takes is one person to "fat finger" a data entry or accidentally modify a calculation and you will spend hours trying to decipher how this happened.

After waking up sweating from nightmares involving large spreadsheets, you may alternatively determine that your organization does not have the in-house expertise or time to conduct a proper customer data analysis. So you decide to bring in outside expertise in the form of consultants. These consultants will eagerly bill your organization at an exorbitant hourly rate as they comb through all of the customer data points you gathered. In the end, they will produce a flashy PowerPoint deck that beautifully summarizes where the best value creation opportunities lie with your customers.

The consultant route will be time-consuming and expensive. Your employees will spend many hours getting them up to speed on your business. Consultants will spend a lot of time (on your dime) manually analyzing all the data. They may even decide to use a spreadsheet.

Consultants are never a long-term solution, particularly if you are short on cash or wish to learn for yourself what your customers want instead of paying someone else to tell you. Nevertheless, you may be satisfied with the work effort of the consulting firm. However, customer discovery is meant to be an ongoing process. So next year, when preparing to embark upon another round of interviews, you will face the same analysis predicament.

If done manually, the analysis document(s) will not be integrated into the Initiatives or work efforts to capitalize on the value creation opportunities. Once again, you are faced with a manual process to enter these Initiatives into your organization's strategic planning system.

You see where this is going. It should be readily apparent now that an automated process is ideal for performing a proper customer analysis. Think of it as Henry Ford's assembly line for manufacturing automobiles. Any redundant data entry should be eliminated, any reports and calculations should be automated, and any integration with your systems should happen silently in the background. The technology exists today to eliminate much of the manual labor involved in customer analysis, which we refer to as software. So where do we start?

In order for you to gather and organize customer interviews, conduct analyses, identify opportunities, document strategic initiatives, and measure their effectiveness, you will need somewhere to store all this information. This information will grow each year as more customers are interviewed. It would also be nice if you could measure the effectiveness of Customer Discovery over several time periods. This brings us to the database, a structured and relational means of organizing vast quantities of data. It may not seem like much, but there may be upward of 200 distinct data points captured from the interview. For only five customers, over the course of five years, that amounts to 5,000 points of data. Processing this information without the help of a database would take two weeks for a single individual.

In addition to the ability to enforce referential and data integrity, you need a database that can be accessed by multiple users at any time. There should also be various levels of access to the data for different users and the database should be managed and optimized by an IT department or organization. These requirements essentially rule out using small office suite databases such as Microsoft Access.

Now that we have decided where to store all this data, we need to determine how to analyze this data. Any software solution will need to automate the analysis of customer data. It would also be helpful if the software could automatically generate the interview materials or kick out other documents and reports related to customer analysis. These hard copies would be ideal for interviews or presentations when having an open laptop is not an option.

Finally, how are we, as users of the software, going to interact with it? To work effectively with customer discovery data, you will need a user interface. This interface will interact with the software in a consistent, visually pleasing manner. The software should facilitate data entry while keeping everything synchronized and removing the pain associated with the spreadsheet solution. It also needs to be accessible throughout the organization for those in the office and those outside the corporate firewall, working in the field. In this situation, a web application is most suitable.

Potentially, the software can guide the users through the process and even train them. Imagine a self-motivated employee being able to interview and log data without any human training. You just saved yourself thousands of dollars in consulting costs.

Using a software-based approach to performing customer analytics will put users in a unique position to be heroes. Without software, identifying key initiatives across numerous customer perspectives may feel like searching for the proverbial needle in the haystack. With software, those key initiatives will surface quickly. The user will also be able to find, filter, sort, or tweak certain data at their own leisure to provide further Customer insights. What once took weeks will now take a few hours or even minutes.

Steeped in rigorous quantitative data analysis and armed with identified opportunities, employees can present a logical course of action for strategic planning. For perhaps the first time, the organization is able to focus and prioritize initiatives with a greater sense of confidence.

Another potential benefit for the use of software is the cultural impact on the company's employee base. People will begin talking in the language of the software, making communication between various subgroups in the corporation more efficient through the use of a common language. The software can do everything from scheduling interviews to sending notifications about new actions, reducing the time required for people to manage responsibilities and deadlines.

When software is used to automate these tasks, employees are more productive. The efficiencies gained in data collection and analysis allow employees more time to think strategically. Letting the software do all the heavy lifting makes for a happier, more engaged employee base. Although there is an initial cost in time and expense to institutionalize the software, the organization is prepared to reap the benefits year after year.

When selecting a tool to use for conducting an outside-in Customer analysis, your organization may decide to build this software yourself, hire someone else to do it, or identify a vendor that already provides the necessary toolkit. The primary goal is to gather insightful Customer analyses in a more quantitative approach. Achieving this goal will involve bridging the common gap between Sales and Marketing. For many organizations, this requires a change in the role of marketing— moving from being solely a communication and sales support function to one that creates demand and delivers profitable revenue growth. Marketing can be viewed as the place where revenue starts, and should thus be held accountable, just like Sales. This is a transformational issue.

And it is an organizational transformation that can happen through the use of applied technology.

Instead of the sales people accessing their data in one place and the marketing department in another, both can go to this software. If a sales interview at a regional store provides valuable insight that the brand is not working, which generates opportunities and initiatives for brand improvement, this should trigger actions for marketing at corporate. By having this kind of collaboration, every data point can potentially become millions of dollars in profits.

In short, technology is your friend and a critical ingredient in the formula to succeed at Winning with Customers!

Summary

You have seen in this chapter that analysis is the key to turning the data you collected into insights to help your entire organization make better decisions. The combination of outside-in data captured during Customer Discovery Interviews Combined with inside-out data resident in your ERP and CRM systems provides all the data you need to answer two critical questions: "How do you help customers make more money?" and "How do you capture your fair share?"

There are several basic analyses that can be performed by analysts within your organization. This capability can be developed within your organization without the need for highly paid consultants—empowering your people (across all functions) to learn more about how to create more value for customers each day during the normal course of their jobs. After all, delivering on what creates more value for customers should be everyone's job.

The learning gained from the analysis will result in powerful insights to be used in your decision making. These decisions (augmented by the data, analysis, and learning) will create real measurable customer value and enable you to capture your fair share. This is the ultimate goal.

And to scale this effort to build a company-wide capability requires the use of technology. Technology is your friend. It is impossible to rapidly expand the effort to create and capture value across multiple value-based customer segments—accelerating your wins—without technology. The use of software will instill confidence in the data used throughout your

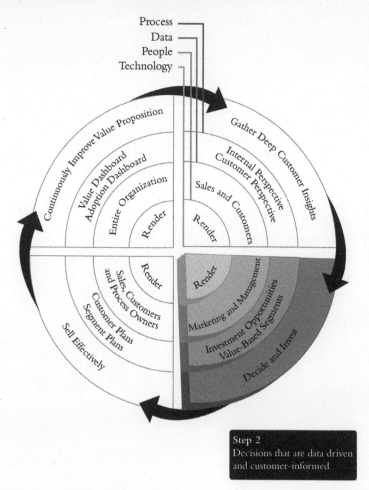

Figure 6.22 CVC Management System

organization to make important decisions. And your people will be enabled to do more faster and spend more of their time thinking strategically about how to grow your business and profits.

Again, in the grand scheme of things, as shown in Figure 6.22, this chapter has been about making investment decisions informed by the needs of your customers. With decisions being made by Marketing, Management, and others, it's time to start moving into action as an aligned organization focused on creating customer value and capturing a fair share.

Chapter 7

Executing Value Creation and Value Capture

I t is time for honesty and vulnerability. This is a hard chapter for us! It is hard because causing people to act and do things differently on a day-to-day basis is one of the most difficult things in the world. Some people look at what we are suggesting when it comes to execution and go, "OMG!" We do not know why. We think it has something to do with the NIMBY (not-in-my-back yard) principle. Generally, NIMBY means people are really agreeable right up until you ask them to do something different. Well, we are going to ask you to consider some different things in this chapter.

After reading this chapter you will be able to answer these questions:

- Why is this approach to execution different and what are the benefits?
- What does a customer plan look like?

- How do you build customer plans out of the information we've discussed so far in the book?
- How do customers and sales react to these plans?
- How do you manage these plans without overloading the organization with work?
- What about getting your fair share (profits) as well?
- What are the things you need to keep in the corporate vault?

If there is any part of you at all that desires to differentiate your company in the eyes of your customer, then dig in and consume every word of this chapter. This is the reward and the fun stuff!

What Is Execute?

Just to make sure we are focused, take another look at the "Why We Win" in Table 7.1. Execute is about customer planning and management.

Table 7.1 Why We Win Playbook

The Big 6	The Playbook
We help customers make more money doing business with us.*	**Discover** Chapter 4: "Winning Metrics" Chapter 5: "What Does Your Customer Think?"
We inject quantitative outside-in customer information into decision making.	**Analyze** Chapter 6: "Informing Decisions"
We develop and execute customer plans that deliver value (the Red Zone).*	**Execute** Chapter 7: "Executing Value Creation and Value Capture"
We predict profit growth.*	**Measure** Chapter 8: "The Scorecard"
We build capability and shape culture.	**Certify** Chapter 9: "Getting Started" Chapter 10: "Sustaining and Scaling: The Maturity Model"
The CVC Management System*	**CVC Management System** "Afterword"

*Breakthrough

In this context, customer planning means anything from changing a service program, launching a new product, increasing sales call frequency, launching a new customer promotion, or anything else that resulted from decision you make in the business relative to your differentiated value proposition. We use these customer plans to drive communication and accountability.

Communication threads through the plan because it contains what the customer said, what we are doing about it, and how we are progressing against improvement plans. Accountability threads through the plan as it becomes a report card to the customer, sales, marketing, management, and the rest of the organization on your ability to achieve meaningful customer outcomes over time.

> *"We sat down as a result of these interviews and we were able to build plans. And there is an interesting thing that happens when you sit down with a customer and you ask them what they think, they tell you, and you come back and you show them that you have taken what they said, you've documented it and you have actually built a plan around it. So there are really two levels of benefit associated with Winning with Our Customers in the context of this conversation. The first is the very organic stuff the customer gets is regards we are moving in the right direction to help them drive business results. The second one is more relationship based and is 'Hey, you guys really heard me, you came in, you asked me what I thought, I told you, and you've actually come back with a plan on a page that addresses the things I said.' You'd be surprised at how many times we've been told by our customers how few of our competitors do this at all. Our experience is that we are one of the few and that means a lot!"*
>
> —Owens Corning executive

A Quick Recap and Chapter Setup

Do you remember the Red Zone analogy we made in Chapter 3?

Well, this is the biggie! Think about where we are on the field of play. We are in scoring position. This is the time to get focused and aligned to turn opportunities into results. A team's performance in this critical area of the playing field determines how many points it scores and how many games it wins. This is where the winners truly outperform the competition."

We probably wrote that short passage on some Sunday afternoon while deep in competitive exuberance. But on reflection it remains true. This is the area of the field where so many fail. There are so many things that can go wrong in the Red Zone. We do not try to cover them all. What we offer up in this chapter are the things that have worked for us and others.

Once more, let us step back a moment and review, using Figure 7.1 as a guide. You took the initiative to find out from your customers how they make money by doing business with you. You developed a cool DVP metric and value attribute trade-off approach for organizing this data. You went on to find out from the customer the things you could do more of and less of to help them make more money. You likely discovered things about your customers and yourself that you did not know before, which resulted in a lot of high-fives. Then you organized many customer interviews together and analyzed them to find business case opportunities for improvement and investment, which yielded the "List." Everyone likes to use the List as shorthand for this area of the field. The list represents the top 5 or 10 things your customers view as adding differential value to them and the worth to their bottom line. This list was submitted with many other inputs to the management team for business and investment planning. During this process, you worked hard to eliminate the overconfidence of the management team regarding their prior beliefs about what customers value. Decisions were made. Some of the decisions were aligned with the customer input and some were not. Now it is time to execute.

The Say-Do Gap

Maybe a little story about the say-do gap will help to further set up this chapter. The say-do gap is just as it sounds . . . The saying and the doing do not come together. The saying and doing of what, you ask. The saying is that the company explicitly states and in fact desires to understand its customers and improve on its performance based on

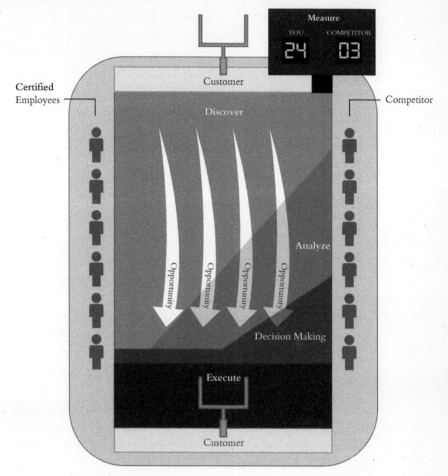

Figure 7.1 The CVC Stadium

that knowledge. The doing is actually changing behaviors and making investments that create value for customers and profits for you. The following is a story we have experienced over and over.

A company uses some kind of customer satisfaction measure, often administered by a third party or an automated questionnaire that just as well could have come from a third party. At best, this information is loosely fed into the business and capital planning process. Executives make decisions, sometimes right and sometimes wrong. There is no clear accountability to improve on what the customer sees as being valuable because there is not a clear road map. Instead, decisions are driven by executives, who are naturally oriented to be overconfident in their beliefs, the very attribute that probably got them to the position they have attained. The gap starts to emerge. The gap is between the investment and resource decisions executives make versus the reality of what drives differential value for the customer. These decisions result in projects for the organization to execute that ultimately marketing needs to market and sales needs to sell.

Marketing goes to work crafting the messages and putting together the selling material, all the while positioning the new initiatives in the context of the company's value proposition. Sales takes all of these inputs and builds an approach to winning with their customer. Sometimes they build great plans and sometimes it is all in their head. Sometimes the plans are consistent from one sales professional to the next and sometimes they are different. In any case, all of the plans are dependent on the company executing on those projects mentioned earlier.

The sales professional goes to the customer and starts selling the plan to the customer, maybe an annual planning meeting kind of deal. It is a crap shoot. Sometimes the customers see themselves in the plan, and other times they do not. Now the sales professional is scrambling to tell her company where it missed the mark on its initiatives relative to her customer base. Or she is scrambling to follow up with those people who own the projects so she can now tell the customer when they are actually going to be receiving the new stuff. Then a few months go by. The sales professional is back in front of those same customers. She is scrambling to find out updates from her own company, putting this into a communication document. She does it, but what chaos.

Then the end of the year comes around. You did not meet the sales and profit goals or maybe you did not take share. The organization is not satisfied or satisfied enough. Sales cannot figure out why the company made the investments it did because they sure were not relevant to her customers. Marketing cannot figure out why sales did not use their stuff. Management cannot figure out why its organization is not beating the pants off the competition. And the customers see an organization doing the same old thing. Old dog, no new tricks! And you step back from all of this and ask, "Why?" Is there a gap between what our customer wants and values relative to what we are delivering? Is there a gap between our stated goals of serving customers versus what we are actually doing?

Now, your story may not be quite like this. Everyone's version is different. But assuming this version of the story, here is what we would have you do different to help bridge the say-do gap and improve your odds of successful execution:

- Instead of having a third party or a nameless survey determine what is valuable to your customers, get sales involved in the process. Check, we did this earlier in the book.
- Instead of surveying customers on your performance, talk to customers about what is valuable to their business and how that value can be improved. Check, we did this earlier in the book.
- Instead of blending all customers together, aggregate customers of like value drivers and create business cases for segments of customers. Who knows—there may be something they all want as well. Check, we did this earlier in the book.
- Instead of leaving it up to interpretation, deliver clear customer business cases to management during capital and business planning to ensure their decisions are clearly informed by what is valuable to the customer. Check, we did this earlier in the book.
- Instead of leaving customers in a lurch on their feedback, create a plan for each customer explicitly showing their input and whether there is an initiative that matches up with their recommended value improvements. Covered in this chapter.
- Instead of thinking that all of your customers want the same thing, sell to customers differently based on what they value. Covered in this chapter.
- Instead of putting the onus on sales to create customer plans, have marketers and initiative owners directly update customer plans throughout the year that sales can use, thereby taking 95 percent of the planning and organizing work off of sales plate. Covered in this chapter.
- Instead of walking from Los Angeles to New York, take a plane. Find or build technology that makes this relatively easy and manageable. Covered in this chapter.

If you get nothing else out of this say-do gap story, we hope it is this: In order to improve execution with customers, you have to work on things that are valuable to them. In order to do that, we need to connect the dots between their input all the way through to having the sales professional walk in the door the next time with a plan that they can see themselves in. Sounds really easy and straightforward, but it is not. It is kind of like that message game— you know, where you tell someone something and have it passed on through 10 other people and then have the 10th person communicate the message? It always winds up being different than the original.

In many ways, this book has been about tightening up this chain of communication and making sure people are accountable for carrying forward the message. Let's move on to building and executing a customer plan.

Building a Plan for Your Customer

"For the execute phase, it is really about how do we take all of this information that we've put through our capital plan, with decisions about those things we will do and those we will not do, how do we take all of that and translate it back down to a customer by customer operating plan. Once again I will make reference to the system we are using, the Valkre team has built, and the system does it automatically. So once we select those things in which we are going to invest to continue driving a difference, then those plans are translated back down to each and every customer operating plan we have interviewed. That gives our field sales team the ability at the push of a button, literally, to prepare a document that they can walk into their customer with and say, we heard you, we've recorded your interview within our system, we've vetted it through the organization, and we have decided these are the things we are going to be able to do. It is also fair for us to say there are also things that are going to be on some of these lists we are not going to be able to get to. We can't do everything. But as long as we communicate with our customers, here are the things we are going to get to, but there are some things we are just not going to be

able to get to . . . That is a fair conversation. It gets us on the same page; it gets Owens Corning and the customers both engaged in value creation for the customer. To a certain extent it puts accountability on them because remember they have already told us what these things are worth. So as we make progress, they know that we know that we are creating value for them."

—Owens Corning executive

We are going to talk about two plans. The first is one that you share with your customers, which focuses on customer value creation. The second is an internal plan that not only considers customer value creation but also gets into the details of how you will capture your fair share. Before we go there, we need to take a quick look at the process flow diagram.

The Process of Building Plans

While the makeup of "Customer Value Creation Plans" is simple and functional, they do not get made by themselves. What you should know about building customer plans is that it is not as linear as a process flow map would lead you to believe. So we do not follow this map, shown in Figure 7.2, exactly in this chapter but it is still a good reference.

An easier way for you to think of constructing the plan is to consider its parts. The customer plan is made up of five major sections:

1. What you said.
2. What are we going to do and what it is worth to the customer in dollars and cents?
3. Other things we are doing to create value for the customer.
4. What are we not going to do?
5. What is the status of our actions?

The plan that is designed for your internal usage looks much the same but contains one additional section. That section, of course, is what is in it for you. So in the next few paragraphs we build the customer plan and finish by discussing what is in it for you. Before

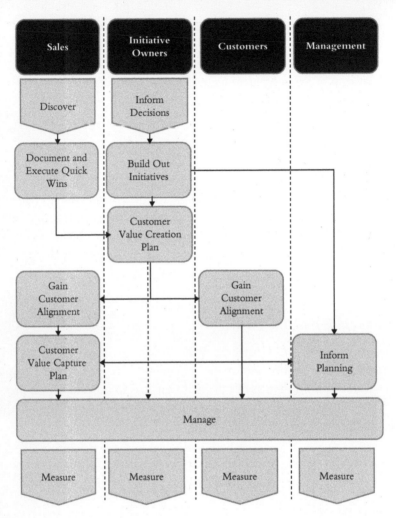

Figure 7.2   Execute Process Flow

we start discussing the plan, we need to apologize for the figures. A book is not a good format to show actual plan figures, tables, and so forth.

What You Said

You have seen what is shown in Figure 7.3 before. This is the first page of the customer plan. We use this page to reestablish with customers

Differential Value Summary
AAA Industries: Widget Contractor

Differential Value Proposition

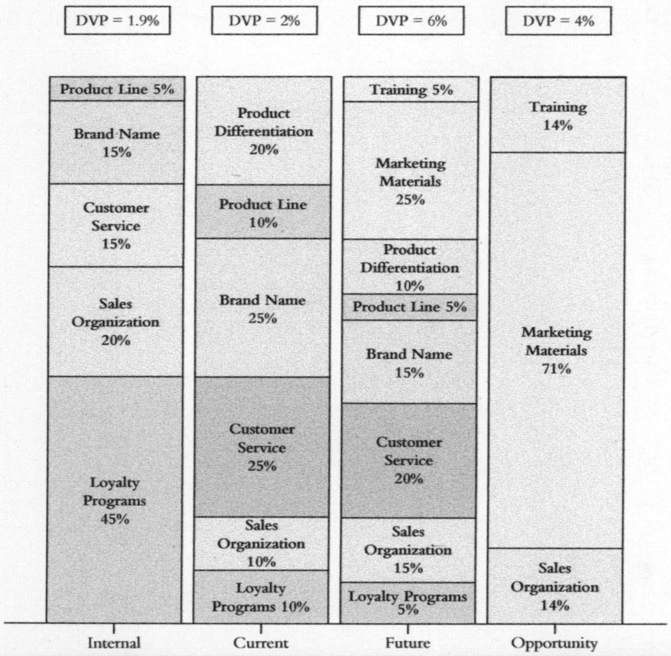

Value Creation Opportunities

Marketing Materials
• With the economy slowing down, need the necessary materials to close a customer when the opportunity arises

Sales organization
• Starting to become respectable. Maybe time to take a strategic approach to down channel selling, rather than a mass market approach.

Training
• Could use some technical training on your products. Would help us sell through the value.

DVP = 1.9%	DVP = 2%	DVP = 6%	DVP = 4%
Product Line 5%		Training 5%	Training 14%
Brand Name 15%	Product Differentiation 20%	Marketing Materials 25%	
Customer Service 15%	Product Line 10%	Product Differentiation 10%	
		Product Line 5%	Marketing Materials 71%
Sales Organization 20%	Brand Name 25%	Brand Name 15%	
Loyalty Programs 45%	Customer Service 25%	Customer Service 20%	
	Sales Organization 10%	Sales Organization 15%	Sales Organization 14%
	Loyalty Programs 10%	Loyalty Programs 5%	
Internal	Current	Future	Opportunity

Figure 7.3 Customer Plan

289

what they told us in the beginning. We have gone through the interpretation of these figures earlier so we will just focus on nuances of
the plan itself at this point. Okay, maybe a little more explanation on
numbers along the way.

On the far left, we start off with our differential value proposition. In
the second bar is what the customer saw as differentially valuable about
us currently. And the third bar shows what the customer believes we
could achieve in 18 to 24 months. To the right of the bars are the value
attributes that offer opportunity for improving your differential value
proposition along with a short description of the associated opportunity.

There is no new data in this figure. What we are really focused on
with this first page is closing the loop with the customer and setting up
a stage of accountability.

What Are We Going to Do?

In this section you detail which of the customer suggestions you
intend to execute. Take a look at Figure 7.4, "Discovery Initiatives."
For this page let's start at the top and work our way down. We
show the customers total purchases from you. The next line, "Value
Creation Opportunity," represents the opportunity to improve the
customers operating income if you were to successfully execute all
of the opportunities the customer identified. The next line, "Value
Creation Plan," shows the value of the initiatives we plan to execute.
You notice the difference. The difference represents those opportunities we will not execute. We are not going to go through the math
again on these. It was boring enough the first time when we did it
in Chapter 6, "Informing Decisions." Go back there if you need a
quick refresher.

Discovery Initiatives		Purchases: $160,000,000 Value Creation Opty: $6,400,000 Value Creation Plan: $5,485,000		Business Unit: Widgets Customer Type: Contractor Market Type: Residential		
DVD Plan $	Value Attribute	Initiative	Team	Owner	Status
$914,000	Sales Organization	Increase focus down channel to drive demand with our customer's customers.	Sales	Maria Burud	Approved
$4,571,000	Marketing Materials	Upgraded materials required to help close the sale with our customer's customers. The materials need to be simplified and widely available in all branches.	Marketing	Brian Kiep	In Progress

Figure 7.4   Discovery Initiatives

Below the financial summary is a short list and description of the initiatives you intend to execute. Each initiative contains the value to the customer, the value attribute of focus and initiative description, the team and owner responsible, and finally a status.

From a data perspective, this page is not hard to complete. You need the customer's total purchases from your company and the decisions management made on which initiatives are going to be executed. Something that is really important to note is that this is not necessarily the sales professional putting this plan together. This is marketing or a business analyst. We actually prefer marketing because it gets them engaged with sales and customer planning. There is an element that generally is sales-related and that is quick wins. If there was something the customer suggested that does not require management decision, then sales can move directly into execution and document it here as a quick win.

Other Initiatives

This is an important portion of the plan. You can see in Figure 7.5, "Other Initiatives," that the format remains similar to the initiatives that are in plan. If you think about the plan so far, it includes "Here is what you said," and based on what you said, "Here is what we are doing." And now here are a few other things we think you should at least know about. There are several subtle and maybe not so subtle things happening right here.

First, the plan starts with what is important to the customer. This customer obviously belonged to a segment of customers that wanted similar things that allowed us to take action on some of their recommendations. So we are now selling to them on a segmented basis based on what they value. But there are other things we are going to do

![VALKRE logo] Other Initiatives

Value Attribute	Initiative	Team	Owner	Status
Loyalty Programs	Implementing Loyalty Program Website to simplify management of account and rewards	Marketing	Jeff Navach	In Progress

Figure 7.5   Other Initiatives

as a company. Some of those things were driven by other segments of customers and some are initiatives we are executing that were not informed by customers at all ... maybe from our own deep R&D research. In this section, we inform the customer of those other actions. This is a great place to cover with your customer what other groups of customers see as being important to their businesses. This is always an interesting conversation. They may see these actions and determine that they are also important to their businesses. It is possible the customer will opt into these other initiatives and redraw what is differentially valuable to them. Now you are having the right conversation!

From a data perspective, there is nothing new here. This is just a matter of including initiatives that are already moving into execution and showing them in the customer plan. We normally start by having marketing determine the initial list and then have individual sales professional decide if they would like to add or delete additional initiatives.

What Are We Not Doing?

These are opportunities you decide to do nothing about. Rather than ignore your customer's thoughts, it is only fair to let the customer know why these opportunities are not being pursued at this time, if known. Often, this is because there is not a business case to justify the investment required to execute. Other times, however, the actions required do not fit with the strategic direction of your company. In any case, it is important to let the customer know why. Figure 7.6, "Opportunities Not in Plan," provides a snapshot on what we are not doing. We call these opportunities rather than initiatives because we are not moving into action. They continue to still just be opportunities for action. Maybe they will become initiatives next year.

Opportunities Not In Plan				
VALKRE				
Value Attribute	Opportunity	DVD Opty $	Reasoning	Contact(s)
Training	Could use some technical training on your products. Would help us sell through the value.	$914,000	Would require 3rd Party Training Curriculum Development. Will Consider at future time due to size of investments.	Bob Jackson & Sally Jones

Figure 7.6   Opportunities Not in Plan

Status of Our Actions

The final section of the plan provides initiative detail, as shown in Figure 7.7, "Initiative Detail." In this case, you can see one of the initiatives, a brief description, initiative owner, actions taken, status, start date, and percent completion along with additional notes.

This starts by ensuring each Initiative is assigned to the right people in the organization and communication is in place such that the Initiative Owners know it. Without full alignment on who owns what, you are in for a major headache trying to keep everyone aligned.

Once the owners are identified, these individuals need to be held accountable for updating the Initiatives to reflect the decisions made. If the decision is to not act on a given Initiative, it is important to detail the reason why. This provides sufficient transparency throughout the organization while providing the sales organization with the necessary information to keep the customer involved in the process.

For each initiative that is going to be acted on, the owner needs to provide enough detail that informs the rest of the organization of the anticipated timeline and progress. These items, which we call actions, should be at a high level and should provide enough information that enables the sales force to keep the customer informed. Remember, the goal of the plan is to help the organization execute while making sure your organization gets the credit for the investments that you are making. The goal is not to develop project plans to manage each initiative, but

VALKRE	Initiative Detail for Upgraded materials required to help close the sale with our customer's customers. The materials need to be simplified and widely available in all branches.		

Owner	Team	Status	Value Drivers
Brian Kiep	Marketing	In Progress	

Action	Team	Owner	Status	Start Date	% Complete
Focus Group to define material requirements	Marketing	Maria Burud	Completed	1/1/2009	100%
Designs created and submitted to graphics firm	Marketing	Jeff Navach	In Progress	3/1/2009	0%
Materials produced and distributed to customers	Sales	Bill Hass	Not Started	10/1/2009	0%
Customer Focus Group to determine effectiveness	Marketing	Maria Burud	Not Started	1/1/2010	0%

Note	Date Added	From
We've approved basic concepts for new marketing materials. Expect to see samples by 6/1/09.	10/19/2009	Brian Kiep
Focus Group Completed on 1/1/2009. Results were fantastic as we were able to design 10 new potential marketing assets that are simple and effective. Next steps include working with graphical design firms for mock-ups.	10/19/2009	Brian Kiep

Figure 7.7   Initiative Detail

rather to give the sales force sufficient updates that inform the customer of progress.

When it comes to maintaining status and managing the plan, there are two particular players we need to discuss in more detail: Initiative Owners and Sales Professionals.

Initiative Owners Who are they? You know them. They are people spread throughout your organization. They manage supply chain initiatives, customer service improvements, product development, quality improvements in manufacturing, and more. It is harder to come up with a functional part of your organization who would not at some time or another be involved in managing a project to improve your differentiated value proposition. Many of these people have never met a customer; some do not know the sales force all that well. They all want to contribute to the success of the company, create value for the customer, and help to capture your fair share. You must get them involved! This group combined with the sales force is the leverage and fabric of the company.

You are going to get them involved by exposing them directly to customer plans and expecting them to update those plans on a routine basis by making them accountable for the "Initiative Detail" section, which is shown in Figure 7.7. Yes, instead of having sales wade through hundreds of e-mail looking for and consolidating updates we are going to have the Initiative Owners take on this accountability. The Initiative Owner is going to update the customer plans directly with the aid of technology we mentioned in the last section. The key is to get the Initiative Owners to communicate in a shorthand that lets customers and sales know they are on the task without writing a book. Sometimes this takes a little training, but the rewards are worth it.

If you have ever been an Initiative Owner you know the drill. You are assigned a project. You are told the project is important to customers but you are not really sure why or to what extent. You are assigned a team, a budget, and everything else involved with running a project. Part of your project includes a communication plan. Maybe the plan is for you to update sales once per month. So when that time rolls around, you send a mass e-mail out to the sales organization. Some of the sales professionals read the update, some do not. I saw a statistic the other day that said sales reads about 30 percent of the e-mail they receive from corporate . . . Probably high! In any case, you never feel comfortable that sales is being updated, or worse, updating the customer on this important initiative you are accountable to deliver.

Well, in our world that is about to change. We look to Initiative Owners to update customer plans directly and to be held accountable to making these updates in a timely, communicative, and clear fashion. Now instead of searching the e-mail for updates, sales simply hits their customer plan technology button and prints a plan that contains the updates that her organization has been executing against. If you have three calls to make tomorrow, then hit three customer plan buttons.

You would not believe how much accountability this creates, how much the communication improves, and how many work hours are eliminated from the process. From an accountability perspective, the Initiative Owners now feel they are directly accountable to the customers. All it takes is one or two pieces of customer feedback to an initiative owner on the poor quality of their updates to cause them to gain a whole new appreciation that there is really a customer on the other end of this string. Right along with accountability goes clarity of communication. The Initiative Owners can no longer use the excuse that sales did not communicate properly or adequately. The ownership is now squarely on the Initiative Owner to communicate in a fashion that is meaningful and gets across their message. Finally, the work hours are eliminated. Think about the wasted time that is involved with having those in your organization write long e-mails to sales about their projects, then having each sales professional read and transcribe this information so they can update the customer. Never mind the consistency of the transcription! We are talking massive hours of potential time savings.

So the Initiative Owners play a critical role in our approach to winning with customers. A role they want to play. A role they have been playing anyway. But now we are giving them a better framework from which to win.

Sales Professionals If you are a sales professional, we are talking directly to you at this point. You have three sales calls to make tomorrow in Philadelphia. Each of the customers is important to your territory.

Quick, do you have plans for each? Are they updated with the best information your company has to offer? Are they each grounded in what that customers feels is valuable to them? Do you know how much your plan is worth to the customer's business? Do you have a plan for improving your own value capture (share, price, etc.)? Does the customer buy into the plan? Have they ever seen the plan? Do your plans look professional and consistent one to the next? Can you communicate how the plans relate to your differential value proposition? Well, we hope so because it turns out your COO is in town and wants to ride around to see these customers with you.

We have both been in this position. This is hard work! Sometimes you do not get to it all and your relationships and pure sales acumen have to carry the day. And you make it work. But would you like it to be easier? Would you like to get all of this blocking and tackling off your plate so you could devote more time to thinking critically about positioning with the customer? Well, that is exactly what we are trying to do for you. We said this earlier in the book but we have covered enough ground now to make this point more explicit. By and large, we aim to take planning off your plate and put it back on the organization whose job it is to work, day in and day out, to change or improve the value proposition you are tasked to sell. We want you to focus on selling it and to understand why we are working on what we are working on.

This is why you were tasked upfront to lead the initial customer discovery interview. No third party was involved, no random questionnaire was sent to your customer without your knowledge, and you gathered and organized the input from your customer and submitted it to your company in a manner that was consistent with a hundred of your colleagues. It might have taken you about two hours to complete and in the process you were learning about your customer and doing something different than your competition! In return for your two hours of work, you are now going to get a plan—the plan we have been building toward for this entire book.

Now you have a plan that has fundamentally been built by your entire organization. This is the right way to do it because your entire organization's sole job is to create differential value for your customer. Management has been involved with making decisions that inform your plan. They understand where the input data came from. They understand the look and feel of your plan. So go get some sleep. In the morning you can print out three plans and go make the calls with the COO.

Now, after you finish your calls tomorrow, there are a few things you need to do to keep your plans up-to-date:

- Update the status on any Quick Wins.
- Add Other Initiatives that have been executed to create customer value.
- Print out the plan each time you are about to walk into a customer's office and share any updates with the Customer.

Here are three additional benefits for you that you will find useful while you are sitting at the customer table:

1. The plan is based on what the customer asked for. If the resulting actions were not successful, both you and the customer are accountable to some extent, limiting the customer's ability to hold it over your head.
2. Successes are economically rigorous and linked to the customer's bottom line. By understanding the impact to your customer's profitability, you are in a better position to collaboratively negotiate your fair share.
3. Documentation makes it difficult for customers to game Winning with Customers. If all of the work you have done is dismissed by the customer and will not provide any real reward, you will learn exactly what type of business you are dealing with. If this happens more than a couple times, it becomes apparent that your investments should be focused in another direction.

Plan Value Capture

Q: *Regarding Big Box. I understand you went through the process of understanding what the customer needed and the customer answered. In my experience, the answer is almost always tied to dollars but is not very clearly tied to actions.*

A: Jim Drew, Owens Corning, sales: *"I think there was a mutual outcome that we identified together. We then went into the planning process together to identify actions. We obviously expected something in return because we don't have unlimited funds ourselves. The point I really want to make here is that the dialogue once it is uncovered generates a lot of discussion that normally would not have happened. And it is mutual, collaborative in nature, it is action-oriented, and there are responsibilities on both sides."*

One day while reviewing the value creation plans for a segment of customers, a prominent executive stopped us and said, "Hey, all of this value creation stuff is great . . . but when do we start talking about what we get in return?" Well, now is the time. Everything we have shown so far in regard to customer planning is intended to be shared with the customer. It was all about creating value for the customer. In order to make all of this work there also needs to be something in it for you: profits! You have to get a return from the investments you make to create customer value or else the whole effort becomes a charity case.

Recall the Growth Cube, shown in Figure 7.8, that we discussed in Chapter 2, "Define Winning." This is the place where it becomes relevant. Just in case you have forgotten, here is a refresher.

In our last book, *Beyond Six Sigma, Profitable Growth through Customer Value Creation* (Plaster and Alderman, 2006), we spent considerable time

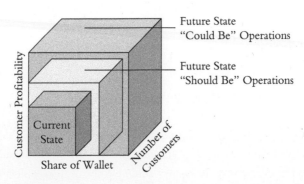

Figure 7.8   Growth Cube

discussing this profitable growth cube. The cube represents all of the customer dimensions that lead to profit improvement with customers.

The three dimensions are:

- Customer profitability
- Share of wallet
- Number of customers

The idea was that the combination of these dimensions represented the sum total of levers you could pull to increase your profits with customers. You could increase the profitability on your current business by increasing price or reducing cost to serve . . . Customer Profitability. You could increase profits by doing more business with the customer you have . . . Share of Wallet. Or you could win new customers to drive additional profits . . . Number of Customers. We had long debates on duration or the length of time you held on to customers. Duration is also an important consideration but share of wallet over time seems to be a better measure.

We are not going to spend much time re-creating the cube in this book but we have learned a few things that relate to the profit growth cube since 2006. Back in 2006, we talked about the three cube dimensions as being equally important. We suggested you should take a close inventory of your business and then decide on which dimension to work. The practical reality of our work with companies since then is suggesting there is a sequence to working on the dimensions. Now, this may be influenced by the economy we have been in since 2006 and all sorts of other factors, but given those disclaimers, here is what we have experienced.

The share of wallet seems to be the dominant dimension. If you can command ever-increasing share of the customer's wallet, it is more often than not related to your ability to deliver value to your customer. Delivering value with customers you know and do business with is the job number one. Customer profitability follows. If you are delivering good value and continue to seek ways to increase that value to customers then opportunities for improving profits at the customer relative to your competitors through price or cost-to-serve reduction is enhanced. As you are figuring out how to increase share with existing customers or maximize profits the formula to winning with new customers seems to just fall out. You will note that during the book we spend 90 percent of our time talking and working on figuring out how you create value for existing customers. But you know what happens—the outcome of this work yields an incredibly powerful approach to winning with new customers.

In our experience the results of understanding the value you deliver to customers generates four benefits in this order:

1. Increase share with existing customers (share of wallet).
2. Reduce cost to serve as you understand the levers that drive value (customer profitability).
3. Improved ability to win new customers (number of customers).
4. Ability to capture price as investments in new value are realized (customer profitability).

We have also found that different industries see themselves differently in the cube and in our work. Deal-based industries such as Technology work differently than On-Going Transaction industries such as Building Materials. This is not a black-and-white sort of difference, but nonetheless, different. In technology getting the big deal can make or break a year. There is tremendous focus on winning the deal, which tends to feel like the new customer dimension. In deal-based situations, there is little chance to work with a given customer to determine what is creating value and improve that value over the long term. For ongoing transactional customers, the entire health of the business is about improving value to that customer over the long term. Our focus is more on the latter than the former. The solution in this book has been built with those who have ongoing relationships with customers where really getting in and understanding what drives value for those customers is important.

With that as a quick refresher let's take a look at a Value Capture Plan. Remember the Capture Plan contains everything we have covered so far in the Value Creation Plan.

A Plan Just for You, Not to Share

Figure 7.9, "Value Summary," is an example of a Value Capture Plan. On the left-hand side of the example is a summary of value creation for

Value Summary

Business Unit: Widgets
Customer Type: Contractor
Market Type: Residential

VALKRE

Value Creation

	Current	Future	Opportunity
%	2%	6%	4%
$	$3,200,000	$9,600,000	$6,400,000

Current

| Product Differentiation 20% |
| Loyalty Programs 10% |
| Sales Organization 10% |
| Product Line 10% |
| Customer Service 25% |
| Brand Name 25% |

Future

| Training 5% |
| Marketing Materials 25% |
| Product Differentiation 10% |
| Loyalty Programs 5% |
| Sales Organization 15% |
| Product Line 5% |
| Customer Service 20% |
| Brand Name 15% |

Opportunity

| Training 14% |
| Marketing Materials 71% |
| Sales Organization 14% |

Value Capture

	Prior	Plan	Change vs. Prior
Sales	$160,000,000	$180,000,000	13%
GM %	25%	25%	0%
GM $	$40,000,000	$45,000,000	13%

Share

Prior Period — $457,142,857
- Unassigned 65%
- –Our– 35%

Plan — $450,000,000
- Unassigned 60%
- –Our– 40%

Height = Total Customer Purchases

Figure 7.9 Value Summary

the customer. On the right-hand side is a summary of value capture for you. In this case you can quickly see the value creation opportunity for the customer is $6.4 million while the value capture for you is $5 million (the change in Gross Margin $). You can see the value capture is being driven by share of wallet. Your sales with this customer are going from $160 million to $180 million at a constant margin of 25 percent. So in this case share of wallet is the value capture lever. If we were using price as the lever then we would expect to see our GM percent change.

This is just one customer. You could imagine this table for teams, regions, businesses all the way up to a company summary. As you summarize, you can bring the investment dollars in and see the Initiative Return on Investment.

For organizations that take a top-down approach, the Value Creation Plan at a minimum provides the road map on how to meet the financial targets identified by management. Often, however, the Value Creation portion of the plan can identify gaps in the financial plan . . . both positive and negative. For organizations that do not do customer planning, or build it from the ground up, customer by customer, the Value Creation Plan provides a great amount of information to build an accurate forecast.

Figuring Out Your Financial Driver

So how do you know if you should focus on price or share when building your value capture plan? Here's a simple example to illustrate:

- Look at the set of Initiatives and think about how they will impact the Customer's bottom line, as shown in Table 7.2. In this case it

Table 7.2   Initiative Financial Impact

Value Attribute	Initiative	Value Creation Driver	DVP Oppty $
Supply Chain	Increase plant inventory levels for top 3 SKUs	Reduce inventory	$161,000
Customer Service	Authorized direct calls to Beth Johnson	Reduce operating costs	$52,000
		TOTAL	**$213,000**

looks to be reducing customer costs and freeing up some cash by reducing inventory levels.

- Based on the Value Creation Drivers, think about how that translates to your bottom line. Reducing Costs and inventory levels do not necessarily translate into sales growth or reducing your costs. By reducing this customer's costs, you may be able to capture a higher price or gain additional share. We call these the potential Value Capture Drivers.

- Take a look at your existing financial position with this customer against the average Customer. In this case, as shown in Table 7.3, it seems the real opportunity is to win additional share.

Now that you have determined the value capture drive to be shared, translate that finding into a plan:

- Set a goal for the main Value Capture Driver. In this case, let's set a goal to increase share from 20 percent to 25 percent.
- Translate the Value Capture Goal into profits. In this case, a 5 percent increase in share amounts to an incremental $2.5 million sales, or $750,000 in incremental GM$ at a 30 percent margin.
- Calculate the Value Capture Ratio by comparing the Value Capture amount to the original Value Creation amount specified by the customer to see how much value you expect to capture for every dollar you create. In this case, we would say the expected Value Capture Ratio would be 3.5 ($750,000/$213,000), or $3.50 for every dollar of value created for the customer
- See if the Value Capture Ratio is reasonable. For example, if you plan on capturing value by increasing price, you would not expect to see a Value Capture Ratio of > = 1. Greater than one would

Table 7.3   Customer Financials versus Average

Metric	Customer Financials	Average Customer
Sales	$10,000,000	$5,000,000
Gross Margin %	30%	26%
Gross Margin $	$3,000,000	$1,300,000
Share %	20%	32%
Total Customer Purchases	$50,000,000	$15,625,000

mean the customer was worse off because they are paying more out of their pocket for the value they receive.

The benefit of going through an exercise like this is that your forecast has been informed by an outside-in Customer perspective, not just a hollow goal. A side benefit to planning Value Capture like this is you tend to see a different attribute in Sales Professionals that are typically "gatherers." The nature of forecasting Value Capture as a result of the activities you do on behalf of the customer creates an environment of "hunting" for incremental profits rather than just managing them.

Our Next Book

There is so much more material to cover on value capture. If you do a few of the simple things we have suggested, you will be ahead of the game on capturing your fair share. Capturing share gets a whole lot easier when you first recognize that you need to create value in order to capture value . . . at least in the long run. Everyone seems to want to jump right into value capture. "Hey, how do I capture more value?" It is like my kids wanting to know when they are going to get more allowance and you know what the answer is: "When you start earning it." So it is natural to spend the bulk of this book on finding out what customers value. As a result, you will capture share and find areas where you can reduce cost. Moving on to use this information to increase price and win new customers is the subject of our next book.

Gain Customer Alignment

"So as we continue to work with customers to exercise the plan we have put on a page one other thing happens and that is the customers themselves become enrolled in the process. They have some account-ability because we have already aligned on what they want us to do; we've already aligned on what they said it is worth. When we present the plan to them we actually, in somewhat of a provocative way include

in the plan the dollar amount that customer said the plan would be worth. So that gives us the means to very much stay on the same page with the customer. We are in action in accordance with the plan we have aligned with them and we are staying on the same page relative to the value being created for the customer."

—Bob Harlan, Director of Business Insights,
Owens Corning

Now that we have a plan, it is time to get back to the customer. We will tell you at this point this whole process goes from something that may have seemed like a good exploratory mission to something that is real. Customers are surprised. They were originally surprised when you talked to them in the first place about how you could help them to make more money. Now they are falling off their chair surprised at the follow up. They are surprised at the organization. They are surprised that their feedback has been baked into your plan for them. All of a sudden they start to feel some sense of accountability. Goes like this: "Wholly smokes, these guys are about to do something I suggested would help my business. I better make sure it actually does." It is really quite something to watch this happen and talk about separating yourself from the competition.

When sitting down with the customer, you can often learn just as much as you did during the Discovery Interview. First of all, your organization will have already started to differentiate itself by taking the time to organize this information in a personalized plan. This helps reinforce the fact to the customer that all of this is more than just market research or a customer loyalty study. As a result, there may be more value creation opportunities identified. Second, the CVC Plans provide a value creation agenda built directly from the Customer's needs. By having what you plan to do on the same page with what the customer asked for, a detailed collaborative discussion focused on getting into action will emerge . . . light years away from a meeting in which you push your agenda.

The "Opportunities Not in Plan" and "Other Initiatives" section of the Plan also become powerful collaboration opportunities. At first, the customer might not be thrilled to see an important Opportunity not in plan, but they will appreciate that it was not just brushed off. In fact, there might be an opportunity for you and your customer to share investment or risk to move the Opportunity into Plan. You find that covering the Other Initiatives with a customer is easier, too. By leading with the Customer's agenda, you will be in a better position to collect feedback from an engaged customer on the Initiatives that we are not necessarily informed by the Customer. As a result, you should leave a sense of alignment and gain additional feedback that can be incorporated into the plan.

Providing a Technology Assist

To close the say-do gap and effectively communicate internally, e-mail alone will not cut it. Sending an e-mail to notify the organization that customer opportunities have been identified, initiatives have been created, or actions are in place is acceptable. But using e-mail to communicate the specifics of those items is a lost cause. In many enterprise organizations, e-mail is becoming a crippling wasteland of lost ideas and reply-all banter. Using e-mail to manage anything, let alone Customer Value Creation, is as effective as sticking a Post-it note on the wall of a cluttered teenager's bedroom. Do not ever expect to see it again, remember what you wrote, or receive any response.

If an e-mail is sent, it should ideally point the reader to a centralized repository of all Customer insights and the processes it encompasses. No matter how information regarding your outside-in efforts are communicated, there is comfort in knowing it all resides in one single location or structure.

Here, software and technology can provide the solution to tracking the Actions and resources required to implement your Initiatives. It can also track your progress to deliver on your promises/initiatives to the customer. Building each customer plan with the appropriate content and accurate value creation/capture metrics and amounts is not a trivial exercise. But the ability to generate a customer plan for external or internal communication with the click of a button is an enormous benefit.

With software providing the central repository for getting into action, the entire organization can be brought together in collaboration. Marketing, finance, operations, and R&D departments can be given account access to view all the information relevant to their respective functions. The technology is not there simply for Sales to use and to benefit from.

The Vault

We do not know where this goes so we are going to put it right here. We have covered enough concepts to make this point. In case you have not noticed, we like to bring in a few random concepts. Sometimes there are constructs you would like to organize the whole book around. This is one of them.

We call this concept "The Vault." The concept is that there are a few things that we should keep in the corporate vault. These are things that really matter to your company and determine the difference between success and not success. Here are those four things:

1. *The value proposition.* This is why we believe customers should buy from us and not our competitors. We need to keep this fresh and real. Worship this thing and keep it in the vault with all of your other most cherished possessions.
2. *Customer input.* What do customers think about your value proposition? This may be the deepest and most valuable secret of all. If we are clear on our belief and understand the gaps our customers see, we have a road map for improvement or a road map for failure . . . your choice.
3. *The investment plan.* This is your plan of allocating resources to close the gaps and reinforce the positives.
4. *The customer plan.* The customer plan is where we get into action. Are we communicating and getting things done.

If you take these four documents you can tell in short order the health of an organization. Sometimes they get lost in the hustle and bustle of day-to-day business. Do not lose them—put them in a vault and look at them often! Go and try and find them for yourself right now and see if they connect.

Summary

Here is another short story from Roger Warren, Owens Corning sales, before summarizing:

> *"Let's move on to what we learned during the interview. First of all it gave us a clear understanding in the customer's words of how they thought. What did they value in us and what could we be. The value creation opportunities were very simple, behavioral and often time when you take new programs or you ask the customer what they need you are faced with a capital investment challenge. These were very small capital investment opportunities. So what did we do. Collaboratively with the customer we agreed on actions based on opportunities that we had identified during the Customer Discovery. They were as simple as training, inventory management, tools and ease of offloading products. So we enrolled the key process areas within Owens Corning. Since we had everyone internally aligned on Customer Discovery getting things done was much easier. We reported out progress to the customer on a regular basis against milestones. At the end of the project we took a measurable result and communicated them out. So what did the customer get? We created an atmosphere of partnering, that we were listening instead of telling. What did we get? We were rewarded with National Vendor of the Year against 270 of the premier brands in the United States. We maintained 100% of share and we moved to long term contracts. The Customer Discovery changed the contract conversation from a short term tactical conversation into an atmosphere that focused on partnering and driving toward a common goal of sales and profit growth."*
>
> —Roger Warren, sales, Owens Corning

In the beginning of the chapter, we suggested these as our learning objectives. How about we look at them one by one:

- Why is this approach to execution different and what are the benefits?

- Fundamentally, we have created a closed-loop process from customer input all the way through to customer plan execution. Execution and results are better when they are aligned with what the customer values.
- We have connected sales, marketing, management, and the rest of the organization in the creation and execution of customer plans. It does take a team to win with customers and the results show up in the win column.
- The process guides you to sell to customers on a segmented basis rather than using a vanilla approach yielding more targeted efforts on a customer-by-customer level.
- Investment planning and customer planning are linked thereby allowing you to track performance and return on investment. This process linkage allows you to get feedback and continuously improve.
- What does a customer plan look like?
  - Check
- How do you build customer plans out of the information we have discussed so far in the book?
  - Check, but with a few holes that just do not work in a book format
- How do customers and sales react to these plans?
  - Check
- How do you manage these plans without overloading the organization with work?
  - This was the purpose of the technology section.
- What about getting your fair share (profits) as well?
  - We started you down the path and promised a next book.
- What are the things you need to keep in the corporate vault?
  - Check

As we said in the beginning of the chapter, much of what we have discussed has been aimed at communication and accountability. Communication runs the gambit from that first conversation with the customer to sitting down with them and reviewing the plan and everything in between. Accountability is created at the executive level relative to investments that are made to create customer value to sales

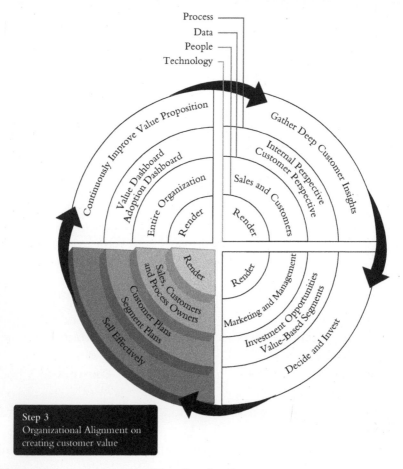

Figure 7.10   The Customer Value Creation System

managing customer plans to marketing and the rest of the organization delivering and updating initiatives. Figure 7.10 shows this chapter's place in the system, which we call "Customer Value Creation." Selling effectively by creating and documenting customer value to capture your fair share comes from building collaborative customer and segment plans directly informed by Discovery Interviews and the resulting Analysis. By doing so, we are ready to tackle Step 4 of the system to measure value to provide insights into future profits and competitive advantage driven by continuous improvement.

Chapter 8

The Scoreboard

There was a young business man who bought a farm that came with a trusty horse. After one long weekend their conversation went like this: Well, I've observed some very effective features of you being a horse," said the businessman/part-time farmer. "You work diligently and faithfully and with good-humor and, if I may ask . . . can you think of any ways of pulling the plow a little faster?"

"No!" said the horse. "I said give me the 'feedbag' not 'feedback.'"

Sorry to say there is no feedbag that goes along with this chapter. It is, however, a chapter about feedback, measurement, and continuous improvement. The Big 6—Playbook Map tells us this has something to do with predicting profit growth. A crystal ball on future profits! That might be overselling the case just a tad but it is the path we are heading down.

If you are a student of decision making, you already know the importance of this section. In order to improve a process, you need to have a feedback loop. At first, the feedback tends to create course process adjustment. Over time, and as you become expert, the adjustments become more like fine-tuning. The beauty of what we have done so far is to create a system that is measureable and capable of receiving feedback.

> *"This really becomes a part of how we look as this data, how do we at Owens Corning look at what we've done for our customer regards building value for them and how do we get into action around trying to capture some of that value. This leads to a very virtuous cycle, which says the more value we create the greater the opportunity for us to capture value. That simply said is the essence of Winning with our Customers. They Win, We Win."*

—Owens Corning Management

This is one of those chapters that could get really crazy with the regressions, correlations, and statistics that some people are telling us would be really cool. Where do these people come from? We are not going there. Our aim is to keep this reasonably simple, as the concept we aim to emphasize is quite straightforward. We will just add the elements of time and continuous improvement to things we have already discussed. If we measure value creation for the customer and value capture over time, you can start to see the relationship between the two. You get better at understanding what investments work, how the meaning of your value proposition changes in good economic times and bad, the lag times between investment and return, and more. As these pictures evolve, you improve your next decision and the relation between investment, value creation and value capture tightens. It is no different than the feedback loop to any other process. This is similar to investing in your house: There is good information out there suggesting that an investment in updating your kitchen or bathroom has a higher return than putting in a new pool. Through this process you are trying to build this similar understanding for your company.

After reading this chapter you will be able to:

- Successfully measure the value you create for your customers.
- Determine whether you are capturing your fair share from the investments you make.
- Track CVC activity in your organization to ensure continuous improvement.

Finding Our Place on the Field

Consider the CVC Stadium again for a moment, shown in Figure 8.1. Measurement is the scoreboard. You can also think of it as the chains along the field. You can think of it as the statistics of the game and from one game to the next.

The scoreboard, in this case, tells you how well you are doing compared to your competition. It provides feedback on whether you are winning or losing with your customers. Over time, if your score is

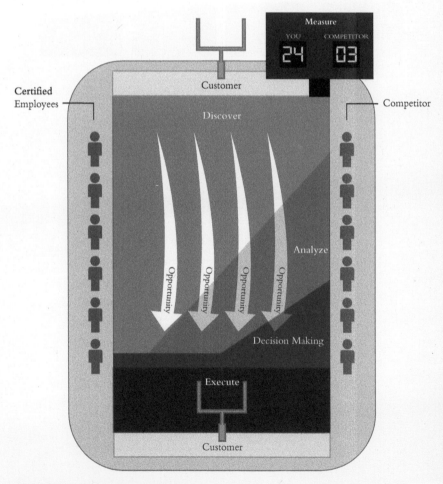

Figure 8.1 The CVC Stadium

continually lower than the competitors, you will understand the business is at risk. The goal of measuring is to continually understand how effectively you are creating value for your customers, and to make sure you are capturing your fair share of the profits all in the context of your competitors.

The Process

In Figure 8.2, we represent the basic process structure for creating your measurement scoreboard. You can see that we are going to

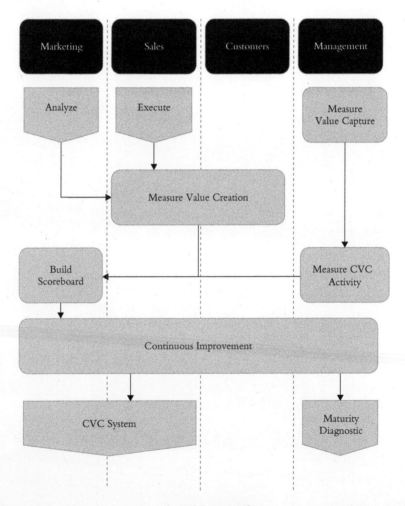

Figure 8.2   Measurement Scoreboard Process Flow

measure ongoing value creation with your sales force and customers. Like we said earlier, this is not a one-and-done deal. Management is going to let us know how we did with value capture. Management is also going to let us know how diligent we have been with the CVC process. Then we will bring these perspectives together, reflect, and map out a path of improvement in our ongoing journey of Customer Value Creation.

Collecting the Scorecard Data

Well, as it turns out, the scorecard does not build itself. We need some data. Let's go get some.

Measuring Value Creation

You did not think you could measure progress without involving the customer did you? Just as with the initial interviews with a customer, it is imperative to gather an outside-in perspective on the value you have created. To successfully measure value creation, we need to identify how well we executed against the original plan. The way outside-in measurement happens is with Ongoing Discovery Interviews that look and feel like the original customer discussions but now are a combination of measurement and discovery. These ongoing Discovery Interviews are the value creation dialogue with your customer, which provides data on the progress you have made since the last conversation and also allows you to reset the value creation road map going forward. Here is how to prepare and execute one of these discussions.

In the first Discovery Interview, the interview team goes in prepared with an Internal Hypothesis on the value you create for a segment of customers, not for each one. This time, you will go into the interview with what the customer said was valuable last time, along with the progress you made on the suggested improvement road map. The benefit of interviewing a customer the second or third time is that you now have the data necessary to build an Interview that builds off the last discussion rather than starting from scratch.

Figure 8.3 shows how you can summarize what the customer said and what you did about it on one page.

Value Creation Progress

Business: Widgets
Market: Residential

Last Interview Date: 10/14/2009

DVP = 2%		DVP = 6%

Bar chart categories (Current / Future):

- Training 5%
- Product Differentiation 20% / Marketing Materials 25%
- Loyalty Programs 10%
- Sales Organization 10% / Product Differentiation 10%
- Product Line 10% / Loyalty Programs 5%
- Sales Organization 15%
- Customer Service 25% / Product Line 5%
- Customer Service 20%
- Brand Name 25% / Brand Name 15%

Current — Future

DVP:	2%	6%

Value Creation Opportunities

Opportunity	Initiatives
Marketing Materials With the economy slowing down, need the necessary materials to close a customer when the opportunity arises	• Upgraded materials required to help close the sale with our customer's customers. The materials need to be simplified and widely available in all branches.
Sales Organization Starting to become respectable. Maybe time to take a strategic approach to down channel selling, rather than a mass market approach.	• Increase focus down channel to drive demand with our customer's customers
Training Could use some technical training on your products. Would help us sell through the value.	**None:** Would require 3rd Party Training Curriculum Development. Will consider at future time due to size of investments.

Other Initiatives

Loyalty Programs	Implementing Loyalty Program Website to simplify management of account and rewards

Figure 8.3 Value Creation Progress

That is it! The process after an ongoing Discovery session is the same. Document your notes and get them back in front of the Customer as soon as possible to verify their perspective. The new data will be fed into new data analysis processes and new "Value Creation Plans" will be built. The side benefit to all of this is that now you have developed a time-based picture of how your DVP is evolving with this customer. As you are about to see, combining this DVP data over time with your own internal financials generates powerful insights that can help predict the investments your customers need rather than just reacting to them.

One final thought on the people side of these Ongoing Discovery Interviews: Even though the agenda and objectives of Ongoing Discovery Interviews are the same, the conversation will be drastically different. First, both your organization and the customer will have already established a working language of value creation. Second, the data available in the conversation will be more robust. These two factors generally decrease the amount of preparation and transition the "interview" into a collaborative investment conversation. Having a common language and data to support also supports greater customer accountability for the resulting dataset. Customers that try and game the system or dismiss the efforts you put into creating customer value will have a much harder time doing so. Customers that continue to try and commoditize your relationship in the face of the data will reveal their true colors during these ongoing interviews and you will learn what not to trust about their perspective.

Measuring Value Capture

The next component to building a scoreboard that drives continuous improvement and informs strategic planning is your internal financials. In Chapter 6, "Informing Decisions," we covered the financial data required to analyze the Discovery Interview dataset . . . The same financials are used to measure progress, as shown in Table 8.1. At a customer level, you are going to want to know Sales, Gross Margin $, and Share. With these three metrics, you can calculate Gross Margin % and the total purchases a customer makes from both you and your competitors. Across all customers, you are going to want to know what the average customer looks like. Note that customer financials should be collected as actuals that coincide with your traditional fiscal calendar.

Table 8.1   Customer Financials

Metric	Customer Financials	Average Customer
Sales	$10,000,000	$5,000,000
Gross Margin %	30%	26%
Gross Margin $	$3,000,000	$1,300,000
Share %	20%	32%
Total Customer Purchases	$50,000,000	$15,625,000

In addition to collecting the data on a Customer Level, it makes sense to assemble the same metrics at a DVP level. This means that you should know your Sales, Profit, and Share Position at the level you are measuring Value Creation. By having this information accessible year over year at a DVP level, you can begin to establish organic changes in the market place. This is especially helpful when trying to distinguish if the improvements you have made to your bottom line are a result of Customer Value Creation or a symptom of general market changes.

Building the Basic Scoreboard

Once the data is collected, it is time to turn that data into an informational scoreboard. Rather than just showing a few charts and graphs, we try to get the idea across in a short story. This story is about measuring value with a particular customer but it could just as well have been a segment of customers or a whole business. The concepts are similar enough for you to get the point.

A Scoreboard Story Setup

This scoreboard story we are about to tell is real. We cannot reveal the names due to the confidential nature of the situation. It is not the most exceptional story we know of or have experienced, but it is strong.

Our story starts with the graphic shown in Figure 8.4. This graphic is one of the more basic and highly used that companies like.

Let's spend time just talking about what is contained in this figure. There are three years of data, 2007 through 2009. There are six stacked bars, two for each year. The first bar in the pair represents the

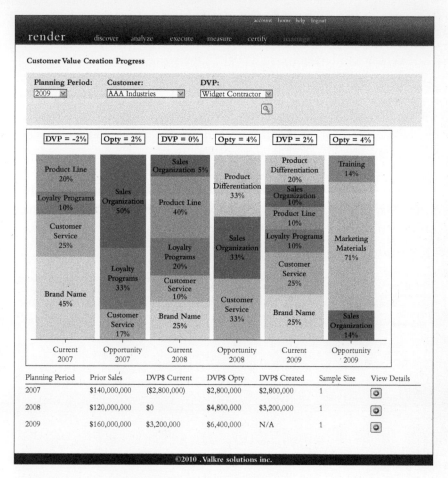

Figure 8.4 Customer's Value Creation Scoreboard

current value being created for a customer, segments of customers, or an entire business. The second bar, Opportunity, represents the road map of improvement from the customer's perspective. The opportunity bar is developed as the difference between the current and future perspectives. Along the top are the DVP%. The first bar has a -2 percent DVP and an opportunity DVP% of 2 percent, meaning our goal for the year from the customer perspective is to get to competitive parity or a DVP of zero percent.

Along the bottom is the financial meaning to your customer. In the Prior Sales column you can see that in 2007 this particular customer purchased $140 million. Under the DVP$ Current column you were negatively impacting the customers operating income by $2.8 million (2 percent of $140 million). The DVP$ Oppty suggests that the customer has created an improvement road map to improve your performance by $2.8 million. And finally, the DVP$ created shows your performance for the year from your customer's perspective; in this case, you created the full $2.8 million for this customer in 2007. Now we add the dimension of time, 2008 and 2009, and measure the change.

Before we start adding color to the story, let's bring in the other side of the equation, your profits. Most of our basic scoreboards use Gross Margin $ as a proxy for this measure. Figure 8.5 shows the actual profit performance that goes along with Figure 8.4.

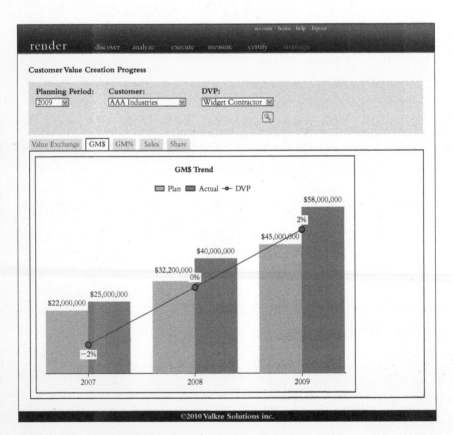

Figure 8.5   Gross Margin $ Trend

This figure is straightforward. Once again we have the years of 2007, 2008, and 2009 and six bars, three pairs of two. The first bar represents your planned GM$ for the account. The planned GM$ takes into consideration market growth, price increases/decreases, and other market factors not associated with customer value creation. The second bar represents the actual GM$ for the account in 2007. The line depicts your DVP% for each of the years. This is your value capture picture.

The Scoreboard Story

Now the story: The year was 2007. You had a large customer with whom things were not going so well. At $140 million this customer was important to the business . . . duh. The relationships were good with the customer but the underlying business performance was stagnant. Sorry, we cannot show you the prior years, but take our word for it. To say that the business was stagnant is an optimistic appraisal of the situation. Characterizing it as a disaster might be closer to the truth.

In 2007, a discovery interview was conducted. The result was a -2 percent DVP. In other words, the customer felt it was losing about $2.8 million by doing business with you relative to a competitive alternative. Ouch! At that time, your GM$ were about $22 million on sales of $140 million or 15.7 percent; 15.7 percent gross margin was lower than your average customer. The customer painted a road map to get back to competitive parity, a DVP improvement of 2 percent. The customer identified three things to work on: Sales Organization, Loyalty Programs, and Customer Service. As you know from earlier chapters, there was much more detail under these three ideas, but we will leave them at a high level for purposes of this scorecard chapter. You worked on these three things during the course of the year and then conducted another discovery interview early in 2008.

During the 2008 discovery interview, you found that the customer had realized results from your work. The company now saw you as being on par with competition and realized the full 2 percent gain of $2.8 million in operating income improvement. This customer was no slouch when it came to measuring its vendors; the improvement numbers were calculated straight from their financial data. On your side of the ledger, GM$ improved from $22 million to $25 million, for an improvement of $3 million. Sales dropped during 2007 by $20 million. The drop in sales was consistent with the path you had been on with this customer and the sales drop was not changed during the year, as the customer had made commitments to other vendors that were performing. The good news was that you were able to get margins up; $25 million on $120 million in sales yielded just over 20 percent, which was in line with your average.

So for 2007, the customer improved its bottom line by $2.8 million and your gross margin dollars improved by $3 million. We define a value capture ratio as your value capture divided by your customer's improvement, or in this case $3 million divided by $2.8 million for a value capture ration of 1.07. Pretty dang good!

During that same interview in early 2008, you can see that the customer's view on your differential value proposition changed. Sales Organization now shows up in your DVP. Loyalty programs went from 10 percent of your DVP in 2007 to 20 percent now in early 2008. You did not do as well with Customer Service, which actually dropped from 25 percent to 10 percent. Luckily, Customer Service was the least heavily weighted on the opportunity list. Net, net you made good improvements and achieved a DVP% improvement of 2 percent, which is really strong. More important, the customer has given you a strong DVP% improvement road map of 4 percent. This would yield an improvement to the customers operating income of $4.8 million. The 4 percent road map is driven by improvements in Product Differentiation, Sales Organization, and Customer Service. You will note in this road map that Loyalty has dropped off. You have made the necessary improvements. Customer Service and Sales Organization continue on from 2007 as opportunities and a new opportunity has been introduced in the way of Product Differentiation.

And so you execute 2008. In early 2009, you go back to the customer for you third formal customer discovery interview. With your customer, you look back at a good year of performance in a difficult market. Sales between your companies were back up to $160 million, reversing a several-years-long declining trend. Of the $4.8 million DVP improvement road map the customer realized $3.2 million. On sales of $160 million, this now represents a full DVP% of 2 percent. You are now outperforming the competition, although not by much. Remember, you would like to see a 4 percent DVP. For your part, gross margin dollars went from a planned level of $32 million to $40 million. Gross Margin % is now a healthy and above average 25 percent. You captured $8 million above plan versus the customer value creation of $3.2 million for a value capture ratio of 2.5, which is remarkable. As a side comment, a value capture ration above 2 is not all that uncommon. There is something about focusing on helping your customers to make money that creates rewards that are multiplicative in their returns.

Note again that your DVP has changed from the customer perspective in the beginning of 2009. Product Differentiation has gone from nonexistent to a full 20 percent of your value proposition. The Sales Organization factor showed continuous improvement going from 5 to 10 percent. And Customer Service really came around, by going from 10 percent to 25 percent. The customer also painted another great DVP% improvement road map for 2009 of 4 percent. This year, the road map is composed of Training, Marketing Materials, and Sales Organization. In 2009, the desire for Training and Marketing Materials are a direct result of the differentiated products that were developed and introduced in 2008. The continued emphasis on Customer Service that continues to thread through is a direct result of poor market conditions and the reliance of the customer on customer service to manage inventories.

The results for 2009 are not in as of this writing but the early indications are positive. So step back for a moment. Eighteen million dollars of margin improvement in two years, reversal of sales decline, and a customer who is actively engaged in helping you to create value creation road maps. Yes, there were investments. As this case currently stands, the ROI is around 300 percent. Not bad at all! I would personally contend that ROI is not even the right measure for developing a capability within an organization to carry out this kind of effort. The measure should be something about winning in the game or as the craft of a business professional.

More Points on This Story

Consider for a moment if you had these statistics through good markets and bad. You would be able to see how your customers value your products and services differently depending on market conditions. We have certainly seen this during the past few years. If you only knew how the value proposition was going to change, you could anticipate the customers' shifting needs and stay ahead of their changing demand and, more important, stay ahead of competitors.

You can start to see the need for a philosophy of continuous improvement. The power really comes from measuring year over year what is a reflection of Discovery, Analysis, Decision Making, and Execution. It is also a reflection on the capability of your people. It has been proven a million times that measurement is key to improvement. Whether you are working with patient outcomes or athletic feats, measurement and visibility of those measures is a necessary ingredient for improvement. In order to improve, you must measure over time and strive for continuous improvement.

One customer at a time is at work. Sure, we are going to measure at all levels, by sales rep, by division, by region, by business unit, and at the company level. But execution occurs one customer at a time. Being able to communicate and understand at the customer level what is happening with value creation and value capture is fundamental to our playbook.

When it comes to managing the business, executives are always searching for understanding of how their investments and strategies result in tangible value creation to customers with resulting financial improvement to their own bottom line. For sales professionals who are always tasked with explaining why a particular customer's profit contribution went up or down, they now have a coordinated measure to explain the customer's viewpoint. Being able to correlate and measure value creation and value capture has implications that are far reaching for an organization.

Advanced Scoreboard Topics

These topics are not so much advanced as they are just ideas that may go on your scorecard. Similar to the Chapter 6, "Informing Decisions," we touch on a few powerful views and insights that can be achieved when you combine Value Creation, Value Capture, and the element of time. Keep in mind that these views can be built Customer by Customer, across all of your customers, and any segment of customers in between.

How Has Our DVP Changed?

Wouldn't it be a boring world if our value proposition never changed? Well fortunately or unfortunately, your differential value proposition is not static. What is valuable to the market and to your customers changes over time. Your job is to make sure your company understands the changes and manages communication and investment to stay ahead of those changes and to ensure that your organization is on the same page. One of the fascinating things we have learned in the past few years is the dynamic nature of a value proposition. Getting really good at managing a value proposition is a capability that you do not hear enough about.

In the example shown in Figure 8.6, you have a track record built with a particular customer. This is your track record on the relevance of your organization with a given customer. Moving a DVP% from a

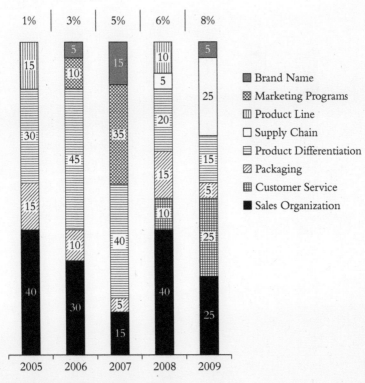

Figure 8.6 Customer DVP over Time

near commodity in 2005 to becoming a value-added partner in 2009 is a big deal, and you should be rewarded for this. If your game is Value Pricing, you need pictures like this to justify the acceptance of price increases. Additionally, images like these create continuity in ongoing relationships in the event of Sales Turnover. When a new Sales Rep takes over an account, this picture says a thousand words. Same goes for a change in management. A good executive when starting out in his or her first 90-day plan should grasp what the organization's competitive advantage is. This one picture goes a long way to speeding up that understanding.

Another critical measurement understands how customer needs have changed and shaped your DVP over the years, as shown in Figure 8.7. This is easily done by lining up the Value Creation Opportunity stacked bars over time. Besides understanding a key driver of

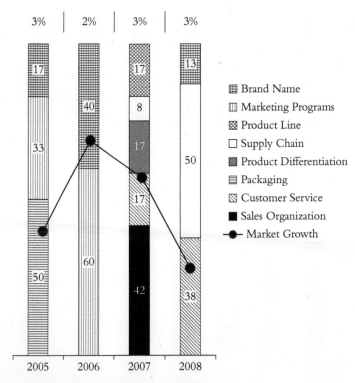

Figure 8.7 Customer Opportunity over Time

how your DVP has evolved, measuring changing customer needs begins to equip your organization with a predictive capability by looking for correlations with other factors. For example, plotting Market Growth against Customer Needs begins to provide insights into what your role should be in a customer's organization as markets ebb and flow. In this example, you start to see requests for investments in Marketing Programs and Brand Names when the market is growing while investments such as Customer Service and Supply Chain become more important as the market slows. This makes intuitive sense, but the availability of data helps bring clarity in efforts to see around the corner.

Are We Being Rewarded for the Value We Create?

The whole point of creating customer value is to be rewarded for it. Measuring progress along both dimensions over time can provide an assessment of your management team as to how well value capture is

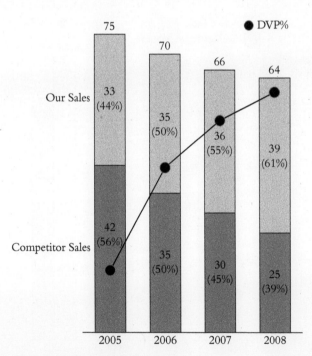

Figure 8.8 Capturing Share over Time

being managed. Assembling views to do this is simple . . . just plot the DVP% against all of your key metrics in a fashion that they can be evaluated simultaneously.

Figure 8.8 is an example on Capturing Share at a Business Unit Level. In 2005, you had a dominant 44 percent market share, but the market has contracted since then. Over the course of the years, the DVP% has increased, allowing you to capture more market share. In this case, your sales have increased by $6 million in a market that has shrunk by $11 million. That is how "Winning with Customers" works.

Do not stop by looking only at share . . . A look at your profitability levels as you capture market share is critical as well. At the end of the game, what pays our bills is not market share—it is the cold hard cash generated by profits.

Take a look at the example in Figure 8.9.

In this case, average profits actually dipped or held flat for a few years as the DVP% was strengthened. Finally, by 2008, margins caught

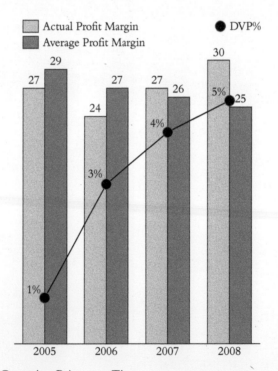

Figure 8.9   Capturing Price over Time

up with a rising DVP% and jumped by almost 10 percent. In this example, the organization was able to capture its fair share of the value created . . . It just comes in different ways over time. At first, it meant maintaining sales in a declining market leading to capturing a higher price once a dominant share position was established.

This same thought process should be applied on a customer-by-customer basis as well. Remember our Winning with Customers 2x2 charts discussed earlier, which classify customers as a Partner Opportunity, Risk, or Transaction? Well, the charts come in handy when tracking the correlation between the value you create and the value you capture over the years. Again, this is easily done by plotting your DVP% over the years by the critical internal financial performance metrics. Here is another simple example that tracks the creation and value capture path for a given customer.

Let's start by looking at customer profitability first. In Figure 8.10, it looks like an organization's investments have been aligned with this customer's economic needs given the fact that the DVP% has increased each year. However, Customer Profitability has not increased in step. It was not until 2008 that value pricing was successfully installed at this customer.

The story Figure 8.11 tells is Customer Share. As you can see, share jumped significantly after the first year.

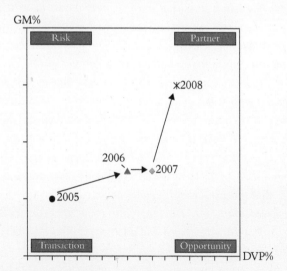

Figure 8.10   Customer Profitability 2x2 Matrix

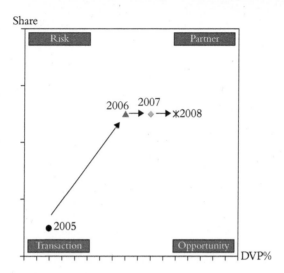

Figure 8.11   Capturing Customer Share 2x2 Matrix

No matter how the value was captured, we always recommend translating back into the metrics that gets us all paid: profit dollars.

"In the measurement phase we can start to put the whole picture together. Remember I started this by talking about the one dimensional view we had which was what our customers meant to us which was in terms of whether or not we had strong margins with that customers, did we have strong share. Now we can combine that with what we mean to them and we can actually start to see a different picture. In some cases we have a situation where we are not making money but our customer is receiving great value. This is an opportunity for us to work on capturing more of the value created. On the other hand, we've identified customers where we thought things were great, and they are great because we are receiving strong margins. But when we looked at it in terms of what we were delivering to them we discovered our value proposition was not strong. And those customers candidly are at risk. These are the customers we've found during the past two years where we have challenged ourselves, we have to get engaged and get engaged quickly or they are at risk and they could fire us. So this has informed us in both ways, situations where we have lost opportunity because we are not capturing enough and

situations where we are at risk because we are not creating enough for customers that we love."

—Owens Corning *Management*

Measuring CVC Activity for the Scoreboard

Another key aspect to measuring value creation is taking a look at Customer Value Creation activity of your organization. Having insight into what work is being done helps bridge any gaps that may appear between value creation and value capture. For example, an organization that collects a lot of data but does not do a great job of documenting the investments it makes may find that its DVP%'s continue to rise, but that it is not able to capture its fair share. Measuring the activity can also direct organizations how to scale or prioritize their Customer Value Creation. An organization that has a hundred Sales Professionals execute a hundred Discovery Interviews and build a hundred CVC Plans will reap the subsequent rewards. That is great, but would it not be better if the rewards were scaled five times? Only by understanding what is being done can you understand what it can be.

Here are some views of the data that we like to keeps tabs on and measure:

- Number of DVPs collected, organized by Business Unit, Customer Type, and Sales Team
- Number of Value Creation Initiatives built, categorized by their status (i.e., cancelled, completed)
- Number of CVC Plans built, categorized by last updated date to understanding if they are being actively managed
- Number of employees trained to lead Discovery Interviews
- Number of sales professionals trained to build and manage CVC plans

Examples

From an organizational capability perspective, after gathering and analyzing data and executing on the results, it is a good idea to assess the activity to determine how aligned your organization is with the market place. Simply put, the more customer needs consistently injected into your decision-making processes, the higher the value creation and value capture opportunity. This includes customers you directly sell to and downstream customers or influencers that you rely on to get your product or service to market.

As a way to measure the activity going on in the organization, we like to break down the market according to the "freshness" of the value creation data. In Figure 8.12, we can clearly see that 27 percent of sales have not been interviewed, while 10 percent of sales have interviews expiring in the next 90 days. Simple views like this keep an organization up-to-date on whether they have the data to create differential customer value.

Similarly, it is imperative to measure the execution aspect of Winning with Customers. A Discovery Interview is required to have a customer plan, but there is a risk that the information is not turned into a Value Creation Plan. Without keeping tabs on this information, you may find yourself asking why your organization is so good

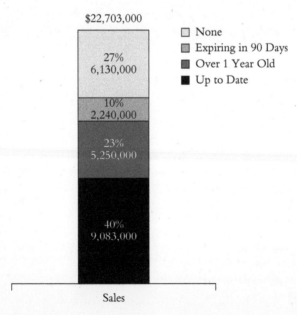

Figure 8.12 Data Status

at creating value, but unable to capture your fair share. Of course, measuring data collection and interviews can happen at many different levels of the organization. We recommend empowering the organization to manage these metrics at a Business, Business Unit, Region, Sales Team, and Sales Professional level. This granularity allows you to quickly understand the drivers behind the Value Creation and Value Capture data.

Continuous Improvement

We introduced the Maturity Model, Table 8.2, in Chapter 3, "The Playbook." The main discussion of the maturity model will come in Chapter 10, "Sustaining and Scaling," when we discuss the trials and tribulations of implementing the CVC Management System. Because it does have specific relevance at this point we will use it to reinforce a point. The point is that you should not expect to become an expert at value creation and value capture overnight.

Take a look at the line that says Measure and Improve Value Proposition. As you scan along the dimension, you will notice it starts by suggesting you will first become proficient at establishing your market value proposition. Then you will move on to better understand your value proposition at a segment level and improve your selling effectiveness. Once you have mastered those concepts, you start to correlate value creation and value capture. Finally, you get to a point where you are managing the business by a value creation and value capture dashboard that will help you to predict profit improvement. Now, it may not happen as linearly as suggested. The point is that there is a progression. A word of advice would be to not set yourself up for disappointment and failure by thinking you will master the science of correlating value creation and value capture in a few short months or even a year. It takes time and work.

Examples of Things That Take Time

The data that we have collected so far will help us better understand our ROI for the investments that we make. In many companies, at the base level, we are able to use value creation data to better inform our

Table 8.2 Maturity Model

Level of CVC Maturity	Reactive	Discrete	Pervasive	Predictive
Understand Value of Products and Services	No documented understanding	Known for select customers	Known for 80% of revenues	Known for 80% of revenues and key influencers
Make Customer-Informed Decisions	Sales decisions	Marketing and management decisions impacted	Organizational decisions impacted	Customer-informed strategic planning
Create Value and Capture Fair Share	No customer planning	Sales creates customer plans	Organizational aligned and accountable	Customer informed organizational planning
Measure and Improve Value Proposition	Market value proposition established	Segment value proposition established	Integration of value creation and value capture	Value management dashboards
Build Capability to Sustain CVC	Employees have hands-on experience	Ability to collect data established	Ability to analyze and get into action	CVC integrated in job description and supported with training
Enable CVC Management System to Scale and Speed	Render® software implemented	CVC processes defined	CVC processes integrated with business processes	Render® software integrated into IT strategy

anticipated ROI. With measure, we are now able to reflect back to identify particular gaps in the process.

Overestimation by Customers Some of the customers that we talk with may overestimate the amount of value they will receive from a particular investment. As we measure the value creation and the DVP % with customers, we will be able to identify those investments that performed according to expectations, and those that did not. Customers that frequently overestimate the return will quickly be identified, and modifications can be made as needed to temper internal expectations.

Not Being Rewarded for the Value We Create For some of the investments that we made, the customer may not have been willing to reward us accordingly. When we measure, we can determine how much value the customer received and what our fair share should be for the investment made. Sometimes, the customer is unaware of the investments that we made. Through this process, we are able to update them on the investments and their anticipated return based on what they told us. We can then determine how best to improve our ROI with these customers.

Risk Reduction We can reduce the risk that we face when making large investments. Though data from the customer is not solely sufficient to determine whether an investment is a good one, items that a large set of customers clearly identifies as beneficial increases the likelihood that investments will be well received in that area. As we invest in these opportunities, we can determine, through measurement, where we are not getting rewarded for the value that we create. We now have the data to support our claims that particular investments that we have made have benefited our customer. We then have the opportunity to gain our fair share of value.

How Technology Helps

The discussion of applying technology to drive operational efficiency and improvement for CVC may sound like a broken record at this point, but it is one that we continue to play. In fact, when it comes time to keep "score" and drive continuous improvement, this is when all your investments in tools and technology become fully realized.

CVC is all about the second Discovery Interview (and third, fourth, fifth, etc.). It is about demonstrating to the customer how effective you performed on identified areas of improvement and investment. It is about tracking what you accomplished, what was not, and quantifying how much value creation you generated for the customer. Clearly, there is a fair amount of data required to reach this level of communication with the customer.

Integrating customer financials, customer needs, and customer plan progress (for initiatives and actions) is required to have any semblance of a scoreboard. Poring through such statistical data can be a daunting task, especially on a yearly basis, without an assist from technology. If you have already made the effort to organize all your discovery, analysis, and execution data in a structured manner, then the measurement effort becomes a rewarding exercise.

If you have created a solid foundation of data collected throughout the "playbook," the measurement possibilities now are endless. Over time, the way your organization keeps score may change, and maybe you wish to integrate the CVC data with other information to produce entirely new market insights. If the goal of CVC is continuous follow up with the customer as market needs change, then tools or software plays a vital role in your organization's ability to keep an ongoing, real-time scoreboard.

Summary

How about a quick review of our learning objectives and how they fit within the larger system of Customer Value Creation:

- *How to successfully measure the value you create for your customers*. The key takeaway is to conduct Discovery Interviews on an ongoing basis. Do not make this a study but rather create an environment of ongoing understanding and delivering value to your customer.
- *How to determine whether you are capturing your fair share from the investments you make*. The big deal here is to line up your profits alongside the value customers receive and to do this over time.
- *How to track CVC activity in your organization to ensure continuous improvement*. The focus here is to drive accountability and to set an expectation that the world is not going to change overnight.

At the highest level, accomplishing these "how-tos" gets at the core of using customer value data to provide insights into future profits and competitive advantage, as shown in the CVC Management System in Figure 8.13. Simply put, this chapter began to touch on how this is accomplished by providing the entire organization Value and Adoption Dashboards that help continuously improve your differentiated value proposition. Although this is labeled "Step 4," measuring value is simply a launching pad for starting the cycle over again.

The Crystal Ball

Yes, this is part of the chapter summary . . . the crystal ball. This is another one of those subjects that will be included in our next book.

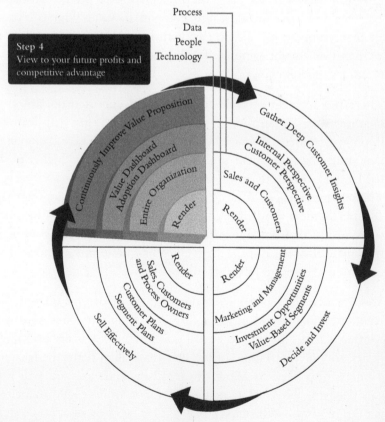

Figure 8.13 CVC Management System

But why not start talking about it right now. The crystal ball concept is that we would like to be able to better predict our profits from customers based on the investments we make and the value we deliver. We have touched on this idea here and there. Mostly, we have focused on just making sure you capture your fair share or at least have a basis to think about your fair share. But step back and think about what we have covered so far in the book.

We track over time the value our customers receive by doing business with us relative to competitors and the resulting profits we receive in return. We track this on a customer level, with segments of customers, product lines, divisions, lines of business, and for the whole company. How would you like for the next $5 million, $20 million, $100 million, or whatever level of investment be able to reduce risk, increase ROI accuracy, and have the information to predict profits at a confidence level that would cause investors to value your company higher than competitors. We do this with cost reduction but when it comes to customers not so much. It can be done.

Consider the following:

- There is a segment of your customers that consistently, over two or three years, identifies improvement road maps that lead to improved profits for you. Would you have increased confidence that your next investment in this group would lead to higher profits? Do you know this group in your business?
- There is a segment of your customers that consistently does not see an improvement road map and yet your investment ROI includes some profit lift from this group. Would you feel more confident in your ROI calculations if these customers were not included? Do you know this group in your business?

You get the idea? Not all customers value what you do now or what you are going to do in the future in the same manner or at the same level. It is not because they are good or bad, it is because their businesses are different. Some of the businesses align better with yours than others. You need to know this. And by knowing you will not only increase the profits you make today but will be able to better predict future results—the crystal ball.

Chapter 9

Getting Started

In the previous chapters you have seen the "cool" and valuable outcomes that are possible—the measurable financial results that can be achieved using the CVC Management System to Win with Customers and set you apart from competitors. Now it is time to discuss how to make this a reality in your business. We know you have been waiting for this. Now that you know *what* to do (technically) and are excited about the possible outcomes, it is time to discuss *how* to get it done in your organization.

We have experienced many different approaches to getting started over our years of working for and with companies to develop an outside-in, customer-driven culture. There is the new CEO who walks into a situation where she or he quickly sees the team is too internally focused. The CEO sets out to drive change in a top-down-oriented fashion. There is the VP of Sales who year after year experiences her company not connecting with the customer, resulting in performance simply not up to her expectations. There is the VP of Marketing who does not feel his department is connected to the field in an organized manner and sets out to change the situation. There is the disaster where a company finds itself losing share year over year, culminating with a big customer loss, causing a broad swath of the management team to move into action. There is the VP of Product Development or R&D who consistently is beaten by competitors with innovations that were available for the taking if only someone would listen. There is the VP of Operations or Continuous Improvement who is charged with bringing consistency and repeatability to work and finds it difficult to deploy an effective solution in the sales and marketing arena.

In each of these instances there is a person or group of people driven to better link their organization with the outside customer world. As you survey your organization, you will likely find people who are committed to making these changes. And you will find these people in a variety of areas throughout the business. Why? This is not a functional issue. Because every part of the business suffers from a lack of outside-in customer input, and likewise, every part of the business can benefit greatly from adding this key input.

Although you may find several people who are interested in taking action to change the organization's approach, there must be champions to truly advance and sustain the effort.

After reading this chapter you will learn how to mobilize the organization to begin Winning with Customers, including:

- How to kickoff a CVC effort in your organization
- How to choose and enroll the team required for success
- The game plan for that first "project"

Kickoff

We start this chapter with words from the professional at Owens Corning who was responsible for getting their program off the ground.

Christian Nolte served as the change agent at Owens Corning. He was the guy who framed the work, established expectations, and gained the buy-in, building a foundation for tremendous success. As you think about getting started, think about Christian Nolte's

A Conversation with Christian Nolte, Sales and Marketing Executive

On why he felt compelled to try something different. We were spending so much energy trying to get the most out of the marketing investments we were making that we really hadn't invested the time and energy to decide if we were making the right decisions. We had plenty of stuff that we were spending money on but we did not feel the expenditures were optimized. This was not about just getting the maximum return on an investment but making sure the investments were right in the first place. We really did excel in execution; we were just not sure if we were pointed in the right direction.

On the necessary qualities of a change agent. In order to do this well, you need change agents. You must have people who think outside the limitations that are inherent in their role. Every person in an organization is given a set of tools, and people are asked to make the most out of it. You can't be paralyzed if your particular toolset does not seem to be getting the job done. A change agent will think outside of the parameters and go get resources. You need to have "intellectual curiosity" and seek to find new ways to solve nagging challenges.

On establishing priorities. You must have an ability to prioritize the challenges that you can go solve. When you're managing a multi-million dollar budget, there is no end to challenges you face. You must find common issue to solve the challenge and look past the hundred challenges to get to the critical few.

On using those change agent qualities to get something like Customer Discovery off the ground. First, you have to identify the opportunity. In our case, the company had defined five critical outcomes and one of them was that we were going to be able to understand and measure the value we delivered to our customers. Once you have your agenda defined, you are then on the hook to find resources to get traction. Once you have it all together, then push relentlessly. Be relentless.

(Continued)

On having champions. You need champions from whom you can seek and solicit feedback and guidance on your efforts. For me, that my leader and our CEO. You need to find sponsors at the highest levels of the company to provide air cover and budgets. It was always necessary for me to talk through those challenges and get help to prioritize action. You need to be able to work with your champions and stay in tune with their priorities. The champions need to carry weight in the organization and be willing to take a risk with you.

On why Customer Discovery is still alive today. In the beginning, we found things that frankly shocked the organization. Within a month, we had discovered loyal customers who were on their way out. We discovered things that were, frankly, shocking. During this time, we had continual communication with executive leaders. The leaders were engaged and learning. We took some relatively quick actions that generated wins and we have been going ever since. Another key was that we did not build this as a marketing initiative or a sales initiative. We learned early on that these sessions with customers were different from sales calls or marketing satisfaction surveys and the resulting information was different and new. The sales and marketing teams grew together as a result.

On some of the big challenges. The whole effort almost died a thousand times. Finding resources to work on this was tough because everyone already has a full-time job. The work was different and for a Fortune 500 company to do something different does not happen every day. The norm is probably to be a little more risk averse and use standard toolsets in standard ways. This was different, maybe a little unproven at the time. A few of our key executives could not envision where we were going with the work. But once they saw a little bit of the work, they quickly got to a point where they could see the potential return.

On what did not go right. I did not anticipate how much people were threatened about what we might find. They were afraid of what they were going to hear. As a result, there were saboteurs, offline conversations, and politics. By getting serious about understanding our customers deeply, we exposed people in the organization who held different ideals. In many ways, the information that creates the most change is also the information that creates discomfort. We needed a better path for giving individuals and groups opportunities to change based on the feedback rather than assigning blame and that should have been laid out upfront.

On what he would have you do different. Speed. I would have personally jumped in with both feet earlier. I would have spent more time really getting to understand the Customer Discovery solution rather than just acting as the brush clearer. I think we would have even greater speed and enrollment had I dedicated myself full time rather than the hour or two a day I had available. In retrospect, it certainly would have been more than worth the time. I would have also challenged us to get more internal resources on the team to participate in the interviews. To see all of this unfold in real time was big learning and we should have included even more people upfront than we did.

On who received the initial benefit. Sales got the first benefit from individual customer wins. We reorganized the sales team as an outcome of the work. Marketing's return came slower.

stories and the following seven-point checklist to start change in your organization:

1. Believe and communicate that now is the time for change.
2. Understand and align with the established organizational needs.
3. Establish champions who can lead change.
4. Take initiative and start doing work.
5. Become an expert to establish yourself as a leader and source of information.
6. Achieve and document early successes.
7. Formally define an executive champion.

Here is a little more on how to get started in your organization.

If Not Now, When?

You and your team need to believe that now is the right time to win with customers. And from our perspective, the time is always now, no matter what your current situation. We have worked with organizations that have adopted this approach only after a crisis. And now they publicly thank God for the crisis that moved them into action. But we suggest that you not wait for the big customer relationship explosion or watch your share dwindle away and become forced into action. Regrettably, it seems that most companies and most people tend not to take action until faced with a crisis. When markets are bad and budgets are tight we fall into the trap of resisting anything new. When markets are good—sales and profits are rising—we get lulled into the false sense that we are really beating the pants off our competitors. While in reality, a rising tide raises all boats—even those that are not well built. Or maybe we get on the path of cutting cost as a way to prosperity and cannot seem to bring balance to our actions—the kind of balanced actions that result in both sales growth and cost reductions or productivity improvements. Last we checked, a growth strategy does not consist of cost-cutting only. Any executive who has been around for 20 or 30 years has gone through this major cost-cutting exercise one or several times during his or her career. And anyone who thinks this is really fun has a warped sense of what is fun about business. Remember, business success at its core is about making investments that create more value for customers than competitors and results in you making more money. In many ways, a cost-cutting strategy is the result of failing to stay in touch with what is valuable to customers and making the best investment decisions to address these customer needs in ways that help you and the customer make more money. This is the ultimate responsibility of senior management and now is the time to begin or accelerate this process in your organization.

To create a sense of urgency, field a team that has an entrepreneurial spirit for building a successful business. Think about an entrepreneur for a moment. A large percentage of them get started by understanding a customer problem better than anyone. And they possess the passion, commitment, and resourcefulness to build a new or different solution working closely with customers. Entrepreneurs operate in this fashion because they understand so clearly that without their customers they will not make payroll, meet other financial obligations, or continue to exist as a viable entity. As a result of this environment, they believe and act as thought the time is now! Your Customer Value Creation team must operate with the same sense of urgency. There are initiatives that companies should wait to pursue—even some of the important ones. This is not one of them. Now is the time.

Understand and Align with the Need

Somewhere in your organization there is a need or an objective already established that you can use to get started. Or, if you happen to be the leader, you may be planning to establish the objective. Either way, you need a platform from which to do your work that aligns with the goals of your company. Here are objectives or problem questions we have found that may apply as you consider how the Customer Value Creation system can help you develop a winning strategy:

- What is your value proposition? Do you really know why customers buy from you? Do you really know what your customers want?
- What is your competitive advantage? Can you reasonably expect to grow your business based on something you are doing better than your competitors?
- Are you improving your value to customers year over year? How much progress have you made in the past few years? How much progress will you make in the next few?
- Are your capital and operational plans aligned with what creates value for your customers?
- Are you getting your fair share? When you create value for your customers do you get anything in return or are you giving everything away?
- Do you really know how your customers think you can improve?
- Do you spend too much time just talking about the product and not all of the other things you do to create value such as brand development, logistics, sales force, customer services, and the rest?
- Do you know why customers view you differently? Why do you have a great relationship with some customers and not others while offering them the same product or solution? Do you know why?

- Does your sales organization really use customer plans? What do you need to do in order to make sales planning more consistent so that it is something that your sales team sees as being easier and helping them in their jobs?
- Are your sales and marketing teams really connected? What can you do to drive them closer together?
- Are you listening to your sales organization? Do you just hear the squeaky wheels of large customers and miss a large perspective of those that are somewhat smaller or less vocal?
- When budgets are tight and you need to make sure you are making investments that matter to your customers, do you really know where to make investments?
- Are you using your understanding of customers to get into action? Is your organization action-oriented? Do you move deliberately from identifying opportunities to taking decisive action?
- Is your organization efficient in its collection and use of customer information?
- Do you really see the "true" picture of what your customers think about you, relative to your competitors?
- Is your sales organization consistently communicating to your customers about what you are doing to improve your business with them?
- Does R&D have a window into what your customers want? Are your R&D activities and investments aligned with what your customers will buy or care about?
- Does your organization feel connected to the customer? Do your manufacturing facilities really have a sense for customer?

We could continue on with this list and you probably have many ideas to add as well. The goal is to identify what is going on in your organization and establish yourself as working to help solve one or several of these key challenges.

Establish Champions

One of the champions may be you! In the beginning, champions are those who take the initiative to get up in the morning and try something different. People who are curious, willing to take a risk, those who look in the mirror and ask themselves, "What have I done about this?" The champions are those who can get past the fun discussion and into the details and actions needed to help drive their organizations to see the opportunity. When we are challenged to drive change within a company, these are the people we seek out as champions.

Sometimes, these champions are already in places of leadership, which sure makes things easier. When the leaders "get it," the help needed with resource allocation, establishing work priority, and marshaling capital fuels the pace of progress. Here is the thing, though—we have seen plenty of cases where the leaders, or some portion of the leaders, are the ones who are stuck in an inside-out mentality. They already know the answers because they have been there and done that . . . even if it was 15 or 20 years ago. So, in some cases, the leaders are those you need to convince to become champions.

The point we are trying to make is that having champions is a necessary ingredient and you can certainly serve as one of them. So, if you truly believe this will help your organization grow and thrive, then when you are looking around for champions—you may be *it*!

> *"One of our lessons on getting the organization engaged was that senior leadership had to embrace the change. This is a cultural change and takes time and commitment. It is not a project but an ongoing way of doing business. You will fail if it is viewed as a marketing effort or a sales effort—it is a commercial effort and takes the entire organization."*
>
> —Chad Fenbert, Sales, Owens Corning

Take Initiative

Once you have identified the key challenges, the effort will not magically begin on its own. It is important to note that whether you are a senior officer in your company, improving performance is driven in large part by taking initiative. Someone has to get the ball rolling. Initiative might also fall into a category called "Don't be afraid to stick your neck out." Take it from a couple of people who have managed many teams and have had leadership roles in varying companies, large and small: The people you want around you are those who take initiative. There is something enjoyable about being around a group of people who are proactive and seek out responsibility and accountability for solving the challenges you face. On the contrary, there is also something draining about working around a team where every little thing needs to be spelled out and managed. Now, we could spend a lot of time discussing leadership qualities and the qualities of people. But all of those discussions notwithstanding, taking it upon yourself to take initiative is a big deal.

Become an Expert

Do not think for a moment that just because you consider yourself a champion and take initiative that you actually have the expertise you need to tackle the challenge. On the other hand, do not let your lack of expertise stop you. Also, do not get caught up in the idea that your company has all of the expertise and therefore there is nothing new you can contribute. There is a vast amount of knowledge in this world that is available to you. Research on the Internet, read a book (oh no, wait, you are already doing that), take a course—continue learning and developing your expertise.

We happen to think that networking is one of the most under-utilized approaches to improving your expertise. It is not so different than the challenge of finding a new job. We all know that the best path to finding a job is networking, networking, and more networking. Take the time to reach out to people in other companies and meet new people at conferences where the topic is consistent with your challenge and make a connection. Find others who are solving or having similar struggles with these challenges and use their insights and approaches to help inform your plan. By doing these things you will establish yourself as an expert and you will find that others will begin to respect your knowledge and ability. We will support your efforts to build expertise through taking courses and engaging with the larger CVC community. The companion web site (www.winningwithcustomers.com) is designed to provide support resources to help you build expertise.

Achieve Early Success

Having a team committed to winning is important. However, as you prepare to assemble, mobilize, and sustain the team to help you win, key executives in the organization must buy in to the effort, or it is doomed. The good news is that no matter who you are in the organization, you can positively impact the creation of the customer value-oriented culture required for success. We have seen executives announce to their organizations their intention to develop a Winning with Customers' culture. Whether you think of this as getting ordered around or developing buy-in, either way it got people aligned and into action. We have also seen change driven from more of a "bottom-up" approach. A few people who believed got into action and showed their organization a better way. We are not really sure that one of the models, "top-down" or "bottom-up," is preferable or more effective. From our experience, the determining factor in a company's success with this approach to Winning with Customers has more to do with achieving early successes than it does with who gets it started.

You have heard the saying "A picture is worth a thousand words." Well, when it comes to helping others in your organization see the real value and possibilities from the use of the CVC Management System, there is no better way than to show them a "picture" of what success looks like—one with real customers in your business. Let's just say that we have seen actual results create some serious "eureka" moments— something that verbal descriptions, impactful presentations, or compelling references cannot achieve.

So, as you prepare to field a team and select the right people to engage in this effort, please remain focused on the critical success factor in gaining buy-in—achieving early successes. You must have a team of people capable of putting early wins on the scoreboard.

Here is a personal experience from Keith.

D. Keith Pigues: A Personal Experience

I was responsible for leading the effort of implementing the new approach across 12 business units of a global Fortune 500 company. The senior management team had given its support for the effort, although the team members did not really know what they were committing to. Each time I provided

(Continued)

an update to the senior executive team members, they would end the review with "What exactly will we get from the investment?" This was an appropriate question; however, I was only able to provide examples from other companies and the general results that the consultants were confident we would receive if we continued to follow the plan.

My team had a well-developed strategy for deploying the tools over multiple years and a committed group of midlevel management that provided people resources that were applying the approach across several business units. After several months of activity, prepping for interviews, conducting interviews, identifying value attributes, and estimating the impact we could have on customer profit, we were losing steam and momentum. The spending was mounting and the organization was growing weary. Then we had what was probably the most significant breakthrough that fueled the effort and elevated it to the short list of key strategic growth opportunities for the company. We decided to focus our efforts on one customer segment of a dozen or so customers within a business unit—to get a win that the entire organization could rally behind.

The update meeting to share the results of our focused effort on the chosen customer segment was a meeting to behold. I remember it as if it were yesterday. This one-on-one update meeting with one of the executive vice presidents to show progress on the CVC initiative was a major breakthrough to gain buy-in. I had only a few printed PowerPoint slides showing the results of our work with customers in the chosen customer segment where we focused our efforts. We had boiled down all of the work into two key insights about how the customers' businesses operate from a financial and operational perspective. We identified areas where we could impact their businesses directly and significantly (with dollars and cents estimates provided by the customers). This represented a depth of knowledge about our customers that did not exist in the organization previously. His response was cautious, yet showed a level of interest in the initiative I had not seen before. He asked, "Are you saying that we know exactly how these customers make money, their revenue drivers and cost drivers, as well as how we can affect them to help these customers make more money?" I said, "Yes." This is the point of the initiative and why we have a team of people working feverishly to get this project completed.

I continued by sharing the balance of the update presentation that included a "back of the envelope" business case for several potential investments that we believed would allow us to impact the customers' profits in the areas we identified, as well as the specific improvements to our value proposition (products, services, sales force, and operational capabilities) that would result from the investments. The business case estimates included an attractive increase in sales and margins from the new offerings that customers were eager for us to develop and launch as soon as possible.

He then asked a second question, as he apparently began to think of the possibilities that sprang from this new customer insight: "Are you telling me that customers have told us how much value they will receive from these investments and that we may have an opportunity to use value-based pricing to get higher margins?" Again, I said, "Yes." This is also an objective of the Customer initiative.

I shared with him that these two observations are what we communicated in previous update meetings with the executive team. And he said, "Yes, but you never had real examples from real customers with real numbers." This was a breakthrough moment for me. We had provided descriptions of what was possible from consultants, case examples from other companies that successfully used the approach, and hypothetical opportunities that might result from our efforts. But it was the real examples from real customers with real numbers that created the "eureka" moment. And having all of the learning wrapped up in a business case truly got the attention and support from this executive.

(Continued)

His final question makes the point: "What will it take to roll this out across the entire company and how long will it take you to get it done?" A "picture" is worth a thousand words.

What made this even more interesting in subsequent discussions with this executive, as he had an opportunity to ponder other possibilities, is the competitive insight gained from the early success. We had been unable to gain a sustained competitive advantage over competitors in the past. As he considered the significant work we had done with customers to identify these opportunities, using an approach that was rigorous and quantitative, he concluded that this approach to engage with customers may well represent a source of competitive advantage. While we believed that the specific new offerings could not be duplicated easily in the marketplace, we felt even stronger about a new way of running the business that could keep us on the forefront of new ways to help customers make more money and get our fair share of the money in return. Fielding a team that can help to create an early success can do the same for you and your organization.

Hopefully, this example brings to life the importance and impact of achieving early successes. Nothing brings a team together like a little success. When people see success, they want to be part of it. The success does not even have to be completely realized. Sometimes, just having a clear picture of what success looks like and a path to get there draws a crowd! So whether you get started from a top-down edict or a bottom-up entrepreneur, the key to developing buy-in is achieving an early success.

Find a Champion

We were not kidding in the previous section about "you are the champion." That said, if you are not the CEO or one of the senior leaders then you need air cover. Air cover means having that executive who says yes; it is worthwhile to spend the time and energy to attack the challenge you have set out to solve. You will need the executive's support when the time comes to navigate an organization filled with professionals who desire involvement and input into your activities. Some of these professionals will agree with your plan and some will not. They are people. Do not venture off into this land of differing opinions and politics until you have gained the support of a champion who recognizes the benefits of your effort.

As you consider potential candidates for champions, remember the distinctive attributes of the CVC Management System and how they can impact the company and its financial results. A champion needs to clearly understand the potential link between the approach and the financial results.

Fielding a Team

Well, once you have identified the champion, it is necessary to field a team.

Winning with Customers Is a Team Sport

You can improve the odds of winning with your customers by executing what we discussed. But you are just one person and you will not be able to win with your customers by fielding a team of one. So, although you may be fired up and ready to take action in your organization, resist the temptation to single-handedly change your company's approach to winning. Trust us—it does not work.

Winning with customers is definitely a team sport. Let us clear something up right now. The improved financial outcomes that are possible from implementing the CVC Management System are not possible without, first, a change in thinking within your organization. You must think "team" to win with customers. Way too often, we run across situations where the attitude or prevailing culture is otherwise—"This is my customer," "You don't talk to this customer unless I am aware," "All customer communication goes through me," and the list continues. What a hoot! Winning requires getting people in your business on the same page and pulling in the same direction. Who are the people who must be involved? Well, that is everyone in your organization who has an impact on whether the customer receives value. Turns out, that is most of the people. In fact, we argue that every person in your business should contribute to your efforts to create value for customers. Each person should know specifically how he or she contributes to customer value creation and feels a part of the winning team. Anything short of this is not a formula for winning.

If manufacturing consistently produces subpar quality or poorly manages the production schedule, you may lose. If customer service is understaffed because of constant turnover and is unable to answer customer questions, or if orders are consistently wrong, then you may lose. If marketing does not market, sales does not sell, product development does not create new products, and management does not make good decisions, your organization may lose with customers. Each member of the team must understand how to create maximum value for customers and capture a fair share of that value for your organization. And team members must be armed with the information and tools to do these two things well.

There are many aspects of your business that determine success with customers. And there is none more important than the people responsible for planning, managing, executing, and continuously improving every aspect of the business. Yes, your success is all about people and having the right team of people to do what is required to win. We will spend considerable time later in this chapter discussing the recommended profile of the winning team. Before focusing on the team members, your organization must first decide how the team you put in place is going to play this game—will they "play not-to-lose" or "play to-win." There is a distinct difference. We advocate playing to win—it is the only way you will be successful. Here is why: Playing not-to-lose is an "every person for himself or herself" approach, with all people or functions in your organization concerned primarily about themselves, rather than the success of the business as a whole. This results in a very "me-centric" model where everyone seems to have his or her own agenda. The individual agendas may be good in its own right (local optima) but do not complement each other to help the team win. Sometimes, people refer to this model as silo thinking, or in other even less positive descriptions, protecting your own turf or covering your backside. This is a natural way to play because each of the functions we described (manufacturing, sales, marketing, etc.) is typically run by some type-A personality who is driven to achieve results that in too many cases are narrow and functional. Unfortunately, many of these functional leaders believe they have all of the answers and do not collaborate well with others who bring different and valuable perspectives. They are not willing to consider alternative approaches that could lead to greater success for the total business. And to further complicate matters, these leaders in some cases only measure success by their function's metrics of success, or the individual recognition or promotions they receive. This approach will not help the company Win with Customers.

Playing to win, however, requires everyone to be on the same page. The organization must be aligned in everything it does and be orchestrated by an integrated plan to achieve a common goal. Playing to win begins with a commitment to a belief that there is power in team. Those who favor this approach understand that it is more likely to produce a winning customer solution than people or functions operating independently. Playing to win becomes less about watching what your competitors are doing and more about understanding and acting on what your customers value. Doing this better than your competitors— staying ahead by crafting a sound (qualitative and quantitative) value proposition and continuously improving it is what this is all about. Playing to win is what this entire book is about.

Playing to win, or playing not to lose? Which will it be? If your organization does not field a team with a commitment to play to win, you may well be wasting your time, energy, and money. We are just keeping it real. Although there are some big-time results ahead for those who adopt this approach to winning, it will be a colossal waste of time for those who are not committed to playing to win.

Stop and think for a moment. The stakes are high!

If you win with your customers, you can achieve levels of sustained profitable growth you have never achieved. As your business grows profitably, you add jobs. In addition to adding jobs, those who delivered the attractive growth will get additional opportunities—lead larger businesses, make more money, lead larger groups of people, and so forth. With more jobs and wealth, the individuals in your company and the people in the communities where you operate prosper. As you ponder these rewards from operating a successful business, they may represent some of the reasons you selected business as your vocation. It is unlikely that you chose this field to cut jobs and reduce wealth for your company, its employees, and the communities in which your business operates. This is certainly the less-than-ideal situation businesses face sometimes, but we believe the CVC Management System will help position your organization to make better decisions that result in more winning and growing, and less losing and cutting.

Winning with customers is indeed a team sport. So you have to field a winning team to be successful in this sport—a team that will play to win. We could probably write an entire book on this subject alone, but we will not.

Choosing the Team

We hope we have made the case that this is really a team sport, and that the much needed buy-in is easier to obtain if you leverage early successes from customers and share their compelling stories. Now, let's turn our attention to selecting the team—members who must work together to get this done.

The work required to move from a great "idea" to one that is supported within the organization and begins to yield results is not for the fainthearted. As you begin to assemble the initial team, people with the following characteristics will provide the essential assets to the team:

Intellectually curious. Those who are truly excited about learning a new topic that is important to the business and will get satisfaction from exploring something new, even if it does not result in major changes in how the business is run.

Seekers of positive change. Those who are willing to pursue the "road less traveled" in pursuit of something new, different, and potentially better for the business—even if it may be controversial—because they believe it is the right thing to do for the business.

Well-respected functional experts. It is important to have people on the team whose involvement suggests this a serious effort whose results are credible and sound. This may require some selling to get these folks involved (they are typically involved in several other key initiatives and much sought after); however, their involvement alone can add credibility to the effort.

Require sound compelling evidence to support change. This is another big one—those who may be keepers of the current way of doing business, but are open to changing their views or perspective with valid and compelling data or information are great members of the initial team. They also represent a good test group. If the newfound ideas can gain support from this group, they will likely be compelling enough to impact other skeptics and senior leaders.

Great communicators. This subject matter is quite different and may represent something many organizations have not pursued previously. As such, great communicators are needed who can translate the approach and learnings to others in the organization—a big part of gaining buy-in is communicating what this is and what it will do for the organization.

Entrepreneurial drive. Above all, members of this team must have entrepreneurial drive that propels them to explore opportunities and find solutions, knocking down barriers, defying the odds, and continuing to push forward in the face of significant challenges or doubt.

There is no more important work that will impact the success of your company, and yes it requires the "A team." It may be difficult to find initial team members that possess all the characteristics or traits. However, the more people you can enlist with these important abilities, the greater your chances of moving from an idea to an initiative that takes hold in the organization and delivers meaningful results.

In addition to these personal aspects of team members, there are more obvious business perspectives that are required to gain input and support from the various functions or units within the organization. And the functional expertise and business knowledge required to perform the work must be resident within the team. The team must be composed of those who bring the skills, experience, and organizational credibility required to lead a change of this magnitude.

Table 9.1 shows the recommended functional expertise or business knowledge that should be resident within the team.

The team members and their contribution or role is fairly straightforward, but there is one particular group worthy of special notice. It represents the "make or break" team member.

Table 9.1   Recommended Team Expertise

Expertise or Knowledge	Team Contribution
Market Research	Access to industry, market, and customer information to form initial customer value hypotheses. Quantitative skills to analyze and interpret data.
Finance	Understanding of customer and company financials and ability to analyze financial impact of business operations improvements.
Operations/ Manufacturing	Knowledge of operations/manufacturing and the impact of operational improvements on financial results.
Customer Service	Knowledge of customer service programs and the impact on customer satisfaction and loyalty. The ability to determine the impact of current gaps in service or new service offerings.
Marketing	Understanding of macro-market and industry drivers, customer segments, company value propositions, and competitive offerings. The ability to develop effective customer solutions (products and services), competitive positioning strategies, pricing strategies, customer communication, and sales support tools.
Product Development or R&D	Knowledge of technologies and how they can be leveraged to develop products to meet customer needs effectively within desirable cost parameters.
General Management	A big picture view of the business—the market forces and drivers, profitable growth strategies, and the business financial structure. In-depth knowledge of the organization's culture, risk profile, and rewards systems—a keen sense of what works (and does not work) within the organization.
Sales	Provides firsthand knowledge of customers' perspectives, as well as what's working and what's not working in selling the current value proposition. Gives the input most critical to developing new customer plans that are executable. The first line of communication to the customer, as well as opportunities for continuous improvement.
Customers	No one can provide the customer perspective, but the customer. The customer must be an integral part of the winning team. Need we say more?

Include Sales or Do Not Proceed

This is another one of those "if you get nothing else from this book" points. This has likely come through loud and clear in previous chapters, but it is worth repeating. We think it is pretty important.

When it comes to winning with customers, you have to have sales on the team. This is nonnegotiable. You might be thinking, yea duh! As obvious as this may seem to some, it does not happen all of the time. Here is the kind of justification we have heard: "Sales is too busy selling to customers to spend time participating on a team exploring new ways of running the business and developing plans to deliver the results." "We will lose sales if even one of the key members of the sales organization spends any time on this effort to shape the customer plans." Yes, we have heard these views and others like them more times than you can imagine. Despite all the good business reasons, here is the bottom line: No sales participation, no initiative.

There is a really good reason for us to hold the line on this one. Unfortunately, we listened to the good business reasons and tried a few of these without sales in the early days. Let's just say we will never do it again. Here is why: When sales is not involved, the experience goes something like this. It is October (if you are on a calendar fiscal year) and the annual strategic planning efforts are completed. The organization is feverishly developing capital, operational, and sales plans for the following year. The plans specify capital investments, align organizational deployment efforts, target new segments to be tackled, and outline new initiatives to be launched. Teams are formed to make sure all the *i*'s are dotted and *t*'s crossed. Presentations are made to management brimming with confidence about the company's ability to outperform competitors and achieve the financial targets in the upcoming year.

Decisions are made and the plans are executed. The following year comes to a close and the results are less than projected. The sales team blames the ivory tower for being disconnected from the reality of the market, customers, and competitors. They knew they never had a chance at executing the plan, and probably lay most of the blame at the feet of the marketing team, who, from their perspective, simply does not understand their customers. General management looks bad and sees to it that appropriate punishment is doled out or bonuses withheld. And where was sales when the ill-fated plans were being created? Well, they were selling because the year was quickly coming to a close (remember, it was October) and they were under the gun to close the gap between last year's financial performance and this year's target. Maybe it does not work quite like this at your company (yea, right). The point is this: This scenario is normal for an inside-out oriented company. But it is an absolute showstopper in making the transition to an outside-in company and winning with customers.

To really drive your company to be outside-in requires getting sales completely involved on the team. The sales organization needs to be as involved with bringing the customer perspective into the organization as it is at delivering the company's value proposition to the market. So, when you are fielding a team, please get sales involved. *Include sales or do not proceed.*

Enrolling the Team: It Is How You Do Business

Invariably, when you start trying to build a team you get the usual "I don't have time for another project," or "We always start these things and nothing ever happens," or "Did the executive or manager who controls resources say it was okay?" There is always a long list of reasons why you should not do things—even things that are critical for your survival or growth as a business. You must find teammates who are willing to take a risk and try something different to accelerate profitable growth in the business. What has worked for us is to not think about winning with customers as a project because it is not. Winning with customers should be and has to be "how you do business."

Consider these 10 questions about your organization. We call this the "CVC Management 10-Point Check-Up." And, if answered truthfully, it is telling. We urge to answer the questions honestly. Here you go:

1. Do you know if your customers make more money by doing business with you?
   (*If you answer yes, give the specific incremental operating margin a given customer or customer segment earns by doing business with your company versus your closest competitor.*)

2. Do you talk to your customers on a regular basis to understand qualitatively and quantitatively what creates value for them?
(If you answer yes, please provide us with a written document from your most recent customer conversation. We will gladly sign a nondisclosure and confidentiality agreement.)

3. Do you use the customer's perspective (both qualitative and quantitative) to inform your management team's collective decision making for capital and operational plans?

4. Do you develop consistent plans across the organization that demonstrates and communicates to customers your commitment and organizational alignment to respond to their input and ideas?

5. Do you measure and track the implementation progress of customer plans and the resulting value you create for customers (from the customer's perspective)?

6. Do you have a clear and quantitative value proposition that addresses the most valuable customer needs?
(If you answer yes, please state the value proposition for an individual or segment of customers. Remember, a true value proposition is expressed in quantitative terms)

7. Do you proactively enhance your value proposition to address changes in what customers value and their new and emerging needs?
(If you answer yes, what change have you made to the value proposition for a customer or customer segment in the past 12 to 18 months? What change in customer value and customer need led to the change?)

8. Do you measure and track the direct financial contribution to your business from the investments you have made, based on direct and unfiltered customer input?

9. Can you accurately forecast or predict your company's financial results from planned changes in your value proposition and the return on the associated investments?

10. Do the key decision makers (and others) in your organization agree on the answers to the previous nine questions?

That was not so bad. We have challenged many organizations to answer these questions. And most of them, when making an honest assessment, have answered *no* to each of these questions. If you are like most of the organizations that have answered these questions, you identified several areas of opportunity to change the way you do business—to truly operate your business to Win with Customers using the principles of Customer Value Creation.

We have spent considerable time with organizations trying to understand why these 10 questions so critical to their success consistently receive *no* answers. And we have uncovered what seems like a million reasons—we will not attempt to list them or prolong the issue. The real question is, "Wouldn't we all rather do business differently— by understanding our customers' perspective and winning with them?" Wouldn't we rather just make this the way we do business?

To be successful, you have to find people who get this concept. The objective is not to complete a "project" and get back to business as usual. The objective is to use this process to set an example (with real examples from real customers with real numbers) and show the organization there is a benefit to operating with outside-in customer knowledge. If the team approaches this effort realizing that it represents a new way of doing business, both the team and management may be convinced that a new way of doing business may be just what is needed to Win with Customers.

Without the Customer There Is No Team

You got the point that the participation of sales is critical to the success of the team. And there is one member of the team whose involvement is even more crucial than sales—the customer.

We are compelled to emphasize again that this book and all of its contents is about Winning *with* Customers. As we listed, the ideal members to include on your team to bring this approach to life within your organization, we recognize that many of you may have raised an eyebrow (or both eyebrows) when seeing the customer listed as a member of the team. Some companies, including some we have worked with, would never consider the customer as a member of such a team without our prompting or urging—okay, demanding. Because of their engrained inside-out approach to running the business, in many cases the customer was considered an enemy (i.e., us versus the customer). Even organizations that professed to be customer-focused fell way short of the level of customer understanding required with this approach. The organizations that have successfully used this approach to win with customers have seen the business insight that only a customer can bring. And they have benefited greatly from this new invaluable input into their decision making. Unfortunately, this is not the case with many (and we would argue most) companies. Herein lies a big part of the problem we are addressing in this book.

If your organization typically excludes the customer from these sorts of efforts and relies solely on your internal perspective, that is a big problem. No one in your organization can adequately represent the customer but the customer—sorry. No one in your organization succeeds or fails with the decisions your customers make, like your customers do. Even the person in your organization who is most knowledgeable about the customer's business cannot provide an accurate assessment of how much money your customer makes doing business with you, relative to your competitor. Although you may be seduced into using your internal perspective as a proxy for the customer, we beg you—do not do it. It is a straight line and a fast path to failure. And we are saddened to say that we have seen and experienced this too often. There is nothing cool about the lack of validity and value of the outcomes when real unfiltered customer input was omitted. When organizations have taken an approach counter to the one we have outlined in Discover honestly, it is ugly and quite embarrassing during the follow-up with the customer. Please spare your organization the drama and embarrassment.

As you have seen in the cases and customer interviews shared throughout this book, so much rich insightful information is captured from direct customer input. More information and more sensitive information than you might ever imagine. It is also fair to say that, in most cases (from our experience), the information provided by customers on the team dismantled many strong and widely held beliefs and assumptions about the customer's business that were simply not true. Things thought to be extremely valuable to customers were found not to be valuable at all. Areas where an assumed competitive advantage exists were viewed quite differently by customers. Future actions and investments planned for new products, services, sales force, marketing programs, and so forth, were considered by customers to be significantly less valuable than the internal views and assessments. Yes, things are likely to change significantly when a true unfiltered customer perspective is included on the team. *No customer, no team.*

Now, we do recognize that this way of working with customers may be new for you and for your customers. So you should choose customers to include on the team wisely. Here are some helpful hints to consider when selecting customers for the team.

Start Small and Grow

Do not think that you can change your entire organization at once. Target a business unit, a product line, a few large customers, or some manageable set of customers that you would like to explore.

Start Small but Not Too Small

Do not hang your success or failure on a conversation with one or two customers and their perspectives. If you are focused on a few customers, then work to get multiple perspectives throughout the customers' organizations. If you start too small, you are likely to fail for two reasons:

1. If you happen to talk with a customer who you will never win with or one who is so cynical that the effort will not be productive, the initiative will lose credibility and come to a screeching halt. Yes, there are some of these customers—avoid them like the plague.
2. You will have to overcome your own organization's overconfidence bias. As we discussed earlier in the book, this is a challenge in most organizations. People within the organization will naturally resist customer information that is contrary to their beliefs (Don't be alarmed or take it personally—it is a human thing.) They will come up with all sorts of excuses why what you have discovered is invalid. We have seen this more often than we would like to remember. The most powerful way to combat your organization's overconfidence bias is to have ample data. It is easy to come up with reasons why one or two customers may have a different perspective. However, it is difficult to argue when you show the results from in-depth conversations outlined earlier in the book with 10,

20, or 30 customers who are suggesting the emperor has no clothes. It will take the weight of the data and the magnitude of the potential implications on the business, whether positive or negative, to get people's attention. And remember, you may only get one shot at this, so go for the weighty data to make the case. It's worth the effort and time required.

Start with "Friendlies"

To develop success, start with customers who are friendly with your organization—those where you have good relationships and who are willing to invest the time and effort to explore new ways of creating and sharing value throughout the industry value chain, new approaches to working collaboratively with suppliers. Having friendly customers on the team allows you to test the process and work out the kinks. This is not to say that you should only communicate with friendly customers in this process, but it is critical to have the first few interviews with these individuals. This approach will also help to build your organization's confidence in the process and provide the momentum and interest needed to gain support as you expand the effort. Friendly customers will be much more forgiving as you become comfortable with this new way of working with customers. In fact, they may even appreciate being selected to work through this new approach with you. As you will find, they also get a lot out of the process and would prefer that they, rather than their competitors, are first to get the value from your improved value proposition.

Bob Harlan on Talking with Multiple Customers

Q: *It seems like you use this process for large progressive customers as well as small business owners. Was it more difficult to get buy-in from small or less progressive customers?*

A: Bob Harlan: *"We had about 500 interviews with experienced customers of all sizes—direct transactional customers and*

(Continued)

> *down-the-value-stream customers. We've had great conversa-*
> *tions with all types. We have had one example out of 500*
> *where the customer was not so forthcoming; 1 out of 500 is*
> *not bad. And when I say down the value stream, an example*
> *would be in our roofing business. We sell to distributors and*
> *distributors sell to contractors. We do not sell directly to roof-*
> *ing contractors yet we go talk to them about the value they*
> *receive from Owens Corning and how it could be improved.*
> *We go all the way down the value stream, we talked to mul-*
> *tiple constituencies."*

At this point in the chapter, you may be asking yourself if proceeding further with the thought of implementing the CVC Management System is worth the effort. Finding the team members with the required traits and skills is no small effort. Getting organized to get the effort going requires additional work. Gaining buy-in will take time and energy (physical and emotional) and is not assured. Oh, and then the budget pressure that makes the thought of trying to justify another expense—a real downer. And now, the added pressure of selecting the right customers.

Why on earth would you move forward now to pursue this? As you consider the breakthrough results achieved by Owens Corning, the chemical manufacturer, the health-care products company, and other unnamed companies, this is something you cannot afford not to do. What other initiatives are you pursuing or considering that can have an impact of this magnitude in both the short term and long term? What other initiatives will allow you to understand customers this deeply, measure and improve your competitive advantage, and capture your fair share of the value you help customers create from your investments? We believe this is the real question. Here is where true visionary and transformational leadership is required to move organizations from the "status quo" to innovation and growth. Again, this is not for the faint-hearted, but it is well worth the effort.

And just to dispel the misconception about the amount of time required, here is a perspective from a sales executive at Owens Corning.

Owens Corning Sales Executive, Roger Warren:

Q: *Does it take more time preparing to have the discussion with customers?*

A: *"We interface with our customers on a regular basis and this has just become part of the conversation and from a time standpoint to get a 90-minute interview completed is very minimal for the return."*

This is not really about spending additional time with customers in many cases. It is about using the time with customers in a more effective and productive way that produces data and outcomes that can improve your customer relationships and profits—with friendlies and unfriendlies alike.

The First Project

Now that you have the concept of Winning with Customers off the ground and the team is selected, it is time to get into action. However, it would be foolhardy to believe an organization can achieve everything written in this book during the first few months of developing the capability. The CVC system impacts many different areas of an organization, and it takes time to fully develop. If that is the case, then what do you get in the beginning? In our experience, the short-term financial impact can be significant. We have had customers that achieved a 600 percent ROI within the first six months of launching the effort.

Yes, there are attractive financial results that can be achieved in both the short term and the long term. The first project is incredibly important to set the organization on a course to realize both. If done well, it can deliver a down payment on the possible financial results, while helping to get buy-in across the organization. There is much riding on this initial project. Here is the list of things the team must do (and do well) to get off to a good start:

1. *Prepare like crazy.* The work necessary to conduct a discovery interview is one of the primary items delivered in the first phase of the

project. The internal hypotheses may be for a single customer, or for multiple customers depending on your approach.

2. *Conduct customer interviews.* Initial conversations with your customers have been held. For each customer, you have identified opportunities for value creation. You will likely find opportunities that you can act upon immediately, without any significant thought. These actions typically are quick, easy to implement, and do not require significant investment of time or money. As reports of these quick opportunities develop, excitement within the organization and within the sales force (in particular) starts to build.

3. *Turn data into actionable plans.* The data collected has been analyzed and initiatives have been identified. The part of your organization exposed to the CVC system has taken a look at the consolidated data, identified specific initiatives that are the most attractive, and decided which warrant an investment.

4. *Get into action.* Take personal responsibility in getting the things done that were decided upon by the organization and document the results.

5. *Communicate findings.* The key stakeholders in your company will be introduced to the results of the interviews to determine what investments they feel are required, and which ones they can delay. It is equally important to communicate the approved plans to address customer opportunities—share these broadly throughout your organization.

6. *Follow-up.* Winning with customers is ongoing and guess what, it involves your customers. After the data has been analyzed, decisions have been made, and plans are put in place, it is critical to follow up with the customers and share the outcomes. Each customer gave you 90 minutes (or more) of their time for the interview—it is the least you can do. You will be pleasantly surprised by the customers' responses.

We have found that there is no time as critical in the success of the team as the kickoff. We share some additional insights and helpful hints from our experience that we believe to be of value as you begin your journey with the CVC Management System.

Prepare Like Crazy

As you prepare for the kickoff, keep in mind that the most valuable portion of this initiative is the input you receive from customers. The quality of interaction you have with customers will be directly correlated to your level of preparedness. If you spend 30 minutes putting together a list of 10 questions with 1 to 10 answers, you will probably get about 30 minutes worth of value—not much! People have uncanny radars that detect when you really care about their businesses or if you are just milking them for information that will improve your own business. If people sense your sincerity you will be successful in your effort to operate your business with the added dimension of outside-in customer knowledge. If you walk into a customer meeting having done your homework, along with a genuine interest, desire, and belief that you can improve his or her business, you will have a successful conversation. The recipe for a fruitful interview has been laid out for you in the early parts of Chapter 5, "Informing Decisions," when we discussed creating an Internal Perspective on how you make your customers more money.

Here is a little story from a recent customer interview that underscores the point: About six months ago I was leading a few interviews for a company that was just getting started in its quest to understand if its customers made more money doing business with them. We were interviewing a scientific equipment distributor in Pennsylvania. There were four of us myself, a sales executive from my client, and two professionals from the distribution company. I started off the conversation with my best stuff and, after about 30 seconds, one of the distribution professionals cut me off and asked, "What do you really know about my business?" Now, you have to realize the question was in the tone of "Why should I talk to you? You don't know anything about me." I took a breath and then honestly told him what I knew. It turns out that I knew quite a lot. I knew the history between the two companies; I knew the growth patterns; I was familiar with the business financials; I understood the investments that had been made over the years targeting a variety of improvements; and I knew the value proposition and the numbers and assumptions behind them like nobody's business. I also knew in my heart that we were there for the right reason. I believed we could help their businesses. After three or four minutes, the distribution professional stopped me. He said he appreciated the preparedness and sort of apologized for the question. He then spent 10 minutes talking about the lame surveys and sessions he had been subjected to over the years that he felt were not really about helping his business. We then went on to have an amazing conversation that lasted two-and-a-half hours—when we had planned only a one-and-a-half-hour meeting. I often reflect on this interview. The positive outcome was not a given. The reason it turned positive was 100 percent due to the fact that we were prepared. We encourage you to be prepared.

Conduct Customer Interviews

Go talk to customers in person. Talking directly with customers is the key to the whole deal. This seems kind of obvious but it is a rule that is often challenged. In order to do this successfully, you need to get into the mind-set of having an investment conversation. The investment you will make as a result of what you discover is one you believe will help your customer make more money—more money than they can make with the competitive alternatives. Think about that for a moment. Before making those investments, would you like to have an in-person conversation and with several people?

Let's take the in-person aspect of customer meetings first. Where should we begin? Well, for starters, you set the tone of importance for this conversation based on how you choose to conduct the meeting. If you take the time to show up in person, then your customer is already in the mind-set that the conversation is important. If you conduct the meeting by phone or send a survey, you have automatically fallen a million miles down the importance scale in their eyes. (Do not take our word for it—ask your customer.) Our view is that of all the trips a company makes to its customer during a given year, one or two of them should be devoted to understanding the business from the customer's perspective and nothing else—no other agenda items.

Some people say, "Yeah, we do that during our annual account planning meeting." Sorry, but those annual account planning meetings are normally about your objectives for the year and have not been informed by a careful consideration for how your customer makes money. Be honest! We have both been around customer account planning for most of our professional careers.

Account Planning, the condensed version: Someone at corporate comes up with a number, the number is spread across the business units or regions, a bunch of meetings happen to determine how those numbers will be divvied up across the account base, a few new great products and services are introduced that will help you be more profitable and you are sent off to create a plan with your customers hoping to get their commitment. That may have come off a little cynical but we have experienced it firsthand over and over and over again.

You should see how account planning is different when you go in with a plan that has been informed by your customer. Here is my plan: You said if we did these four things we could improve your business by $1 million. Well, we could not do all four, but we are investing in the three that will improve your business by $750,000. Is that okay with you? It seems like we are wandering off point. Getting back to the point . . . this type of truly effective account planning begins with your taking the time to have an in-person conversation with your customers. You just do not get the input needed to decide on investment strategies with these types of quantifiable financial opportunities any other way.

And there is another interesting phenomenon about in-person communication. We all know communication is as much nonverbal as it is verbal. So many times we have been in sessions with customers that would have gone badly had we not been there in person. They would have gone badly because you could tell by the person's body language that something was not quite right. They did not understand what we were trying to do—maybe they understood but did not believe, or they were just having a bad day, and so on. Being there in person allowed us to redirect and satisfy the human dimension before diving back into the business task at hand. We are all just people. Advancements in communication technologies have advantages in some settings; effective Customer Discovery Interviews have to be conducted the old fashion way—in person.

In the second part of Chapter 5, we went into pretty good detail of how to use your Internal Perspective to create Interview Guides. Do this. Do not take the shortcut and go in with a blank piece of paper and ask, "How can we create more value for you?" This will lead to a confusing and unproductive conversation—one that customers will describe as a waste of time. Do not do it. Follow the plan—build the Interview Guides and use them to facilitate the conversation. You will get the right information in a format that can be analyzed later.

Turn Data into Actionable Plans

Now, remember we are just talking about getting started. We are not dealing with hundreds of customers that intersect with hundreds of sales professionals that will be involved as the effort expands in larger organizations. At the outset, we are dealing with a manageable set of customers. During this time you need to play a hands-on role in building success. Here is what we mean.

Now that you have collected the customer perspective take those top five or six things that will help your customer make money and build a business case for change. Do not let the accountability drop for making sure your own organization takes action. If you think someone else is doing it, you should look at the nameplate by your office door; it says "Someone." If you run into resistance in getting the organization to commit to a few actions then leverage your champion.

Once you have received commitment to action, work with the sales professionals to build a plan for those few customers who were engaged. Show them exactly what they suggested and detail those ideas where you are taking action, as well as those actions you have chosen not to act on. Do the math. What is the value of the opportunities you are tackling? Work with the sales professionals to have them present the plans to their customers on their next visit. And then be prepared for your first success story.

We guarantee that when you present the plan the customer will say, "You know what, in 20 years of business, no one has ever done this before." The customer might go on to tell you that if you even complete one item on the list you will be ahead of the competitive field. Whatever they say, we guarantee you it will be positive. You have taken the time to have a rigorous conversation with them about how they make money. You listened to their suggestions on how to help them make even more money. You followed up with them to make sure you had the story right. You took their case to your own company and moved it into action on a few key ideas. You developed a plan that details what you intend to accomplish and how much money your customer will make as a result. You will get a nice success story out of this work. As soon as you have that story, go to a high mountaintop and tell everyone. You might be thinking to yourself, "I would rather wait until we have achieved some tangible benefit or outcome." No, do not wait and here is why.

At this point, you have created accountability and ownership with the customer reps. They have told you what to do and you have confirmed with them your intention to execute on a few of their ideas. Through this process, the customer reps feel accountability and ownership in the plan. If you execute on your end, they will feel compelled to follow through on their end as well. The party you likely do not have completely hooked yet is your own organization. What you are accomplishing by going to the highest mountain and proclaiming success in the process so far is aimed squarely at establishing ownership and accountability within your own company. When your company feels it has established a process that provides input and ideas that others may not have, and that the customer loves the path you are on then you will start to get attention and a following. People will start to become interested and may well want to share in the success. We have seen this happen over and over again. This is when you will start to feel some momentum, do not let it fizzle!

Delivering on this portion of the CVC Management system can be done by following the playbook outlined in Chapter 6, "Informing Decisions," and Chapter 7, "Executing Value Creation and Value Capture." Take the data, analyze it, and summarize your insights. Make decisions based on those insights and create customers plans.

Get into Action

Not too many things happen with a big bang. In fact, success often happens slowly enough that it goes unnoticed. Your job now is to make sure success does not go unnoticed. Stay on top of the actions the company has committed to accomplishing with the handful of companies. Ensure they get done! Whatever it takes, get them done.

Take personal ownership and get them done. If you get roadblocks then find help from your champion to get them removed. Just get them done. There will be a hundred reasons why things cannot get done. You job is to find 101 reasons why they will get done.

As you get things done, make sure they are communicated to your customers. Continue to work with your sales professionals and the customers to keep track of how the customer is benefiting. Success stories will start to emerge. As they do, have that sales professional go to the highest mountaintop and declare their successes. You have just established your first evangelist. Continue to do this and multiply the successes. Your job now is to make others successful. Nothing creates believers like winning with customers.

Communicate Findings

A potential trap for some people is staying in their own little world of successes. Throughout the project it is important to have clear and direct communication with the project team and champions. During the project, keep everyone up-to-date on which customers have been interviewed and what the customers said. After the data is analyzed, bring the team together in a workshop setting to facilitate learning and make decisions. After customer plans are built, keep the team up-to-date on the Initiatives being pursued and the resulting successes.

Finally, create customer stories in a one-page format that can be shared. The powerful one-pagers should include your initial thoughts about how you create value for customers, the customer's perspective of how you create value currently and future opportunities, and the economic successes so far for both the customer and your organization. These customer stories are a catalyst for change. In the next chapter, we get into how an organization matures with regard to Winning with Customers. Individual customer stories enable that to happen, and to happen more quickly.

Follow Up with Customers

This step is where the pretenders are separated from those who are genuinely interested in operating their businesses with an outside-in customer perspective. And it is also the step where your customer may start to realize you are serious.

After you finished the session with the constituencies at your customer, put the quantitative and qualitative data into a presentable format and share it with those you interviewed to make sure you captured their input. This is magic stuff. You see it turns out that most of the time when customers take the time to provide input and feedback they never see follow-up of any kind. They may ask their sales professionals what happened to their input and the sales professionals will come up with a good cover story but in reality both are left unsatisfied. The customers do not feel like their time was well spent and the sales professionals do not feel like their customers were heard. Not good. Actually following up will surprise everyone in a good way. You know what happens then: The customer reflects on the conversation and adds more detail; they will tell you that this is right; you did not quite understand what I was saying here; I thought of these two additional ideas; I was talking to someone else and we need to add this perspective; and so on. The moment you follow up you are creating separation between yourself and 95 percent of those with whom you are competing. You are actually experiencing what it is like to Win *with* Customers.

Summary

In the chapters leading up to this point, there has been a lot of content thrown at you. Simply put, this chapter's aim was to bottle that up into a few checklists that help you get your arms around the process of getting started. It is not that hard to do. You need to gain buy-in from a part of your organization, enroll a team to help, and execute a first project. That first project will generate the data and insights required to see the path to Winning with Customers in your organization. We mentioned this a few times already, but we will reinforce it here. The companion web site to this book (winningwithcustomers.com) has exercises, templates, forums, and additional networking/learning opportunities. Combining this chapter with the web site will get you on your way.

As a brief review of this chapter, here are some of the key points that you should have walked away with:

- Getting started required three things: gaining organizational buy-in, enrolling a team to help, and having a successful first project.
- Organizational buy-in starts with believing that now is the time to start. Once that occurs, it helps to attach Winning with Customers as a solution to an established organizational need.
- Identifying champions who can take initiative and becoming an expert who can guide the process are two important steps you can take to drive change.
- Winning with Customers is a team sport. It requires sales, support of different parts of the organization, and, of course, your customers.
- The first project is all about generating early success and the resulting customer stories. These customer stories drive high initial ROI and are the catalyst for change in your organization.

Chapter 10, "Sustaining and Scaling: The Maturity Model," gets into what happens after a first project. How have companies like Owens Corning embedded Winning with Customers into the fabric of their organization? We will explore a CVC maturity road map, the organizational leadership, as well as many of the tactics required for your success and to make CVC the way you do business.

Chapter 10

Sustaining and Scaling

The Maturity Model

In the last chapter, we talk about how to get Customer Value Creation (CVC) off the ground in your organization—it is simple to do. Installing the system in your organization takes a little more work, of course. The stories earlier in the book do a good job of highlighting the keys to implementation—getting started and building momentum.

The purpose of this chapter is to help you understand what successful implementation of the CVC Management System looks like in an organization. Specifically, after reading this chapter you will understand:

- The CVC Maturity Model as a framework for setting expectations and guiding organizations through implementation.
- Tools and tactics to sustain and scale a system of CVC in an organization.

The Hurdles We Faced

Before jumping into the discussion on sustaining and scaling, let's hear what several individuals at Owens Corning thought were their biggest hurdles in implementing the approach:

Q: *What was the biggest hurdle in implementing this approach overall and how did you overcome it?*

A: Bob Harlan, Director of Business Insights, Owens Corning: *"I'm thinking about that. The biggest hurdle . . . I don't know that it would be fair for me to characterize the biggest hurdle. There are hurdles, and when we think about where we are today in terms of building an overall capability across several hundred people, it requires persistence, some investment in training of those folks. Everyone is familiar with the work required to drive change and we had to exercise our best thinking in managing change across the organization. But I think it is fair to say that once we got a taste of this and saw what it was capable of, to a large extent it was a self seller. We had many early adopters; we had some that were not so early, sort of the normal curve. I don't think there is any magic bullet. You get started and you take the first step, the second step, and you decide if you want to keep going. We did and we are glad we did."*

A: Steve Persinger, Owens Corning, sales executive: *"I talk to my customers about what they value every single day. Some sales leaders may fall into a mind-set that says, 'Wait a minute, I don't need to go through this; this is just a process. I do what this process mandates automatically; I do it in my sleep; I've been doing this all of my life.' Well, I'm going to tell you, you cannot underestimate the power of having a common language that engages the entire organization from top to middle to bottom. Our plant guys are enrolled, our supply chain people, and our CEO. It is that common language that drives our ability to attain resources that will have an impact for our customer and for Owens Corning. I will conclude by saying customer discovery opportunities are baked directly into our operational plans year after year. So the hurdle you have to watch out for is: Well, I do this anyway."*

Sticking to It: Maturity Model

In addition to being a team sport, Winning with Customers is also a marathon, not a sprint. Before the initial team is selected to take on this exciting challenge, it is important to appropriately set the organization's expectations—what you will likely get from your efforts and when you are likely to get it. Those involved must understand what to expect over time—during the initial pilot, as well as with broader implementation and on complete adoption throughout the organization. We introduced the Winning with Customers Maturity Model earlier in the book (shown again in Table 10.1). This is a good time to take a closer look at the model and set the expectations for what your organization will experience as you grow and mature with this new way of doing business.

Looking at maturity models in general can be overwhelming, but they are great tools to help set expectations for progress. They are particularly helpful for organizations that expect magic to happen on Day 1. When implementing a CVC management system within your organization, you should have four expectations:

1. This is not a project. It is a system that is easy to start, something you can get really good at, and has the potential to create a real competitive advantage.
2. The path to maturity begins with being *Reactive* and advances to a mature stage when the organization becomes *Predictive* across the six dimensions of Winning with Customers.
3. The team's make-up will change as the system grows and develops— different people with different skills in different parts of the organization are required for continued success over time.
4. A change in the organization's culture will occur as maturity happens—continuously moving to a customer-value centric culture.

This Is Not a Project

This is not a "one-shot" deal. If it were that easy, every company would adopt this approach to doing business. And your organization would not have an opportunity to set yourselves apart from competitors by building

Table 10.1 Maturity Model

Level of CVC Maturity	Reactive	Discrete	Pervasive	Predictive
Understand Value of Products and Services	No documented understanding	Known for select customers	Known for 80% of revenues	Known for 80% of revenues and key influencers
Make Customer-Informed Decisions	Sales decisions	Marketing and management decisions impacted	Organizational decisions impacted	Customer-informed strategic planning
Create Value and Capture Fair Share	No customer planning	Sales creates customer plans	Organizational aligned and accountable	Customer informed organizational planning
Measure and Improve Value Proposition	Market value proposition established	Segment value proposition established	Integration of value creation and value capture	Value management dashboards
Build Capability to Sustain CVC	Employees have hands-on experience	Ability to collect data established	Ability to analyze and get into action	CVC integrated in job description and supported with training
Enable CVC System to Scale and Speed	Render® software implemented	CVC processes defined	CVC processes integrated with business processes	Render® software integrated into IT strategy

this new organizational capability to accelerate profitable growth. So we want to be direct by saying that this is not about launching a retrospective customer loyalty measurement study, or developing a static product development road map. It is not as simple as conducting a comparative analysis of competitors, performing a pricing study, or crafting traditional customer or account plans. None of these one-shot, short-term tactics or programs will get you what you need to win with customers over and over again. And they will not individually or collectively help your customers make more money by doing business with you, or help you develop a systematic approach to running your business differently—with outside-in information.

This perspective on how the Customer Discovery process has evolved and gradually become a more significant part of the decision-making processes at Owens Corning is an example of what happens when this and other tools are used as part of an effort to build capability throughout the organization.

> *"During the initial roll out (of Customer Value Creation), Customer Discovery played a significant part in informing what our organization needed to be and helped shape the current org structure. May sound trivial but it gave us information from the customers' perspective on what we needed to be working on, how we needed to be organized to get it done and to make ourselves easier to do business with took out some of the complexity and moved decisions closer to the customer. Today, Customer Discovery is in our planning processes, our customer management, our strategic planning, it is becoming more consistently part of our language . . . you see, feel and hear a more outward focus as a company and organization."*
>
> —Chad Fenbert, sales, Owens Corning

You will not become world-class at Customer Discovery or any other aspect of CVC overnight. This is a multiyear effort that impacts every part of your business—providing a truly integrated approach to winning. However, as adopters of this approach have experienced, you will continually learn and the learning will build and spread throughout the organization as you progress along the path of maturity to become proficient with the CVC Management System.

Owens Corning Progression: Bob Harlan, Director of Business Insights, Owens Corning

This is a story that begins a couple years ago. When we look back at 2005 and 2006, we were enjoying a robust building economy. Then, like the rest of America, we started to see that market soften. Now, Owens Corning is an organization that has gotten pretty good over the years as a process-based organization. We've done a lot of work with Lean and Six Sigma. We know how to operate in a disciplined fashion. When we looked at the challenge of a softening economy, we started to ask ourselves a different question. We started to ask ourselves how we regard our customers. Traditionally, Owens Corning, like many companies, has regarded our customers through the lens of what we see and what we know. So we had some good customers based on their profitability, and our share. And we had some great customers. But as the economy softened we knew that was not enough; we needed to leverage our experience of operating a process and get to know our customers differently.

So at the beginning of 2007, the company defined a goal for itself that was very simple, very concise, and very meaningful—and that was in 2007—we were going to understand the value we deliver to customers and determine a means to measure it. And the operative word in the goal is *measure*! So we set out to find a measure. We looked at a lot of the available measurement schemes in the market. We talked to Gallup, we talked to Bain, JD Powers—we talked to a lot of different people. We found a lot of those schemes were not going to achieve our goal. They were largely retrospective, they were largely based in things like satisfaction and loyalty and engagement but they really didn't help us understand our value. We really wanted to get to the universal standard of value, which is money. So we challenged ourselves with the question "Do we know if our customers are making more money doing business with us versus the other guy?"

And as we challenged ourselves with that question—we really thought that this is the ability to crack the code. If we could answer this question, we could move our company, in terms of having our customers make more money doing business with us than with the competition, and that our ability to capture some of that value would increase as well. And it would be truly what we had established as a mantra, which was "winning with our customers."

So we set our sights on how we measure the value of Owens Corning through the lens of making money with our customers. As we looked around we found a scheme that we thought made a lot of sense. It was brought to us by the Valkre team and is encompassed in a phenomenon called differential value. In Owens Corning today, if you were to walk around the hallway or sit in any of our meetings you'd be likely to hear the citation of differential value.

We saw how powerful it was and just decided it should become the way we do work. So we've worked for the last two years to create this as a culture and a capability within Owens Corning. I can say that two years later, from a start in 2007, we are at a place whereby this is how we engage with customers, this is how we marshal the resources, this is how we spend money, and this is how we Win with Our Customers.

This story was shared earlier in the book, but now that you better understand what winning with customers is all about, it might make more sense. The progress at Owens Corning has been quite impressive. Their journey underscores our point that this is an evolutionary process that builds on itself—gaining momentum as you learn more and more about what creates value for customers and using a disciplined approach to move beyond a pilot to broader implementation. And their journey highlights the benefits of a rigorous and quantitative approach to capture, analyze, and act on outside-in customer information. In the company's case, it truly has become a new way of doing business.

Maturity Happens in Four Stages

We have been involved in many of these efforts with many customers over the years. A real "ah-ha" for us and the teams we have worked with is that while the road to success may be a little different for every organization, *a successful journey will be shaped by six critical areas of development to help you get better at using the CVC Management System, embedding it into the organization and delivering results consistently.*

These six areas of development align with the Big 6 reasons why we win with customers. We introduced these earlier in the book. The maturity model provides a way to assess your organization's degree of proficiency in mastering each of the Big 6 reasons or requirements to win with customers. For each critical area you are able to assess the things you actually do that contribute to or advance your ability to bring each of the Big 6 reasons to life in your organization in a tangible way and build organizational capability. As you see this again in Table 10.2,

Table 10.2   Why We Win Playbook

The Big 6	The Playbook
We help customers make more money doing business with us.★	**Discover** Chapter 4: "Winning Metrics" Chapter 5: "What Does Your Customer Think?"
We inject quantitative outside-in customer information into decision making.	**Analyze** Chapter 6: "Informing Decisions"
We develop and execute customer plans that deliver value (the Red Zone).★	**Execute** Chapter 7: "Executing Value Creation and Value Capture"
We predict profit growth.★	**Measure** Chapter 8: "The Scorecard"
We build capability and shape culture.	**Certify** Chapter 9: "Getting Started" Chapter 10: "Sustaining and Scaling: The Maturity Model"
The CVC Management System.★	**CVC Management System** "Afterword"

★Breakthrough

each of the Big 6 reasons why we win with customers is paired with the six concrete capabilities your organization must develop and assess as you grow and mature with Customer Value Creation.

As your organization's capability continually improves in each of these six areas, you will experience four stages of development as you work to embed this new way of doing business into your organization. It is important to note that this is not designed to be an "all or nothing" assessment of where you are in each area. It is about celebrating your learning and progress, while identifying the next key steps you must take on the road to continuous improvement. The Maturity Model serves as a useful tool to help set continuous improvement goals for your organization and to benchmark your development against other organizations that are also on the journey. Refer back to Table 10.1, "CVC Management Maturity Model." Here is a description of what you can expect at each stage of development:

Reactive As you begin, you work through the process—learning a ton about your customers and your organization. You uncover the good, the bad, and the ugly, and begin doing something to improve. Armed with this new insight, you begin to react to the opportunities. In fact, we call this first stage of organizational development *Reactive*. There is no documented understanding of the value of your products and services, from the customer's perspective. You begin to make customer informed decisions; however, they are limited to decisions made by the sales organization. You recognize there is a void of true customer planning in the organization. And you recognize that to measure and improve your value proposition, you must first establish a value proposition. Organizations typically react to this finding by swiftly using the output of this process to establish a value proposition. Your people jump right in and begin to "get their hands dirty" building the capability, albeit on a small scale, to keep the organization's efforts going. And as you begin to understand the cool and powerful outcomes, you quickly realize that attempting to do this without robust software is virtually impossible.

Discrete As you gain more experience, you begin to take real and meaningful action with impressive results on a small scale. At this juncture, your organization's capability is *Discrete*—it shows up in one or several areas of the business as you build momentum. You understand the value that your products and services provide for select customers. Customer-informed decisions move beyond the sales organization and into marketing and management. Real customer plans are created by the sales organization. Value propositions are now developed for each segment of customers and you have developed the ability to collect customer data. At this stage, the CVC processes within your organization are defined, and your organization has tweaked the playbook and made it your own as it begins to take shape across the organization. You have moved from reacting to new outside-in customer information to applying CVC in pockets of the business. This is where you begin to transition from a pilot to broader implementation.

Pervasive The third stage of maturity is what we call "Pervasive." At this stage, you are in full-blown implementation of CVC. You understand the measurable value your products and services create for customers representing over three-quarters of your sales. All decisions across your organization are impacted by the outside-in customer information you have collected and analyzed. The functions throughout the organization are on the same page and working in concert to create and capture value and are held accountable for doing so. Your analytical ability has moved into full swing, generating more and more valuable and actionable insights from the customer data you collected. The CVC process is embedded in the company's business processes. It has become a way of doing business.

Predictive The fourth and final stage of CVC maturity is "Predictive." Organizations that reach this stage have mastered the use of CVC to win with customers by fully integrating all aspects of the system into its strategy, planning, and operations. These organizations are able to measure the value of its products to customers and influencers and have deep understanding of value creation and capture along the industry value chain. Its strategic planning and organizational planning efforts are driven by outside-in customer data and value management dashboards are used to monitor the organization's efforts. The competencies and skills required to be successful with CVC shape both the selection and training of employees across the organization. And everything is IT-enabled allowing you to operate this system and to operate it efficiently. Reaching this stage signals complete adoption.

The path to CVC maturity is indeed a journey. These stages of maturity serve as markers to gauge your progress along the way as you move from a pilot to full implementation to adoption of this new way of doing business.

The Team Will Change

As you move from one stage of development to the next, the team's make-up will change—moving from transformational entrepreneurs to skilled specialists. As you build the capability over time, the team will grow and expand as you move from exploration, to an initial group of customers, to segments of customers, to customers throughout the business.

The team will likely begin with part-timers driving the charge in addition to their other full-time jobs in the company. You know those jobs that were originally crafted to support the inside-out approach to doing business. As the outside-in approach to running the business begins to emerge and take hold, more and more people will experience job transformation and take on full-time positions with responsibilities that are more directly aligned with Customer Value Creation. This will be a key sign that the organization is on the path to success.

As these changes take place, embrace—even force—these changes. If you operate with the principle "the more the merrier," you will be successful. Get as many people involved in this effort as possible as it grows. Also, as you move beyond the pilot, be intentional about bringing in specialists who possess the skills to handle specific responsibilities on the team and make it their job.

The Culture Will Change

An organizational culture should emerge that places customer value at the center of everything it does. As you begin the process with the initial team and as the team expands to support the organizational transformation, there are some things that the organization must absolutely "stick to" to ensure success over the long term.

The culture shift starts in earnest as everyone in the organization begins to truly understand customer value—what it is (from the customer's perspective) and how it can be created and managed. The knowledge and insight gained from conducting interviews and analyzing the results must be disseminated to people throughout the organization. Each person should know how the company creates value for its customers, and how more value can be created in the future. Without this, CVC will not deliver maximum benefit, as people will likely operate in two systems—the old and the new. What is worse is that your employees—those responsible for creating value for customers—will fail to fully understand the real meaning of the company's success and the role they play in creating this success. It is crucial to have everyone rowing in the same direction toward a common goal and helping everyone in your organization understand customer value is essential to make this happen.

The culture shifts also occur as the people in your organization follow up with customers, execute on the value creation initiatives, and begin to see how they have impacted the customer's bottom line. We should point out that there is something magical about the Discovery Interview with customers to kick off the second year of working with them in this new way—lightbulbs come on in a big way when customers share the measurable value they have received from your efforts.

As people throughout the organization gain a deep understanding of the concepts and begin using them in their daily routines, this is also a sign of cultural change. People will develop a common language of "stacked bar charts," DVP, and so forth, simplifying day-to-day communications and creating a customer value vocabulary.

Finally, it happens as success is evaluated. The customer stories of additional value creation, marketing programs that work, new products that deliver customer value, and so on. These success stories are a catalyst for behavioral and cultural change—the change that is inevitable as customer value takes root in the organization.

When asked a question about getting executives involved in understanding the customer: *"I'll share a lack of senior management engagement example. I have major customers that identified as part of the value discussion 'we don't know your senior leaders. We'd like to see more of your senior leaders. We would like to engage more with your senior leaders.' I had a heck of a time personally getting my senior leader to go to this customer even though they were substantial in terms of their strategic contribution. It was through this discussion, by using this process that enabled me to go to that customer with that senior leader. And that senior leader was thankful and appreciative of the fact they were engaged with a customer they normally wouldn't have. So, all kinds of positive things come out of this over and above the financial metrics we have been primarily focusing on."*

—Jim Drew, sales executive, Owens Corning

Sustaining and Scaling

Okay, now that we understand how maturity happens, let's take a look at some of the change management tools and tactics we have found over the years to help guide this process:

- Connect all employees to Customer Value
- Align leadership with Stage of Maturity
- Create an Organizational Capability
- Define and Establish Process
- Define Scope and Set Expectations
- Implement Technology

Using these tools and tactics, along with the maturity model, will set you on a path to successfully drive change in your organization. Let us explore these further.

Connect All Employees to Customer Value

Here is a perspective on the importance to connect all employees to customer value from Owens Corning:

"As I analyze the data and have visibility to the specific customer opportunities I can't help but think about the value that this information would have brought me in my past role as a Team Leader in our Customer Service organization. I spoke with customers on

a regular basis but it was always regarding an issue that needed to be resolved and was not focused on what we could do differently to positively impact their business and ensure that we were focused on and investing in the right things. By improving the visibility of this information to all functional areas within the supply chain we are better positioning ourselves to execute against the initiatives that matter most to our customers and differentiate ourselves from our competition.

In order to fully integrate and adopt a system of value creation, each functional area needs to have visibility to the information coming in that impacts their area so they can act accordingly. We are looking to communicate each value creation opportunity to the functional area leader following the interview along with the key initiatives that come from the data analysis. By combining the two we will be able to execute on the quick wins as they come in but also leverage the larger opportunities in our strategic planning to validate that we are focused on the right things. We are positioned to keep the customer updated on the progress being made and value being created through individual customer plans. Not only will this process help streamline our communication to our customers but it will help us communicate internally what each area is focused on to differentiate ourselves from our competition and win in the market."

—Dave Longmuir, operations, Owens Corning

To truly change your company to one that uses outside-in customer information to improve business performance, you need to connect large portions, and maybe all of your employees to the customer. We think about this as being similar to Six Sigma. Those companies who did and still do use Six Sigma in successful ways have many people in their organizations trained in the art and science of Six Sigma. The Six Sigma management system includes language, tools, methods, and problem-solving approaches to ensure variation, waste, and ultimately cost levels are continuously improved. The organization understands the language as significant portions or maybe all employees are trained as Green Belts. The Green Belts understand the language and tools deeply enough so they can participate, communicate, and work effectively with others on their teams to accomplish desired outcomes.

There are also Black Belts and Master Black Belts. The Black Belts determine which initiatives to tackle and lead the work. They also continue to train Green Belts and help them to achieve Black Belt status—working to support their efforts on specific projects. The Green and Black Belts are not contained to a department or function. Rather, they are distributed across many or all functions of the organizations. By having multiple departments speaking the same language, seeing opportunities for improvement through common lenses, and using standard tools to do the work, the organizations have become execution machines.

Sales and marketing never got the Six Sigma fever, although some organizations made valiant efforts. This is not a surprise since Six Sigma is more about cost, manufacturing, and operations than it is about revenue and customer. What we would like to do is ensure that the lesson learned from implementing Six Sigma is leveraged in our approach to Winning with Customers. One lesson we have learned for sure is that the team is larger than sales, marketing, and management. In order to really get this approach to Winning with Customers to stick, you will need the help of logistics, R&D, product development, manufacturing, customer service, finance, and more.

Having come to this conclusion we set out on a journey to establish a Customer Value Creation Institute with several other companies. We think of it in terms of building your own capability. We, and the anti-consultants in your organization, understand the economic benefit to your organization by using this approach.

Align Leadership with Stage of Maturity

In Chapter 9, "Getting Started," we focused on getting started and creating a few wins or success stories. Congratulations! You have come a long way. At this point you have the attention of the organization. Some within the organization may be eager to get involved. Others in the organization are probably skeptical. Much of the organization is somewhere in between. Now you are ready for what is the hardest and yet most rewarding work of all—scaling your approach to the rest of the organization.

At this point of the journey, you probably have a reasonably small team and the work still feels like a project. If you were to stop, the work would stop right with you. You could continue to carry the ball on your own, but you know deep down that your entire company could benefit greatly by using this approach. You must get others involved to help propel the effort forward into new areas of the company and establish CVC as a key strategic priority for the entire company.

Before we go on let us just say that we have been in this spot many times ourselves. Everything we discussed in this book so far we have done on our own on multiple occasions. We would do the work we have described, take a breather, and do it again. Value was being created. We learned a ton. We were good individual contributors.

At some point in your career being an individual contributor is not enough. Your job becomes more about teaching and leading others. Your job becomes focused on helping others to create their own capabilities. This is not an easy transition for many of us. It is sort of like raising kids. Those of you who have had the good fortune of raising kids to become adults know exactly what we are talking about. From the moment they are born, you develop a set of hopes and dreams for their lives. You nurture those hopes and dreams for decades, give them access to all of the experiences you believe necessary to help them in their journey. You pour your heart and soul into instilling values that you know they will need down the road. And then one day, you find they are grown up. All of a sudden they are making important life decisions without your help. Sometimes they make decisions with which you disagree. You wish you could help them to see the wisdom you have gained through having made a few of those bad decisions yourself. But you cannot. They have to learn on their own. You have to let go in many ways to allow them to grow and stand on their own. They will not be exactly like you, but probably better. In the end, all you can hope for is to have instilled a set of values and helped to build capabilities to support and guide their life journey. It is hard to let go.

Some of you may be thinking to yourselves, wow, we are getting a little sappy here. We are supposed to be talking about business not family. You see, the thing is, we are not so sure it is all that different. In order to scale, you have to let go. You must be willing to let others develop skills to win with customers on their own. The only thing you can do is to provide them with the methods, processes, and tools—the system if you will. In order to be successful in leading your organization to a place of scale you need to "change your stage." We will elaborate.

Dr. Harry Davis has several famous speeches he shares with graduate students at the University of Chicago. The two we remember best are "The Journey" and "The Stage." Both are metaphors for life and business. "The Stage" is particularly relevant as we consider how to scale. Here we go. The central point of focus of a play is the stage. There are many moving parts. The lead cast, the supporting cast, the orchestra, the producers, and you get the picture. Each of these people plays critical roles at different times to ensure that what you see on stage is brilliant. In the production the director and producer play critical roles. They pick the cast, shape the story, resolve creative conflict, coach the actors, and nurture the cast toward opening night. The actors and actresses play a much different role in facing the public. They get into their characters and bring the audience into the story. The scripts pull the curtains, move the set, and orchestrate the scenes in a manner seamlessly integrated into the overall production while not distracting the audience from the story itself. The orchestra plays and adds to the experience but the story is not about them. Dr. Davis paints this picture in a far more eloquent manner but his point is that life and business are like the stage. Sometimes in business you find yourself on the stage as the lead actor. On the next stage you may be the director. Then on the next you are in the orchestra. Each time you find yourself needing to draw on different skills to be successful. As you make the transition from kickoff to scaling you have just stepped onto a different stage. Instead of the lead actor you were likely playing in "Getting Started" you are now the producer and director in "Scaling." You may still have a scene or two on the acting stage but for the most part you are operating outside of the view of the camera.

So, the first step in scaling is acknowledging that you have to change your stage.

Create a Capability

We believe strongly in the philosophy that companies need to have their own capabilities to do all of the things we have and will discuss in this book. Winning with Customers should not be a consulting project. Winning with a customer is not a market study or any other activity routinely outsourced to third-party vendors. You might use these third parties to augment your approach, but the core capability of Winning with Customers is something you must develop and own for yourself.

Building your own capability is what drives leverage. There is no way that any third-party vendor can cost effectively deliver the same results that are achievable by your own organization. The power of Winning with Customers is created by leveraging your own organization to continuously improve its efforts and approaches on a daily basis. This requires the development of an internal core capability.

How do you go about creating a core capability? Let's assume you have fielded a small team and created a couple of nice successes. Now the General Manager or CEO or some other direction setter says, "Wow, I want more of this!" What do you do? What a loaded question! Maybe we should break this question down into a few manageable chunks. An effective way to answer this question is to address the *Who*, *What*, *When*, and *How* questions.

- *Who in the organization should be equipped with the skills to perform the responsibilities of CVC?*
- *What level of training is appropriate for various people throughout the organization?*
- *When should each team member be trained to maximize the value of the training?*
- *How will the training be conducted to make it most effective?*

Who. In short, employees in all functions must be equipped to expand the effort—everyone who can impact customer value creation. Employees ranging from manufacturing leaders to R&D management, from sales professionals to customer service managers, from logistics specialists to financial analysts—the cross-functional team must be equipped for success.

What. Here we take a page from Six Sigma. You obviously cannot have everyone trained at the highest level. We would like to have the management team, as well as the entire sales and marketing staffs, trained at the Green Belt level. It is also important to have Black Belts in both sales and marketing—the areas where the highest skill level is required. Getting significant parts of the balance of the organization up to Green Belt status should be the goal to enable everyone to operate in this new way of doing business.

When. We have found great value in starting with the sales force. The sales force always seems to have practical questions that are unique to their role of interacting directly with customers. The sales force is always most interested in their direct role of collecting the information from their customers in a credible manner and understanding their role in follow-up and execution. Other parts of the organization seem to be more similar in their approach to learning. So we like to begin with the sales professionals and then move to the rest of the organization. We also think it is valuable for selective members of management to become familiar with the tools and outcomes relatively early in the process.

How. The companies we are working with that are most effective use a combination of learning methods. They use computer-based learning as a way to establish baseline skills and maintain the online material for reference and ongoing refresher. For the Green Belt level, they typically use a two-day in-classroom session composed of some instruction, a lot of practice case application, and some tools familiarity. The Black Belt training consists of advanced application learning, and each Black Belt must demonstrate the ability to generate success using the Winning with Customers methods and tools. They, in turn, lead the continued capability development within the organization serving as resident experts.

Define and Establish Process

People need to know what is expected of them. If you jump into scaling without a good process, people will be left confused as to what they are supposed to do and when. Some of those people will come up with their own processes, while others will throw up their hands. If you jump into this without having a defined process, you will significantly increase the odds of failure. If you have one group following a process and another group following a different process, you will have a difficult time getting them on the same page.

The pace of adoption is also important. Establish your timeline. Do you want to accomplish objectives ahead of this fall's operational planning meetings so the group you are targeting can use the approach to augment their normal business routine, or are you looking to develop additional success stories in other areas of the business to help increase process adoption?

Process also includes how CVC integrates with the routines of your organization. The objective here is to make Winning with Customers part of how you do business, not something that is in addition to how business is done. A common organizational push back is "Well, how are we going to get this done with everything else we have going on?" This is a legitimate point because there is only so much an organization can accomplish at any given time. The trick is to incorporate the strategies we have discussed into the normal routine and position them as merely a way of continuously improving what is currently being done.

Define Scope and Set Expectations

When it comes to "scope," we mean how many of your customers, businesses, geographies, and so on are involved. To start, we personally like the approach of going wide but not deep. This means touching most of the people in the sales organization while not expecting each member of the sales organization to manage more than one or two of their customers using the winning with customers approach. This allows the sales organization to learn and experience the approach but not create an expectation that it changes everything it does overnight. By taking this approach you will quickly see those who embrace the strategies and tactics we have discussed. These adopters will be good spokespeople as the process gains traction. Once a baseline is established and the organization becomes more comfortable with the tools and methods, the organization will want to incorporate more customers. A mature organization will continuously manage value for 80 percent of its revenues and the key influencers located in the value chain.

Final point on scope . . . set expectations. This can come in several forms, from management communications to integrating the new expectations into job descriptions. In our experience, human resources gets jazzed about including this new level of accountability for creating customer value as part of a job description because they finally have a means to measure it using CVC metrics. Yes, even human resources gets value from this system.

Implement Technology

You have almost finished reading this playbook and I know you are excited to kick open your office door and hop on a plane to talk to your biggest customer (your biggest "friendly" customer). Playing the game is always more fun than practicing. However, playing this game is much easier with the use of technology. Determining the proper customer set to interview, formulating your internal hypotheses, and preparing for interviews are critical parts of this game, as is proper customer follow up. And although it may seem that the need for software or tools is minimal at this point, we assure you this is not the case— the devil is in the details. And these details cannot be managed well without the aid of software.

The bottom line is that it will be almost impossible to sustain and scale Winning with Customers without the help of technology. Technology is an enabler, making everything easier, faster, and more standardized. Initially, spreadsheets and presentations can do the job, but you will quickly become overwhelmed by data. Technology also helps connect the organization to customer value creation with instant access to data, the charts described in Chapter 6, "Informing Decisions," the plans, initiatives, and so forth. An environment of visibility is only obtained with the aid of technology.

Beyond the work efficiencies gained, technology helps institutionalize the process. Recall that one of the key aspects of the CVC system is a standardized mechanism for conducting interviews and collecting data. As the process is scaled, more employees will become users of these tools. As the user base expands, the software is there to reinforce adherence to the process. Without a controlled approach, things can quickly spin out of control—leading to confusion, disparate collections of data and practices, and inconsistent metrics and reporting of customer value creation and capture. These will severely limit the ability to scale the CVC capability throughout the organization.

Summary

That is it! Well, almost. We summarize the book for you in the Afterword. Congrats, though, on taking the initiative to learn about how leading B2B companies are changing the way they work and win with their customers. In this chapter, the goal was to provide you with a high-level view of what it takes to successfully install a system of CVC in your organization. As the Owens Corning stories suggested to kick off this chapter, it is easy to get started and generate results. You can take the first nine chapters of this book and its companion web site and do some nice work. Installing CVC in your organization is so impactful that it can literally change your organization and create a sustainable competitive advantage in the process.

Installing CVC starts with understanding the big picture and sticking to it. We outlined a maturity model that provides a path for your organization to grow along the six dimensions of customer value creation. These dimensions line up with the six reasons we win, introduced way back in Chapter 2, "Define Winning." When embarking on this path, it is important to set four expectations with your organization:

1. This is not a project. It is a system that is easy to start, something you can get really good at, and has the potential to create a real competitive advantage.
2. The path to maturity begins with being reactive and advances to a mature stage when the organization becomes predictive across the six dimensions of Winning with Customers.
3. The team's make-up will change as the system grows and develops— different people with different skills in different parts of the organization are required for continued success over time.
4. A change in the organization's culture will occur as maturity happens—continuously moving to a CVC culture.

Finally, we covered some tools and tactics required to successfully adopt CVC and create a competitive advantage in your organization. By combining the maturity model with these basic change management principles, you will be on a path to implementation in your organization:

- Connect all employees to Customer Value
- Align leadership with Stage of Maturity
- Create an Organizational Capability
- Define and Establish Process
- Define Scope and Set Expectations
- Implement Technology

The next and final chapter simply summarizes all of the content in this book for you. Take the time to read it, step back from all of this information, and think about how to get started on your CVC journey—it will be an exciting and profitable ride.

Afterword

It seems like it has taken us forever to complete this book! We started talking about tackling the project at the annual Business Marketing Association (BMA) conference in the summer of 2008. As we are writing some of these final words, it is now New Year's Eve 2009. By the time we go through the rest of the publishing process it will surely be summer 2010. Wow! Maybe it would have gone faster if we were better writers or clearer thinkers. We are certainly clearer thinkers after having spent nearly a year documenting what we have lived for more than 15 years.

In the Beginning

A good way to finish the book might be to go back to the beginning and reread some of the opening words and reflect now that you've had a chance to get a little deeper with us. Glenn Dalhart wrote the preface. Glenn has followed us closely for almost 10 years. He has a great perspective on the big picture of what we are up to. He wrote:

"I believe that CVC draws its power from the ingenious combination of three powerful business principles: outside-in thinking,

competitive advantage, and continuous improvement (e.g., Kaizen/ Six Sigma). First, CVC is absolutely focused on understanding and measuring value from the customer's point of view. This point of view is critical and is differentiated from the approach taken by most businesses that ask the question: 'How profitable (to me) is this customer?' CVC turns that table and asks a much different and more powerful question: 'Do you (the customer) make more money doing business with us than with our competitors?' Second, CVC embraces the well-established principle of relative performance when it comes to understanding competitive advantage. CVC applies this principle at the customer level by measuring its value proposition relative to its competitors—as you will learn this measurement is central to the CVC solution and is called the differential value proposition (DVP). Lastly, CVC embraces the continuous improvement principles of Kaizen/Six Sigma by embedding DVP measurement within a closed-loop process: Discover—Analyze—Execute—Measure.

The CVC solution is truly unique. While it resides primarily in the 'Customer Intelligence' space, the CVC solution is truly different from the typical 'Customer Loyalty,' 'Customer Satisfaction,' 'Voice of Customer' or 'Customer Relationship Management' solutions. CVC is differentiated through the analytical rigor of its DVP measurement process and through the 'relative to competition' measurement framework. Perhaps most importantly, CVC is an active, forward-looking solution that answers the question: 'What can we do to create additional value for our customers?' Most 'Customer Intelligence' solutions are passive, backward looking asking: 'How loyal/satisfied are our customers?' The collection of answers to the CVC question from many customers across the value chain and from various channels provides valuable enterprise level perspectives that inform critical investment decisions. In this way, CVC morphs into a powerful closed loop management decision-making system that aligns and impacts all function areas of a business."

—Glenn Dalhart, Retired Partner, Ernst &
Young management consulting

Now that you have read the book, we hope that you agree with Glenn. We have indeed borrowed from the best of business science to build our CVC Management System.

At the beginning, we also promised to provide you with a combination of understanding and practical how-to approaches for these concepts Glenn references. The truth of the matter is that we could have written much more on theory and understanding and we could have also written much more on the how-tos. It seemed like there was a constant tension between writing for understanding versus creating a how-to guide. We attempted to strike the right balance to make the book both informative and enjoyable. In the end, we tried to follow a line somewhere between tactical boring and conversational fun that delivered on our original promise, which was:

- *If you are* interested in helping improve the financial performance of your company and learning more about "how to" use a proven new business management system to win with customers, this book is for you.
- *If you are* an executive who would like to feel more confident that your company's investment decisions will actually create value for your customers and your company—this book is for you.
- *If you are* a sales professional who would like to have your customer heard by your company, and want to sell products and services that are truly differentiated in the market—this book is for you.
- *If you are* a marketer who would like to hear your organization's value proposition communicated by the sales force on a consistent basis, achieve alignment with sales on key customer needs, and develop communication that is used proficiently by the sales force in their selling efforts—this book is for you.
- *If you are* in Product Development or R&D and would like to improve the connection between your development efforts and the operational and financial success of your customers, short circuiting the process from idea to product development to successful launch—this book is for you.
- *If you work* in manufacturing and would like to increase your organization's understanding of quality and its importance and value from the customer perspective, and would like to know that

your efforts are directly linked to the success of your customers—this book is for you.

- *If you work* in customer service and would like to bring what customers actually care about into the center of what you do each day, feeling confident that making changes to continually improve will result in greater value for customers and more profits for your business—this book is for you.
- *If you work* in logistics and have a desire to increase the value that your sales organization and customers place on the effort you expend to keep service programs in order and deliver what is expected, bringing innovation to your efforts that customers need and are willing to pay for—this book is for you.

We are writing the book for each of these perspectives and more. One of the lessons we've learned is that including many functions in the journey to an outside-in approach improves the chances for success. Sure, it is important to have an executive sponsor and that strong champion and all of the rest, but real momentum occurs when a large portion of the organization sees itself through the eyes of the customer and has an organizing approach for action and measurement.

So whatever your role happens to be in your organization, we trust that you got something out of this book. Creating value for customers and helping your organization to capture its fair share is not bestowed on you. You have to work for it and it takes a team.

A Few Highlights

It feels like we could write another 30-page chapter summarizing everything we've covered . . . let's not. Instead, we will just cover a few of the organizing frameworks and concepts to refresh your memory or for you to use as a cheat sheet to share with others.

Why We Lose—Why We Win

If you can still remember the beginning of the book—we opened the book with a discussion on why companies lose their customers, based on our experience. We then offered a winning formula that has worked for us and organized the rest of the book around the winning ideas—the Big Six Reasons Why We Win, shown again in Table AW 11.1.

We stressed the importance of understanding the business from your customer's perspective—"outside-in." The critical question: "Does your customer make more money by doing business with you?" was introduced and explored. We hope this question is forever etched in your mind and serves as a constant reminder of what it takes to win. As we tackled this question, we discussed how we get beyond an interesting concept and purely qualitative information and move into action based on a quantitative understanding of what creates value for customers. The Differential Value Proposition (DVP%) metric was introduced along with value attribute tradeoffs—helping you for the first time to understand and measure your competitive advantage. This is a big deal. We believe this separates our approach from all others and

Table AW 11.1 Why We Win Playbook

The Big 6	The Playbook
We help customers make more money doing business with us.★	**Discover** Chapter 4: Winning Metrics Chapter 5: What Does Your Customer Think?
We inject quantitative outside-in customer information into decision making.	**Analyze** Chapter 6: Informing Decisions
We develop and execute customer plans that deliver value (the red zone).★	**Execute** Chapter 7: Executing Value Creation and Value Capture
We predict profit growth.★	**Measure** Chapter 8: The Scoreboard
We build capability and shape culture.	**Certify** Chapter 9: Getting Started Chapter 10: Sustaining and Scaling: The Maturity Model
The CVC Management System★	**CVC Management System** Afterword

★Breakthrough

gives you a sound basis to build a profitable growth strategy for your business—please use it to separate your business from the pack.

Another critically important point we made is to develop an understanding of where you've been (retrospective), as well as the opportunities for improvement with the customer in the future. We provided some insight into how to collect the data to shape this understanding using your own people—essential to making this a part of the fabric of your business. The biggest secret here is that you are talking to your customer about what is important to their business—every day. A novel idea.

We then moved into a rather quantitative discussion about using this outside-in customer perspective to inform decisions and get into action. Remember to embrace analytical rigor—it is essential to identify the most valuable opportunities to create value for customers. And, yes, one of the cool outcomes: "The List." The invaluable document that quantifies the Top 10 opportunities customers believe will help them make more money doing business with you. Everyone loves that list— some organizations keep it in the vault for safekeeping. We moved beyond the general discussion of value with customers in general and shared the various ways of understanding the segments of our customer base. The point—only value-based customer segments really matter. This helps us identify the customers that value our current offerings and see a bright future, as well as those who don't see as bright a future, and most importantly why? After layering on the profitability we enjoy with customers, we created some interesting frames from which to better understand your business and develop targeted activities and plans. The big "ah-ha" in this section is that overconfidence bias in decision making (which we all suffer from) can be eliminated by using outside-in customer data. The so what—you can make better decisions using your current decision making frameworks. It's the outside-in customer data that makes the difference.

We then moved on to execution as we entered the CVC Stadium or the Field of Play, shown in Figure AW1.1. This is where the rubber meets the road, the time to put up or shut up, to get it done—to execute!

We made reference to how some teams play around in the middle of the field and lose because they never execute, falling prey to "analysis paralysis." By the way, that is still one of our favorite passages in the book.

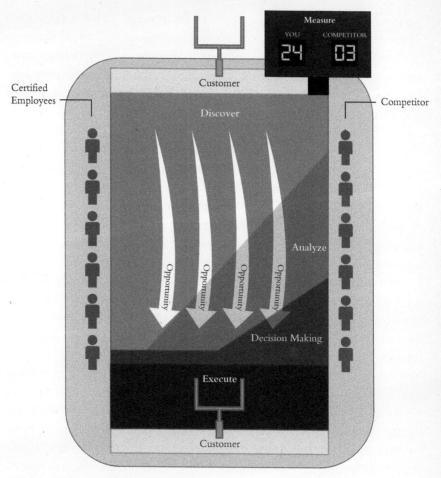

Figure AW 1.1 The CVC Stadium

There are a couple of important points worth highlighting from this section as we moved down the field attempting to score and win. First, this is a process in which you need to strive for continuous improvement in order to consistently win with your customers and against your competitors—this is not a one shot deal. The second point is that it is critical to get into scoring position (the Red Zone) and *score*! From our experience, execution gets easier and becomes more effective when the organization buys into the process that incorporates the customer perspective throughout every aspect of their work, including customer discovery, analyzing data, developing opportunities, making investment decisions, customer planning, as well as the day-to-day conversations and interactions throughout the organization and with your customers.

One of the key aspects of this approach that makes it work so well is accountability. Accountability is demonstrated in your own organization by developing customer plans based on what the customer told you they value—you will become a star in your customers' eyes when you do this. Most companies just do not do it—we continue to be baffled by this. Accountability is also demonstrated by customers as they execute the opportunities resulting from their suggestions. This closes the loop and you are rewarded for your investments. The shared accountability between you and your customers makes the system go and serves as the fuel that helps you win over and over again.

We covered the scoreboard or measurement that helps you keep track of the wins. As you become experienced at running the plays in the Playbook, you gain insight into what works and how much value each play creates for you and the customer. This leads you to a path of predicting profit growth, which may seem like a pipedream. It is not! You can get better at aligning your decision making with those things that create value for your customers. You can get better at understanding what creates value for your customers. You can get better at coordinating the communication and information flow from customer discovery to creating and executing customer plans. The way to get better is to measure, provide feedback, and improve. Yes, a part of the "secret sauce" is continuous improvement. The ongoing improvements will indeed reduce risk and increase your confidence in getting the return on investment you anticipate from the customer facing investments. The scoreboard is also used to measure the impact on the customer's business as you continue to increase the DVP% customer by customer—putting more money in your customers' bank account. If we are going to get better at creating and managing value, you must continuously improve your own organization skills and help customers measure and improve theirs as well. You must use metrics for both.

CVC provides the process, the data, and the metrics. However, the big secret here is to "just do it." Do not let the cynics, naysayers, been there done that attitudes, do not have time excuses, and the other 101 reasons that this cannot work stand in the way of managing the value you create for customers. This is a proven approach to help you capture profits your competitors cannot. This is why you are in business!

Doing this once or twice is fine, but it is not what will get you on the path of sustainable profitable growth in your business. The secret to continued success is building capability and culture. The cold hard reality is that you cannot do everything we have discussed in one fell swoop. It takes time, you need to build capabilities, you may need cultural shifts and you will need a plan to guide you on your journey. Here is where we introduced the Maturity Model. There is nothing magical about the maturity model. All it does is to help you find a path, establish reasonable expectations, and measure progress along the journey of making this the way you do business. The big deal we emphasize with the maturity model is that you should build your own capability and not rely on third-party vendors to do the work we have outlined. Our point of view is that this work is foundational and a necessary core competence to drive sustained competitive advantage for your company. You can get third-party help early on to get started but as soon as you can, walk on your own, allow for a few stumbles, and get on the maturity path. Before you know it you will be under the big lights.

The approach we have described is a system. It is not only about process, or people, or data, or technology. Managing value with customers requires all of these elements coordinated in a system—the CVC Management System. Building this system has been our professional journey, as well as that of our teams for many years. We continue adding layers, ways to do things better, new customers, new employees, new tools, new partners and collaborators, and now *you*. We welcome you to the family.

During the course of the book we have spent the bulk of our time on the process, data, and the people. And, we spent some time on technology. The message we delivered on technology is, "hey, use technology, it makes things easier." We intentionally did not provide many of the specifics because we felt it could be better addressed in a different medium. However, it is important to note that technology will be a key part of your success. In fact, we believe it can be a force multiplier of your efforts to win with customers. Using technology to make everything we have discussed easier and more manageable has been a big part of our lives for the past few years. The software we have built to support the system is called Render®. We think of Render® as the easy button!

Get into Action

The book is done, hurray, but it is just another milestone in a journey of learning and sharing. Tomorrow we will be working on "Winning with Customers"—it is what we do. If you, like us, need to get past the reading and into action delivering business results, then we offer you a path to get going. The path begins at www.winningwithcustomers.com.

We have designed this site as a place of resources, learning, and sharing to support your efforts to get into action . . . not a book sales site. Here are a few of the things you find there:

- Information on how to connect to thought leaders and other companies who are moving down the road on their journey of winning with customers.
- If you would like to talk with others in your organization about what you have discovered in the book, we have built a few PowerPoint slides containing many of the relevant topics.
- As of this writing we have discussed putting a few exercises on the site so you can get started on your own. We do not have this one completely figured out but take a look. If they are not there you can feel free to give one of us a call and we will get you set up.
- If you are interested in learning more about the Render® software, you will find a link to a demo that will provide more insights into how it works.
- We will also post conferences and webinars where you can learn more on this topic.
- And finally, if you would like to buy a million books you can do that as well. We would certainly appreciate it.

That's everything for now. Thanks for spending the time with us. We hope to meet you soon on your journey winning with Customers!

About the Authors

D. Keith Pigues, Senior Vice President and Chief Marketing Officer, Ply Gem, Inc.

D. Keith Pigues is senior vice president, chief marketing officer, and member of the executive committee for Ply Gem Industries, a leading provider of building products brands. He is also an adjunct professor of Leadership at the University of North Carolina Kenan-Flagler Business School.

He has held executive positions at Monsanto, CEMEX, RR Donnelley, ADP, and Honeywell International.

He has more than 25 years of experience in marketing, strategic planning, mergers and acquisitions, and sales leadership in companies ranging from the Fortune 500 to midmarket private-equity-backed ventures in a range of industries, including information technology, health care, agriculture biotechnology, automotive manufacturing and retailing, commercial printing, and building products. He has been recognized as a leader of strategic growth and marketing—developing new growth strategies and marketing capabilities, creating valuable brands, building effective global marketing teams, and increasing profitable revenue growth through strategy and marketing excellence.

Pigues received an MBA from the University of North Carolina Kenan-Flagler Business School in Chapel Hill and a bachelor of science degree in electrical engineering from Christian Brothers University in Memphis, Tennessee.

He is past chairman of the board of directors for the Business Marketing Association and a member of the Executive Leadership Council. In 2007, he received the Frost & Sullivan Marketing Lifetime Achievement Award and was recognized by *BtoB* magazine as one of the leading senior marketing practitioners and is a member of Who's Who in B to B. Pigues speaks, writes, and teaches on the topics of business growth strategy, marketing, and leadership. Find out more about Keith at www.dkeithpigues.com.

Jerry Alderman, Chief Executive Officer, Valkre Solutions, Inc.

Jerry Alderman is an entrepreneur, founder, and chief executive officer of Valkre Solutions, Inc. (www.valkre.com). Valkre was founded in 2008 and is in Chicago, Illinois. Valkre is a software tools and services company whose primary mission develops capability within B2B companies to use "deep customer understanding" to build and execute customer-driven strategies and operating plans. The software product Render®, which makes this possible, is revolutionizing the way B2B companies interact with their customers and has driven results. Alderman and his team have worked with a who's who of companies, including Owens Corning, Kimberly Clark, Turtle Wax, RR Donnelley, and more.

Prior to founding Valkre, Inc., Alderman was a senior vice president for Exogen. During his tenure dating to 2001, Alderman led and developed his innovative approach to building corporate competitive advantage through using and executing on unique, deep customer insights. During this time, Alderman has shown that whether in good markets or bad, the benefits of operating with an advantaged customer perspective yields results. In down markets, the benefits are knowing better than competitors how value is created and the waste of nonvalue-adding activities and investments. During good markets, the results come from making smarter investments than competitors. In all cases, Alderman has built a reputation for getting sales and marketing organizations into action on initiatives that have been customer informed.

Alderman started his business career at Boise Corporation. He spent 12 years with Boise, learning and experiencing the unique challenges of B2B companies. During his time at Boise, he served in many roles, including manufacturing engineer, sales professional, sales and marketing management, product development, and general management.

Before starting his business career, Alderman served six years on nuclear submarines as a Naval Officer through the Admiral Rickover program. During this time, Mr. Alderman participated in special operations on fast-attack subs and stealth missions on ballistic missile submarines. Through these experiences, Alderman gained a deep respect for the capability of high-performing teams and the power of technology and innovation to drive the outcome of events. These experiences, combined with a bachelor degree in Civil Engineering, a master's in Nuclear Engineering, and an MBA from the University of Chicago provide a broad base of problem-solving skills from which Alderman grounds his work.

Alderman's recognition as a thought leader is growing and he continues to contribute to the advancement of business science through his practice, speaking, writing, and academic contributions.

About the Contributors

Brian Kiep, Vice President, Valkre Solutions, Inc.

Brian Kiep is a vice president of Valkre Solutions and is responsible for solution development and customer engagements. Over the past several years, Brian has worked directly with the authors and Owens Corning to expand on Customer Value Creation theory and turn it into products and capabilities that organizations can own. To do so, Kiep leaned on deep experience in the strategies, processes, and technologies surrounding Customer Value Management and Customer Relationship Management across many industries, including telecommunications, health care, financial services, building materials, and technology. As a result, Kiep has developed extensive skills in general management, e-commerce, B2B marketing and sales, and change management. Kiep is a graduate of the Chicago Booth School of Business (MBA) and the University of Illinois at Urbana-Champaign (Engineering). In his spare time, he enjoys time with his family, cheers on the Fighting Illini and the Chicago Bears, and plays golf with his friends.

Alex Monacelli, Vice President,
Valkre Solutions, Inc.

Alex Monacelli is a vice president at Valkre Solutions and is responsible for customer engagements. Over the past several years, Monacelli has worked directly with Owens Corning and various Fortune 500 clients to develop their internal Customer Value Creation capabilities. Through this work, Monacelli has developed expertise in project management, change management, and B2B marketing and sales, as well as with the strategies and processes surrounding Customer Value Management. A graduate of the Chicago Booth School of Business (MBA) and Brown University, Monacelli enjoys spending time with his family, playing basketball, and skiing with friends.

Matthew Cobb, Director of IT,
Valkre Solutions, Inc.

Matthew Cobb is the director of IT at Valkre Solutions. He is responsible for all engineering processes and software development within the organization, and ensures their strategic alignment with the needs of the business. From proof of concept to implementation, Cobb serves a leading role in translating the intellectual theory of Customer Value Creation into a commercial software product. A technical enthusiast, he provides extensive experience in developing software solutions, as well having a passion for application design and usability, to Valkre.

A graduate of Vanderbilt University, Cobb currently resides in Chicago with his wife, daughter, cat, and a whole bunch of computers.

Gabriel Lerner, Lead Software Architect,
Valkre Solutions, Inc.

Gabriel Lerner is the lead software architect at Valkre Solutions. His responsibilities include everything from design to deployment in the lifecycle of Valkre's software. He brings experience from a variety of environments, including small start-ups and large corporations, and is proficient in a multitude of programming languages. Ever since he began programming at the age of eight, his interest in technology has kept him on the cutting edge. All this and more has helped Lerner influence Customer Value Creation's success as a software product.

After graduating from the University of Illinois at Urbana-Champaign, Lerner moved to Chicago and lives there to this day. When he's not online, Lerner plays tennis and takes photographs.

Index